5th Workshop on Computational Approaches to Discourse 2024

St. Julian's, Malta
21 March 2024

ISBN: 978-1-7138-9451-3

Printed from e-media with permission by:

Curran Associates, Inc.
57 Morehouse Lane
Red Hook, NY 12571

Association for Computational Linguistics
209 N. Eighth Street
Stroudsburg, Pennsylvania 18360

Phone: 1-570-476-8006
Fax: 1-570-476-0860

acl@aclweb.org

Additional copies of this publication are available from:

Curran Associates, Inc.
57 Morehouse Lane
Red Hook, NY 12571 USA
Phone: 845-758-0400
Fax: 845-758-2633
Email: curran@proceedings.com
Web: www.proceedings.com

CODI 2024

5th Workshop on Computational Approaches to Discourse

Proceedings of the Workshop

March 21, 2024

The CODI organizers gratefully acknowledge the support from the following sponsors.

Sponsor

HITS
Heidelberg Institute for Theoretical Studies

Association for Computational Linguistics (ACL)
209 N. Eighth Street
Stroudsburg, PA 18360
USA
Tel: +1-570-476-8006
Fax: +1-570-476-0860
acl@aclweb.org

Preface

Welcome to the 5th Workshop on Computational Approaches to Discourse, CODI!

CODI provides a venue to bring together researchers working on all aspects of discourse in Computational Linguistics and NLP. Our aim is to provide a venue for the entire discourse processing community where we can present and exchange our theories, algorithms, software, datasets, and tools.

The workshop consists of invited talks, contributed papers, extended abstracts, and EACL Findings presentations. We received paper submissions that span a wide range of topics, addressing issues related to discourse representation and parsing, reference and coreference resolution, summarization, dialogue, pragmatics, applications, and more. As the workshop is hybrid this year, papers are presented live either in person or remotely and discussed during live Q&A sessions. We received 28 submissions, including 14 regular long papers, 6 regular short papers and 8 non-archival communications (Findings, extended abstracts and direct submissions). We accepted 16 articles among the 20 regular submissions and 6 are presented orally. We also organize two poster sessions this year, in order to encourage discussions.

We thank our invited speakers, **Hannah Rohde**, Professor in Linguistics & English Language at the University of Edinburgh, who works in experimental pragmatics, focusing on aspects of communication such as ambiguity, redundancy, deception, and the establishment of discourse coherence. Her presentation is entitled: *Inferences of additional coherence-driven meaning within and across clauses*. Our second invited speaker is **Manfred Stede**, Professor of Applied Computational Linguistics at the University of Potsdam and head of the Applied CompLing Discourse Research Lab, who works on text structure and automatic text analysis, currently mainly for social science issues. His presentation is entitled: *Connectives and Arguments*. They helped us to prepare an excellent and well-rounded workshop program. We would also like to thank the EACL 2024 workshop chairs Zeerak Talat and Nafise Moosavi who organized the ACL workshops program.

Finally, we thank our sponsor HITS, Heidelberg Institute for Theoretical Studies https://www.h-its.org.

The CODI Organizers,

Chloé Braud, Christian Hardmeier, Chuyuan Li, Junyi Jessy Li, Sharid Loáiciga, Michael Strube, and Amir Zeldes

Program Committee

Program Committee

Giuseppe Carenini, University of British Columbia
Jackie Chi Kit Cheung, Mila / McGill University
Vera Demberg, Saarland University
Elisa Ferracane, Abridge AI, Inc.
Mark Finlayson, FIU
Annemarie Friedrich, University of Augsburg
Jie He, University of Edinburgh
Freya Hewett, University of Potsdam
Ryuichiro Higashinaka, Nagoya University/NTT
Cassandra L. Jacobs, University at Buffalo
Sungho Jeon, Heidelberg Institute for Theoretical Studies
Yangfeng Ji, University of Virginia
René Knaebel, University of Potsdam
Ekaterina Lapshinova-Koltunski, University of Hildesheim
Yang Janet Liu, Georgetown University
Wanqiu Long, The University of Edinburgh
S. Magalí López Cortez, University at Buffalo
Philippe Muller, IRIT, University of Toulouse
Jingcheng Niu, University of Toronto
Maciej Ogrodniczuk, Institute of Computer Science, Polish Academy of Sciences
Massimo Poesio, Queen Mary University of London and University of Utrecht
Hannah Rohde, University of Edinburgh
Ahmed Ruby, Uppsala University
Tatjana Scheffler, Ruhr University Bochum
Manfred Stede, University of Potsdam
Francielle Vargas, University of São Paulo
Suncheng Xiang, Shanghai Jiao Tong University
Wen Xiao, University of British Columbia
Frances Yung, Saarland University
Deniz Zeyrek, Middle East Technical University
Haopeng Zhang, University of California, Davis
Zheng Zhao, University of Edinburgh

Table of Contents

An Algorithmic Approach to Analyzing Rhetorical Structures
Andrew Potter 1

SciPara: A New Dataset for Investigating Paragraph Discourse Structure in Scientific Papers
Anna Kiepura, Yingqiang Gao, Jessica Lam, Nianlong Gu and Richard H.r. Hahnloser 12

Using Discourse Connectives to Test Genre Bias in Masked Language Models
Heidrun Dorgeloh, Lea Kawaletz, Simon Stein, Regina Stodden and Stefan Conrad 27

Projecting Annotations for Discourse Relations: Connective Identification for Low-Resource Languages
Peter Bourgonje and Pin-Jie Lin 39

Experimenting with Discourse Segmentation of Taiwan Southern Min Spontaneous Speech
Laurent Prévot and Sheng-Fu Wang 50

Actor Identification in Discourse: A Challenge for LLMs?
Ana Barić, Sebastian Padó and Sean Papay 64

Quantitative metrics to the CARS model in academic discourse in biology introductions
Charles Lam and Nonso Nnamoko 71

Probing of pretrained multilingual models on the knowledge of discourse
Mary Godunova and Ekaterina Voloshina 78

Feature-augmented model for multilingual discourse relation classification
Eleni Metheniti, Chloé Braud and Philippe Muller 91

Complex question generation using discourse-based data augmentation
Khushnur Jahangir, Philippe Muller and Chloé Braud 105

Exploring Soft-Label Training for Implicit Discourse Relation Recognition
Nelson Filipe Costa and Leila Kosseim 120

The ARRAU 3.0 Corpus
Massimo Poesio, Maris Camilleri, Paloma Carretero Garcia, Juntao Yu and Mark-Christoph Müller 127

Signals as Features: Predicting Error/Success in Rhetorical Structure Parsing
Martial Pastor and Nelleke Oostdijk 139

GroundHog: Dialogue Generation using Multi-Grained Linguistic Input
Alexander Chernyavskiy, Lidiia Ostyakova and Dmitry Ilvovsky 149

Discourse Relation Prediction and Discourse Parsing in Dialogues with Minimal Supervision
Chuyuan Li, Chloé Braud, Maxime Amblard and Giuseppe Carenini 161

With a Little Help from my (Linguistic) Friends: Topic segmentation of multi-party casual conversations
Amandine Decker and Maxime Amblard 177

Program

Thursday, March 21, 2024

09:15 - 09:30 *Opening Remarks*

09:30 - 10:30 *Invited Talk - Hannah Rohde: Inferences of additional coherence-driven meaning within and across clauses*

10:30 - 11:00 *Coffee Break*

11:00 - 12:00 *Poster Session 1*

Discourse Structure Annotations for the Minecraft Dialogue Corpus
Kate Thompson, Julie Hunter and Nicholas Asher

Syntactic Preposing and Discourse Relations
Yunfang Dong, Xixian Liao and Bonnie Webber

Learning Label Embeddings for Mapping Discourse Relations of Different Annotation Frameworks (Extended Abstract)
Yingxue Fu

Actor Identification in Discourse: A Challenge for LLMs?
Ana Barić, Sebastian Padó and Sean Papay

Exploring Soft-Label Training for Implicit Discourse Relation Recognition
Nelson Filipe Costa and Leila Kosseim

Projecting Annotations for Discourse Relations: Connective Identification for Low-Resource Languages
Peter Bourgonje and Pin-Jie Lin

Probing of pretrained multilingual models on the knowledge of discourse
Mary Godunova and Ekaterina Voloshina

Complex question generation using discourse-based data augmentation
Khushnur Jahangir, Philippe Muller and Chloé Braud

Thursday, March 21, 2024 (continued)

12:00 - 13:30 *Lunch*

13:30 - 14:30 *Invited Talk - Manfred Stede: Connectives and Arguments*

14:30 - 15:30 *Poster Session 2*

Zero-shot learning for multilingual discourse relation classification
Eleni Metheniti, Philippe Muller, Chloé Braud and Margarita Hernández Casas

Exploiting Questions Under Discussion for Discourse Relation Recognition in Dialog
Shuhaib Mehri, Chuyuan Li and Giuseppe Carenini

Quantitative metrics to the CARS model in academic discourse in biology introductions
Charles Lam and Nonso Nnamoko

On Measuring Context Utilization in Document-Level MT Systems
Wafaa Mohammed and Vlad Niculae

An Algorithmic Approach to Analyzing Rhetorical Structures
Andrew Potter

SciPara: A New Dataset for Investigating Paragraph Discourse Structure in Scientific Papers
Anna Kiepura, Yingqiang Gao, Jessica Lam, Nianlong Gu and Richard H.r. Hahnloser

The ARRAU 3.0 Corpus
Massimo Poesio, Maris Camilleri, Paloma Carretero Garcia, Juntao Yu and Mark-Christoph Müller

Discourse Relation Prediction and Discourse Parsing in Dialogues with Minimal Supervision
Chuyuan Li, Chloé Braud, Maxime Amblard and Giuseppe Carenini

15:30 - 16:00 *Coffee Break*

Thursday, March 21, 2024 (continued)

16:00 - 17:30 *Session - Oral presentations*

Using Discourse Connectives to Test Genre Bias in Masked Language Models
Heidrun Dorgeloh, Lea Kawaletz, Simon Stein, Regina Stodden and Stefan Conrad

Experimenting with Discourse Segmentation of Taiwan Southern Min Spontaneous Speech
Laurent Prévot and Sheng-Fu Wang

Feature-augmented model for multilingual discourse relation classification
Eleni Metheniti, Chloé Braud and Philippe Muller

Signals as Features: Predicting Error/Success in Rhetorical Structure Parsing
Martial Pastor and Nelleke Oostdijk

GroundHog: Dialogue Generation using Multi-Grained Linguistic Input
Alexander Chernyavskiy, Lidiia Ostyakova and Dmitry Ilvovsky

With a Little Help from my (Linguistic) Friends: Topic segmentation of multi-party casual conversations
Amandine Decker and Maxime Amblard

17:30 - 17:45 *Closing Remarks*

An Algorithmic Approach to Analyzing Rhetorical Structures

Andrew Potter
Computer Science & Information Systems Department
University of North Alabama
Florence, Alabama, USA
apotter1@una.edu

Abstract

Although diagrams are fundamental to Rhetorical Structure Theory, their interpretation has received little in-depth exploration. This paper presents an algorithmic approach to accessing the meaning of these diagrams. Three algorithms are presented. The first of these, called *Reenactment*, recreates the abstract process whereby structures are created, following the dynamic of coherence development, starting from simple relational propositions, and combing these to form complex expressions which are in turn integrated to define the comprehensive discourse organization. The second algorithm, called *Composition*, implements Marcu's strong nuclearity assumption. It uses a simple inference mechanism to demonstrate the reducibility of complex structures to simple relational propositions. The third algorithm, called *Compression*, picks up where Marcu's assumption leaves off, providing a generalized fully scalable procedure for progressive reduction of relational propositions to their simplest accessible forms. These inferred reductions may then be recycled to produce RST diagrams of abridged texts. The algorithms described here are useful in positioning computational descriptions of rhetorical structures as discursive processes, allowing researchers to go beyond static diagrams and look into their formative and interpretative significance.

1 Introduction

It has been shown that rhetorical structures and relational propositions are interchangeable (Potter, 2023a). The structure of an RST diagram can be restated as a relational proposition and relational propositions can be returned to RST diagrams. Relational propositions, as defined by (Mann & Thompson, 1986a, 1986b, 2000), are implicit assertions arising between clauses within a text and are essential to the functioning of the text. They can be considered as an alter ego of RST relations, with each assertion consisting of a predicate (or relation) and two variables (representing a satellite and nucleus). Because the predicate notation developed for relational propositions is Python conformant (Potter, 2023a, 2023b), mapping RST diagrams to relational propositions opens the possibility of exploring rhetorical structures algorithmically, presenting a range of analytic possibilities. The immediate effect of rendering RST diagrams as code is to unlock the picture: If, as the saying goes, a picture is worth a thousand words, the diagram now becomes a movie. It is a story about what is happening in a text. The objective of the research described in this paper was to investigate some of these possibilities.

Three algorithms are presented, each addressing a distinct aspect of Rhetorical Structure Theory. The first of these is called *Reenactment*. This algorithm replays the abstract process of structure formation, demonstrating the step-by-step construction of discourse formation starting with elementary relational propositions, and combining these to form complex expressions which are in turn integrated to define the comprehensive discourse organization. The second algorithm, referred to as the *Composition* algorithm, implements Marcu's strong nuclearity assumption and demonstrates the reducibility of complex structures to simple relational propositions. The third algorithm, called *Compression*, picks up where Marcu leaves off, providing a generalized scalable method for progressive reduction of relational propositions down to their simplest possible forms.

These algorithms provide the opportunity for a direct and deep look into information implicit in

Proceedings of the 5th Workshop on Computational Approaches to Discourse (CODI 2024), pages 1–11
March 21, 2024

RST diagrams. A benefit of this is that it should set aside any notion that RST diagrams are incapable of articulating in-depth aspects of discursive development, or that they are merely static specifications (Martin, 1992). On the contrary, although RST is only a partial explanation of discourse coherence, the part it plays is an important one. If we can restate RST diagrams in computational terms and allow these terms to describe what a diagram is doing, then perhaps we can begin to enjoy a deeper appreciation for what they are telling us about the text, and that these diagrams, far from static depictions of discourse structure, are actually renderings of a dynamic process, showing how a discourse germinates from its elementary units to become a whole that is greater than its parts.

2 Framework

The interlocking property of rhetorical structures, where a satellite's support for a nucleus creates a span which in turn becomes the satellite for yet another nucleus, suggests that the typical rhetorical relation is rhetorically transitive, with the consequence that their intended effects develop cumulatively across complex structures, ultimately converging on an identifiable locus of effect. This abstract process is an assumption of the research described here; otherwise, the algorithms would fail to achieve produce their expected results. Potter's (2023a) algorithm for transforming RST analyses into relational propositions is used to provide the input for this framework. Throughout this process, these propositions maintain their structural isomorphism with RST diagrams.

Marcu's strong nuclearity assumption, also known as the strong compositionality criterion, says that when two complex text spans are connected through a rhetorical relation, the same rhetorical relation holds between the nuclei of the constituent spans (Marcu, 1996, 2000). This means that from relations between spans, simple structures may be inferred. The algorithmic implementation of this supports its application to RST analyses of any size. The reenactment algorithm implements a bottom-up perspective on RST structures by enacting the dynamic process of structure development, starting with elementary relational propositions, and combining these to form a complex expression ultimately of the comprehensive discourse organization. The Compression algorithm implements a technique previously proposed by Potter (2023b). As a generalization of strong nuclearity, it progressively eliminates the precedent satellite within the RST nuclear path to reduce the relational proposition to its simplest possible expression. The technique specifies delimited transitivity for handling multinuclears and unrealized relations. Taken together the three algorithms provide a foundational set of capabilities for analyzing rhetorical structures and exploring various features of the theory, such as inference, transitivity, reducibility, intentionality, and structural dynamics. In short, the algorithms can be used for investigating a range of discourse characteristics following a well-defined algorithmic approach. These algorithms are neither large nor complex. They are of interest more for what they do rather than for how they do it. What they do is offer insights into the nature of discourse. How they do this is largely reliant on the representation of RST structures as Pythonic relational propositions. I believe their simplicity is a by-product of the alignment of the theory with the discursive organizations it describes.

3 Related Work

While the literature on Rhetorical Structure Theory is vast, only a rather narrow strand of that research is relevant to this study. This naturally encompasses the founding RST documents, including but not limited to Mann and Thompson (1988) and Mann and Thompson (1987). These publications define Rhetorical Structure Theory (RST) as a descriptive theory of text organization, as a tool for describing and characterizing texts in terms of the relations that hold among the clauses within a text. A detailed exemplification of the theory can be found in Mann, et al.'s (1992) analysis of a fund-raising text. Matthiessen and Thompson (1987) provide an in-depth discussion of the theoretical foundations of RST.

Of continuing research interest in RST has been the possibility that it could be used as a text summarization technology. Most prominent in this area has been the works of (Marcu, 1997, 1998a, 1998b, 1998c, 1999, 2000). There has also been ongoing work in extending and refining the RST relation set. Generally this has been aimed at enhancing the ability of parsers to correctly identify relations while at the same time increasing the

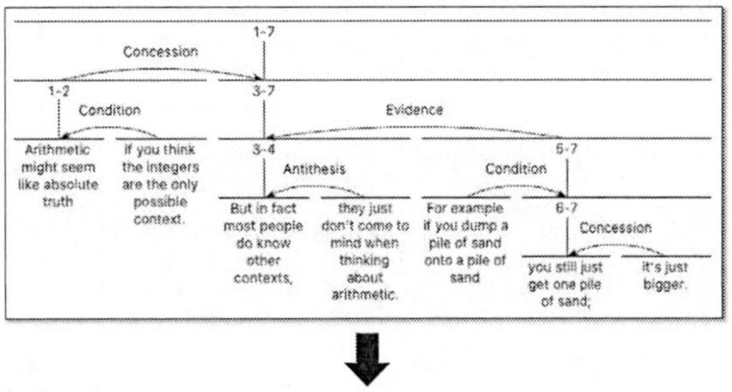


```
condition(2,1)
concession(7,6)
condition(5,concession(7,6))
antithesis(4,3)
evidence(condition(5,concession(7,6)),antithesis(4,3))
concession(condition(2,1),evidence(condition(5,concession(7,6)),antithesis(4,3)))
```

Figure 1: Reenacting a Rhetorical Structure (text from Cheng, 2022)

specificity of relations (Carlson & Marcu, 2001; Zeldes, 2017).

Other research has been aimed at enriching the theory. In particular, Marcu is known for articulating the aforementioned strong nuclearity assumption. Stede (2008) explored the problems of nuclearity. In his investigation of different types of salience phenomena, he found that nuclearity as defined in RST tends to conflate information from different realms of description within a single structure. He proposed a multilevel analysis approach that would reconcile these issues. A variety of formalisms have been developed that would address limitations in RST (e.g., Asher & Lascarides, 2003; Webber & Prasad, 2009; Wolf & Gibson, 2005). An assumption made for this paper is that the theory and practice of RST is sufficiently well developed as to produce useful and interesting analyses.

In a parallel but lesser-known universe is the theory of relational propositions. This theory is an antecedent to the conceptualization of RST. With relational propositions, relations between satellites and nuclei are treated as implicit coherence-producing assertions (Mann & Thompson, 1986b). A relational proposition consists of a predicate and a pair of arguments. The predicate corresponds to the RST relation, and the arguments correspond to its satellite and nucleus. A shortcoming in the early work in relational propositions was its limitation to elementary expressions. There were no provisions for complex structures. Mann and Thompson (2000) attempted to address this but without success. That leaves off where this research begins.

Potter (2019a, 2023b) devised a functional notation to support representation of complex relational propositions. The original objective was to develop a deductive interpretation of RST, one that would support investigation of logical operations such as transitive implication in discourse. That work provided an initial proof of concept for the algorithms described in this paper. However, rather than rely on propositional logic, the discourse features of interest were accessed directly.

This was expedited by using Potter's (2023a) program for mapping of RST diagrams to relational propositions. Automating this step enables scalability, reduces the likelihood of error, and eliminates a lot of tedium. Because the notation used for these relational propositions is conformant with the Python programming language, the algorithm effectively converts a diagram into machine processable code. An RST analysis like the *Arithmetic* analysis shown in Figure 1 can be automatically converted to its relational proposition:

```
concession(
   condition(
      2,1),
   evidence(
      condition(
         5,
         concession(
            7,6)),
      antithesis(
         4,3)))
```

These encoded relational propositions are the drivers for the algorithms described here. Each relation has a corresponding function within the code, called a relation handler, so that performance of the relational proposition causes execution of the defined functions.

4 Algorithmic Analyses of Rhetorical Structures

As introduced earlier, this paper describes three algorithms for analyzing rhetorical structures. *Reenactment* models the bottom-up production of discourse organization. *Composition* implements Marcu's (2000) strong nuclearity. And *Compression* leverages the asymmetry of RST relations to implement transitive inference directly into relational propositions.

Each of these algorithms uses Pythonized relational propositions as input. For each algorithm there is a set of functions called *relation handlers*, one handler per relation. Typically, these functions return a tuple-formatted relational proposition, i.e., the name of the relation and a nested tuple containing satellite and nucleus identifiers, including the relation names and tuple information for any relational propositions nested within them. At runtime the handlers are invoked in order of precedence as specified by the relational proposition. Each algorithm defines a collector function that manages the values returned by the relation handlers. The output consists of one or more relational propositions, constituting the reenactments, inferences, or compressions as determined by the algorithm.

Input to each algorithm starts with RST analyses created using RSTTool or RST-Web (O'Donnell, 1997; Zeldes, 2016). These analyses are transformed into relational propositions using Potter's (2023a) conversion tool. The relational propositions are then input to the algorithms which transform them into reenacted, inferred, or compressed relational propositions. These relational propositions may be analyzed as is, or they may be used to construct new RST analyses. The following sections provide detailed descriptions of the algorithms and their applications.[1]

4.1 Reenactment Algorithm

The hierarchical appearance of RST diagrams encourages the impression of top-down tree structures. But these trees do not sprout branches as it were from a root, branch, or stem. On the contrary, from a functional perspective, the diagrams are upside down: the segment nodes at the lower part of the diagram combine to form composite structures. These composite structures become increasingly complex at higher levels of the diagram. Although a completed diagram might seem to depict a static situation, what is revealed there is the end-state of a dynamic process. By modeling the abstract bottom-up process of discourse organization, the reenactment algorithm provides guidance for reading RST diagrams. The replay of a rhetorical structure shows how elementary discourse units combine logically to form relational propositions and how these propositions combine with other relational propositions to create increasingly complex expressions until a comprehensive analysis emerges. It is this comprehensive analysis that is modeled in an RST analysis.

The *reenactment algorithm* performs a bottom-up evaluation of a nested relational proposition. The design of the algorithm is simple. A relational proposition is evaluated as a Python expression. A relation handler is invoked whenever the relation occurs within an expression. These relation handlers convert a relational proposition from code to data. The function returns the name of the relation and a nested tuple containing identifiers for its satellite and nucleus. The contents of the tuple reflect the depth of the nesting of the relational proposition. The tuple representation of the relational proposition is assembled in precedence order, working from the inside out. The replay

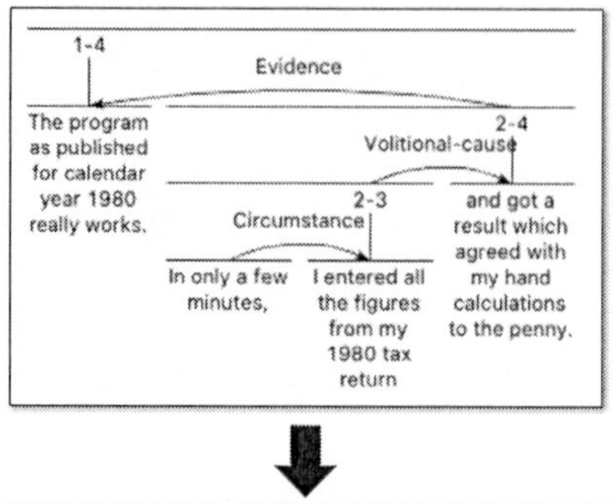


```
evidence(volitional_cause(circumstance(2,3),4),1)
evidence(volitional_cause(3,4),1)
evidence(4,1)
1
```

Figure 2: A Fully Compressible Analysis

[1] https://github.com/anpotter/aaars

manages the recursion of the expression and collects the output.

As the function makes its way through the relational proposition, it constructs the expression as it goes. In other words, it performs the relational proposition. A completed relational proposition can thus be thought of not as a static entity but as the result of an abstract process. And because relational propositions are isomorphic with their respective RST diagrams, the interpretation of the diagram can be understood as consistent with the performance of the relational proposition. As the reenactment in Figure 1 shows, RST structures define themselves from elementary relational propositions which combine to form complex expressions, enacting a logical process through which rhetorical intentionality emerges. This abstract process follows the precedence of the relational proposition.

4.2 Composition Algorithm

The *composition algorithm* is an implementation of Marcu's strong compositionality criterion. The criterion states that any relation between two spans will also hold between the nuclei of those spans (Marcu, 2000). Thus, simplified structures may be inferred from complex structures. In discussions of the criterion, it seems to be assumed that both the satellite and nucleus are themselves complex spans (e.g., Das, 2019; Demberg, Asr, & Scholman, 2019; Egg & Redeker, 2010; Marcu, 1996; Sanders et al., 2018; Stede, 2008). However, for the criterion to be delimited in this way suggests that relations between elementary units and relations between complex spans are in some way fundamentally different from one another. While there would be no difficulty in limiting the algorithm to comply with this, I have adopted a broader interpretation: nuclearity arises as a result of the relation of a unit or span to some other unit or span; hence the criterion is more broadly applicable. The only constraint is that at least one part of the relation be a span. Otherwise, any inference would be a simple repetition. Thus, the algorithm as written permits inferences in which either the satellite or the nucleus is an elementary unit, so that, for example, from the relational proposition:

```
volitional_cause(
   circumstance(
      2,3),4)
```

the algorithm makes the inference:

```
volitional_cause(3,4)
```

The algorithm evaluates the relation handlers for the relational proposition, collects the relational tuples, and determines which of those meet the compositionality criterion. The set of inferences generated from the RST analysis shown in Figure 1 are listed in Table 1.

Relational Proposition	Inference
`concession(` `  7,6)`	`6`

`condition(`
`  5,`
`  concession(`
`    7,6))`
	`condition(5,6)`

`antithesis(` `  4,3)`	`3`

`evidence(`
`  condition(`
`    5,`
`    concession(`
`      7,6)),`
`  antithesis(`
`    4,3))`
	`evidence(concession(7,6),3)`

`concession(`
`  condition(`
`    2,1),`
`  evidence(`
`    condition(`
`      5,`
`      concession(`
`        7,6)),`
`    antithesis(`
`      4,3)))`
	`concession(1,antithesis(4,3))`

Table 1: Inferences Generated by Composition Algorithm

4.3 Compression Algorithm

The *compression algorithm* is a procedure for progressive reduction of relational propositions to their simplest accessible form. By evaluating the expression in precedence order, the expression is progressively reduced from the innermost relational propositions outward. With each iteration the relation and satellite of the precedent proposition is eliminated. In effect, the relational proposition collapses inward. Usually, but not always, the ultimate reduction will be the single elementary discourse unit identifiable as the locus of intended effect. When not, it will be the simplest accessible relational proposition containing the nucleus that would have been the locus of intended effect, were that relation realizable. In other words, the algorithm takes the compression as far as it can, and yet acknowledges that some relations are by

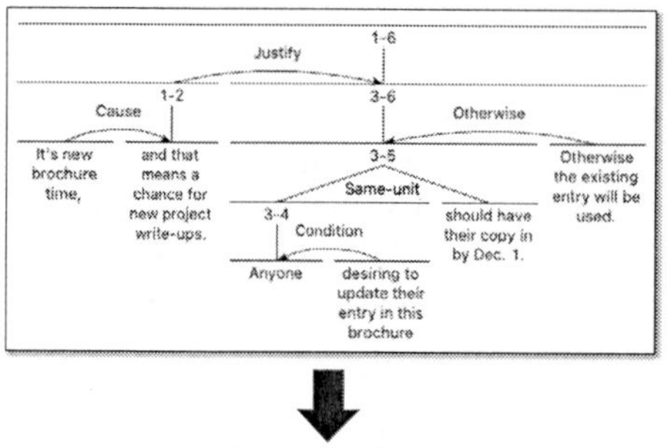


```
justify(cause(1,2),otherwise(6,same_unit(condition(4,3),5)))
justify(2,otherwise(6,same_unit(condition(4,3),5)))
```

Figure 3: A Partially Compressible Analysis

definition or by position resistant to reduction. The *Tax Program* analysis (Figure 2, above) provides a simple example of a fully compressible analysis. With each step, the innermost relation and its satellite are eliminated. The CIRCUMSTANCE and its satellite are dropped first. Next VOLITIONAL-CAUSE and its satellite are dropped, followed by elimnating the satellite from the EVIDENCE relation, ultimately leaving only segment 1: *the program as published for calendar year 1980 really works*. Applying this procedure to a variety of RST analyses has yielded positive results. However, not all RST analyses are as simple as the Tax Program.

Some relations are not compressible and require special treatment. These include multinuclears, relations with unrealized satellites, and attribution relations. While multinuclears may seem syntactically and semantically simple, they present complications. The nuclei within a multinuclear relation may consist solely of elementary discourse units, but quite commonly these nuclei are complex relational propositions that must themselves be reduced. So, on one level multinuclears may be treated as unanalyzable virtual units, but on the other, it is necessary to analyze the members of the relation, subjecting each to the compression process.

Relations with unrealized satellites include CONDITION, PURPOSE, UNLESS, and OTHERWISE. Unrealized relations do not permit inference or realization of the nucleus from the satellite. With the CONDITION relation the satellite presents a hypothetical, future, or otherwise unrealized situation such that realization of the nucleus is dependent on it. Hence the nucleus remains hypothetical. Similar dependencies hold for UNLESS and OTHERWISE. With PURPOSE, the nucleus is an activity that must be performed in order for the satellite to be realized. The relation between the satellite and nucleus holds but has not been realized. The compressibility of these relations depends on their position within a relational proposition. If the relation is positioned as the satellite of a relational proposition, it may be eliminated, but if it is the nucleus, it may not. This is because the process of reduction involves the progressive elimination of satellites. This, particularly when combined with multinuclear relations, can result in structures that are resistant to compression. *The New Brochure Time* analysis shown in Figure 3 is an example of this. There the OTHERWISE relation cannot be reduced because neither the satellite nor the nucleus is realized. SAME-UNIT is a pseudo-relation used for linking discontinuous text fragments that are really a single discourse unit. It is modeled on the multinuclear schema. The compression completes after only one reduction.

Alternatively, it can be useful to relax the reducibility constraint in order to focus on intentional development. For example, this can be of interest when the unrealized relations involve actions that might be taken by the reader. This is the case for the CONDITION and OTHERWISE relations for the *New Brochure Time* analysis shown above in Figure 3, presumably the writer of the text expected that these conditions would hold for to

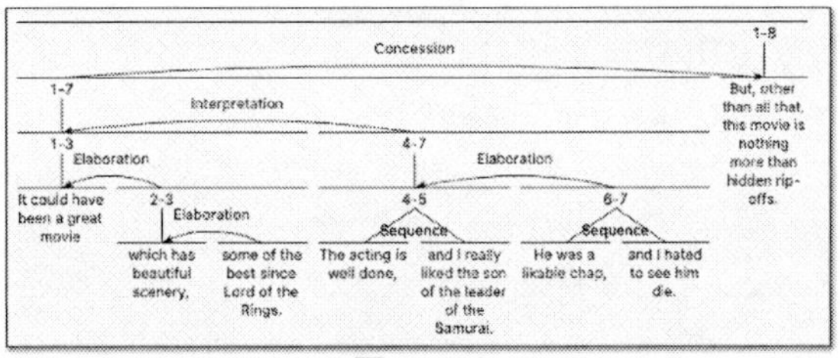


```
concession(interpretation(elaboration(sequence(6,7),sequence(4,5)),elaboration(elaboration(3,2),1)),8)
concession(interpretation(sequence(4,5),elaboration(elaboration(3,2),1)),8)
concession(interpretation(sequence(4,5),elaboration(2,1)),8)
concession(interpretation(sequence(4,5),1),8)
concession(1,8)
8
```

Figure 4: Reduction of Multinuclear Relations (Adapted from Lu et al., 2019)

some readers. With the constraints removed, the analysis reduces to `same_unit(3,5)`, or *Anyone...should have their copy in by December 1.*

Sometimes, as a compression proceeds, a non-compressible relation will be shifted from a nuclear to a satellite position. When this occurs, the relation can be eliminated. This can be observed in the process shown in Figure 4. There are two SEQUENCE relations in the analysis, one as satellite and the other as nucleus of an ELABORATION relation. When the ELABORATION is eliminated, it takes with it its satellite, thus eliminating the first of the SEQUENCE relations. The remaining SEQUENCE is now satellite to the INTERPRETATION relation, making it eligible for elimination, which occurs when it becomes the precedent relational proposition. The status of the ATTRIBUTION relation has been debated from time immemorial, so perhaps it is fitting that it should require special attention here. Mann and Thompson (1987) rejected it as a legitimate relation, but it was subsequently instated and refined by Carlson and Marcu (2001), as well as by Zeldes (2023), and yet provisionally rejected by Stede, Taboada, and Das (2017) and reduced to alternative relations by (Potter, 2019b). For the present research, ours is not to reason why, but rather to process any and all analyses as they presented. ATTRIBUTION is treated (at least optionally) as irreducible in part because sourcing of information is often part of the intended effect, particularly when the intention of the attributed material differs from that of the writer.

In order to assess the algorithm's applicability over larger texts, the compression algorithm was tested on several analyses from the GUM corpus (Zeldes, 2017). Because these analyses make frequent use of multinuclear relations, this resulted in reduced compressibility, so that the results are sometimes lengthy in their own right. Code was added to the algorithm to enable recovery of compressed texts. The results of this suggest coherence is preserved, albeit with some irregularities in surface cohesion and punctuation. For the *GUM Academic Thrones* analysis, the original contains 87 segments, and compression reduced this to 17 segments. The compressed text was mapped to its relational proposition to create an RST analysis relationally consistent with the source. The compressed text generated by the compression is shown in Figure 5. For readability, line breaks were inserted for each of the ORGANIZATION-HEADING relations. This text, along with the relational proposition, was used to create the RST analysis shown in Figure 6. The original segment identifiers are preserved for

> A Comparative Discourse Analysis of Fan Responses to Game of Thrones
>
> For us , as digital humanists , defining the " transmedia fan " is of particular relevance
>
> Methodology
>
> As a first step the current project undertakes a comparative discourse analysis of online conversations of Game of Thrones fans . As a pilot project , the current work takes the content of both comment threads and analyzes each thread separately Through this analysis , a categorization of themes emerges A comparison of categories and sub-categories between both groups provides preliminary findings to support an emergent model , or models , of the " transmedia fan " .
>
> Conclusion
>
> The present research represents a first step The question is , fundamentally , an examination Future research should explore the negotiation tactics The current study will contribute to the development of further qualitative and quantitative research This project is of relevance to researchers in media studies , fan studies , information studies and digital humanities.

Figure 5: Academic Thrones Compressed Text

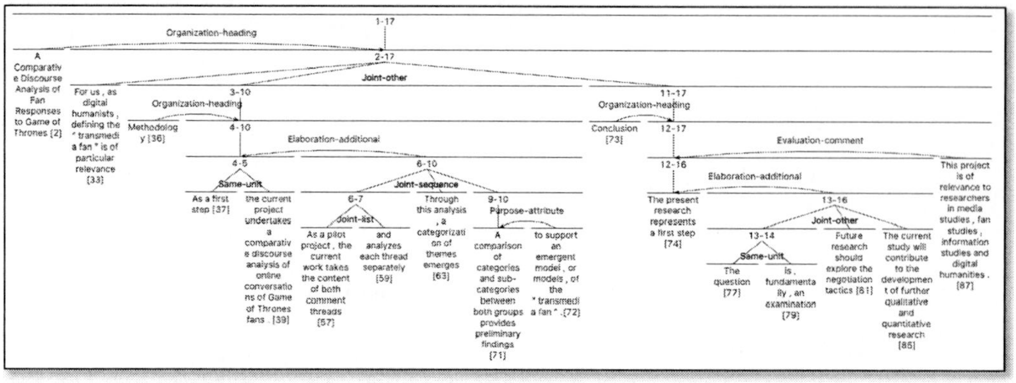

Figure 6: Compressed GUM Academic Thrones RST Analysis

reference. The rhetorical structure as well as the text survived the compression process. For the complete original text, see Forcier (2017).

The compression algorithm supports a longstanding view about nuclearity: simple summarizations should be possible merely by lopping off satellites. Moreover, this is reflected in a limitation that surfaced during testing. In analyses of longer documents where the JOINT relation and its variants are necessary to hold the structure together, guideposts such as ORGANIZATIONAL-HEADING become helpful for assuring readability. This is as true for the compressions as it is for the original texts.

In compressions of longer texts, such as the GUM analysis of Nancy Pelosi's speech on George Floyd, where such guideposts are lacking, minor digressions which work well in the original spoken medium become difficult in the transcript, and these difficulties are apparent in the compressions. That these reflect the features of the original should be understood as an affirmation of RST as an explanation of discourse coherence. The features of the document are carried forward through multiple layers of analysis.

As to whether the compression algorithm's contribution provides anything new or unique, I would argue that it affirms claims often left to intuition, and that it does so in a systematic and repeatable manner. The code is freely available to anyone who cares to take it for a test drive. Moreover, the approach is generalizable to other RST problems – once their solutions can be stated algorithmically, they can be readily evaluated and applied to a wide range of cases.

5 How it Works

The algorithms described here all share a common design. Each consists of two parts: a set of *relation handlers* and a *core algorithm*. A handler is provided for each relation in the RST relation set. These handlers are functions evaluated in response to each occurrence of their corresponding relation in a relational proposition. They are simple one-liners. Each handler returns a tuple containing the function's name and a nested tuple containing its satellite and nuclear identifiers. The functions obtain their names at runtime using a system call. Thus, in the reenactment and composition algorithms, an occurrence of the relational proposition `concession(1,2)` will return the tuple: `('concession',(1,2))`, and an occurrence of the relational proposition `evidence(3, concession(1,2))` will return the tuple: `('evidence',(3,('concession',(1,2)))`

When a relational proposition is evaluated, each handler is called in precedence order, with each function returning its name and arguments to the calling function. In this way, the program essentially *performs* the relational proposition, starting with the innermost (hence higher precedence) functions, working outward to the edges of the expression. The reenactment algorithm exploits that process.

The compress algorithm is only slightly more complicated. Each of its relation handlers makes a call to the core compression algorithm, passing it its relation name and arguments. Special handling for nonreducible relations is specified syntactically in the handler functions. The evaluation of the

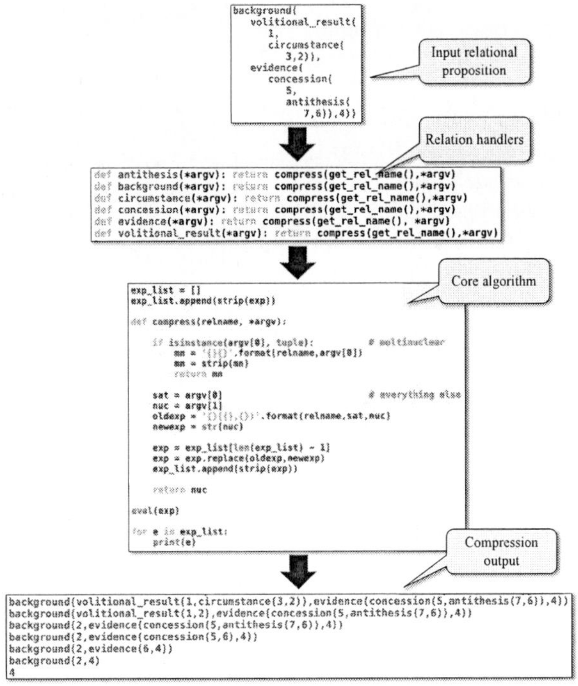

Figure 7: How it Works

relational proposition shown at the top of Figure 7 invokes each of the cited relation handlers and each of these call the `compress` function, first `circumstance`, followed by `volitional_result`, `antithesis`, `concession`, `evidence`, and finally the outermost relation, `background`. This leaves little for the core algorithm to do. Since multinuclears are non-compressible, the algorithm simply formats them and returns the formatted expression. For compressible relations, the algorithm simply replaces the current relational proposition with its nucleus, thus for each step eliminating the relation and satellite. Functionally, it infers the nucleus from the relational proposition. This is consistent with Marcu's strong nuclearity assumption. Because this process is implicit within the relational proposition, we can say it is also implicit within the RST diagram from which the proposition is derived, and therefore inferable from within the text itself. Figure 7 shows the complete code for the compress algorithm. For space reasons, the list of relation handlers has been limited to what is required for the example.

6 Conclusion

An RST analysis can be understood as an explanation of the organizational composition of a text. By identifying the text structure, by showing how its elements come together, an RST analysis explains how the text accomplishes what it is intended to do. The algorithms described in this paper contribute to that explanation. Reenactment is a step-by-step articulation of coherence development. The composition algorithm identifies relational propositions implicit within the text. The compress algorithm performs a deconstruction of the structure from its totality down to its intentional essence. These algorithms show that rhetorical structures can be studied in terms of their relational propositions. The relational propositions generated by the algorithms are inferences which follow directly from the source rhetorical structure. For each inference there is an isomorphic RST analysis and a corresponding text, that is, a structure within the structure and a text within the text. Thus, these simple algorithms provide interpretations of rhetorical structures as discursive processes, enabling the analyst to move beyond static diagrams and study formative and interpretative features of rhetorical structure. By positioning the algorithms within the framework of relational propositions, considerable simplicity is achieved. The algorithms extend the scope of RST as a tool for explaining discourse organization.

References

Nicholas Asher, & Alex Lascarides. 2003. *Logics of conversation*. Cambridge, UK: Cambridge University Press.

Lynn Carlson, & Daniel Marcu. 2001. *Discourse tagging reference manual* (TR-2001-545). Retrieved from Marina del Rey, CA: ftp://ftp.isi.edu/isi-pubs/tr-545.pdf

Eugenia Cheng. 2022. *The Joy of Abstraction*. Cambridge: Cambridge University Press.

Debopam Das. 2019. Nuclearity in RST and signals of coherence relations. In Amir Zeldes, Debopam Das, Erick Maziero Galani, Juliano Desiderato Antonio, & Mikel Iruskieta (Eds.), *Proceedings of the Workshop on Discourse Relation Parsing and Treebanking 2019* (pp. 30-37). Minneapolis, Minnesota: Association for Computational Linguistics.

Vera Demberg, Fatemeh Torabi Asr, & Merel Scholman. 2019. How compatible are our discourse annotations? Insights from mapping RST-DT and PDTB annotations.

Markus Egg, & Gisela Redeker. 2010. How complex is discourse structure? In *Proceedings of the Seventh conference on International Language Resources and Evaluation (LREC'10)* (pp. 1619-1623). Valletta, Malta: European Languages Resources Association (ELRA).

Eric Forcier. 2017. Re(a)d wedding: A comparative discourse analysis of fan responses to Game of Thrones. *Digital Humanities*.

Ruqian Lu, Shengluan Hou, Chuanqing Wang, Yu Huang, Chaoqun Fei, & Songmao Zhang. 2019. Attributed Rhetorical Structure Grammar for domain text summarization. *arxiv.org*.

William C. Mann, Christian M. I. M. Matthiessen, & Sandra A. Thompson. 1992. Rhetorical structure theory and text analysis. In William C. Mann & Sandra A. Thompson (Eds.), *Discourse description: Diverse linguistic analyses of a fund-raising text* (pp. 39-78). Amsterdam: John Benjamins.

William C. Mann, & Sandra A. Thompson. 1986a. Assertions from discourse structure. In *HLT '86: Proceedings of the workshop on strategic computing natural language* (pp. 257-270). Morristown, NJ: Association for Computational Linguistics.

William C. Mann, & Sandra A. Thompson. 1986b. Relational propositions in discourse. *Discourse Processes, 9*(1), 57-90.

William C. Mann, & Sandra A. Thompson. 1987. *Rhetorical structure theory: A theory of text organization* (ISI/RS-87-190). Retrieved from Marina del Rey, CA:

William C. Mann, & Sandra A. Thompson. 1988. Rhetorical structure theory: Toward a functional theory of text organization. *Text - Interdisciplinary Journal for the Study of Discourse, 8*(3), 243-281.

William C. Mann, & Sandra A. Thompson. 2000. *Toward a theory of reading between the lines: An exploration in discourse structure and implicit communication.* Paper presented at the Seventh International Pragmatics Conference, Budapest, Hungary.

Daniel Marcu. 1996. Building up rhetorical structure trees. In *Proceedings of the Thirteenth National Conference on Artificial Intelligence* (Vol. 2, pp. 1069-1074). Portland, Oregon: American Association for Artificial Intelligence.

Daniel Marcu. 1997. From discourse structures to text summaries. In *Proceedings of the ACL'97/EACL'97 Workshop on Scalable Text Summarization* (pp. 82-88). Madrid, Spain.

Daniel Marcu. 1998a. Improving summarization through rhetorical parsing tuning. In *The Sixth Workshop on Very Large Corpora* (pp. 206-215). Montreal, Canada.

Daniel Marcu. 1998b. *The rhetorical parsing, summarization, and generation of natural texts.* (Doctor of Philosophy dissertation), University of Toronto, Toronto, Canada.

Daniel Marcu. 1998c. To build text summaries of high quality, nuclearity is not sufficient. In *Working Notes of the AAAI-98 Spring Symposium on Intelligent Text Summarization.* Stanford, CA: AAAI.

Daniel Marcu. 1999. Discourse trees are good indicators of importance in text. In *Advances in automatic text summarization* (pp. 123-136).

Daniel Marcu. 2000. *The theory and practice of discourse parsing and summarization.* Cambridge, MA: MIT Press.

J. R. Martin. 1992. *English text: System and structure.* Philadelphia: John Benjamins.

Christian M.I.M. Matthiessen, & Sandra A. Thompson. 1987. The structure of discourse and 'subordination'. In John Haiman & Sandra A. Thompson (Eds.), *Clause combining in grammar and discourse* (pp. 275-329). Amsterdam: John Benjamins.

Michael O'Donnell. 1997. RST-Tool: An RST analysis tool. In *Proceedings of the 6th*

European Workshop on Natural Language Generation. Duisburg, Germany: Gerhard-Mercator University.

Andrew Potter. 2019a. Reasoning between the lines: A logic of relational propositions. *Dialogue and Discourse, 9*(2), 80-110.

Andrew Potter. 2019b. The rhetorical structure of attribution. In Amir Zeldes, Debopam Das, Erick Maziero Galani, Juliano Desiderato Antonio, & Mikel Iruskieta (Eds.), *Proceedings of the Workshop on Discourse Relation Parsing and Treebanking (DISRPT2019)* (pp. 38-49). Minneapolis, MN: Association for Computational Linguistics.

Andrew Potter. 2023a. An algorithm for Pythonizing rhetorical structures. In Sara Carvalho, Anas Fahad Khan, Ana Ostroški Anić, Blerina Spahiu, Jorge Gracia, John P. McCrae, Dagmar Gromann, Barbara Heinisch, & Ana Salgado (Eds.), *Language, data and knowledge 2023 (LDK 2023): Proceedings of the 4th Conference on Language, Data and Knowledge* (pp. 493-503). Vienna, Austria: NOVA CLUNL.

Andrew Potter. 2023b. Text as tautology: an exploration in inference, transitivity, and logical compression. *Text & Talk, 43*(4), 471-503. doi:doi:10.1515/text-2020-0230

Ted J M Sanders, Vera Demberg, Jet Hoek, Merel C.J. Scholman, Fatemeh Torabi Asr, Sandrine Zufferey, & Jacqueline Evers-Vermeul. 2018. Unifying dimensions in coherence relations: How various annotation frameworks are related. *Corpus Linguistics and Linguistic Theory, 17*(1), 1-71.

Manfred Stede. 2008. RST revisited: Disentangling nuclearity. In Cathrine Fabricius-Hansen & Wiebke Ramm (Eds.), *'Subordination' versus 'coordination' in sentence and text – from a cross-linguistic perspective* (pp. 33-58). Amsterdam: Benjamins.

Manfred Stede, Maite Taboada, & Debopam Das. 2017. *Annotation guidelines for rhetorical structure*. Retrieved from Potsdam and Burnaby: http://www.sfu.ca/~mtaboada/docs/research/RST_Annotation_Guidelines.pdf

Bonnie Webber, & Rashmi Prasad. 2009. Discourse structure: Swings and roundabouts. *Oslo Studies in Language, 1*(1), 171-190.

Florian Wolf, & Edward Gibson. 2005. Representing discourse coherence: A corpus-based analysis. *Computational Linguistics, 31*(2), 249-287.

Amir Zeldes. 2016. rstWeb – A browser-based annotation interface for Rhetorical Structure Theory and discourse relations. In *Proceedings of NAACL-HLT 2016 (Demonstrations)* (pp. 1-5). San Diego, California: Association for Computational Linguistics.

Amir Zeldes. 2017. The GUM corpus: Creating multilayer resources in the classroom. *Language Resources and Evaluation, 51*(3), 581-561.

Amir Zeldes. 2023, November 20. Rhetorical Structure Theory annotation - RST++. Retrieved from https://wiki.gucorpling.org/gum/rst

SciPara: A New Dataset for Investigating Paragraph Discourse Structure in Scientific Papers

Anna Kiepura[†], **Yingqiang Gao**[†], **Jessica Lam**[†], **Nianlong Gu**[‡]
Richard H.R. Hahnloser[†]
[†]Institute of Neuroinformatics, University of Zurich and ETH Zurich, Switzerland
{akiepura, yingqiang.gao, lamjessica, rich}@ini.ethz.ch
[‡]Linguistic Research Infrastructure, University of Zurich, Switzerland
nianlong.gu@uzh.ch

Abstract

Good scientific writing makes use of specific sentence and paragraph structures, providing a rich platform for discourse analysis and developing tools to enhance text readability. In this vein, we introduce SciPara[1], a novel dataset consisting of 981 scientific paragraphs annotated by experts in terms of sentence discourse types and topic information. On this dataset, we explored two tasks: 1) discourse category classification, which is to predict the discourse category of a sentence by using its paragraph and surrounding paragraphs as context, and 2) discourse sentence generation, which is to generate a sentence of a certain discourse category by using various contexts as input. We found that Pre-trained Language Models (PLMs) can accurately identify Topic Sentences in SciPara, but have difficulty distinguishing Concluding, Transition, and Supporting Sentences. The quality of the sentences generated by all investigated PLMs improved with amount of context, regardless of discourse category. However, not all contexts were equally influential. Contrary to common assumptions about well-crafted scientific paragraphs, our analysis revealed that paradoxically, paragraphs with complete discourse structures are less readable.

1 Introduction

Writing a scientific paper that is understandable to readers is a challenging task. Well-written scientific papers not only facilitate the comprehension of scientific discoveries but also reduce the risk of disseminating inaccuracies and misconceptions in research (Freeling et al., 2021).

As a rhetorical unit of writing, paragraphs contain valuable information regarding the logical and narrative connections among sentences (Nunan, 2015). Scientific papers with many well-written

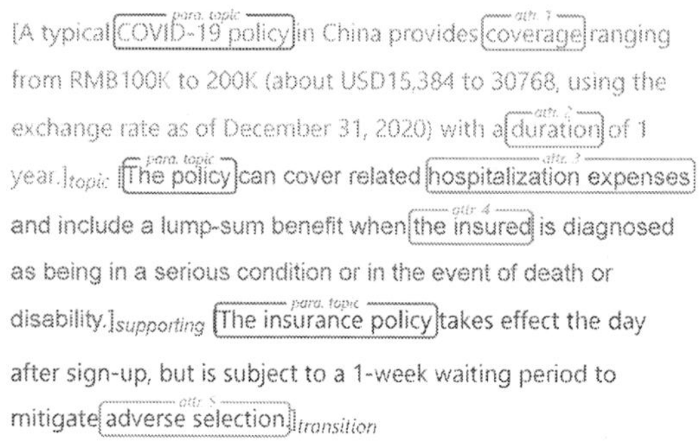

Figure 1: An example (taken from Feng et al. (2023)) annotated paragraph with one Topic Sentence (green), one Supporting Sentence (grey), and one Transition Sentence (blue). The paragraph topic is indicated in red and the topic attributes are indicated in orange.

paragraphs are easier to understand. In those paragraphs, related sentences are grouped and information is stitched in a thematically progressing manner (Weissberg, 1984).

In recent years, significant efforts have been directed at utilizing NLP technologies to process and comprehend scientific texts. For instance, research has focused on automatic summarization (Gu et al., 2022), text generation (Hu and Wan, 2014; Wang et al., 2019; Chen et al., 2021), as well as argument mining and discourse analysis (Fergadis et al., 2021; Gao et al., 2022; Achakulvisut et al., 2019), all in the context of scientific papers. However, few efforts have been devoted to identifying well-written scientific paragraphs from the perspective of discourse structure.

In this work, we propose **Sci**entific **Para**graphs (**SciPara**), a novel dataset specifically curated for studying the structure of scientific paragraphs. SciPara is a collection of scientific paragraphs that have been manually annotated by professional editors with strong biomedical backgrounds. The annotations include paragraph-level discourse com-

[1]Code and data are available at https://github.com/annamkiepura/SciPara.

Proceedings of the 5th Workshop on Computational Approaches to Discourse (CODI 2024), pages 12–26
March 21, 2024

pleteness, sentence-level discourse categories, and word-level occurrences of the paragraph topic. By training various language models on SciPara, we address the following research questions (RQs):

RQ1 Can language models distinguish sentences of different discourse categories?

RQ2 Can Topic, Concluding, and Transition Sentences be generated from the rest of the corresponding paragraphs?

RQ3 Are paragraphs with complete discourse structure more readable?

Our main **contributions** are as follows: 1) We propose a manually annotated dataset of scientific paragraphs, which is, to the best of our knowledge, the first dataset specifically designed for the study of the discourse structure of scientific paragraphs; 2) We fine-tune language models to perform sentence classification and generation tasks on our dataset; 3) We perform an in-depth analysis of the paragraph discourse structure with respect to our experimental results.

2 SciPara: A New Dataset for Discourse Structure of Scientific Paragraphs

Our goal is to facilitate the analysis of scientific paragraph discourse structure on two levels:

Sentence level How do individual sentences relate to the paragraph's discourse structure?

Subsentence level What are the paragraph's topic and its corresponding attributes?

In this section, we outline the protocol given to the annotators for creating SciPara (see Figure 2a).

2.1 Initial paragraph filtering

To preserve the coherence of the paper's narrative, annotators processed paragraphs in their order of occurrence. We instructed annotators to skip paragraphs that had parsing errors, such as incorrect sentence splits, or that contained less than three sentences. The annotators were required to label such paragraphs as "Bad Parse" and "Too Short" respectively.

2.2 Sentence-level annotation

We tasked annotators with categorizing each sentence of a paragraph into one of the following six discourse categories:

Topic Sentence A sentence that encapsulates the central theme of the paragraph. The information presented in a Topic Sentence is typically expanded upon in the other sentences of the paragraph (McCarthy et al., 2008).

Supporting Sentence A sentence that bolsters the Topic Sentence(s) with relevant information such as explanations, elaborations, and examples.

Concluding Sentence A sentence that summarizes and closes the narrative of the paragraph.

Transition Sentence A sentence that connects the current paragraph to the next paragraph, thereby maintaining the coherence of the paper.

Off-Topic Sentence A sentence that lacks information pertinent to the topic of the paragraph.

Redundant Sentence A sentence whose content has already been stated in an earlier sentence of the paragraph.

We refer to paragraphs with at least one Topic Sentence and at least one Concluding or Transition Sentence as paragraphs with *complete* discourse structure. All other paragraphs are considered to have an *incomplete* discourse structure (see Table 2).

During the annotation, a few paragraphs turned out to have no Topic Sentences. We instructed annotators to halt the annotation of such paragraphs and to proceed to the next.

2.3 Subsentence-level annotation

The annotators then moved on to the subsentence-level task, see Figure 2b. The first step was to identify noun phrases in the Topic Sentence(s) that pertained to the topic of the paragraph. Inspired by Ajjour et al. (2023), we defined the paragraph topic hierarchically:

Topic Ontology A noun phrase that best encapsulates the topic of the paragraph.

Topic Attribute A noun phrase that describes an aspect of the Topic Ontology.

We allowed for exactly one Topic Ontology and up to seven unique Topic Attributes per paragraph. A handful of paragraphs had multiple Topic Sentences; however, in all cases, the multiple Topic Sentences had the same Topic Ontology and Topic Attributes.

Next, the annotators identified all re-occurrences of the paragraph topic (both Topic Ontology and

Topic Attributes) in the other sentences of the paragraph. Re-occurrences could be either exact matches or semantically similar noun phrases.

When a sentence s did not contain the paragraph topic, we asked annotators to identify links between s and the other sentences of the paragraph. Links are noun phrases that can be found in both s and at least one other sentence of the paragraph that contains the paragraph topic annotations. Finally, we asked annotators to label sentences that contain neither the paragraph topic nor links as "Off-Topic Sentences".

2.4 Data sources

We obtained 62 scientific papers from two datasets: Semantic Scholar Open Research Corpus (S2ORC) (Lo et al., 2020) and Europe PMC[2]. S2ORC is a comprehensive repository consisting of 81 million scientific papers in English. Europe PMC is an open-access repository containing 43 million publications and preprints enriched with links to supporting data, reviews, and other relevant sources.

We investigated paragraphs from INTRODUCTION and DISCUSSION sections only. This is because these sections aim to deliver narratives, as compared to, say, RESULTS sections, which typically aim to list but not necessarily analyse the papers' findings (Nair et al., 2014).

Due to the need for clear sectioning, we only used papers from the fields of medicine and biomedicine. Papers from such fields often follow the IMRaD format and contain INTRODUCTION, METHODS, RESULTS, and DISCUSSION sections (Nair et al., 2014).

For the annotation tasks, we enlisted the expertise of four proficient biomedical editors who are members of the European Medical Writers Association (EMWA)[3]. Annotation was performed on the interactive data annotation platform *Doccano* (Nakayama et al., 2018).

2.5 SciPara statistics

The SciPara dataset consists of 981 paragraphs and 4071 sentences, see Table 1. Across these paragraphs, the annotators identified more than 700 instances of Topic Ontologies and over 2800 instances of Topic Attributes. In total, 432 paragraphs have complete discourse structure and 309 paragraphs have incomplete discourse structure, see Table 2. We kept the 240 paragraphs that were not annotated for discourse completeness so that we could study the influence of context information in the discourse sentence generation task.

Statistic	Count	Statistic	Count
# Papers	62	# Topic Sentences	724
# Paragraphs	981	# Supporting Sentences	2,869
# Sentences	4,071	# Concluding Sentences	273
# Topic Attribute	2,821	# Transition Sentences	188
# Topic Ontology	724	# Off-topic Sentences	3
-	-	# Redundant Sentences	14

Table 1: Overall statistics of our SciPara dataset.

Topic Sentence	Concluding Sentence	Transition Sentence	Discourse Structure	Count
✓	✓	✗	Complete	250
✓	✗	✓	Complete	177
✓	✓	✓	Complete	5
✓	✗	✗	Incomplete	284
✗	✓	✗	Incomplete	7
✗	✗	✓	Incomplete	4
✗	✗	✗	Incomplete	14

Table 2: Structure assessment for sentence-level annotation. We exclude paragraphs with both Concluding and Transition Sentences but no Topic Sentences on purpose, since subsentence-level annotation for this type of paragraphs was not possible (Topic Ontology must be labeled from the Topic Sentence).

Due to the unexpected absence of annotator 3, we present the inter-annotator agreement (IAA) results for annotators 1, 2, and 4 only, see Table 3. For sentence-level annotation, we calculated Cohen's Kappa coefficients (Cohen, 1960) for each pair of annotators. As for subsentence-level annotation, where Topic Ontology and Topic Attributes do not have fixed discourse categories and can vary in length, we evaluated the IAA based on lexical overlap of annotations measured by ROUGE scores (Lin, 2004). High ROUGE-1 and ROUGE-2 scores therefore indicate better agreement between pairs of annotators.

Sentence-level annotations of Topic, Supporting, and Concluding discourse categories showed a high agreement among annotators when compared against a reference rubric for Cohen's Kappa scores interpretation (McHugh, 2012), which we summarize in the legend of Table 3. For example, for Topic Sentence identification, all of the analyzed data subsets fall into the "strong agreement" category. This indicates that the task of identifying these discourse types was clearly defined and the annotators understood the instructions well. The

[2] https://europepmc.org/

[3] https://www.emwa.org

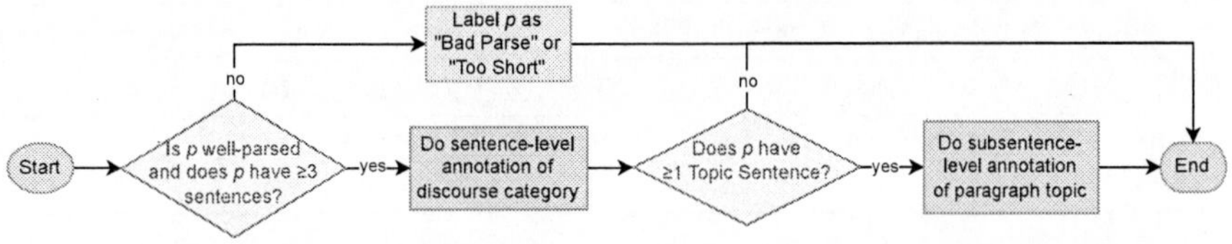

(a) Sentence-level annotation process for a paragraph p. The process starts with an initial filtering to determine whether p is well-parsed and has at least three sentences. Next, the annotators identify the discourse category of each sentence in p. If p has at least one Topic Sentence, then annotators perform subsentence-level annotation to locate all occurrences of the paragraph topic.

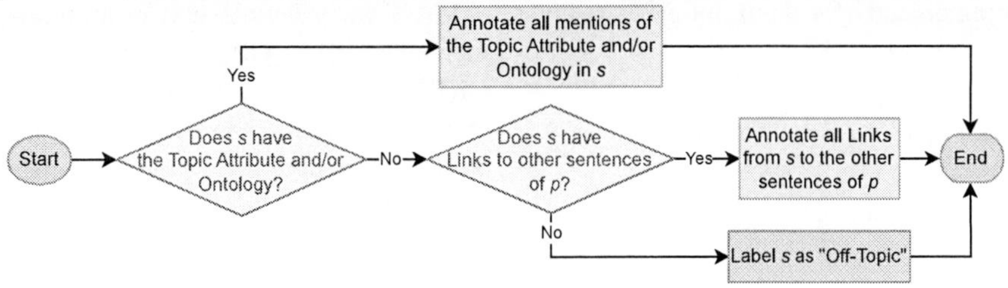

(b) Subsentence-level annotation process for a paragraph p. Starting with labeling the Topic Ontology in the Topic Sentence s, the subsentence-level annotation identifies Topic Attributes throughout the paragraph.

Figure 2: Overview of the SciPara data annotation process for a given paragraph p.

Subset	A			B	C
Annotator Group	1&2	2&4	1&4	1&4	1&4
κ - Topic Sent.	0.79	0.72	0.92	**0.97**	0.96
κ - Supp. Sent.	0.75	0.68	**0.78**	0.68	**0.78**
κ - Concl. Sent.	0.69	**0.78**	0.60	0.64	0.53
κ - Trans. Sent.	**0.69**	0.40	0.22	0.08	0.26

(a) IAA results for sentence-level annotation.

Subset	A			B	C
Annotator Group	1&2	2&4	1&4	1&4	1&4
R-1 (f-measure)	0.59	0.61	**0.67**	0.63	0.61
R-2 (f-measure)	0.43	0.48	**0.50**	0.45	0.41

(b) IAA results for subsentence-level annotation (stopwords are removed for all measures).

Table 3: Inter-annotator agreement (IAA) results for sentence-level and subsentence-level ($\kappa \leq 0.4$ = poor agreement; $0.4 < \kappa \leq 0.6$ = fair agreement; $\kappa > 0.6$ = strong agreement). Subsets A, B, and C contain 36, 36, and 50 paragraphs, respectively.

agreement was considerably lower for Transition Sentences, which we discuss in more detail in Limitations.

For subsentence-level annotations, given that the average length of Topic Ontology and Topic Attributes was around 3 to 4 words, a lexical overlap score above 0.4 is considered as high. Thus, it suggests that the subsentence-level task was also well understood by the annotators, suggesting that the curated dataset has good quality.

3 Methods

In the following section, we detail the experimental methods applied to the SciPara dataset to address our research questions. Notably, our experiments primarily utilized the annotations corresponding to the sentence-level task, and the Topic Ontology annotations from the subsentence-level task. We plan to incorporate other annotation types, such as Topic Attributes and links, in future studies.

3.1 Discourse category classification

Underlying RQ1 is the following sequential sentence classification task (Cohan et al., 2019): Identifying the discourse category of a sentence Y based on the context of Y. By context, we refer to the paragraph P containing Y and the subsequent paragraph P'. We ignored Off-Topic and Redundant Sentences because of their rarity and considered only Topic, Concluding, Transition, and Supporting Sentences.

For each sample, we concatenated the paragraph P and the subsequent paragraph P', then we indicated Y by wrapping it with the special token [SENT]. We also inserted a [PARASEP] token between P and P' to indicate the paragraph boundaries. The sample was then presented as input to two language models we explored: BioBERT (Lee et al., 2020) and SciBERT (Beltagy et al., 2019). To compute the probability of each discourse category in either model, we presented the [CLS] embedding as input to a Softmax classifier.

Model	Topic Sent.			Concluding Sent.			Transition Sent.			Supporting Sent.		
	P	R	F1	P	R	F1	P	R	F1	P	R	F1
BioBERT	**98.85**	**97.73**	**98.29**	**11.69**	33.33	**17.31**	**7.52**	**50.00**	**13.07**	93.91	**55.10**	**69.45**
SciBERT	**98.85**	**97.73**	**98.29**	7.41	**74.07**	13.47	4.76	5.00	4.88	**94.63**	35.97	52.13

Table 4: Results on discourse category classification in terms of Precision (P), Recall (R), and F1 score.

The training objective was to minimize the following log cross-entropy loss:

$$\mathcal{L} = -\log\left(\frac{\exp(s_p)}{\sum_{j=1}^{|\mathcal{C}|}\exp(s_j)}\right),$$

where $\mathcal{C}$ represents the discourse categories of Topic, Concluding, Supporting, and Transition Sentences, s_j is the logit for the j-th discourse category label ($j = 1, \dots, 4$), and s_p is the logit for the positive label (p is the index of the correct label).

To avoid over-representing Supporting Sentences in the Discourse Category Classification task, we balanced the label distribution in the Train and Dev sets. However, we did not perform this balancing for the Test set to determine the real-world performance of the classifiers. Note that we also tried other balancing methods, such as weighting the loss per category based on their frequency, but none worked as well.

3.2 Discourse sentence generation

To address RQ2, we investigated the influence of context on the generation of Topic (resp. Concluding, Transition) Sentences. As context we used either the remainder of the corresponding paragraph P, or we additionally included other information X, such as the Topic Ontology, or out-of-paragraph information, such as the paper's abstract and the subsequent or previous paragraph.

We describe the generation task formally here. Let P be a paragraph and let Y be a Topic (resp. Concluding, Transition) Sentence in P. The training objective is to minimize the following negative log-likelihood:

$$\begin{aligned}\mathcal{L} &= -\log p\,(Y|P\setminus Y, X)\\ &= -\sum_{i=1}^{|Y|}\log p\,(y_i|y_{1:i-1}, P\setminus Y, X)\,,\end{aligned}$$

where y_i is the i-th token of Y, $P \setminus Y$ represents the paragraph P without Y, and X represents additional information.

We explored two classes of Pre-trained Language Models (PLMs): 1) causal language models (CLMs) that generate text in an auto-regressive manner, such as OPT (Zhang et al., 2022) and GPT-Neo (Black et al., 2022), and 2) sequence-to-sequence models (Seq2Seq) that learn mappings between the input and output sequences, such as BART (Lewis et al., 2020) and T5 (Raffel et al., 2020). To ensure a fair comparison, we chose models with a similar number of parameters (OPT-base and GPT-Neo both have 125M parameters, BART-base has 140M, and T5 has 220M). The inputs to all models were formed as $P \setminus Y$ concatenated with X. For CLMs, we additionally appended a separation token <|endoftext|>. For Topic Sentence generation with BART and T5, we prepended the input with "Truncated Paragraph:" and also appended "Topic Sentence:". The inputs for BART and T5 for generating Concluding and Transition Sentences were formed analogously.

For the discourse sentence generation task and each discourse category, we used only paragraphs that had at least one sentence of the corresponding discourse category, see Table 5.

Discourse category classification	Train	Dev	Test
# Topic Sentences	124	44	88
# Supporting Sentences	141	27	392
# Concluding Sentences	136	32	27
# Transition Sentences	137	31	20
Discourse sentence generation	**Train**	**Dev**	**Test**
# Topic Sentences	579	85	60
# Concluding Sentences	216	25	32
# Transition Sentences	129	34	25

Table 5: Statistics of datasets created for discourse category classification and discourse sentence generation.

3.3 Evaluation

For the discourse category classification task, we report the precision, recall, and F1 score for each discourse category. Higher scores indicate better performance. For the discourse sentence generation task, we compared the generated discourse sentences against the ground-truth sentences using summarization metrics such as ROUGE scores

(Lin, 2004) and BERTScore (Zhang et al., 2019), as well as the translation metric METEOR (Banerjee and Lavie, 2005). Higher scores indicate that the generated discourse sentences more closely resemble the ground-truths.

To quantify the readability of paragraphs, we used three automatic readability metrics, namely, Flesch-Kincaid Grade Level (FKG, Kincaid et al. (1975)), the New Dale-Chall Readability Formula (NDC, Chall and Dale (1995)), and the Automated Readability Index (ARI, Senter and Smith (1967))[4]. For these metrics, higher scores indicate higher reading difficulty and thus lower readability.

3.4 Implementation details

For the classification task, the BioBERT and SciBERT models were trained for 3 epochs with a learning rate of 2e-5, a dropout rate $p = 0.1$, and a batch size of 1.

For the generation task, all PLMs were trained for 2 epochs using the Trainer and TrainingArguments classes from the Transformers library[5]. We used the AdamW optimizer (Loshchilov and Hutter, 2017) with a learning rate of 2e-5 and early stopping. The batch size was set to 2. For the inference step, we used beam search with $num\_beams = 3$, $top\_k = 10$, and $temperature = 0.95$.

All models were fine-tuned using a single A100 GPU provided by Google Colab. We kept batch sizes low to allow for experimenting with various context sizes.

Model	R-1	R-2	R-L	F_{BERT}	MTR
Topic Sentence Generation					
OPT-base	21.64	4.44	17.40	18.62	15.20
GPT-Neo	22.26	4.77	17.52	18.25	15.60
BART-base	24.33	4.72	18.49	24.67	15.39
+ PP	25.82	5.83	19.54	25.75	17.32
+ PP + A	24.90	6.15	18.98	24.78	16.88
+ PP + A + TO	**33.50**	**16.72**	**28.12**	**30.67**	**25.05**
T5-base	23.23	5.12	17.61	18.19	15.74
+ TO	30.92	15.20	26.55	24.89	23.57
Concluding Sentence Generation					
OPT-base	22.06	4.55	**18.90**	21.17	14.96
GPT-Neo	19.84	3.98	15.36	23.75	13.13
BART-base	24.11	2.84	15.55	24.52	15.39
+ PP	22.50	3.91	16.87	26.11	15.42
+ PP + A	**24.52**	**5.23**	18.84	**29.89**	**16.07**
T5-base	17.35	3.34	13.26	6.25	11.64
Transition Sentence Generation					
OPT-base	15.50	2.21	12.31	6.42	9.50
GPT-Neo	15.38	2.18	11.77	3.40	7.88
BART-base	17.00	3.27	11.35	13.99	16.33
+ NP	**23.85**	**4.51**	**15.94**	**17.80**	**19.86**
+ NP + A	21.43	3.21	14.54	13.72	15.92
T5-base	12.22	2.70	8.71	2.59	8.86

Table 6: Results on discourse sentence generation. For ROUGE scores, we report the f-measures for ROUGE-1, ROUGE-2, and ROUGE-L. For BERTScore, we report the F1 score (F_{BERT}). MTR denotes the METEOR score. PP indicates the addition of the **P**revious **P**aragraph to the input, whereas NP, A and TO indicates the addition of the **N**ext **P**aragraph, the **A**bstract, and the **T**opic **O**ntology, respectively.

4 Results and Discussion

4.1 PLMs accurately identify Topic Sentences

As shown in Table 4, on the discourse category classification task, both BioBERT and SciBERT achieved the highest scores of 98.29 F1 on Topic Sentences, indicating that this discourse category is the easiest to identify. Because 98.86% of Topic Sentences in our Test set were the first sentence of their respective paragraphs, a possible explanation of this finding is that the positional information of Topic Sentences can be easily captured and learned by the models.

The second-highest scores were recorded for Supporting Sentences, and the lowest scores for Transition and Concluding Sentences. We hypothesise that the poor performance on Concluding and Transition Sentences may be because both types of sentences tend to appear at the end of paragraphs, which means the model cannot rely on learning positional information alone in distinguishing the two classes. In the Appendix A, when considering Concluding and Transition Sentences as a single class, performance across all metrics improved.

Based on the confusion matrices in Figure 3, BioBERT and SciBERT respectively tended to misclassify Supporting Sentences as Transition and Concluding Sentences. A possible explanation is that Supporting Sentences may be very diverse, and because we heavily downsampled Supporting Sentences to balance the four discourse categories for this task, our models were not able to learn this diversity.

4.2 Influence of context

On the discourse sentence generation task, both CLM and Seq2Seq models achieved the highest ROUGE F1 scores on Topic Sentences and the low-

[4] All metrics were computed with the Python package *py-readability-metrics*.

[5] `https://github.com/huggingface/transformers`

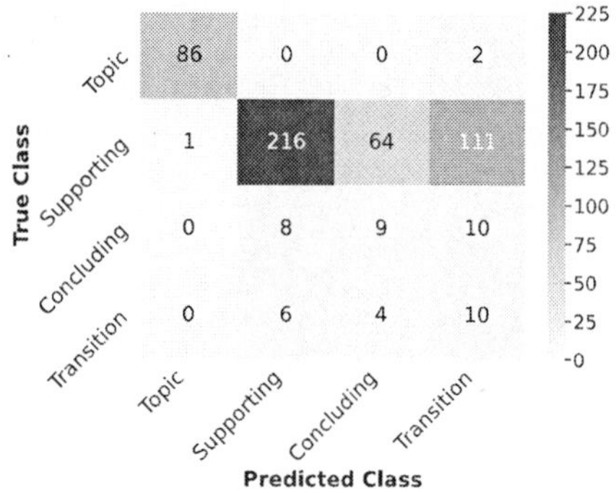

(a) BioBERT

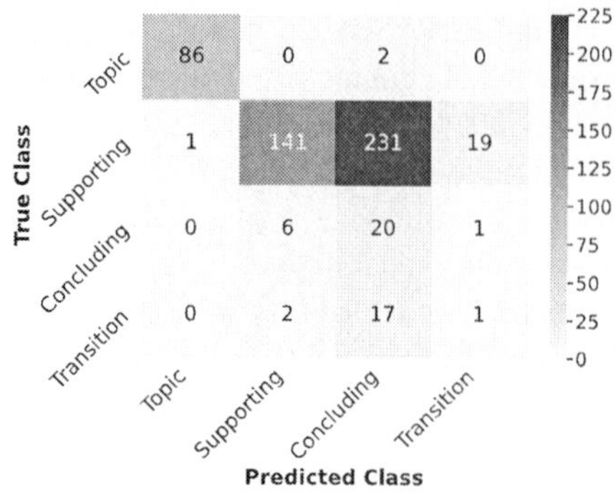

(b) SciBERT

Figure 3: Confusion matrices for discourse category classification with BioBERT and SciBERT.

est scores on Transition Sentences, see Table 6. This finding was true regardless of whether context contained additional information or not, although the best generation scores across all discourse categories were achieved when additional information was included.

To delve deeper into whether sentences of a given discourse category carry information beyond the current paragraph, we conducted training of separate Seq2Seq models on text beyond the current paragraph (namely, using previous/next paragraphs and the abstract) as part of the input).

The BART model generated the best Concluding Sentences when the input contained the previous paragraph and the abstract in addition to the current paragraph. BART also generated the best Topic Sentences when the context included the Topic Ontology, abstract, and the previous paragraph.

As for Transition Sentences, incorporating the next paragraph resulted in the greatest improvement, but including the abstract deteriorated the performance. These findings suggest that pertinent information related to Topic, Concluding, and Transition Sentences can be found at diverse positions in a discourse category-dependent manner.

4.3 Trade-off between discourse structure and text readability

Text readability refers to the ease with which a reader can understand a written text (Zamanian and Heydari, 2012). The relationship between the completeness of discourse structure and text readability offers valuable insights. It sheds light on how the organization of a paragraph influences a reader's comprehension, engagement, and retention of information from a written piece.

To understand how discourse structure completeness relates to readability, we compared the readability across two groups of paragraphs: paragraphs with complete discourse structure and paragraphs with incomplete discourse structure. We filtered out paragraphs containing less than 100 words[6]. Then, we computed the readability of remaining paragraphs using the three previously mentioned metrics (FKG, NDC, and ARI).

Structure	FKG	NDC	ARI
Complete	16.75	12.68	17.98
Incomplete	***15.82**	**12.60**	***16.75**

Table 7: Readability measures for paragraphs with complete and incomplete discourse structures. Higher scores indicate that the paragraph is more challenging to read. * indicates statistical significance at $p < 0.05$.

We found that the paragraphs in SciPara are generally difficult texts to read, regardless of discourse structure completeness. This is evident by the average FKG scores of around 16 (see Table 7), which means that a university-level education would be required to comprehend these SciPara paragraphs. This result is not surprising, given that SciPara was constructed from scholarly works that are written for the scientific community.

Additionally, our results revealed that paragraphs with complete discourse structure are associated with greater reading difficulty than incompletely structured paragraphs. This is consistent with the work of Plavén-Sigray et al. (2017), who found that abstracts, which typically have complete discourse structures, are more challenging to read than the full text. As a complete discourse structure indicates a tightly connected reasoning chain, our

[6]As required by *py-readability-metrics*.

results imply a paradoxical trade-off between text readability and discourse structure: well-crafted scientific texts with complete discourse structures are inherently more difficult to comprehend.

5 Related Work

Previous works on automatic classification of discourse category of sentences from scientific papers are Dernoncourt and Lee (2017), Cohan et al. (2019), Gonçalves et al. (2020), Dayrell et al. (2012), Fisas et al. (2015), and Li et al. (2022). The discourse categories used reflected various roles within the scientific paper. For example, Dayrell et al. (2012) used BACKGROUND, GAP, PURPOSE, METHOD, RESULT, and CONCLUSION as discourse categories, and Fisas et al. (2015) used BACKGROUND, CHALLENGE, APPROACH, OUTCOME, and FUTURE WORK. Li et al. (2022) analyzed sentence roles specifically in RELATED WORK sections, introducing categories like "multi-document summarization" and "transition" for sentences bridging various topics. Our work distinguishes itself by examining discourse sentences in relation to their function in paragraph development, with annotations for "Transition Sentences" allowing us to comprehend how discourse expands over consecutive paragraphs, which is fundamental to our proposed research questions.

Moreover, there is a scarcity of research on generating sentences across these discourse categories. Shieh et al. (2019) and Song et al. (2022) conducted related studies, with the former generating abstract "conclusions" and the latter generating topic-word-constrained sentences. Our approach, however, explores generating "Topic Sentences" and other categories from the remainder of the corresponding paragraph and varying additional contexts, such as preceding paragraphs, thus addressing a research gap.

6 Conclusion

We introduced the SciPara dataset which comprises scientific paragraphs with expert annotations of sentence discourse category and of topic information. Leveraging pre-trained language models, we explored two tasks: discourse category classification and discourse sentence generation. While the models demonstrated high accuracy in identifying Topic Sentences, they encountered challenges in distinguishing Concluding, Transition, and Supporting Sentences, underscoring the inherent complexities in automating discourse category classification.

We also examined the influence of contextual input on generating discourse sentences. Our findings indicate that language models perform better with increased context, but that the context most useful depends on the sentence discourse category. For instance, Topic Ontology plays the most crucial role for Topic Sentence generation, whereas the next paragraph has the largest influence on Transition Sentence generation.

We also assessed the readability of SciPara paragraphs. Surprisingly, our analysis reveals an intriguing paradox on the relationship between discourse structure and readability. Scientific paragraphs containing at least one Topic Sentence and at least one Concluding or Transition sentence are commonly perceived as well-written. However, such paragraphs are more challenging to read.

7 Limitations

The limitations of our work include:

- SciPara is a high quality dataset. However, the acquisition of expert-annotated data is a resource-intensive process, which made expanding SciPara to a larger size difficult. This has resulted in a limited number of samples for certain discourse categories, notably Concluding Sentences (273) and Transition Sentences (188).

- Our annotation protocol exclusively targets scientific paragraphs within the INTRODUCTION and DISCUSSION sections because these sections are likely to have narrative structures. However, we refrained from including other sections due to the associated complexity.

- The readability metrics FKG, NDC, and ARI were developed to assess general domain text, not academic texts. Even so, we used them in this work because we were unable to find more fitting readability metrics.

Our future work will delve into a more comprehensive examination of the discourse structure across various sections of scientific papers. We are committed to finding innovative approaches to mitigate the cost and effort associated with human annotation, enabling the collection of a more extensive and diverse set of samples.

References

Titipat Achakulvisut, Chandra Bhagavatula, Daniel Acuna, and Konrad Kording. 2019. Claim extraction in biomedical publications using deep discourse model and transfer learning. *arXiv preprint arXiv:1907.00962*.

Yamen Ajjour, Johannes Kiesel, Benno Stein, and Martin Potthast. 2023. Topic ontologies for arguments. In *Findings of the Association for Computational Linguistics: EACL 2023*, pages 1381–1397.

Satanjeev Banerjee and Alon Lavie. 2005. Meteor: An automatic metric for mt evaluation with improved correlation with human judgments. In *Proceedings of the acl workshop on intrinsic and extrinsic evaluation measures for machine translation and/or summarization*, pages 65–72.

Iz Beltagy, Kyle Lo, and Arman Cohan. 2019. Scibert: A pretrained language model for scientific text. In *Proceedings of the 2019 Conference on Empirical Methods in Natural Language Processing and the 9th International Joint Conference on Natural Language Processing (EMNLP-IJCNLP)*, pages 3615–3620.

Sid Black, Stella Biderman, Eric Hallahan, Quentin Anthony, Leo Gao, Laurence Golding, Horace He, Connor Leahy, Kyle McDonell, Jason Phang, Michael Pieler, USVSN Sai Prashanth, Shivanshu Purohit, Laria Reynolds, Jonathan Tow, Ben Wang, and Samuel Weinbach. 2022. Gpt-neox-20b: An open-source autoregressive language model.

Jeanne Sternlicht Chall and Edgar Dale. 1995. *Readability revisited: The new Dale-Chall readability formula*. Brookline Books.

Hong Chen, Hiroya Takamura, and Hideki Nakayama. 2021. SciXGen: A scientific paper dataset for context-aware text generation. In *Findings of the Association for Computational Linguistics: EMNLP 2021*, pages 1483–1492, Punta Cana, Dominican Republic. Association for Computational Linguistics.

Arman Cohan, Iz Beltagy, Daniel King, Bhavana Dalvi, and Dan Weld. 2019. Pretrained language models for sequential sentence classification. In *Proceedings of the 2019 Conference on Empirical Methods in Natural Language Processing and the 9th International Joint Conference on Natural Language Processing (EMNLP-IJCNLP)*, pages 3693–3699, Hong Kong, China. Association for Computational Linguistics.

Jacob Cohen. 1960. A coefficient of agreement for nominal scales. *Educational and psychological measurement*, 20(1):37–46.

Carmen Dayrell, Arnaldo Candido Jr., Gabriel Lima, Danilo Machado Jr., Ann Copestake, Valéria Feltrim, Stella Tagnin, and Sandra Aluisio. 2012. Rhetorical move detection in english abstracts: Multi-label sentence classifiers and their annotated corpora. In *Proceedings of the Eight International Conference on Language Resources and Evaluation (LREC'12)*, Istanbul, Turkey. European Language Resources Association (ELRA).

Franck Dernoncourt and Ji Young Lee. 2017. PubMed 200k RCT: a dataset for sequential sentence classification in medical abstracts. In *Proceedings of the Eighth International Joint Conference on Natural Language Processing (Volume 2: Short Papers)*, pages 308–313, Taipei, Taiwan. Asian Federation of Natural Language Processing.

Jingbing Feng, Xian Xu, and Hong Zou. 2023. Risk communication clarity and insurance demand: The case of the covid-19 pandemic. *Journal of Economic Dynamics and Control*, 146:104562.

Aris Fergadis, Dimitris Pappas, Antonia Karamolegkou, and Harris Papageorgiou. 2021. Argumentation mining in scientific literature for sustainable development. In *Proceedings of the 8th Workshop on Argument Mining*, pages 100–111.

Beatriz Fisas, Horacio Saggion, and Francesco Ronzano. 2015. On the discoursive structure of computer graphics research papers. In *Proceedings of the 9th Linguistic Annotation Workshop*, pages 42–51, Denver, Colorado, USA. Association for Computational Linguistics.

Benjamin S. Freeling, Zoë A. Doubleday, Matthew J. Dry, Carolyn Semmler, and Sean D. Connell. 2021. Better writing in scientific publications builds reader confidence and understanding. *Frontiers in Psychology*, 12.

Yingqiang Gao, Nianlong Gu, Jessica Lam, and Richard HR Hahnloser. 2022. Do discourse indicators reflect the main arguments in scientific papers? In *Proceedings of the 9th Workshop on Argument Mining*, pages 34–50.

Sérgio Gonçalves, Paulo Cortez, and Sérgio Moro. 2020. A deep learning classifier for sentence classification in biomedical and computer science abstracts. *Neural Computing and Applications*, 32.

Nianlong Gu, Elliott Ash, and Richard Hahnloser. 2022. Memsum: Extractive summarization of long documents using multi-step episodic markov decision processes. In *Proceedings of the 60th Annual Meeting of the Association for Computational Linguistics (Volume 1: Long Papers)*, pages 6507–6522.

Mateusz Hohol, Kinga Wołoszyn, and Krzysztof Cipora. 2022. No fingers, no snarc? neither the finger counting starting hand, nor its stability robustly affect the snarc effect. *Acta Psychologica*, 230:103765.

Yue Hu and Xiaojun Wan. 2014. Automatic generation of related work sections in scientific papers: An optimization approach. In *Proceedings of the 2014 Conference on Empirical Methods in Natural Language Processing (EMNLP)*, pages 1624–1633, Doha, Qatar. Association for Computational Linguistics.

J Peter Kincaid, Robert P Fishburne Jr, Richard L Rogers, and Brad S Chissom. 1975. Derivation of new readability formulas (automated readability index, fog count and flesch reading ease formula) for navy enlisted personnel. Technical report, Naval Technical Training Command Millington TN Research Branch.

Jinhyuk Lee, Wonjin Yoon, Sungdong Kim, Donghyeon Kim, Sunkyu Kim, Chan Ho So, and Jaewoo Kang. 2020. Biobert: a pre-trained biomedical language representation model for biomedical text mining. *Bioinformatics*, 36(4):1234–1240.

Mike Lewis, Yinhan Liu, Naman Goyal, Marjan Ghazvininejad, Abdelrahman Mohamed, Omer Levy, Veselin Stoyanov, and Luke Zettlemoyer. 2020. Bart: Denoising sequence-to-sequence pre-training for natural language generation, translation, and comprehension. In *Proceedings of the 58th Annual Meeting of the Association for Computational Linguistics*, pages 7871–7880.

Guiming Li, Joanne Domenico, Yi Jia, Joseph Lucas, and Erwin Gelfand. 2009. Nf-κb-dependent induction of cathelicidin-related antimicrobial peptide in murine mast cells by lipopolysaccharide. *International archives of allergy and immunology*, 150:122–32.

Xiangci Li, Biswadip Mandal, and Jessica Ouyang. 2022. CORWA: A citation-oriented related work annotation dataset. In *Proceedings of the 2022 Conference of the North American Chapter of the Association for Computational Linguistics: Human Language Technologies*, pages 5426–5440, Seattle, United States. Association for Computational Linguistics.

Chin-Yew Lin. 2004. ROUGE: A package for automatic evaluation of summaries. In *Text Summarization Branches Out*, pages 74–81, Barcelona, Spain. Association for Computational Linguistics.

Kyle Lo, Lucy Lu Wang, Mark Neumann, Rodney Kinney, and Daniel Weld. 2020. S2ORC: The semantic scholar open research corpus. In *Proceedings of the 58th Annual Meeting of the Association for Computational Linguistics*, pages 4969–4983, Online. Association for Computational Linguistics.

Ilya Loshchilov and Frank Hutter. 2017. Decoupled weight decay regularization. *arXiv preprint arXiv:1711.05101*.

Philip M. McCarthy, Adam M. Renner, Michael G. Duncan, Nicholas D. Duran, Erin J. Lightman, and Danielle S. McNamara. 2008. Identifying topic sentencehood. *Behavior Research Methods*, 40:647–664.

Mary McHugh. 2012. Interrater reliability: The kappa statistic. *Biochemia medica : časopis Hrvatskoga društva medicinskih biokemičara / HDMB*, 22:276–82.

PK Ramachandran Nair, Vimala D Nair, PK Ramachandran Nair, and Vimala D Nair. 2014. Organization of a research paper: The imrad format. *Scientific writing and communication in agriculture and natural resources*, pages 13–25.

Hiroki Nakayama, Takahiro Kubo, Junya Kamura, Yasufumi Taniguchi, and Xu Liang. 2018. doccano: Text annotation tool for human. Software available from https://github.com/doccano/doccano.

David Nunan. 2015. *Teaching English to speakers of other languages: An introduction*. Routledge.

Shiro Otake, Shotaro Chubachi, Ho Namkoong, Kensuke Nakagawara, Hiromu Tanaka, Ho Lee, Atsuho Morita, Takahiro Fukushima, Mayuko Watase, Tatsuya Kusumoto, Katsunori Masaki, Hirofumi Kamata, Makoto Ishii, Naoki Hasegawa, Norihiro Harada, Tetsuya Ueda, Soichiro Ueda, Takashi Ishiguro, Ken Arimura, and Koichi Fukunaga. 2021. Clinical clustering with prognostic implications in japanese covid-19 patients: Report from japan covid-19 task force, a nation-wide consortium to investigate covid-19 host genetics. *SSRN Electronic Journal*.

Pontus Plavén-Sigray, Granville James Matheson, Björn Christian Schiffler, and William Hedley Thompson. 2017. The readability of scientific texts is decreasing over time. *Elife*, 6:e27725.

Colin Raffel, Noam Shazeer, Adam Roberts, Katherine Lee, Sharan Narang, Michael Matena, Yanqi Zhou, Wei Li, and Peter J Liu. 2020. Exploring the limits of transfer learning with a unified text-to-text transformer. *The Journal of Machine Learning Research*, 21(1):5485–5551.

RJ Senter and Edgar A Smith. 1967. Automated readability index. Technical report, Cincinnati Univ OH.

Alexander Te-Wei Shieh, Yung-Sung Chuang, Shang-Yu Su, and Yun-Nung Chen. 2019. Towards understanding of medical randomized controlled trials by conclusion generation. In *Proceedings of the Tenth International Workshop on Health Text Mining and Information Analysis (LOUHI 2019)*, pages 108–117.

Tianbao Song, Jingbo Sun, Xin Liu, Jihua Song, and Weiming Peng. 2022. Topic-word-constrained sentence generation with variational autoencoder. *Pattern Recognition Letters*, 160:148–154.

Sadia Sultan and Syed Irfan. 2016. Adult primary myelodysplastic syndrome: Experience from a tertiary care center in pakistan. *Asian Pacific journal of cancer prevention: APJCP*, 17:1535–7.

Qingyun Wang, Lifu Huang, Zhiying Jiang, Kevin Knight, Heng Ji, Mohit Bansal, and Yi Luan. 2019. PaperRobot: Incremental draft generation of scientific ideas. In *Proceedings of the 57th Annual Meeting of the Association for Computational Linguistics*, pages 1980–1991, Florence, Italy. Association for Computational Linguistics.

Robert C Weissberg. 1984. Given and new: Paragraph development models from scientific english. *Tesol Quarterly*, 18(3):485–500.

Mostafa Zamanian and Pooneh Heydari. 2012. Readability of texts: State of the art. *Theory and Practice in Language Studies*, 2:43–53.

Susan Zhang, Stephen Roller, Naman Goyal, Mikel Artetxe, Moya Chen, Shuohui Chen, Christopher Dewan, Mona Diab, Xian Li, Xi Victoria Lin, et al. 2022. Opt: Open pre-trained transformer language models. *arXiv preprint arXiv:2205.01068*.

Tianyi Zhang, Varsha Kishore, Felix Wu, Kilian Q Weinberger, and Yoav Artzi. 2019. Bertscore: Evaluating text generation with bert. *arXiv preprint arXiv:1904.09675*.

A Merged Confusion Matrix

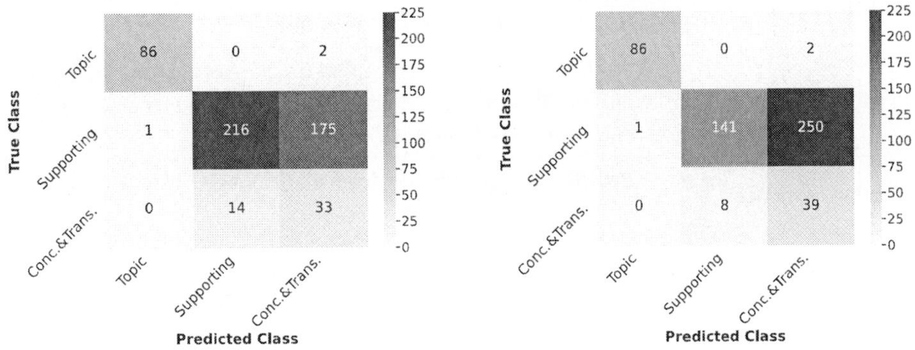

(a) BioBERT (b) SciBERT

Figure 4: Confusion matrix after merging the categories of Concluding and Transition Sentences.

B Dataset Example

Discourse category	Sentence
Topic Sentence	(#1) This study was the first in Japan to perform a **cluster analysis** of *COVID-19 patients*.
Supporting Sentence	(#2) We identified four clinical **sub-phenotypes**, namely the **"young healthy cluster" (Cluster 1)**, **"middle-aged cluster" (Cluster 2)**, **"middle-aged obese cluster" (Cluster 3)**, and **"elderly cluster" (Cluster 4)**, which were associated with different outcomes in Japanese *patients with COVID-19*.
Supporting Sentence	(#3) Previous reports, including ours, have shown that *comorbidities* and *mortality rates* in Japan differed from *inpatient* studies in other countries.
Supporting Sentence	(#4) Thus, the identification of the meaningful **sub-phenotypes** of *Japanese COVID-19 patients* is important.
Supporting Sentence	(#5) Notably, our study used simple baseline characteristics as variables for **cluster analysis**.
Supporting Sentence	(#6) Several previous studies have shown that **cluster analysis** is useful for **phenotyping** and predicting COVID-19 outcomes.
Supporting Sentence	(#7) However, most of these studies used complicated variables, combining a wide range of blood test results for **clustering**.
Supporting Sentence	(#8) Promptly indefinable is an important feature of defining *COVID-19* **sub-phenotypes**.
Concluding Sentence	(#9) We believe that the present simple clustering may be of great help to clinicians in predicting *prognosis* and performing individualized *therapy*.

Table 8: An example paragraph with one Topic Sentence, seven Supporting Sentences, and one Concluding Sentence. Paragraph topic is marked with bold font, while topic attributes are marked with italics. Source: Otake et al. (2021)

Discourse category	Sentence
Topic Sentence	(#1) Among other factors, the **SNARC effect** is considered to be **linked to the finger counting direction**.
Supporting Sentence	(#2) Fischer (2008) has shown that the **SNARC effect** was not significant (associated p-value of .061) in *participants starting finger counting with their right hand (right-starters).*
Supporting Sentence	(#3) It differed significantly from the **SNARC effect** observed in *left-starters*.
Supporting Sentence	(#4) The latter group also revealed a significant **SNARC effect**.
Supporting Sentence	(#5) Moreover, the variance in the **SNARC effect** was greater among *right-starters*.
Supporting Sentence	(#6) This observation was only partly replicated in a large-scale online study (Cipora, Soltanlou, et al., 2019), which showed a difference between *left- and right-starters* in the same direction.
Supporting Sentence	(#7) Still, it was associated with a negligibly small effect size (Cohen's d = 0.12).
Supporting Sentence	(#8) However, Bayesian analysis has shown that the result was inconclusive and was leaning towards supporting the null hypothesis.
Supporting Sentence	(#9) At the same time, unlike in Fischer (2008), a robust **SNARC effect** was found in *right-starters*, and there was no significant difference in variance between *left- and right-starters*.
Supporting Sentence	(#10) Further studies have also demonstrated a robust **SNARC** in *right-starters* (Fabbri, 2013; Prete & Tommasi, 2020).
Supporting Sentence	(#11) Additionally , in several countries where the majority of *people start finger counting with their right hand* (e.g., Belgium and Italy), the **SNARC effect** has been observed in multiple studies (e.g., Cutini, Scarpa, Scatturin, Dell'Acqua, & Zorzi, 2014; Gevers, Ratinckx, de Baene, & Fias, 2006; Mapelli, Rusconi, & Umilta, 2003).
Concluding Sentence	(#12) To sum up, there seems to be some evidence, however mixed, that finger counting is associated with the **SNARC effect** (see also Riello & Rusconi, 2011).
Supporting Sentence	(#13) Having seen these results, one might ask why the **SNARC effect** should be **related to the finger counting direction**.
Transition Sentence	(#14) The research on the *embodiment of numerical cognition* can illuminate this issue.

Table 9: An example paragraph with one Topic, Transition, Concluding, and Transition Sentence each. Paragraph topic is marked with bold font, while topic attributes are marked with italics. Links are marked with underline. Source: Hohol et al. (2022).

Discourse category	Sentence
Topic Sentence	(#1) In December 2019, a **disease outbreak** was noticed after a massive admission of *patients* with common clinical symptoms of *pneumonia* in the local hospitals of Wuhan City, China.
Supporting Sentence	(#2) Upon further investigations, the *World Health Organization* confirmed that the novel *coronavirus, severe acute respiratory syndrome coronavirus 2 (SARS-CoV-2)*, was responsible for these clinical symptoms and further denominated this disease as *coronavirus disease (COVID-19)*.
Supporting Sentence	(#3) Its clinical course is diverse, ranging from mild self-limited *illness* to life-threatening organ dysfunctions.

Table 10: Example badly-structured paragraph with only one Topic Sentence and two Supporting Sentences. Paragraph is marked with bold font, while topic attributes are marked with italics. Source: Otake et al. (2021).

Discourse category	Sentence
Supporting Sentence	(#1) Most published data on MDS is from Western countries.
Supporting Sentence	(#2) Published local data are scarce.
Supporting Sentence	(#3) There are few studies available from Pakistan (Irfan et al., 1998; Ehsan et al., 2010; Rashid et al., 2014).
Transition Sentence	(#4) The purpose of this study is to demonstrate demographical, clinical and the hematological features of adults primary MDS patients who visited our tertiary care center from 2010 till the end of 2014.

Table 11: An example paragraph with only one Transition Sentence and four Supporting Sentences. As this paragraph does not contain a Topic Sentence, the subsentence level part of the annotation task was not completed. Source: Sultan and Irfan (2016).

Discourse category	Sentence
Supporting Sentence	(#1) It was determined that CRAMP expression in BALB/c-derived mast cells was inducible by LPS, which also induces production of certain cytokines, including IL-13.
Supporting Sentence	(#2) This is of interest since IL-13 (and IL-14) can reportedly suppress induction of cathelicidin production by some cell types, such as antigen-exposed keratinocytes.
Supporting Sentence	(#3) In contrast, activation of mast cells with IL-4 appears to increase accumulation of cathelicidin protein.
Supporting Sentence	(#4) It was also reported that skin obtained from patients with atopic dermatitis have decreased cathelicidin LL-37 levels compared to normal skin and thus supports high levels of vaccinia virus replication, as is characteristic of eczema vaccinatum.
Supporting Sentence	(#5) Atopic dermatitis skin is characterized by overexpression of IL-4 and IL-13.
Concluding Sentence	(#6) Thus, although mast cells may be a source of cathelicidins, as described above, their presence and activation in skin could in fact, through production of certain cytokines, result in suppression of production of the antimicrobial peptides by other cell types.

Table 12: An example paragraph with only one Concluding Sentence and five Supporting Sentences. As this paragraph does not contain a Topic Sentence, the subsentence level part of the annotation task was not completed. Source: Li et al. (2009).

Using Discourse Connectives to Test Genre Bias in Masked Language Models

Heidrun Dorgeloh[1], **Lea Kawaletz**[1], **Simon David Stein**[1],
Regina Stodden[2] and **Stefan Conrad**[3*]
[1] Department of English and American Studies – Faculty of Arts and Humanities
[2] Department of Computational Linguistics – Faculty of Arts and Humanities
[3] Department of Computer Science – Faculty of Mathematics and Natural Sciences
Heinrich Heine University Düsseldorf, Germany
{firstname.secondname}@hhu.de

Abstract

This paper presents evidence for an effect of genre on the use of discourse connectives in argumentation. Drawing from discourse processing research on reasoning-based structures, we use fill-mask computation to measure genre-induced expectations of argument realisation, and beta regression to model the probabilities of these realisations against a set of predictors. Contrasting fill-mask probabilities for the presence or absence of a discourse connective in baseline and finetuned language models reveals that genre introduces biases for the realisation of argument structure. These outcomes suggest that cross-domain discourse processing, but also argument mining, should take into account generalisations about specific features, such as connectives, and their probability related to the genre context.[1]

1 Introduction

Argumentative structures in discourse, which comprise a claim and a supporting or attacking premise, exhibit significant variation in their realisation. Notably, as argumentative coherence can be achieved by alternative signals (Cabrio et al., 2013; Das and Taboada, 2018), arguments vary in whether the claim and premise are linked by a discourse connective or not. For example, *because* in item 1a explicitly conveys a causal relation. In contrast, item 1b, where two sentences are separated by punctuation, leaves the relation implicit, with the claim indicated only by the deontic modal *should*.[2]

(1) a. Masking should be mandated *because* it keeps everyone safe.

b. Masking should be mandated. It keeps everyone safe.

The explicit or more implicit realisation of argumentation is a challenge for an understanding of argumentative discourse. However, the processing of arguments is likely not random and should conform with general discourse processing principles. In particular, it can be assumed that, following the Uniform Information Density (UID) hypothesis (Frank and Jaeger, 2008), relations within discourse, such as the one between a claim and a premise, are more likely to be expressed explicitly when they are unexpected, and more likely to be implicit when a relation can be anticipated (Torabi Asr and Demberg, 2012).

The factors that shape expectations in discourse are diverse. Local cues within a phrase or sentence, such as the use of the connective *because* in item 1a, play a role. However, more global forces, such as the overall nature of the document, also drive expectations and, with that, information density (Meister et al., 2021). Knowing that genres guide expectations and influence human discourse understanding on many levels of a text (Giltrow, 2010), we explore in this paper how genre creates a bias for the ways argument structures are realised. These structures are based on relations of subjective causality, a coherence relation that is particularly likely to be driven by contextual signals, including the genre (e.g. Canestrelli et al., 2016; Scholman et al., 2020). For example, for a reader of a newspaper editorial these argumentative structures will be much more expected than for one of a novel or monograph.

Our study compares the predicted presence or absence of discourse connectives in arguments taken from New York Times (NYT) editorials. Due to the UID principle we hypothesise that,

*Contributions: Linguistic background, conception of work and discussion: Heidrun Dorgeloh; conception of work, design and preparation of study: Lea Kawaletz; computational modelling: Regina Stodden; statistical modelling and statistical analysis: Simon David Stein; computational background and discussion: Stefan Conrad. All authors contributed to manuscript revision, read and approved the submitted version.

[1]The data and code for the present study can be found at https://osf.io/n6hq5/.

[2]These are constructed examples based on item 2.

Proceedings of the 5th Workshop on Computational Approaches to Discourse (CODI 2024), pages 27–38
March 21, 2024

in genres with predictable argumentative structures, such as editorials, there is a lower likelihood of making a relation explicit with a connective. We also assume that an LM finetuned with data from such genres is likely to show a stronger effect of this tendency. To test our hypothesis, we compare baseline (non-finetuned) masked language models (MLMs) with the corresponding finetuned models genre-adapted to editorials. The comparison of models enables us to disregard frequency effects. In this way, the approach allows to verify genre-induced expectations for argument realisation and produces insights which could in the future improve cross-domain discourse processing.

2 Background

2.1 Defining *arguments*

Our understanding of what constitutes argumentative discourse follows established terminology, especially from the field of argument mining (e.g. Stab and Gurevych, 2017; Stede and Schneider, 2018), where an argument, such as exemplified in item 2, consists of two kinds of argumentative discourse units (ADUs): a controversial statement, the *claim* (marked in bold), and another statement which supports or attacks the claim, the *premise* (underlined).

(2) **[M]asking should be mandated and enforced.** It's not just about your individual risk tolerance, but about keeping everyone safe.

ADUs can occur in a single sentence or span multiple sentences, as in item 2. Also, multiple premises may refer to the same claim, forming a single argument. For simplicity, the data analysed for this project only included arguments consisting of one claim and one premise.

2.2 Connectives and discourse relations

Discourse connectives cover the syntactic classes of coordinators (e.g., *and*, *but*), subordinators (e.g., *because*, *while*), as well as connective adjuncts (e.g., *therefore*, *however*) (Dorgeloh and Wanner, 2022). They make the coherence relation between two (or more) ADUs explicit, which is why they are a prominent feature both for studies of discourse coherence and of argumentation structure (Marcu and Echihabi, 2002; Xu et al., 2012; Goudas et al., 2014; Shi and Demberg, 2019; Crible and Demberg, 2020; Kurfalı and Östling, 2021). However, the extent of the actual presence of connectives is often surprisingly low. For example, in the RST Signalling Corpus (Carlson et al., 2002; Das et al., 2015) or the Penn Discourse Treebank (Prasad et al., 2008) – both based on Wall Street Journal texts that in all likelihood contain argumentative texts – more than half of the discourse relations are not marked by a discourse connective. One possible reason for their absence is that there are numerous other options of signalling a coherence relation (Cabrio et al., 2013; Das and Taboada, 2018).

Another reason is that the support or attack relation within arguments has a subjective "source of coherence", that is, the relation does not exist at the propositional content level but at the level of reasoning (Sanders et al., 2021), as in item 2. For these relations, connectives serve as processing instructions, enabling a reader or listener to evaluate how a premise supports or attacks a given claim (Wei et al., 2021a). Psycholinguistic evidence has shown that overly explicit marking of subjective coherence relations triggers a "forewarning effect", alerting the reader to a persuasion attempt (Kamalski et al., 2008). In that sense, connectives can potentially induce resistance against argumentation. Given this effect, it is plausible to assume that argumentative structures are not made more explicit than necessary.

How the needs for explicitness are balanced likely aligns with the UID hypothesis (Frank and Jaeger, 2008). It suggests that discourse relations, including support or attack within arguments, "should be expressed explicitly with a discourse connector when they are unexpected, but may be implicit when the discourse relation can be anticipated" (Torabi Asr and Demberg, 2012, 2669). If expectations are crucial in that sense, a major factor driving explicitness must be the genre, as genres can be seen as schemata "referring to a set of expectations" (Piata, 2016, 255). It follows that, in argumentative texts, such as editorials, the relation between two ADUs is less likely to be expressed with a connective, since the presence of argumentation in this genre can be expected. For illustration, consider item 2 again, where the ADUs are not linked by means of a connective. By contrast, in the adapted variant in item 2′, the argument relation is made explicit by adding the connective *because*.

(2′) **[M]asking should be mandated and enforced** [because] [i]t's not just about your individual risk tolerance, but about keeping everyone safe.

Following the UID hypothesis, item 2′ is the less likely argument pattern in argumentative texts compared to item 2.

2.3 Connectives and language modeling

Argument realisation is a classic issue for the automatic retrieval of arguments, i.e., in argument mining. Connectives, in this context also commonly referred to as *discourse markers*, are seen as indicators of argumentative structure (e.g., Eckle-Kohler et al., 2015; Stab and Gurevych, 2017; Sileo et al., 2019), but "missing" discourse markers are also known to be the rule rather than the exception (Moens, 2018). One reason is that explicitness in argumentation goes beyond using connectives; it also involves other stance markers, as every argument expresses a stance toward its topic (Stein and Wachsmuth, 2019). Connectives and other markers thus together play a role in facilitating the processing of subjective coherence relations (Wei et al., 2021b), but how they interact is still not fully explored. Stodden et al. (2023) also argue that connectives can play a prominent role in stance detection. They extract the probabilities of connectives for a claim-premise relation from a MLM and show that training a simple classifier using these values as features is capable of optimising stance detection. Our approach here uses a similar line of research.

Another reason why the presence or absence of discourse connectives as indicators of arguments is not fully understood is the lack of cross-genre generalisations. In a recent paper, Rocha et al. (2023) report that introducing connectives as signals of the relation between a claim and a premise has the potential to improve argument mining. They employ finetuned LMs trained on both real and constructed arguments to introduce connectives between ADUs, which improves cross-genre transfer. However, their approach does not consider genre-specific associations of explicit indicators like connectives and the context. To address this, we aim to incorporate genre generalisations through genre-induced fine-tuning.

Our approach is to explore the presence or absence of a discourse connective for the claim-premise relation in arguments using BERT (Devlin et al., 2019) and RoBERTa (Liu et al., 2019). In the task of these MLMs, the objective is akin to a cloze test; the model learns to predict words for randomly masked tokens in the original input texts (Devlin et al., 2019). Unlike a causal LM, which predicts the next word solely based on the previous context, an MLM can predict a word in the middle of a sequence based on both left and right context. We use the cloze position between the claim and premise by extracting probabilities for connectives and, as a proxy for their absence, punctuation marks. In doing so, we refrain from using causal LM prompting methods and instead compare the probabilities of different types of marking in a statistical analysis, which necessitates more than just listing the top n markers.

2.4 Hypotheses

We compare the predictions made by different models, first for the difference between explicit connective and no marking and, then, for the comparison between baseline models and models finetuned for editorials. In this context, we make three predictions. First, given that newspaper editorials are a genre whose primary goal it is to persuade and which are therefore "one of the purest forms of argumentative text" (Al-Khatib et al., 2016, 3440), the discourse relations that are characteristic of this type of discourse are subjective causal relations, i.e., discourse relations that do not refer to propositional content, but to reasoning (see subsection 2.2). Due to the forewarning effect, we assume that these relations are not marked more explicitly than necessary ($\rightarrow$ H1 below). Second, if a genre as a whole involves argumentation, the UID hypothesis suggests that argument relations are expressed more implicitly in this genre than in other, less persuasive genres. It follows that, in LMs finetuned on strongly persuasive discourse, argumentation is even more likely to occur without a connective ($\rightarrow$ H2). Third, regarding the magnitude of this effect, we predict that it depends on the models' baselines, given their varied training data. LMs trained on comparatively non-argumentative texts (e.g., books and Wikipedia, for BERT) should show a more pronounced difference between finetuned and baseline versions than those whose training already included a certain proportion of texts from more argumentative genres (e.g., news and web-based texts, for RoBERTa; $\rightarrow$ H3).

H1 The absence of a connective (here: indicated by a punctuation marker) is more likely than the presence of an explicit discourse connective.

H2 LMs that have been finetuned on argumentative genres (here: editorials) predict a lower probability for a discourse connective than the baseline ones.

H3 This effect is more pronounced in LMs trained on non-argumentative texts (here: BERT) than in those trained on a larger portion of argumentative texts (here: RoBERTa).

3 Methodology

Our method involves comparing explicit to non-explicit realisations of the claim-premise relation in a set of arguments. We use different LMs to quantify the acceptability of the presence of a discourse connective as probabilities of the masked-tokens. These can be seen as a placeholder for the realisations in MLMs.

The bidirectional architecture of these models enables the prediction of token probabilities based on both ADUs (claim and premise). This prediction is dependent on the training data of an LM. To adapt the model to a genre of argumentative texts, we finetuned the LM on additional NYT editorials which are not part of our annotated data, which enables us to compare finetuned with non-finetuned models.

3.1 Data

The data set was manually selected with the aim to test this new approach for exploring genre generalisations. The data set consists of 81 arguments from a corpus of 2,508 NYT editorials (3,227,122 tokens). These were published between January 2020 and June 2021 with at least one of the NYT tags 'coronavirus (2019-ncov),' 'vaccination and immunization,' or 'epidemics.' The selection followed a "purposeful sampling" approach (Patton, 2015), which means we did not aim for a representative sample of all arguments attested in the corpus. Instead, we identified arguments in a subset of 50 editorials (55,603 tokens) and chose 81 arguments in an elaborate and resource-intensive process tailored towards the proof-of-concept nature of our analysis. The process took place in several steps that we describe in detail in our guidelines for annotation (Kawaletz et al., 2023). The selection of arguments was based on the following principles: Not only did all arguments have to adhere to the semantic classification of arguments we have developed (Kawaletz et al., 2022), but they were, at a minimum, identified by two out of three annotators, and subsequently confirmed by two curators, all possessing linguistic training.

Table 1 provides a summary of the data set properties, outlining the features that were integrated into our statistical analysis (Kawaletz et al., 2022): connective (are claim and premise connected by a connective?), relation (does the premise support or attack the claim?), and category (does the claim state that something is or is not the case, or does it mandate an action or prohibition, or does it evaluate something positively or negatively?). As expected, most claim-premise pairs lack a connective (74.07%), reflecting the tendency of argumentative discourse to favour implicit relations (see subsection 2.2). It also becomes obvious that support relations dominate (86.42%), and that most arguments in the data set are epistemic in nature (71.60%).

Property	Option	Count	Per cent
Connective	Present	60	74.07%
	Absent	21	25.93%
Relation	Support	70	86.42%
	Attack	11	13.58%
Category	Epistemic	58	71.60%
	Deontic	19	23.46%
	Ethical	4	4.94%

Table 1: Properties of the data set

Finally, the arguments span a broad range of lengths, from the shortest at 11 words to the longest at 90 words, with an average of approximately 44.05 words and a median of 42 words.

3.2 Extraction of probabilities

In order to calculate the probability for the presence or the absence of a connective, we conducted the following preprocessing steps: i) The last character from ADU1 is truncated to prevent the punctuation character from affecting the predictions. ii) If ADU2 starts with a connective , the connective of ADU2 is truncated to prevent the concatenation of two connectives in a row or of a connective and punctuation mark.

Connectives		Punctuation markers	
although	unless	.	-
because	while	;	–
but	yet	,	−
since	anyway^{B}	:	...
so	consequently^{B}	?	. . .
still	hence^{B}	—	!
and	however^{B}		_^{B}
as	nevertheless^{B}		..^{R}
for	therefore^{B}		
thus	whereas^{B}		

Table 2: Presence or absence of explicit marker queried in the LMs' output. Bold face markers also occur in the NYT data set. Markers with ^{B} are used only for BERT, while those with ^{R} are exclusive to RoBERTa.

Next, both ADUs were concatenated with model-specific masked tokens: *[MASK]* for BERT and *<mask>* for RoBERTa. For instance, item 2 was input to BERT as in item 3.

(3) Masking should be mandated and enforced [MASK] it's not just about your individual risk tolerance, but about keeping everyone safe.

We calculated the probabilities of the masked-token for each possible token (or subword) with a Python pipeline for "fill-mask" included in the Huggingface `transformers` package (Wolf et al., 2020).[3] As opposed to the approach of Rocha et al. (2023), the method does not involve filling the gap between claim and premise with an explicit marker, but at extracting the probabilities of a list of tokens.

From the resulting probabilities list, we extracted the probabilities of 34 tokens of interest (see Table 2)—20 discourse markers (for explicit realisations) and 14 punctuation marks (indicating the absence of a connective). A connective was added to the list of explicit markers if it is a single-word connective, and i) a coordinating or subordinating conjunction expressing a support or attack relation, or ii) a "linking adverbial" (Biber et al., 2021, 755) expressing a support or attack relation. A punctuation mark was added to the list if it occurs in our masked data, and/or if it was in the list of the top 10 predicted tokens of the LM using our data.

We did not include multi-token connectives (e.g., *for this reason* or *on the other hand*) as the fill-mask approach is only available for one-(sub)token prediction. Compound connectives had to be excluded because most LMs are using subword tokenizers, hence, they would be split into several subtokens (e.g., *anyway* would be tokenized as *any* and *way*) and cannot be predicted as a whole token in the fill-mask task.[4]

3.3 Language models and finetuning

For our experiments, we chose BERT-large-uncased (Devlin et al., 2019) and a derivative model, RoBERTa-large (Liu et al., 2019).[5] While sharing the same architecture they are pre-trained on different genres: BERT is pre-trained on 16 GB of data from English books and Wikipedia, whereas RoBERTa is pre-trained additionally on 144 GB of news and web texts. Our selection of these specific LMs was driven by a focus on the impact of genre. However, the differences between BERT and RoBERTa extend beyond their training data. For instance, a) RoBERTa is solely trained for language modelling, unlike BERT, which also includes next sentence prediction; b) they employ different tokenisation methods: RoBERTa uses Byte-Pair Encoding, while BERT uses WordPiece; c) RoBERTa is case-sensitive, whereas the version of BERT we chose is not. Despite these variations, BERT and RoBERTa were the most suitable models for our research objectives. For example, XLM-RoBERTa-base (Conneau et al., 2020) shares the same architecture as BERT and RoBERTa, but includes multilingual training, and DistilBERT-base-uncased (Sanh et al., 2019) is trained on the same data as BERT, but has fewer tunable parameters.

We then applied *domain-adaptive finetuning* (Han and Eisenstein, 2019), an unsupervised method that adapts the LM to a new or under-represented genre. We chose this approach to adapt the LMs for argumentative texts because they are primarily trained on non-argumentative data while also incorporating argumentative data to varying extents. Specifically, we fine-

[3]The determination of the probabilities is limited to the top_k, where k is the length of the vocabulary. Following this, some probabilities are close to 0 (very unlikely).

[4]We are comparing models with the same tokenizer, i.e., the baseline model and the finetuned model. Hence, for a different set of connectives, we would not expect a strong effect on our results.

[5]As previously mentioned, we are not using autoregressive LMs (e.g., ChatGPT or Llama) and prompting methods as we are interested in the probabilites of different types of marking for further statistical analysis. MLMs have the advantage over autoregressive LMs to provide the probabilities of a word at any position within a sequence by considering both the left and right context, rather than solely predicting next words at the end of a sequence.

tuned on the 2,458 NYT editorials from our corpus (but excluding those 50 from which we selected the arguments for our data set). This way, the finetuned LMs are more likely to mirror the lower likelihood of a connective for editorials and, in that, for an argumentative genre.[6]

3.4 Statistical analysis

We fitted generalised additive models of the beta regression family to the data, using the `mcgv` package (Wood, 2017) in `R` (R Core Team, 2023). Beta regression is uniquely suited to model proportional values (see, e.g., Ferrari and Cribari-Neto, 2004). These models also allow us to include a number of important control variables.

Response variable We name our response variable PROBABILITY, referring to the probability of masked tokens estimated by the LMs. For each argument in our data set we calculated two probability measurements, one for the presence of an explicit discourse marker and one for its absence. The probability of an explicit discourse marker was calculated by taking the sum of the estimated probabilities of all connectives. The probability of the absence of marking was the sum of the estimated probabilities of all punctuation marks. Each of these two measurements was paired with the value `present` or `absent` in an additional variable CONNECTIVE. This coding enables us to investigate both types of probabilities in a single statistical model.

Predictor variables Our two predictor variables of interest are CONNECTIVE and MODEL. CONNECTIVE specifies whether we look at the probability for the presence or absence of explicit marking. MODEL specifies which LM estimated these probabilities: `baseline BERT`, `finetuned BERT`, `baseline RoBERTa`, or `finetuned RoBERTa`.

We use the control variable N_TOKENS, the number of word tokens in the sentence, to gauge sentence length and complexity. It may be expected that longer and more complex sentences will exert greater pressure to use punctuation marks, thereby disfavouring marking.

Additionally, we control for RELATION and CATEGORY. RELATION specifies the relation between premise and claim (`attack` or `support`). We expect that, compared to support relations, attack relations favour explicit marking, since contrasting relations are cognitively more complex, requiring more cues (Crible and Demberg, 2020). CATEGORY specifies the semantic argument category (`epistemic`, `ethical`, or `deontic`). We expect deontic arguments to exhibit the strongest dispreference for explicit marking because claims demanding an action often contain a deontic modal, expressing necessity (e.g., *should*), which already implies the presence of a premise (Kawaletz et al., 2023).

Furthermore, we specify with HASNECESSITYMODAL and HASDEMDET whether the sentence contains at least one necessity modal (*must*, *should*, or *ought*) or at least one demonstrative determiner (e.g., *this*, *these*), respectively. Both are features that could reduce the likelihood of explicitness by way of a connective, as they are also known to be linguistic features of persuasion and argumentation (Biber, 1989; Petch-Tyson, 2000).

Finally, we include SOURCEID, the identifier of the source document of the target sentence, to control for potential variation in probabilities introduced by different authors or texts.

Modelling We fitted six types of beta regression model: i) one for baseline BERT, ii) one for finetuned BERT, iii) one for baseline RoBERTa, iv) one for finetuned RoBERTa, v) one that compares baseline BERT and finetuned BERT, and vi) one that compares baseline RoBERTa and finetuned RoBERTa. The first four types of model investigate the difference in probability between the presence or absence of explicit marking for each LM individually. They do not include MODEL as a predictor. Models v and vi investigate the difference between finetuned and baseline models. They include MODEL as a predictor of interest.

We fitted each type of model as a simple version and a complex version. The simple versions include only the predictors of interest (CONNECTIVE for the four individual models and an interaction of CONNECTIVE and MODEL for the two comparisons). The complex versions include interactions of CONNECTIVE with each of the covariates described above (SOURCEID was not included in an interaction).

Following standard procedure, we reduced the models by removing non-significant terms (at the .05 alpha level) in a stepwise fashion

[6]You can find the hyperparameters in Appendix A and the code with more details in the osf repository.

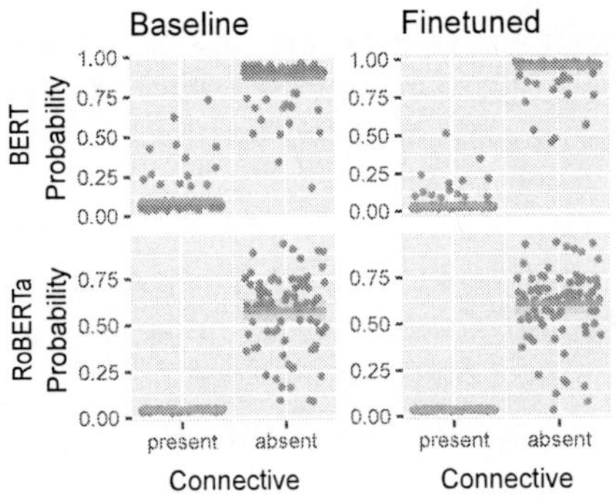

Figure 1: Probability of the presence and absence of explicit argument marking for the four LMs.

(highest p-value first) until only predictors remained of which at least one level reached significance.

4 Results

Figure 1 plots the results of the simple versions of the four models, which predict the probabilities of explicit marking being present or absent for each LM individually.[7] This reality check confirms our expectation that explicit marking is disfavoured across models. In all four cases, we find very highly significant effects (at $p < .001$) of CONNECTIVE on PROBABILITY in the expected direction. Note that this effect is likely in part a frequency artefact. The proxy measure by which we gauge the absence of marking, i.e., punctuation, will naturally yield higher probabilities than the proxy by which we measure explicit marking , i.e., connectives.

In the complex versions of these four individual models, which include interactions of the predictors with CONNECTIVE, the interactions and main effects of the covariates mostly do not reach significance. One exception is N_TOKENS. Figure 2 shows that in three out of four complex models our expectations are confirmed: With increasing ADU length, the absence of marking becomes even more probable, while explicit marking becomes even less probable. In some models we also find the occasional expected interaction with other covariates, such as RELATION: Support relations feature even higher probabilities for `absent` or even lower probabilities for `present` compared to attack relations. Details can be found in the supplementary materials.

[7] The interested reader can view all full models in the supplementary materials at the osf repository.

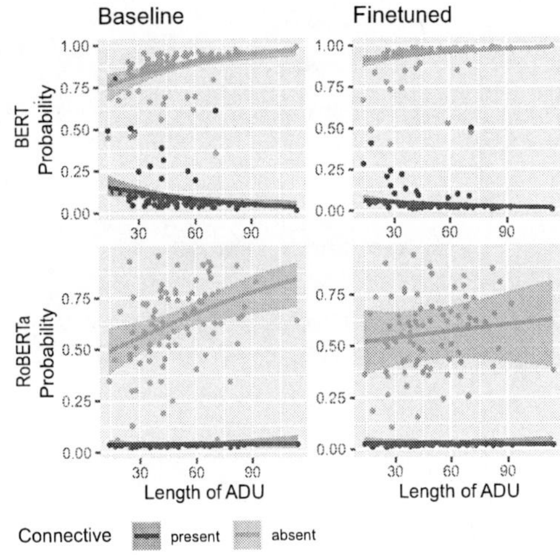

Figure 2: Interaction of CONNECTIVE with sentence length for the four LMs. Greyed out effects did not reach significance and were eliminated in the statistical model.

Let us now turn to the question of genre, i.e., the comparison of baseline LMs with finetuned LMs. Figure 3 plots the main result from each of the two complex beta regression models, the top panel showing the interaction of CONNECTIVE with the BERT LMs, the bottom panel showing its interaction with the RoBERTa LMs (the results are the same in the two simple versions of each regression model).

Both BERT LMs disfavour explicit marking, but the finetuned version prefers such marking to be absent significantly more than does the baseline version of BERT. Again, frequency effects likely amplify the strong dispreference for connectives. However, a general bias for punctuation exists for both baseline and finetuned LMs, enabling us to compare them directly. Moving down to the bottom panel, we can observe that RoBERTa, too, prefers the absence of explicit marking even more when finetuned, but here, the effect fails to reach significance. As it is difficult to interpret the absence of an effect in the frequentist framework, we used the BIC approximation to the Bayes Factor (Wagenmakers, 2007) to compare the model for RoBERTa against a null hypothesis model without MODEL and its interaction with CONNECTIVE. This analysis indicates that the data are more likely under the null hypothesis (finetuning RoBERTa does not affect the presence of a connective) than under the hypothesis (finetuning RoBERTa does affect the presence of a connective) ($BF_{01} = 32.79$). If we assume that it is

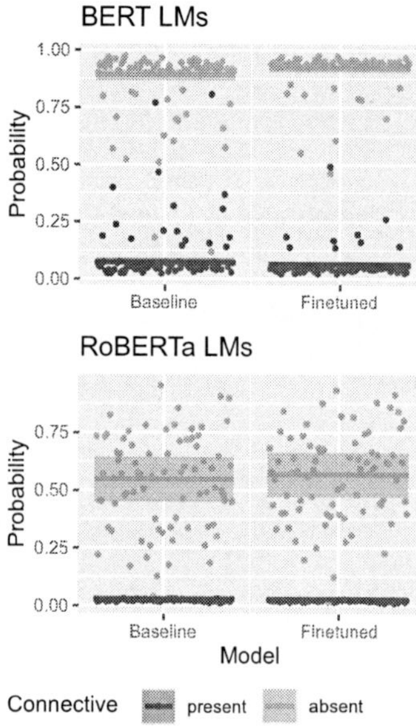

Figure 3: Interactions of CONNECTIVE with MODEL, each comparing the baseline version of the model with the finetuned version. Greyed out effects did not reach significance and were eliminated in the statistical model.

a priori equally likely that finetuning RoBERTa does and does not have an effect, the posterior probability we find ($Pr_{H_0}|D = .97$) constitutes "strong" evidence for the null, according to the Raftery (1995) classification scheme. We can thus be confident that while we find a finetuning effect for BERT, we are dealing with a true null result for RoBERTa.

5 Discussion

The LMs have shown a clear preference for the absence of a discourse connective, which overall confirms a characteristic of argument structures, i.e. their subjective causal relations, in line with the psycholinguistic background to our approach (H1). Also, in line with our expectations, after finetuning, the LMs both showed a decreased probability for an explicit connective compared to the baseline ones (H2).

However, only BERT, but not RoBERTa, shows a clear, i.e., statistically significant, increase. We believe the fact that we find a significant finetuning effect for BERT but not for RoBERTa is a true effect of genre (H3): The baseline version of BERT was trained on less argumentative texts (specifically, books and Wikipedia only) compared to RoBERTa, which also includes news and websites in its training data. The increase in the "argumentativeness" of genres from baseline to finetuned is thus higher for BERT than for RoBERTa, which has already seen many argumentative texts before having been finetuned. For RoBERTa, then, the finetuning effect is less pronounced. This difference that we observed is in line with the assumption that genre does create a bias for the realisation of argument structure in discourse.

Several effects we have presented suggest that the approach covers the use of connectives and genre conditions, as far as they are identifiable for an LM, reasonably well. The fact that the absence of a connective is highly likely across all models (H1) is likely a frequency effect. However, we were able to disregard this effect by focusing on the comparison of baseline and finetuned versions (H3), since it applies to both equally. Our modelling also showed that, in line with expectations, absence of a connective becomes overall more likely with increased sentence length (number of tokens) – a finding which suggests that length is not only a control variable, in the sense of reflecting the complexity of the pairing of claim and premise. The effect of length also suggests that there are other features relevant for the explicitness of an argument, and their presence will become more likely the longer an argument gets. For example, other markers known to typically connect an argument's second constituent are features at the sentence beginning, the so-called "theme zone", such as adjuncts or demonstrative expressions (Fetzer, 2018; Petch-Tyson, 2000). In general, a clear effect of overall length of the discourse units confirms the relevance of information density for the use of connectives.

Our results also indicate that argument mining could profit from genre generalisations. So far, approaches are typically developed and trained using data either from one genre (e.g., persuasive essays in Stab and Gurevych, 2017) or mixed-genre corpora with no systematic cross-genre transfer (e.g., Morio et al., 2022). In the former case, while high accuracy is often achieved within the same genre, the transfer to another genre usually weakens the results. In the latter case, the approach often achieves moderate accuracy across genres without excelling in any specific genre. This indicates a general oversight of genre as a systematic factor in current methodologies. However, genre generalisations are crucial for dealing with a potential problem of LMs when dealing with argumentative discourse: the genre-specific use of explicit marking may lead LMs to learn only the markings used within the genre(s) available in the training data, thereby possibly overlooking or neglecting other patterns.

6 Conclusion and outlook

In this study, we have presented a method for testing genre bias in LMs, and we have shown that discourse expectations as driven by the genre have an impact on the explicit linking of ADUs by way of discourse connectives. We used two discourse processing principles – forewarning and UID – to account for a general preference for the absence of a connective. Testing this preference in the form of fill-mask probabilities of our LMs enabled us to identify an expected genre bias after finetuning.

Even if the computational approach piloted with this work is not without its limitations – being based on a very small data set and focusing solely on single-word connectives while excluding other discourse markers – it successfully quantifies the influence of genre on discourse-structure realisation. In that sense, the method can serve as a role model for investigating genre effects. However, most argumentative discourse will contain many other cues for realising argumentation, which aligns with the identified effect of argument length. Extending the approach to multi-word connectives, to combinations of connectives and punctuation, or to more complex "alternative lexicalizations" that equally express coherence relations (Knaebel and Stede, 2022) would therefore be a promising endeavour. In addition, from a computational standpoint, it would be beneficial to apply our approach to other LMs, particularly considering that only BERT, not RoBERTa, incorporates next-sentence prediction.

Overall, this work shows that both cross-domain discourse processing and argument mining can benefit from genre generalisations. While recent work in argument mining has aimed at making LMs less genre-dependent by way of using connectives (Rocha et al., 2023), our approach highlights a method of revealing genre bias in the use of connectives and could thus be a template for future, more genre-dependent work.

References

Khalid Al-Khatib, Henning Wachsmuth, Johannes Kiesel, Matthias Hagen, and Benno Stein. 2016. A news editorial corpus for mining argumentation strategies. In *Proceedings of COLING 2016, the 26th International Conference on Computational Linguistics: Technical Papers*, pages 3433–3443, Osaka, Japan. The COLING 2016 Organizing Committee.

Douglas Biber. 1989. A typology of English texts. *Linguistics*, 27(1):3–44.

Douglas Biber, Stig Johansson, Geoffrey N. Leech, Susan Conrad, and Edward Finegan. 2021. *Grammar of Spoken and Written English*. John Benjamins.

Elena Cabrio, Sara Tonelli, and Serena Villata. 2013. From discourse analysis to argumentation schemes and back: Relations and differences. In *Computational Logic in Multi-Agent Systems*, volume 8143, pages 1–17. Springer, Berlin, Heidelberg.

Anneloes Canestrelli, Pim Mak, and Ted Sanders. 2016. The influence of genre on the processing of objective and subjective causal relations: Evidence from eye-tracking. In Ninke Stukker, Wilbert Spooren, and Gerard Steen, editors, *Genre in Language, Discourse and Cognition*, pages 51–74. De Gruyter.

Lynn Carlson, Daniel Marcu, and Mary Ellen Okurowski. 2002. *RST Discourse Treebank LDC2002T07*. Linguistic Data Consortium, Philadelphia. Web Download.

Alexis Conneau, Kartikay Khandelwal, Naman Goyal, Vishrav Chaudhary, Guillaume Wenzek, Francisco Guzmán, Edouard Grave, Myle Ott, Luke Zettlemoyer, and Veselin Stoyanov. 2020. Unsupervised cross-lingual representation learning at scale. In *Proceedings of the 58th Annual Meeting of the Association for Computational Linguistics*, pages 8440–8451, Online. Association for Computational Linguistics.

Ludivine Crible and Vera Demberg. 2020. The role of non-connective discourse cues and their interaction with connectives. *Pragmatics & Cognition*, 27(2):313–338.

Debopam Das and Maite Taboada. 2018. Signalling of Coherence Relations in Discourse, Beyond Discourse Markers. *Discourse Processes*, 55(8):743–770.

Debopam Das, Maite Taboada, and Paul McFetridge. 2015. *RST Signalling Corpus LDC2015T10*. Linguistic Data Consortium, Philadelphia. Web Download.

Jacob Devlin, Ming-Wei Chang, Kenton Lee, and Kristina Toutanova. 2019. BERT: Pre-training of deep bidirectional transformers for language understanding. In *Proceedings of the 2019 Conference of the North American Chapter of the*

Association for Computational Linguistics: Human Language Technologies, Volume 1 (Long and Short Papers), pages 4171–4186, Minneapolis, Minnesota. Association for Computational Linguistics.

Heidrun Dorgeloh and Anja Wanner. 2022. *Discourse Syntax: English Grammar Beyond the Sentence*. Cambridge University Press.

Judith Eckle-Kohler, Roland Kluge, and Iryna Gurevych. 2015. On the role of discourse markers for discriminating claims and premises in argumentative discourse. In *Proceedings of the 2015 Conference on Empirical Methods in Natural Language Processing*, pages 2236–2242, Lisbon, Portugal. Association for Computational Linguistics.

Silvia Ferrari and Francisco Cribari-Neto. 2004. Beta regression for modelling rates and proportions. *Journal of Applied Statistics*, 31(7):799–815.

Anita Fetzer. 2018. The encoding and signalling of discourse relations in argumentative discourse. *The construction of discourse as verbal interaction*, pages 13–44.

Austin F. Frank and T. Florian Jaeger. 2008. Speaking rationally: Uniform information density as an optimal strategy for language production. In *Proceedings of the 30th Annual Meeting of the Cognitive Science Society*, pages 911–916, Washington, DC, USA. Cognitive Science Society.

Janet Giltrow. 2010. Genre as difference: The sociality of linguistic variation. In Heidrun Dorgeloh and Anja Wanner, editors, *Syntactic Variation and Genre*, volume 70, pages 29–52. DE GRUYTER MOUTON, Berlin, New York. Series Title: Topics in English Linguistics.

Theodosis Goudas, Christos Louizos, Georgios Petasis, and Vangelis Karkaletsis. 2014. Argument extraction from news, blogs, and social media. In *Artificial Intelligence: Methods and Applications*, pages 287–299, Cham. Springer International Publishing.

Xiaochuang Han and Jacob Eisenstein. 2019. Unsupervised domain adaptation of contextualized embeddings for sequence labeling. In *Proceedings of the 2019 Conference on Empirical Methods in Natural Language Processing and the 9th International Joint Conference on Natural Language Processing (EMNLP-IJCNLP)*, pages 4238–4248, Hong Kong, China. Association for Computational Linguistics.

Judith Kamalski, Leo Lentz, Ted Sanders, and Rolf A. Zwaan. 2008. The forewarning effect of coherence markers in persuasive discourse: Evidence from persuasion and processing. *Discourse Processes*, 45(6):545–579.

Lea Kawaletz, Heidrun Dorgeloh, and Stefan Conrad. 2023. Annotation guidelines for the project *Probing patterns of argumentative discourse*. Manuscript.

Lea Kawaletz, Heidrun Dorgeloh, Stefan Conrad, and Zeljko Bekcic. 2022. Developing an argument annotation scheme based on a semantic classification of arguments. In *Proceedings of the 23rd Annual Meeting of the Special Interest Group on Discourse and Dialogue*, pages 62–67, Edinburgh, UK. Association for Computational Linguistics.

René Knaebel and Manfred Stede. 2022. Towards identifying alternative-lexicalization signals of discourse relations. In *Proceedings of the 29th International Conference on Computational Linguistics*, pages 837–850, Gyeongju, Republic of Korea. International Committee on Computational Linguistics.

Murathan Kurfalı and Robert Östling. 2021. Let's be explicit about that: Distant supervision for implicit discourse relation classification via connective prediction. In *Proceedings of the 1st Workshop on Understanding Implicit and Underspecified Language*, pages 1–10, Online. Association for Computational Linguistics.

Yinhan Liu, Myle Ott, Naman Goyal, Jingfei Du, Mandar Joshi, Danqi Chen, Omer Levy, Mike Lewis, Luke Zettlemoyer, and Veselin Stoyanov. 2019. Roberta: A robustly optimized bert pretraining approach. *arXiv*, abs/1907.11692. Version 1.

Daniel Marcu and Abdessamad Echihabi. 2002. An unsupervised approach to recognizing discourse relations. In *Proceedings of the 40th Annual Meeting of the Association for Computational Linguistics*, pages 368–375, Philadelphia, Pennsylvania, USA. Association for Computational Linguistics.

Clara Meister, Tiago Pimentel, Patrick Haller, Lena Jäger, Ryan Cotterell, and Roger Levy. 2021. Revisiting the Uniform Information Density hypothesis. In *Proceedings of the 2021 Conference on Empirical Methods in Natural Language Processing*, pages 963–980, Online and Punta Cana, Dominican Republic. Association for Computational Linguistics.

Marie-Francine Moens. 2018. Argumentation mining: How can a machine acquire common sense and world knowledge? *Argument & Computation*, 9(1):1 – 14.

Gaku Morio, Hiroaki Ozaki, Terufumi Morishita, and Kohsuke Yanai. 2022. End-to-end argument mining with cross-corpora multi-task learning. *Transactions of the Association for Computational Linguistics*, 10:639–658.

Michael Quinn Patton. 2015. *Qualitative research & evaluation methods: integrating theory and practice*, fourth edition edition. SAGE Publications, Inc, Thousand Oaks, California.

Stephanie Petch-Tyson. 2000. Demonstrative expressions in argumentative discourse. *Corpus-Based and Computational Approaches to Dis-*

course Anaphora, Studies in Corpus Linguistics*, 3:43–64.

Anna Piata. 2016. *Genre "out of the box": A conceptual integration analysis of poetic discourse*, pages 225–250. De Gruyter Mouton, Berlin, Boston.

Rashmi Prasad, Nikhil Dinesh, Alan Lee, Eleni Miltsakaki, Livio Robaldo, Aravind Joshi, and Bonnie Webber. 2008. The Penn Discourse TreeBank 2.0. In *Proceedings of the Sixth International Conference on Language Resources and Evaluation (LREC'08)*, Marrakech, Morocco. European Language Resources Association (ELRA).

R Core Team. 2023. *R: A Language and Environment for Statistical Computing*. R Foundation for Statistical Computing, Vienna, Austria.

Adrian E. Raftery. 1995. Bayesian model selection in social research. *Sociological Methodology*, 25:111–163.

Gil Rocha, Henrique Lopes Cardoso, Jonas Belouadi, and Steffen Eger. 2023. Cross-genre argument mining: Can language models automatically fill in missing discourse markers? *arXiv*, abs/2306.04314. Version 1.

Ted J.M. Sanders, Vera Demberg, Jet Hoek, Merel C.J. Scholman, Fatemeh Torabi Asr, Sandrine Zufferey, and Jacqueline Evers-Vermeul. 2021. Unifying dimensions in coherence relations: How various annotation frameworks are related. *Corpus Linguistics and Linguistic Theory*, 17(1):1–71.

Victor Sanh, Lysandre Debut, Julien Chaumond, and Thomas Wolf. 2019. DistilBERT, a distilled version of BERT: smaller, faster, cheaper and lighter. In *5th Workshop on Energy Efficient Machine Learning and Cognitive Computing @ NeurIPS 2019*.

Merel C. J. Scholman, Vera Demberg, and Ted J. M. Sanders. 2020. Individual differences in expecting coherence relations: Exploring the variability in sensitivity to contextual signals in discourse. *Discourse Processes*, 57(10):844–861.

Wei Shi and Vera Demberg. 2019. Learning to explicitate connectives with Seq2Seq network for implicit discourse relation classification. In *Proceedings of the 13th International Conference on Computational Semantics - Long Papers*, pages 188–199, Gothenburg, Sweden. Association for Computational Linguistics.

Damien Sileo, Tim Van De Cruys, Camille Pradel, and Philippe Muller. 2019. Mining discourse markers for unsupervised sentence representation learning. In *Proceedings of the 2019 Conference of the North American Chapter of the Association for Computational Linguistics: Human Language Technologies, Volume 1 (Long and Short Papers)*, pages 3477–3486, Minneapolis, Minnesota. Association for Computational Linguistics.

Christian Stab and Iryna Gurevych. 2017. Parsing Argumentation Structures in Persuasive Essays. *Computational Linguistics*, 43(3):619–659.

Manfred Stede and Jodi Schneider. 2018. Argumentation mining. *Synthesis Lectures on Human Language Technologies*, 11(2):1–191.

Benno Stein and Henning Wachsmuth, editors. 2019. *Proceedings of the 6th Workshop on Argument Mining*. Association for Computational Linguistics, Florence, Italy.

Regina Stodden, Laura Kallmeyer, Lea Kawaletz, and Heidrun Dorgeloh. 2023. Using masked language model probabilities of connectives for stance detection in English discourse. In *Proceedings of the 10th Workshop on Argument Mining*, pages 11–18, Singapore. Association for Computational Linguistics.

Fatemeh Torabi Asr and Vera Demberg. 2012. Implicitness of discourse relations. In *Proceedings of COLING 2012*, pages 2669–2684, Mumbai, India. The COLING 2012 Organizing Committee.

Eric-Jan Wagenmakers. 2007. A practical solution to the pervasive problems of p values. *Psychonomic Bulletin & Review*, 14(5):779–804.

Yipu Wei, Jacqueline Evers-Vermeul, Ted M. Sanders, and Willem M. Mak. 2021a. The role of connectives and stance markers in the processing of subjective causal relations. *Discourse Processes*, 58(8):766–786.

Yipu Wei, Jacqueline Evers-Vermeul, Ted M. Sanders, and Willem M. Mak. 2021b. The role of connectives and stance markers in the processing of subjective causal relations. *Discourse Processes*, 58(8):766–786.

Thomas Wolf, Lysandre Debut, Victor Sanh, Julien Chaumond, Clement Delangue, Anthony Moi, Pierric Cistac, Tim Rault, Remi Louf, Morgan Funtowicz, Joe Davison, Sam Shleifer, Patrick von Platen, Clara Ma, Yacine Jernite, Julien Plu, Canwen Xu, Teven Le Scao, Sylvain Gugger, Mariama Drame, Quentin Lhoest, and Alexander Rush. 2020. Transformers: State-of-the-art natural language processing. In *Proceedings of the 2020 Conference on Empirical Methods in Natural Language Processing: System Demonstrations*, pages 38–45, Online. Association for Computational Linguistics.

Simon N. Wood. 2017. *Generalized additive models*, 2 edition. Chapman and Hall, Boca Raton.

Yu Xu, Man Lan, Yue Lu, Zheng Yu Niu, and Chew Lim Tan. 2012. Connective prediction using machine learning for implicit discourse relation classification. In *The 2012 International Joint Conference on Neural Networks (IJCNN)*, pages 1–8.

A More details on finetuning

hyperparameter	value
mlm probability	0.15
batch size	32
learning rate	0.00002
weight decay	0.01

Table 3: Hyperparameters for finetuning

Projecting Annotations for Discourse Relations: Connective Identification for Low-Resource Languages

Peter Bourgonje and **Pin-Jie Lin**
Saarland University, Saarbrücken, Germany
{peterb,pinjie}@lst.uni-saarland.de

Abstract

We present a pipeline for multi-lingual Shallow Discourse Parsing. The pipeline exploits machine translation and word alignment, by translating any incoming non-English input text into English, applying an English discourse parser, and projecting the found relations onto the original input text through word alignments. While the purpose of the pipeline is to provide rudimentary discourse relation annotations for low-resource languages (for which no annotations exist at all), in order to get an idea of performance, we evaluate it on the sub-task of discourse connective identification for several languages for which gold data are available. We experiment with different setups of our modular pipeline architecture and analyze intermediate results. Our code is made available on GitHub.

1 Introduction

Uncovering coherence relations in texts, also referred to as *discourse parsing*, is a complex task. It is comparably difficult and time-consuming for humans to annotate such relations, and as a result, relatively little training data is available for machines to train a system on. Most of this data is in English. Although recent shared tasks (Zeldes et al., 2019, 2021; Braud et al., 2023) have had a strong multilingual focus and included up to 13 different languages, there is still a large variety of languages that are seriously under-resourced when it comes to research on discourse and coherence.

In this paper, we attempt to address this issue by presenting an end-to-end, multi-lingual discourse parser. Our parser essentially consists of a processing pipeline that exploits machine translation, an English discourse parser, and a word aligner, to project discourse relation annotations onto any non-English input text, without a need for any language-specific training data. The goal of our pipeline is to kick-start the annotation of discourse relations in languages for which little to no resources are available, or to provide rudimentary discourse relation annotations for downstream applications where accuracy is not the main concern.

To get an idea of performance, we experiment with various different configurations of our modular architecture and evaluate on the sub-task of connective identification. We compare our results against a lexicon-based baseline that needs no training data either, and a state-of-the-art connective identification system trained specifically on the language and domain. Our pipeline mostly outperforms the lexicon-based baseline, by a factor of up to 2.7, and while a system specifically trained on the task outperforms our pipeline for all languages and corpora for which training data is available, we retain up to 81% of performance for some of those corpora. We analyze the (intermediate) results from different system configurations, in order to investigate which components of our processing pipeline are the most error-prone. We hope that our system proves to be a useful tool for researchers working on automated approaches to Shallow Discourse Parsing for languages for which little to no gold data is available.

The rest of this paper is organized as follows: Section 2 discusses related work, focusing mainly on discourse parsing. Section 3 explains our system architecture. Section 4 presents the results, which are discussed in Section 5. Finally, Section 6 sums up our main contributions and discusses directions for future work.

2 Related Work

In 2015 and 2016, two consecutive CoNLL shared tasks (Xue et al., 2015, 2016) caused a spark in interest in the discourse parsing task. The 2015 iteration worked with English only, the 2016 iteration was multi-lingual by adding Chinese. Both followed the Shallow Discourse Parsing paradigm proposed by the Penn Discourse TreeBank (PDTB,

Proceedings of the 5th Workshop on Computational Approaches to Discourse (CODI 2024), pages 39–49
March 21, 2024 ©2024 Association for Computational Linguistics

Prasad et al. (2008, 2019)). This approach is often referred to as *Shallow Discourse Parsing* since contrary to other discourse parsing frameworks such as Rhetorical Structure Theory (RST, Mann and Thompson (1988)) or Segmented Discourse Representation Theory (SDRT, Asher and Lascarides (2003)), it makes no commitment to overall text structure, and deals with coherence relations on a local level.

PDTB parsing is often done in end-to-end fashion, with plain text as input and a list of discourse relations as output, where each relation consists of a relation type (*explicit, implicit, alternative lexicalization* or other), arguments and relation sense. Since the introduction of a pipeline architecture by Lin et al. (2014), many systems adopted this setup (Wang and Lan, 2015; Oepen et al., 2016; Knaebel, 2021). The majority of systems work on English, with some systems focusing on Chinese (Kang et al., 2016; Kong and Zhou, 2017; Chuan-An et al., 2018). Beyond that, to the best of our knowledge, the only other supported language for end-to-end parsing is German (Bourgonje, 2021).

With a series of shared tasks, the Discourse Relation Parsing and Treebanking workshops (DISRPT, Zeldes et al. (2019, 2021); Braud et al. (2023)) strongly encouraged a multi-lingual approach and moreover, attempted to converge work on different parsing paradigms, by including corpora following the annotation guidelines from both the PDTB, RST and SDRT. The shared task setup moved away from an end-to-end approach, and system submissions (Liu et al., 2023; Metheniti et al., 2023; Anuranjana, 2023) focused on particular sub-tasks.

Our contribution aims to enable discourse parsing for an even larger variety of languages, without the need for any language-specific discourse annotations. We hope that this opens up research into discourse parsing for seriously under-resourced languages. We integrate the end-to-end PDTB parser from Knaebel (2021), but in principle, an end-to-end RST parser (Joty et al., 2015; Heilman and Sagae, 2015; Ji and Eisenstein, 2014) could be plugged in as well. The components we implemented for both machine translation and word alignment were mostly selected because of their user-friendly APIs. However, our system architecture is modular by design, and systems focusing on particular, low-resource languages can easily be plugged in. A good example for machine translation is presented by Lin et al. (2023), whereas good examples for word alignment are provided by Procopio et al. (2021); Chen et al. (2021).

Using annotation projection for (sub-tasks of) discourse parsing is not novel. Laali and Kosseim (2017) use annotation projection from English to French on a parallel corpus (Europarl) and improve f1 score for discourse connective identification in French by 15 points. Sluyter-Gäthje et al. (2020) employ machine translation in combination with word alignment, in order to create a German corpus automatically annotated for discourse relations. However, in contrast to Laali and Kosseim (2017), we include machine translation and thereby dynamically enable discourse parsing for any language. In contrast to Sluyter-Gäthje et al. (2020), we focus on the pipeline itself and make that available, instead of focusing on curating and publishing the output of the process (e.g., a corpus annotated for discourse relations in a particular language).

3 Pipeline Architecture

The following subsections explain the three different components of our pipeline to annotate any non-English text with discourse relations, following the PDTB framework. We use a modular setup, such that individual components can be swapped out for alternatives that perform better for particular languages or domains. The system architecture is illustrated in Figure 1. The rounded boxes on the right depict the individual modules. The listed components are the ones we implemented, but for every module, additional components can easily be integrated. For machine translation, using a custom model, trained specifically for a low-resource language (pair) can improve performance. For the discourse parsing module, relevant alternatives that work end-to-end can be integrated. For word alignment, tools that can be trained on or tuned for specific language pairs might return better results. See Section 2 for some suggestions. As long as these components accept and return input/output in the same format, they can easily be interchanged. A detailed description of the modules and the components that we integrated into our pipeline is provided in the following subsections.

3.1 Machine Translation

The first step is translating any non-English input text into English. We integrated both the DeepL[1] and Google Tranlate[2] APIs. At time of writing

[1] https://github.com/DeepLcom/deepl-python
[2] https://pypi.org/project/googletrans/

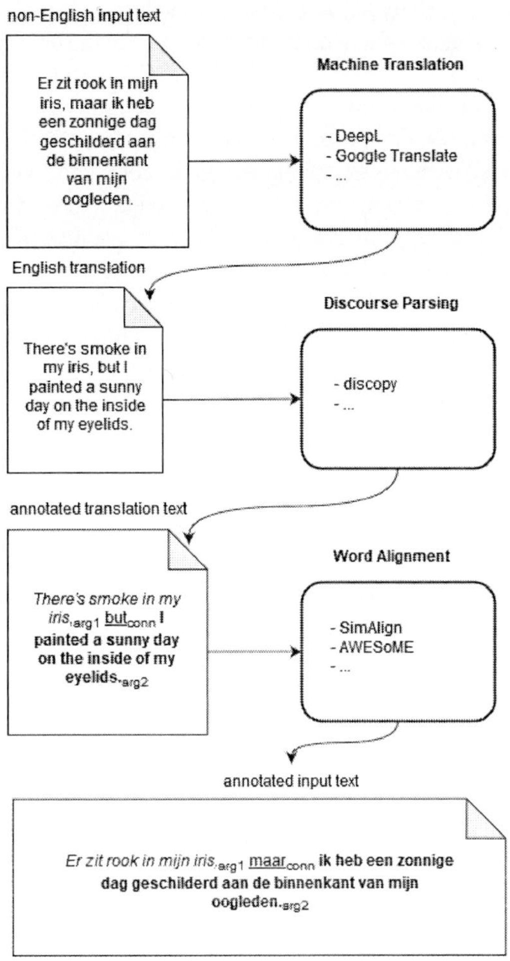

Figure 1: System architecture.

this, DeepL and Google Translate offer translations from/to 30 and 133 languages, respectively. For languages not included in either of those, or for domains where a specialized machine translation engine performs better, this module can easily be replaced by a custom machine translation engine.

Both the input and output format of this first module are a list of sentences; the original input text must be split into sentences, translation is then done sentence-by-sentence, and the output is a list of English sentences. The length of both input and output lists has to be identical.

The reason for translating sentence-by-sentence is that 1) the performance of word alignment is expected to be better when done sentence-based as opposed to text-based, and that 2) doing word alignment on longer texts rapidly leads to memory issues or long execution times. The drawback is that the English translation might be less fluent in cases where it might come more naturally to either merge or split up multiple sentences during translation.

3.2 Discourse Parsing

The second step in our pipeline is applying an end-to-end discourse parser on the English equivalent of the original input. We opted for English as an intermediate language because most training data annotated with PDTB-style discourse relations is available in English. For particular language pairs, if an end-to-end discourse parser is available in a language that is syntactically closer, using that might make sense, as word alignment can be expected to perform better in such a scenario. In our pipeline, we integrated discopy (Knaebel, 2021), because of its state-of-the-art performance and ease of use, accepting pre-tokenized input and running as a Docker container.

```
[
  ['There', "'s", 'smoke', 'in', 'my', 'iris', '.'],
  ['But', 'I', 'painted', 'a', 'sunny', 'day', 'on',
        'the', 'inside', 'of', 'my', 'eyelids', '.']
]
```

Listing 1: Example of discopy input format.

```
{"relations": [
    {
      "Arg1": {
        "CharacterSpanList": [
      [0, 25]
    ],
        "RawText": "There's smoke in my iris,",
        "TokenList": [0, 1, 2, 3, 4, 5, 6]
      },
      "Arg2": {
        "CharacterSpanList": [
          [30, 80]
        ],
        "RawText": "I painted a sunny day on the
             inside of my eyelids.",
        "TokenList": [8, 9, 10, 11, 12, 13, 14, 15,
             16, 17, 18, 19]
      },
      "Connective": {
        "CharacterSpanList": [
          [26, 29]
        ],
        "RawText": "but",
        "TokenList": [7]
      },
      "DocID": -2650724294676803157,
      "ID": 0,
      "Sense": [
        "Comparison.Contrast"
      ],
      "Type": "Explicit"
    }
  ]
}
```

Listing 2: Example of discopy output format.

This module takes the translated and tokenized text as input. The input must be a list of sentences, which in turn consist of lists of tokens. Sentences are already segmented in the previous step. Tokenization can be done with whatever method is most convenient to the user (e.g., spaCy, Stanza, UDPipe). An example of the required input format is included in Listing 1.

The output of this module is a JSON object, indicating where in the (English) input text, discourse relations have been found, indicated through both character offsets and token indices (based on the pre-tokenized input). An example is included in Listing 2.

3.3 Annotation Projection

The third and final step is that of projecting discourse relation annotations back onto the original input text. We integrated SimAlign (Jalili Sabet et al., 2020) and AWESoME (Dou and Neubig, 2021), but any word aligner that accepts sentence-segmented input and returns output in "Pharaoh format" can be used here. The Pharaoh format indicates which token in the source text corresponds to which token in the target text, and the example displayed in Figure 2 would be represented as follows:

```
[(0, 0), (1, 1), (2, 6), (3, 3), (4, 4), (5, 5)]
```

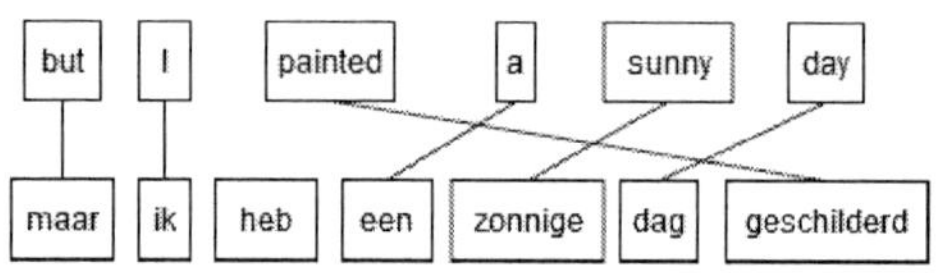

Figure 2: Word alignment example.

In this third and final step, we combine the results of the previous steps, with annotations all based on token indices and character offsets, to project the discourse relation annotations for the English translation back onto the original input text. For this, we use the same JSON format that discopy uses (see Listing 2), but now the annotations are on the original, non-English input text.

4 Results

Our pipeline is specifically targeted at low-resource languages for which no discourse relation annotations exist at all. However, without *any* gold data, we cannot get any idea of performance of our setup. So, in order to assess this across various languages and domains, we use the PDTB-style corpora featured in the 2023 DISRPT shared task (Braud et al., 2023) as gold data to evaluate our pipeline.

The shared task includes two sub-tasks, one focusing on segmentation and another focusing on relation sense classification. For PDTB-style corpora, the segmentation task is essentially about identifying connectives. The sense classification task assumes gold annotations for connective and relation arguments. While our pipeline returns discourse relations, fully specified with a connective, arguments and a relation sense, we decided to evaluate only on the segmentation task, i.e., connective identification, for now, as there is significant room for error propagation in our pipeline and we first want to get an idea of performance on the most upstream and comparably simpler task.

The segmentation sub-task for PDTB-style corpora includes five (non-English) languages (Italian, Portuguese, Turkish, Thai and Chinese), distributed over seven different corpora. An overview is included in Table 1.

Corpus	Domain
ita.pdtb.luna	IT helpdesk dialogs
por.pdtb.crpc	news, fiction
por.pdtb.tedm	TED talks
tha.pdtb.tdtb	news
tur.pdtb.tdb	news, fiction
tur.pdtb.tedm	TED talks
zho.pdtb.cdtb	news

Table 1: Overview of evaluation corpora.

In the task setup, the participants were provided with a train, dev and test set. Systems could therefore be trained and tuned for the relevant language using the train and dev sets. Since we do not train our system in any way for a particular language or domain, we do not expect to match performance of the trained systems that participated in the task, but for comparison, we do include results for DisCut (Kamaladdini Ezzabady et al., 2021; Metheniti et al., 2023), as this is the only system that submitted results for connective identification in the plain track, a setup that most resembles ours. We consider this the upper-bound of expected performance. To compare against a reasonable baseline that also does not require any pre-training and is aimed at low-resource/no-resource languages, we use a lexicon-based approach. This comprises simple pattern-matching using connective lexicons bundled on a dedicated platform[3]. Lexicons for all evaluation languages except Thai are available

[3]http://connective-lex.info/

on this platform. Similarly, because DeepL does not support Thai, the corresponding results are not included either. For all (other) corpora, we experiment with different configurations for the individual modules and their integrated components. We calculate precision, recall and f1 scores for all corpora, based on the *.test.conllu files from the shared task[4]. Since our system needs no training data, we could in principle evaluate against all available data (including train and dev sets), but to make a direct comparison to DisCut's performance possible, we evaluate on the test sets only. The results are included in Table 2.

5 Discussion

As illustrated by the performance of DisCut, with f1 scores generally in the 80s to 90s, given the availability of training data, identifying connectives is relatively easy, at least when compared to other subtasks in discourse parsing. We included the lexicon- and pattern-matching-based baseline, performing considerably worse, to indicate performance when no training data is used at all, since this much more resembles the targeted application scenario of our pipeline.

The mid section of Table 2 represents the results of experimenting with different system configurations. Overall, we can see that our annotation projection approach performs considerably better than the baseline, except for on **zho.pdtb.cdtb** and **ita.pdtb.luna**. However, a trained classifier performs significantly better still. Based on this relatively small set of languages and corpora, there does not seem to be a trend with regard to individual languages performing better or worse, as the difference within languages (46 and 64 for the two Portuguese corpora, and 42 and 48 for the two Turkish corpora, both for **deepl-discopy-awesome**) does not seem to be significantly smaller than the difference between languages.

The following sections discuss the influence of different system configurations with regard to machine translation and word alignment.

5.1 Machine Translation

By looking at the pairs for **deepl-discopy-simalign** and **googletrans-discopy-simalign** first, and **deepl-discopy-awesome** and **googletrans-discopy-awesome** second, we can see the influence of a difference in machine translation alone. For all languages except Chinese, the setup using DeepL performs better than the setup using Google Translate, with the difference in final f1 score ranging from 1 point (42 for **deepl-discopy-awesome** vs. 41 for **googletrans-discopy-awesome** on **tur.pdtb.tdb**), to 6 points (64 for **deepl-discopy-awesome** vs. 58 for **googletrans-discopy-awesome** on **por.pdtb.tedm**). For Chinese, the setup using Google Translate outperforms the setup using DeepL by up to 4 points. Recall that DeepL does not support Thai, hence no results using this in the setup can be provided for **tha.pdtb.tdtb**.

As noted in Section 3.1, the machine translation module only accepts input that is already split into sentences, and translation proceeds on a sentence-by-sentence basis. Translating sentences in isolation is likely to have a negative impact on translation output quality, since it will be less context-aware. This is particularly unfortunate as we are dealing with coherence relations, which are often realized beyond sentence boundaries. We consider it an important next step in the development of our system to feed the sentence-segmented input into the machine translation engine in batch-wise fashion. In this way, we can take context into account, but still force it to return the same number of output sentences as are present in the input, to allow for sentence-based word alignment.

5.1.1 Implicitation and Explicitation

Since we are translating discourse relations and are evaluating on the sub-task of connective identification, an issue known from the literature (Meyer and Webber, 2013; Lapshinova-Koltunski and Carl, 2022; Lapshinova-Koltunski et al., 2022; Yung et al., 2023) to take into account is *implicitation* and *explicitation*, where discourse connectives are either removed (explicit relations in the source text become implicit relations in the target text) or added (vice-versa) during translation. Especially implicitation has a negative effect on performance, as discourse connectives just disappear. Explicitation presumably does not affect performance that much in our evaluation setup, as in most cases, word alignment will not find any tokens in the source text that align to the newly added connectives in the target text. Both implicitation and explicitation are known to play out differently, depending on whether text is translated by machines or by humans, i.e., Meyer and Webber (2013) find an implicitation rate of up to 18% in human trans-

[4]https://github.com/disrpt/sharedtask2023data

	ita.pdtb.luna			**por.pdtb.crpc**			**por.pdtb.tedm**			**tha.pdtb.tdtb**		
	p	r	f1	p	r	f1	p	r	f1	p	r	f1
baseline	28	**58**	**38**	58	13	22	48	15	23	-	-	-
deepl-discopy-simalign	50	30	**38**	68	33	44	**85**	**52**	**64**	-	-	-
deepl-discopy-awesome	**51**	30	**38**	73	**34**	**46**	**85**	**52**	**64**	-	-	-
googletrans-discopy-simalign	48	29	36	72	28	41	81	46	58	52	20	29
googletrans-discopy-awesome	48	29	36	**75**	28	41	81	46	58	**61**	**21**	**32**
DisCut	*66*	*78*	*72*	*78*	*81*	*79*	*75*	*85*	*79*	*85*	*59*	*70*

	tur.pdtb.tdb			**tur.pdtb.tedm**			**zho.pdtb.cdtb**		
	p	r	f1	p	r	f1	p	r	f1
baseline	27	18	22	49	13	21	51	**30**	**38**
deepl-discopy-simalign	37	35	36	69	33	45	46	26	33
deepl-discopy-awesome	42	**42**	**42**	**79**	**34**	**48**	50	24	33
googletrans-discopy-simalign	36	34	35	64	21	42	57	28	37
googletrans-discopy-awesome	**45**	38	41	71	31	43	**58**	27	36
DisCut	*90*	*92*	*91*	*51*	*89*	*65*	*92*	*89*	*90*

Table 2: Results of four system configurations on seven non-English corpora. We compare our parser with a lexicon-based **baseline** and language-specific, trained system (**DisCut**). The reported scores are in percentages (%).

lations, and up to 8% in machine translations.

To investigate to what extent this effect may have negatively impacted performance of our system, we select one corpus where our pipeline did not outperform the baseline (**ita.pdtb.luna**) and one where it outperformed the baseline by quite some margin (**por.pdtb.tedm**). We look at implicitation, by selecting sentences that contain one or more connectives, and then checking if their English translation contains a *potential* connective, using Eng-DiMLex, an inventory of English discourse connectives (Das et al., 2018). If there is no match, we consider this a case of potential implicitation, and manually investigate further.

In **ita.pdtb.luna**, there are 202 sentences containing one or more connectives (of 1.304 sentences in total). Using the procedure described above, we find 23 instances of possible implicitation. Out of these 23 instances, 8 are cases where the input is too short to return a reasonable translation. Because the corpus consists of IT helpdesk dialogs, these include (possibly interrupted) turns in a dialog, such as *ma tanto noi* ("but we") and *perchè* ("why"). 4 instances contain *cioè*, which is consistently translated to "i.e." in English, which is not in Eng-DiMLex. This is basically a design decision (to not include abbreviations), since the semantically identical *for example* is included in Eng-DiMLex and would be annotated according to PDTB guidelines. Of the remaining 12 cases, 7 are cases of actual implicitation, and the other 5 are originating from the fact that the connective in Italian is one word, and corresponding candidates in English are phrasal. A frequent example is *che*, where the English equivalent *that* is present in the translation. But although Eng-DiMlex includes *given that*, *so that* and *after that*, for example, it does not include *that* in isolation.

In **por.pdtb.tedm**, there are 122 sentences containing one or more connectives (of 246 sentences in total), and 7 instances of possible implicitation. Upon manual investigation, we found that this includes 4 cases of actual implicitation, with the remaining 3 being border line cases, which according to the English, PDTB annotation guidelines (Eng-DiMLex is largely extracted from the PDTB) are not considered connectives. An example is *Agora podem vê# -la a desenrolar.* ("Now you can watch it unfold."), where *Agora* is annotated as a connective, whereas "Now" would probably not be annotated according to PDTB guidelines.

In all corpora except for **tur.pdtb.tdb**, recall is considerably lower than precision. We suspect that the reason for this is that we can "lose" connectives in our processing pipeline (which negatively impacts recall), but we can never "gain" new connectives to compensate for this. If discopy finds new connectives in the English translations (i.e., explicitation), they will not be projected back onto the original text, because they are implicit there. Upon investigation, we found that for **tur.pdtb.tedm**, with 247 connective tokens, only 119 were found in the English translations, resulting in an upper-bound (if all instances found are correct) of 48% for recall. The subsequent annotation projection step actually retained all 119 instances. This suggests that the largest source of error is running discopy on the English translations.

Ultimately, it might be more relevant to consider a more holistic evaluation, focusing on which *relations* (including arguments and senses) have been found, instead of which *connectives* have been found. As explained earlier though, we first want to get an idea of performance of comparably simpler tasks, before we move to such a more abstract evaluation.

5.2 Discourse Parsing & Word Alignment

In our current setup, we only include one discourse parser, hence cannot experiment with different setups for this module. By investigating the rows **deepl-discopy-simalign** and **deepl-discopy-awesome** first, and **googletrans-discopy-simalign** and **googletrans-discopy-awesome** second, we can see the influence of a difference in word alignment alone. The setup using AWESoME outperforms the setup using SimAlign on all data sets except **zho.pdtb.cdtb**, where only in the setup using Google Translate, SimAlign returns better results. AWESoME outperforming SimAlign overall is in line with the findings of Dou and Neubig (2021), who compare their results to SimAlign as well.

In an attempt to isolate the effect of discourse parsing and word alignment quality on our final f1 score, we zoom in on one document from one particular corpus. We select talk_1976 from **por.pdtb.tedm** and investigate the best-performing setup for this corpus (**deepl-discopy-awesome**). Talk_1976 contains 59 connectives in its gold annotation. In the English translation of this document, discopy finds 38 relations, 34 of which are explicit (i.e., contain a connective). We found that all 34 connectives were true positives, and they were correctly aligned to the source connective. This is in line with the relatively high precision (85) for this corpus. During manual analysis, we noticed that most instances of explicit relations that were found, featured fairly frequent connectives like *e* ("and"), *mas* ("but"), *se* ("if") and *porque* ("because"), but less frequent connectives were missed by the parser. A case in point is *Agora* ("now") in *Agora podem vê# -la a desenrolar.* ("Now you can watch it unfold."), which was missed by discopy, although as mentioned in the previous section, this might actually not be considered a connective, according to the PDTB guidelines, and recall that discopy is trained on the PDTB.

Another example of this kind, resulting from the fact that the corpus discopy is trained on, might use a different definition than the corpus it is applied on, is *Bem, imaginemos que pegamos no Telescópio Espacial Hubble e o rodamos e o deslocamos para a órbita de Marte.* ("Well, let's imagine we take the Hubble Space Telescope and rotate it and move it into orbit around Mars."), where *imaginemos* ("let's imagine") is annotated as a connective. Similarly, in *Seria o mesmo se erguesse o meu polegar e bloqueasse o ponto luminoso à frente de_ os meus olhos* ("It would be the same if I raised my thumb and blocked the light spot in front of my eyes"), *Seria o mesmo* ("It would be the same") is annotated as a connective. Such examples would most likely be annotated as alternative lexicalizations in the English PDTB, but other corpora might have different definitions. We refer to Danlos et al. (2018) for a detailed discussion, and furthermore note that because in this paper, we are evaluating on connectives specifically, this issue is particularly challenging. For users interested in discourse parsing in general (without specifically looking at connectives), it might be less important whether some relation is found as an Explicit or as an AltLex type relation, as long as it is found.

5.3 Domain Transfer

Based on the 7 corpora, distributed over 5 different languages, we do not observe a significantly larger variance in f1 score across languages, compared to within languages. The two best-scoring corpora are both from the TED Multilingual Discourse Bank (Zeyrek et al., 2018). This raises the question as to whether expected performance is determined by original language or, rather, by original domain. Discopy has been trained on the original, English PDTB corpus, which represents the financial news domain (Wall Street Journal articles). The two TED corpora **por.pdtb.tedm** and **tur.pdtb.tedm** contain *"prepared, formal monologues (...) delivered to a live audience"* (Zeyrek et al., 2018, pp.1915), on a variety of topics. At first glance, this does not necessarily resemble WSJ articles. While one of the corpora for which our pipeline does not outperform the baseline, **ita.pdtb.luna**, is from an even less similar genre (spoken dialogs from the IT helpdesk domain (Tonelli et al., 2010)), the other corpus, **zho.pdtb.ctdb** consists of newswire text

(Zhou et al., 2014), which at first glance seems very similar to the domain discopy was trained on. In the 2023 shared task, **por.pdtb.tedm** and **tur.pdtb.tedm** corresponded to the "Out of Domain" setting. For Turkish, this seems to have had a major impact on a system trained on a different domain, as demonstrated by the performance drop from 91 (**tur.pdtb.tdb**) to 65 (**tur.pdtb.tedm**) for DisCut. However, such a drop is not observed for DisCut's performance on Portuguese, with both corpora having the same f1 score.

6 Conclusion & Future Work

We present a multi-lingual Shallow Discourse Parsing pipeline that makes use of machine translation, an English discourse parser and word alignment to project annotations onto the original, non-English input text. We specifically aim to support low-resource scenarios and make rudimentary discourse parsing possible for languages without any available training data, since our pipeline needs no training data at all. Our code is made available online.[5]

We evaluate our approach on the sub-task of connective identification and compare different configurations of our pipeline to a lexicon-based baseline, and to a system specifically designed for the task and trained on in-language, in-domain data. Our system outperforms the baseline in most cases, and for individual corpora improves f1 score by a factor of 2.7. We find that a trained system still performs considerably better, but for the best-scoring corpus, we retain 81% of the upper-bound f1 score.

In our current architecture, translation is done sentence-by-sentence, so as to keep sentences aligned for better word alignment performance. We consider more context-aware translation (Herold and Ney, 2023) the most important piece of future work. In addition, further investigation of error propagation, as well as the effect of domain transfer, are promising venues for future work. In this paper, we evaluate our approach on the sub-task of connective identification only. Our pipeline returns fully specified relations (with a type, arguments and relation sense), and we leave it to future work to evaluate on more than just connective identification. Relevant related work in this respect is represented by Kurfalı and Östling (2019), who work on implicit relation classification without exploiting any (language-specific) training data, and we consider it an important next step to experiment with zero-shot transfer (Kurfalı and Östling, 2019, 2021) for other sub-tasks of discourse parsing.

Our system architecture is modular by design, with relatively common exchange formats (Pharaoh for word alignments, PDTB-style JSON for discourse relations) across modules, and where individual components fine-tuned to a particular language are available, these can easily plugged in. Furthermore, our current architecture includes only a PDTB parser and another possible extension is the integration of RST parsers.

7 Limitations

In our pipeline, we integrated two alternatives for machine translation, and two alternatives for word alignment. Due to the limited availability of end-to-end Shallow discourse parsers, we only include one such parser in our setup and evaluation. Since we see systematic differences in performance for both machine translation and word alignment, depending on which module is used, integrating more components would provide a broader perspective. Especially since both alignment components are designed to work out-of-the-box, without any fine-tuning, which most likely means that they will work best on languages not too dissimilar to English.

Since we use a discourse parser trained on one specific English corpus, from one domain (financial news), we consider this the most prominent limitation of our system. While through this very work, we attempt to open up discourse research to under-resourced languages, we recognize that we may actually end up enforcing principles and paradigms that happen to work well for English onto languages where discourse relations may be realized in different ways. We already observe and discuss examples of this kind in Section 5.2. While we believe that our work may support the creation of corpora in other languages, it is important to keep this in mind and attempt to minimize bias when using the output of our system in annotation campaigns.

Acknowledgments

This research was funded by the German Research Foundation (DFG), Project-ID 232722074 – SFB 1102: Information Density and Linguistic Encoding. We thank the reviewers for their comments on an earlier version of this manuscript.

[5]https://github.com/PeterBourgonje/projan-disco/

References

Kaveri Anuranjana. 2023. DiscoFlan: Instruction Fine-tuning and Refined Text Generation for Discourse Relation Label Classification. In *Proceedings of the 3rd Shared Task on Discourse Relation Parsing and Treebanking (DISRPT 2023)*, pages 22–28, Toronto, Canada. The Association for Computational Linguistics.

Nicholas Asher and Alex Lascarides. 2003. *Logics of Conversation*. Studies in Natural Language Processing. Cambridge University Press.

Peter Bourgonje. 2021. *Shallow Discourse Parsing for German*. Doctoral thesis, Universität Potsdam.

Chloé Braud, Yang Janet Liu, Eleni Metheniti, Philippe Muller, Laura Rivière, Attapol Rutherford, and Amir Zeldes. 2023. The DISRPT 2023 Shared Task on Elementary Discourse Unit Segmentation, Connective Detection, and Relation Classification. In *Proceedings of the 3rd Shared Task on Discourse Relation Parsing and Treebanking (DISRPT 2023)*, pages 1–21, Toronto, Canada. The Association for Computational Linguistics.

Chi Chen, Maosong Sun, and Yang Liu. 2021. Mask-Align: Self-Supervised Neural Word Alignment. In *Proceedings of the 59th Annual Meeting of the Association for Computational Linguistics and the 11th International Joint Conference on Natural Language Processing (Volume 1: Long Papers)*, pages 4781–4791, Online. Association for Computational Linguistics.

Lin Chuan-An, Hen-Hsen Huang, Zi-Yuan Chen, and Hsin-Hsi Chen. 2018. A Unified RvNN Framework for End-to-End Chinese Discourse Parsing. In *Proceedings of the 27th International Conference on Computational Linguistics: System Demonstrations*, pages 73–77, Santa Fe, New Mexico. Association for Computational Linguistics.

Laurence Danlos, Katerina Rysova, Magdalena Rysova, and Manfred Stede. 2018. Primary and Secondary Discourse Connectives: Definitions and Lexicons. *Dialogue and Discourse*, 9(1):50–78.

Debopam Das, Tatjana Scheffler, Peter Bourgonje, and Manfred Stede. 2018. Constructing a Lexicon of English Discourse Connectives. In *Proceedings of the 19th Annual SIGdial Meeting on Discourse and Dialogue*, pages 360–365, Melbourne, Australia. Association for Computational Linguistics.

Zi-Yi Dou and Graham Neubig. 2021. Word Alignment by Fine-tuning Embeddings on Parallel Corpora. In *Proceedings of the 16th Conference of the European Chapter of the Association for Computational Linguistics: Main Volume*, pages 2112–2128, Online. Association for Computational Linguistics.

Michael Heilman and Kenji Sagae. 2015. Fast rhetorical structure theory discourse parsing. *CoRR*, abs/1505.02425.

Christian Herold and Hermann Ney. 2023. Improving long context document-level machine translation. In *Proceedings of the 4th Workshop on Computational Approaches to Discourse (CODI 2023)*, pages 112–125, Toronto, Canada. Association for Computational Linguistics.

Masoud Jalili Sabet, Philipp Dufter, François Yvon, and Hinrich Schütze. 2020. SimAlign: High Quality Word Alignments without Parallel Training Data using Static and Contextualized Embeddings. In *Proceedings of the 2020 Conference on Empirical Methods in Natural Language Processing: Findings*, pages 1627–1643, Online. Association for Computational Linguistics.

Yangfeng Ji and Jacob Eisenstein. 2014. Representation Learning for Text-level Discourse Parsing. In *Proceedings of the 52nd Annual Meeting of the Association for Computational Linguistics (Volume 1: Long Papers)*, pages 13–24, Baltimore, Maryland. Association for Computational Linguistics.

Shafiq Joty, Giuseppe Carenini, and Raymond T. Ng. 2015. CODRA: A Novel Discriminative Framework for Rhetorical Analysis. *Computational Linguistics*, 41(3):385–435.

Morteza Kamaladdini Ezzabady, Philippe Muller, and Chloé Braud. 2021. Multi-lingual Discourse Segmentation and Connective Identification: MELODI at Disrpt2021. In *Proceedings of the 2nd Shared Task on Discourse Relation Parsing and Treebanking (DISRPT 2021)*, pages 22–32, Punta Cana, Dominican Republic. Association for Computational Linguistics.

Xiaomian Kang, Haoran Li, Long Zhou, Jiajun Zhang, and Chengqing Zong. 2016. An End-to-End Chinese Discourse Parser with Adaptation to Explicit and Non-explicit Relation Recognition. In *Proceedings of the CoNLL-16 shared task*, pages 27–32, Berlin, Germany. Association for Computational Linguistics.

René Knaebel. 2021. discopy: A Neural System for Shallow Discourse Parsing. In *Proceedings of the 2nd Workshop on Computational Approaches to Discourse*, pages 128–133, Punta Cana, Dominican Republic and Online. Association for Computational Linguistics.

Fang Kong and Guodong Zhou. 2017. A CDT-Styled End-to-End Chinese Discourse Parser. *ACM Trans. Asian Low-Resour. Lang. Inf. Process.*, 16(4).

Murathan Kurfalı and Robert Östling. 2019. Zero-shot transfer for implicit discourse relation classification. In *Proceedings of the 20th Annual SIGdial Meeting on Discourse and Dialogue*, pages 226–231, Stockholm, Sweden. Association for Computational Linguistics.

Murathan Kurfalı and Robert Östling. 2021. Probing multilingual language models for discourse. In *Proceedings of the 6th Workshop on Representation Learning for NLP (RepL4NLP-2021)*, pages 8–19, Online. Association for Computational Linguistics.

Majid Laali and Leila Kosseim. 2017. Improving Discourse Relation Projection to Build Discourse Annotated Corpora. In *Proceedings of the International Conference Recent Advances in Natural Language Processing, RANLP 2017*, pages 407–416, Varna, Bulgaria. INCOMA Ltd.

Ekaterina Lapshinova-Koltunski and Michael Carl. 2022. Using Translation Process Data to Explore Explicitation and Implicitation through Discourse Connectives. In *Proceedings of the 3rd Workshop on Computational Approaches to Discourse*, pages 42–47, Gyeongju, Republic of Korea and Online. International Conference on Computational Linguistics.

Ekaterina Lapshinova-Koltunski, Christina Pollkläsener, and Heike Przybyl. 2022. Exploring Explicitation and Implicitation in Parallel Interpreting and Translation Corpora. *The Prague Bulletin of Mathematical Linguistics*, 119:5–22.

Pin-Jie Lin, Muhammed Saeed, Ernie Chang, and Merel Scholman. 2023. Low-Resource Cross-Lingual Adaptive Training for Nigerian Pidgin. In *Proceedings of INTERSPEECH 2023*, pages 3954–3958.

Ziheng Lin, Hwee Tou Ng, and Min-Yen Kan. 2014. A PDTB-Styled End-to-End Discourse Parser. *Natural Language Engineering*, 20:151–184.

Wei Liu, Yi Fan, and Michael Strube. 2023. HITS at DISRPT 2023: Discourse Segmentation, Connective Detection, and Relation Classification. In *Proceedings of the 3rd Shared Task on Discourse Relation Parsing and Treebanking (DISRPT 2023)*, pages 43–49, Toronto, Canada. The Association for Computational Linguistics.

William Mann and Sandra Thompson. 1988. Rhetorical Structure Theory: Towards a Functional Theory of Text Organization. *TEXT*, 8:243–281.

Eleni Metheniti, Chloé Braud, Philippe Muller, and Laura Rivière. 2023. DisCut and DiscReT: MELODI at DISRPT 2023. In *Proceedings of the 3rd Shared Task on Discourse Relation Parsing and Treebanking (DISRPT 2023)*, pages 29–42, Toronto, Canada. The Association for Computational Linguistics.

Thomas Meyer and Bonnie Webber. 2013. Implicitation of Discourse Connectives in (Machine) Translation. In *Proceedings of the Workshop on Discourse in Machine Translation*, pages 19–26, Sofia, Bulgaria. Association for Computational Linguistics.

Stephan Oepen, Jonathon Read, Tatjana Scheffler, Uladzimir Sidarenka, Manfred Stede, Erik Velldal, and Lilja Øvrelid. 2016. OPT: Oslo–Potsdam–Teesside—Pipelining Rules, Rankers, and Classifier Ensembles for Shallow Discourse Parsing. In *Proceedings of the 20th Conference on Computational Natural Language Learning: Shared Task (CoNLL Shared Task 2016)*, pages 20–26, Berlin.

Rashmi Prasad, Nikhil Dinesh, Alan Lee, Eleni Miltsakaki, Livio Robaldo, Aravind Joshi, and Bonnie Webber. 2008. The Penn Discourse TreeBank 2.0. In *Proceedings of the Sixth International Conference on Language Resources and Evaluation (LREC'08)*, pages 2961–2968, Marrakech, Morocco. European Language Resources Association (ELRA).

Rashmi Prasad, Bonnie Webber, Alan Lee, and Aravind Joshi. 2019. Penn Discourse Treebank Version 3.0, LDC2019T05.

Luigi Procopio, Edoardo Barba, Federico Martelli, and Roberto Navigli. 2021. MultiMirror: Neural Cross-lingual Word Alignment for Multilingual Word Sense Disambiguation. In *Proceedings of the Thirtieth International Joint Conference on Artificial Intelligence, IJCAI-21*, pages 3915–3921. International Joint Conferences on Artificial Intelligence Organization. Main Track.

Henny Sluyter-Gäthje, Peter Bourgonje, and Manfred Stede. 2020. Shallow Discourse Parsing for Under-Resourced Languages: Combining Machine Translation and Annotation Projection. In *Proceedings of the Twelfth Language Resources and Evaluation Conference*, pages 1044–1050, Marseille, France. European Language Resources Association.

Sara Tonelli, Giuseppe Riccardi, Rashmi Prasad, and Aravind Joshi. 2010. Annotation of Discourse Relations for Conversational Spoken Dialogs. In *Proceedings of the Seventh International Conference on Language Resources and Evaluation (LREC'10)*, Valletta, Malta. European Language Resources Association (ELRA).

Jianxiang Wang and Man Lan. 2015. A Refined End-to-End Discourse Parser. In *Proceedings of the 19th Conference on Computational Natural Language Learning: Shared Task (CoNLL Shared Task 2015)*, pages 17–24. Association for Computational Linguistics.

Nianwen Xue, Hwee Tou Ng, Sameer Pradhan, Rashmi Prasad, Christopher Bryant, and Attapol Rutherford. 2015. The CoNLL-2015 Shared Task on Shallow Discourse Parsing. In *Proceedings of the Nineteenth Conference on Computational Natural Language Learning - Shared Task*, pages 1–16, Beijing, China. Association for Computational Linguistics.

Nianwen Xue, Hwee Tou Ng, Sameer Pradhan, Attapol Rutherford, Bonnie Webber, Chuan Wang, and Hongmin Wang. 2016. CoNLL 2016 Shared Task on Multilingual Shallow Discourse Parsing. In *Proceedings of the CoNLL-16 shared task*, pages 1–19, Berlin, Germany. Association for Computational Linguistics.

Frances Yung, Merel Scholman, Ekaterina Lapshinova-Koltunski, Christina Pollkläsener, and Vera Demberg. 2023. Investigating Explicitation of Discourse Connectives in Translation using Automatic Annotations. In *Proceedings of the 24th Annual Meeting of the*

Special Interest Group on Discourse and Dialogue, pages 21–30, Prague, Czechia. Association for Computational Linguistics.

Amir Zeldes, Debopam Das, Erick Galani Maziero, Juliano Antonio, and Mikel Iruskieta. 2019. The DISRPT 2019 Shared Task on Elementary Discourse Unit Segmentation and Connective Detection. In *Proceedings of the Workshop on Discourse Relation Parsing and Treebanking 2019*, pages 97–104, Minneapolis, MN. Association for Computational Linguistics.

Amir Zeldes, Yang Janet Liu, Mikel Iruskieta, Philippe Muller, Chloé Braud, and Sonia Badene. 2021. The DISRPT 2021 Shared Task on Elementary Discourse Unit Segmentation, Connective Detection, and Relation Classification. In *Proceedings of the 2nd Shared Task on Discourse Relation Parsing and Treebanking (DISRPT 2021)*, pages 1–12, Punta Cana, Dominican Republic. Association for Computational Linguistics.

Deniz Zeyrek, Amália Mendes, and Murathan Kurfalı. 2018. Multilingual Extension of PDTB-Style Annotation: The Case of TED Multilingual Discourse Bank. In *Proceedings of the Eleventh International Conference on Language Resources and Evaluation (LREC 2018)*, Miyazaki, Japan. European Language Resources Association (ELRA).

Yuping Zhou, Jill Lu, Jennifer Zhang, and Nianwen Xue. 2014. Chinese Discourse Treebank 0.5 LDC2014T21.

Investigating Discourse Segmentation in Taiwan Southern Min Spontaneous Speech

Laurent Prévot[1,2]
[1]CNRS & MEAE, CEFC
[2]CNRS & Aix Marseille Université, LPL
Taipei, Taiwan
laurent.prevot@cefc.com.hk

Sheng-Fu Wang
Institute of Linguistics
Academia Sinica
Taipei, Taiwan
sftwang@gate.sinica.edu.tw

Abstract

In recent years, discourse segmentation has received increased attention; however the majority of studies have focused on written genres and languages with abundant linguistic resources. This paper investigates discourse segmentation of a spontaneous speech corpus in Taiwan Southern Min. We compare fine-tuning a Language Model (LLM) using two approaches: supervised, taking advantage of a high-quality annotated dataset, and weakly-supervised, which requires only a small amount of manual labeling. The corpus used here is transcribed in both Chinese characters and romanized script. This allows us to assess the impact of the written form on the discourse segmentation task. Moreover, the dataset includes manual prosodic break labeling, allowing an exploration of the role prosody can play in contemporary discourse segmentation systems grounded in LLMs. In our study, the supervised approach outperforms weak-supervision; the character-based version demonstrates better scores compared to the romanized version; and prosodic information proves to be an interesting source to increase discourse segmentation performance.

1 Introduction

Discourse segmentation consists in breaking down texts or conversations into functional units that better corresponds to participants' intentions than sentences or simple speech activity chunks. We will use the term discourse unit (DU) (Asher and Lascarides, 2003) to designate a minimal speech act or communicative unit. Each DU corresponds roughly to a clause-level content that denotes a single fact or event.

While the segmentation of discourse units (DUs) in written documents has received a lot of attention from the discourse and NLP community, the same cannot be said for the segmentation of spontaneous speech. In this study, we approach the segmentation of discourse units in a corpus of spontaneous speech in Taiwan Southern Min.

Southern Min is a sino-tibetan language spoken by over 50 million people, and includes Taiwan Southern Min, which is one of the official language of Taiwan. We take advantage here of an existing discourse segmented corpus of spoken interviews for running discourse segmentation experiments.

We develop DU segmenters based on different principles and evaluate their performance. More precisely, we compare fine-tuning an LLM with hand labeled data vs. employing a data programming approach (Ratner et al., 2017) that requires only a fraction of annotated data. While fine-tuning LLMs for language well represented in the LLM training data proved to be a very efficient solution (Gravellier et al., 2021; Prevot et al., 2023), it remains to be seen whether this approach is relevant for languages, particularly their spontaneous speech variants, less represented in the training data. Finally, we investigate the impact of using either romanization or Chinese characters in our dataset, as well as the potential contribution of prosody.

2 Related Work

In recent years, there has been a renewed interest in discourse parsing and discourse unit segmentation within the NLP community. As in other subdomains, Large Language Models have proven highly beneficial and allowed to reach unprecedented scores for these tasks. However, discourse segmentation within these deep learning approaches has been applied to only a few langauges, until the recent initiative of DISRPT campaigns started (Zeldes et al., 2019, 2021; Braud et al., 2023). The work conduced within the framework of these campaigns has equipped the community with a set of powerful tools and frameworks to perform DU segmentation using these contemporary approaches.

Proceedings of the 5th Workshop on Computational Approaches to Discourse (CODI 2024), pages 50–63
March 21, 2024

As discussed in Braud et al. (2023), even for written genres, discourse segmentation performance drops in languages other than English and when gold sentences are not given, due to sentence segmenters being far from perfect (Braud et al., 2017). Considering spontaneous conversational speech, the related tasks of dialogue-act segmentation and tagging yiels various interpretation regarding the definition of base units. For instance, some models explain that dialogue acts being multi-functional, several segmentations can be considered depending on the aspects of dialogue being considered at the time of segmentation (Petukhova et al., 2011).

A recent trend involves approaching discourse segmentation with sequential models over contextual embeddings (Wang et al., 2018; Muller et al., 2019). Turning specifically to spontaneous speech discourse segmentation, (Gravellier et al., 2021) applied a weak-supervision approach (Ratner et al., 2017) and reached an f-score of 73.7 while having access to gold turn segmentation. More specifically, manual heuristic rules, including some rules exploiting the discourse segmentation model trained on a written dataset (Muller et al., 2019), were created to annotate noisily the entire dataset. This noisy data was then used to fine-tune an LLM, BERT (Devlin et al., 2018) in that case. In Prevot et al. (2023), a larger amount of manual annotation allowed to compare fine-tuning with larger amount of training data and a weakly-supervised approach. For this French dataset, it was concluded that more than 7000 annotated DUs were required in the supervised training approach to beat the weakly-supervised approach (f-score: 70.6). When more data was used, supervised fine-tuning reached slightly higher scores (f-score: 73.9). These f-score results are $10 - 15\%$ than the scores obtained on written genress, which is expected as sentence splitters leveraging punctuation provide substantial assistance for discourse unit segmentation. In speech, particularly spontaneous interactional speech, pauses are useful but are by far less reliable in predicting discourse units since they are involved in many other dimensions and are subject to significant inter-individual variability. Recently Metheniti et al. (2023)[1], an improvement over Muller et al. (2019) has been developed, allowing to reach new state-of-the-art results for discourse segmentation in various languages. Our paper reuses the technical framework of this paper.

Segmenting speech into Discourse and Prosodic units has been the focus of numerous studies across various languages, including high-resource languages like English (Hirschberg and Grosz, 1992; Hirschberg and Nakatani, 1996), Dutch (Swerts, 1997), French or Mandarin (Degand and Simon, 2009; Prévot et al., 2015) as well as low-resource languages (Mettouchi and Vanhove, 2021). Discourse-prosodic interface research has also been developed for better understanding turn-taking mechanisms (Hu and Degand, 2023; Botinis et al., 2007). The deep connection between discourse and prosody has led researchers to explore prosodic cues for discourse tasks with some success (Pierrehumbert and Hirschberg, 1990; Shriberg et al., 2000). However, to our knowledge, there are no studies in which modern LLM-based systems described above, which achieve high scores based solely on transcripts, have benefited from incorporating acoustic-prosodic cues. An interesting attempt was made in (Gravellier et al., 2021), which validated the weak-supervision approach exploiting silent pauses among other elements, but the results did not improve with the inclusion of other acoustic-prosodic features. This is likely due to (i) the already high scores obtained from text alone, which would require cues coming from other sources to yield very high precision; and (ii) to the challgenge of automatic extracting reliable prosodic cues, such as speech rate, pitch or even intensity, from conversational speech.

Discourse Studies on Southern Min (and related language like Hakka or Cantonese) have focused on final particles (Lien, 1988; Li, 1999; Fung, 2000; Chappell, 2019), which can carry an interesting range or semantic and pragmatic functions. Moreover, there have been specific corpus studies examining discourse markers in Taiwan Southern Min (Chang, 2002, 2008; Chang and Hsieh, 2017). However, to the best of our knowledge, there has been no attempt to automatically segment discourse units in this language.

Additionally, there have been specific corpus studies examining (Chang, 2002, 2008; Chang and Hsieh, 2017). However, to the best of our knowledge, there has been no attempt to automatically segment discourse units in this language.

[1]Code at https://github.com/phimit/jiant/

3 Dataset

3.1 Base data

The discourse segmentation data used in this paper comes from an 8-hour corpus of monologue-like spontaneous speech elicited in sociolinguistic interviews as part of a larger project that collected Min-Mandarin bilingual speech recordings all over Taiwan between 2004 and 2010 (Wang and Fon, 2013; Fon, 2004). This subset of the corpus, also used in phonetic studies on phenomena including pre-boundary lengthening (Wang, 2023, 2022; Wang and Fon, 2012) and tone sandhi (Chen, 2018), contained speech materials from 16 speakers, who each contributed around 30 minutes of recording. The speakers were evenly split in gender and two age groups (old and young). At the time of recording, the old speakers were between 50-65 years old, and the young speakers were between 20-35 years old. Due to the original recording setup, the transcripts only focused on speech from the interviewee, with the interviewer's turns being labeled with a 'turn' token. The transcripts follow the convention used in a dictionary [2] administered by the Ministry of Education in Taiwan, along with a romanized version. The transcripts were aligned with the recordings at the syllable level using EasyAlign (Goldman, 2011) with manual corrections from a trained phonetician. During the manual correction process, pauses annotation was incorporated in the transcripts that are used in this study. In addition to pauses, the corpus also contains annotations on prosodic breaks, with a main goal of identifying the presence of two levels of breaks (intonational phrases and intermediate phrases), as well as breaks resulted in from hesitations and disfluencies. Data from two of the speakers were used to calculated cross-labeller agreement (kappa: 0.86). We observe that although done completely independently discourse and prosodic units exhibit a relationship : 45% of the prosodic breaks are also discourse breaks while 82% of the discourse breaks also correspond to a prosodic break.

Due to the lack of widely available text-processing tools in this language, dictionary-based method was used to perform word segmentation (maximal length matching) and POS tagging, the latter of which follows a multihot format, i.e., a word that is ambiguous between multiple POS tags according to the dictionary is annotated as '1' for all those tags.

[2]https://sutian.moe.edu.tw/zh-hant/

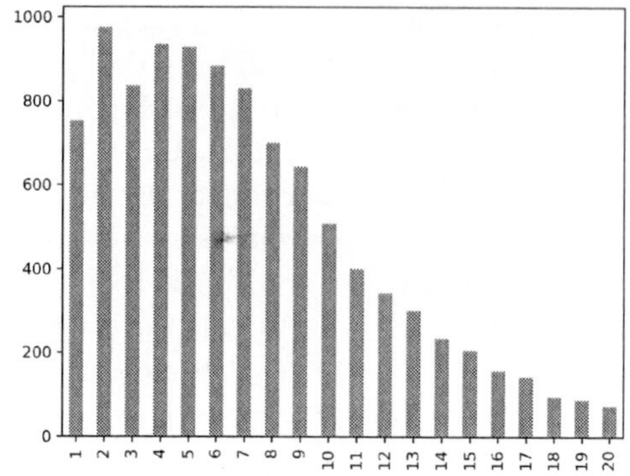

Figure 1: DU lengths in tokens.

The corpus contains 88.5K words at the word level with pause (#) and specific interviewer turn symbols included.

3.2 Discourse Segmentation Annotation

The corpus contains annotation of discourse units, which are defined as units that contain a verb and its core arguments, a criterion that is also used in other studies on the interaction between discourse and prosody (e.g., (Chen and Tseng, 2019; Prévot et al., 2015)). Crucially, discourse annotation in this corpus was performed independently from the recordings, i.e., the annotators only saw the transcripts, with turn information but no precise timing information, when they performed the task. Similarly to the prosodic labeling, two annotators labeled transcripts from two of the speakers for examination of interlabeller agreement (kappa: 0.96), and one annotator labeled the remaining transcripts. See Table 1 for examples of discourse units.

Disfluencies were not segmented apart and were instead included within discourse units. Discourse labellers had access to gold turn segmentation but were not told to use them systematically. As a result a few discourse units manually labeled span over more than one turn.

Taking a more quantitative perspective, the distribution of the annotated discourse units lengths in terms of tokens is provided in 1. We can see a fairly balanced distribution of lengths that are shorter than 10 tokens with a mean of 7.5 tokens per discourse unit. Truly conversational corpora

char:	[其實 # 我 相信]	[別人 會使] #	[咱 就 一定 會使]
roman:	[ki5-sit8 # goa2 siong-sin3]	[pat-lang5 e7-sai2]	[lan2 to it-teng7 e7-sai2]
gloss:	[actually (pause) I believe]	[others can]	[we PART must can]
trans:	['actually I believe']	['(if) others can (do it)']	['we must be able to (do it as well)']

Table 1: Examples of three discourse units. Note how the pause (#) may occur within a discourse unit

tend to present a different bimodal distribution with a mode of very short units (made of 1 token) corresponding to feedback and back-channels and a second mode of units made of 4-6 tokens. The dataset here is a corpus of interviews for which only the interviewee is transcribed. While being truly spontaneous, this explains why there are less extremely short interactional units as well why the mode of the distribution includes longer lengths than purely dialogic genres.

4 Methodology / Experiments

The corpus includes interviews of 16 speakers. We made 8 folds composed of two speakers each and ran a cross-validation over the 8 folds with different test / dev / train splits. Given our corpus, this is a method that maximizes the distance between training and testing data.

Two main approaches are evaluated for segmenting automatically our dataset : (i) directly fine-tuning a LLMs with all the data at our disposal (in a supervised way) (*Supervised* setting), (ii) create a noisily annotated datasets thanks to manual heuristic rules (See Figure 2) and a model to combine them.

More specifically, we used ROBERTA (Liu et al., 2019) and the framework fine-tuning it was DISCUT (Metheniti et al., 2023), grounded in JIANT environment (Pruksachatkun et al., 2020).

The weak-supervision framework uses SKWEAK (Lison et al., 2021) rather than SNORKEL (Ratner et al., 2017). SKWEAK natively allows the model to exploit the sequential nature of our task. On the technical side, SKWEAK relies on SPACY (Honnibal and Montani, 2017) documents. In order to keep all the relevant information (timing, pos-tags, prosody labels) linked to the tokens and to use them in the labeling rules, we made use of SPACY extensions attributes.

In the weak supervised approach, we use SKWEAK's ability to build a generative model

name	label	conflict	precision	recall
#_begpos	BDU	0.14	0.86	0.19
turn	BDU	0.16	0.84	0.11
beg_char	BDU	0.25	0.75	0.21
conj	BDU	0.36	0.64	0.24

Table 2: Profiles for a few labeling rules

from noisy labels provided by the labeling rules. SKWEAK allows to choose an HMM to perform this sequence labeling task. While this approach can be adopted without annotated data, a small development set is useful for testing and crafting the heuristic labeling rules. We can decide more efficiently which manual rules should be retained, dropped or improved thanks to the metrics that are computed on the development set. Besides precision, recall and f-score, *overlaps* and *conflicts* (with other rules) metrics are also useful to take decisions over the usage of these rules (See table 2).

To summarize, the weakly supervised approach is performed as follows:

1. write the labeling rules (See Figure 2) ;
2. apply and evaluate them on the `dev set` (iterate with the previous step until satisfied with labeling rules profiles on `dev set`) (See profiles in Table 2);
3. apply the labeling rules to the `train set`;
4. fit the HMM SKWEAK (rules aggregation) model;
5. apply the resulting model to the `test set`.

For the time being, the labeling rules crafted are extremely simple. They are using (i) pause duration and turn information; (ii) frequent tokens present at discourse boundaries; (iii) POS-tags overrepresented at discourse boundaries. Moreover, manually annotated prosodic units boundaries are included in the dataset and we use them for some experiments. As mentioned above, POS-tags are encoded in a multihot format. The labeling rules

```
def pause_and_begin_char(doc):
    for idx, token in enumerate(doc):
        if idx > 0:
            if (doc[idx-1].text == '#') and (doc[idx-1]._.dur > PAUSE)
                   and (doc[idx].text in BEGIN_CHAR):
                yield idx,idx+1,'BDU'
            else:
                yield idx,idx+1,'ABS'
        else:
            yield idx,idx+1,'BDU'
```

Figure 2: Labelling Function example (pause combined with a DU-initiating character)

exploiting POS are formulated accordingly to this ambiguous situation.

Characters vs. letters The corpus we are working with includes two versions of the transcription: characters and romanization (as seen in example 1). All our experiments were realized in both written forms.

Prosodic boundaries This corpus comes with prosodic break expert manual annotations. For the gold dataset, we created two versions of the dataset : one without any kind of prosodic information; and one with a special token corresponding to the presence / absence of a prosodic break. This special token was added to the transcript in all datasets (train / test / dev).

5 Results

The results comparing the general approach are presented in figure 3; the one related to the impact of the written form used are in figures 4 and 5 and the results of the prosody experiments are visualized in 6. All the numbers can be checked in Annex 3.

Supervision or weak-supervision Our results[3] (presented in Figure 3) shows that our weak-supervision approach remains behind from the supervised approach. This is true with large amount of manually annotated training data (~70K tokens)[4] but the difference is already significant with smaller amounts of training data (~7K tokens) for precision, recall and f-score (P:70.8/R:63.0/F:66.7). Weak supervision does better only if extremely limited amount of training data is available (~700 tokens).

Which base units? The results of the experiments show that different written forms (characters vs. romanized) for the corpus yielded signicantly different results. The difference between the two versions of the corpus lies in the fact some romanized tokens correspond to several characters (e.g., 'ah' corresponds to '啊', an utterance-initial/final particle, and '矣', a sentence-final particle and perfective aspect marker; 'e5' corresponds to '的', a possessive marker and sentence-final particle, '个', a classifier, and '鞋', a noun for 'shoe'.), while there are also some, but much less, characters that correspond to different romanizations (e.g., '嘛' correspond to 'ma7', which means 'also', and 'mah', a final particle). This situation conduced us to propose several hypotheses. First of all, when there is not a lot of fine-tuning data, having less symbol types can help to get faster a robust model. When more annotated data is available, having more specific symbols should bring better results by revolving some ambiguities. However, a second fact to consider is that the LLM we are fine-tuning (ROBERTA) includes Mandarin Chinese but not Southern Min. We therefore hypothesized that the character version should have an advantage when very little amount is provided since the base symbols are present in the model to fine-tune while the romanized symbols featuring tone digits should be something completely new for the model.

The results presented in Figure 4 show an advantage to character based corpus with large amount of fine-tuning data (Characters: 77.0/80.5/78.7 ;

[3]In all the paper, the significance labels included in the figures are corresponding to *p-values* of a *t-test* done on the folds of the experiment. A difference between two conditions is said to be significant (*/**/***) if t-testing the two series of values coming from the folds for both conditions, yielded the corresponding threshold p-values (0.05 / 0.01 / 0.001).

[4]For characters, supervised approach gives an f-score of 78.7 (p:77.0/r:80.5) while weak supervision only reaches a 52.0 f-score (p:55.7/r:50.4).

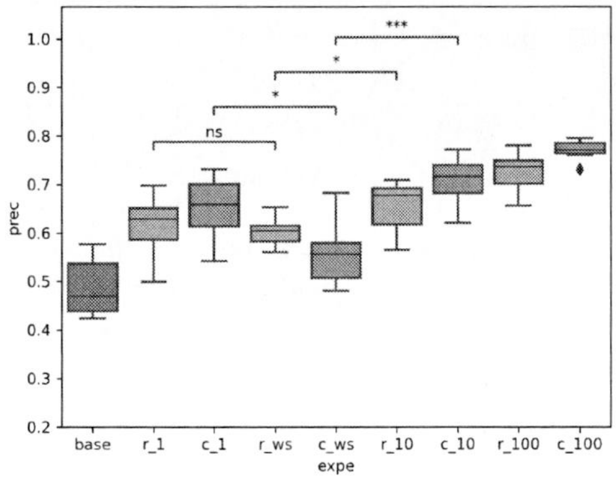

(a) Precision

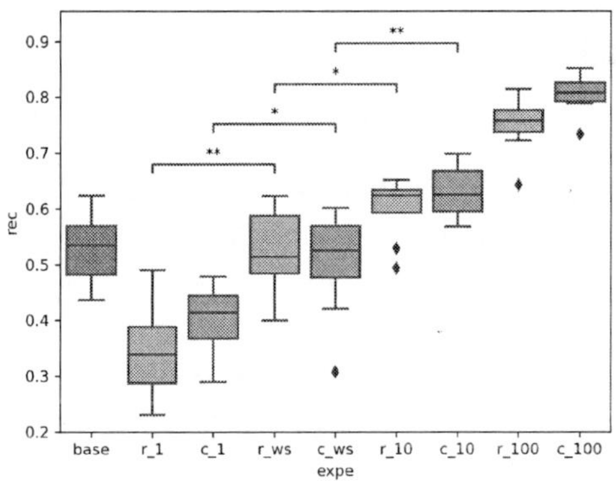

(b) Recall

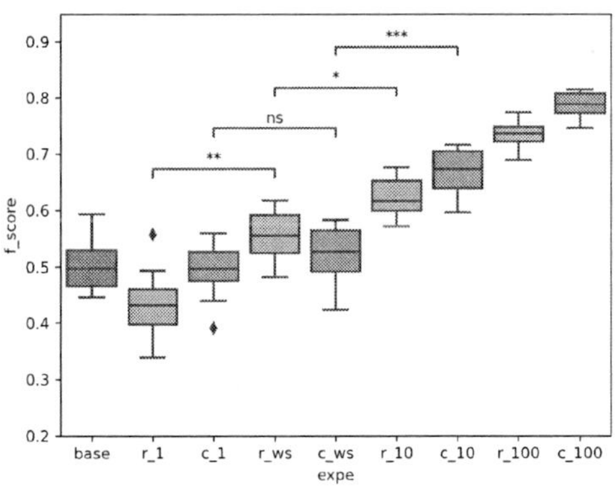

(c) F-score

Figure 3: Supervised vs. Weakly-supervised. *blue : 200ms pause baseline; orange : romanized; green: characters. From left to right _1:1% training data (~700 toks), _10:~7K toks), _100:~70K toks)*

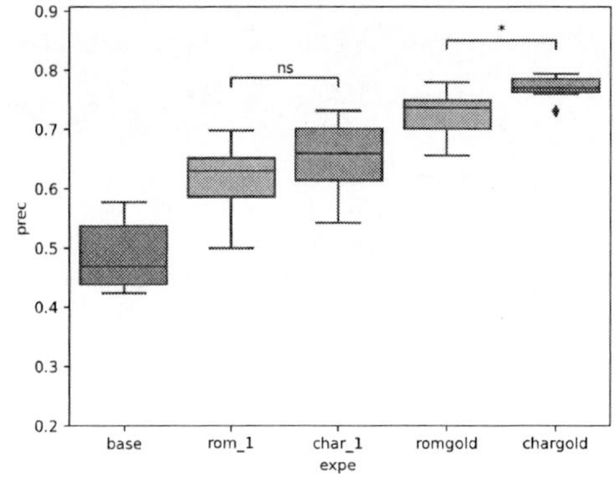

(a) Precision

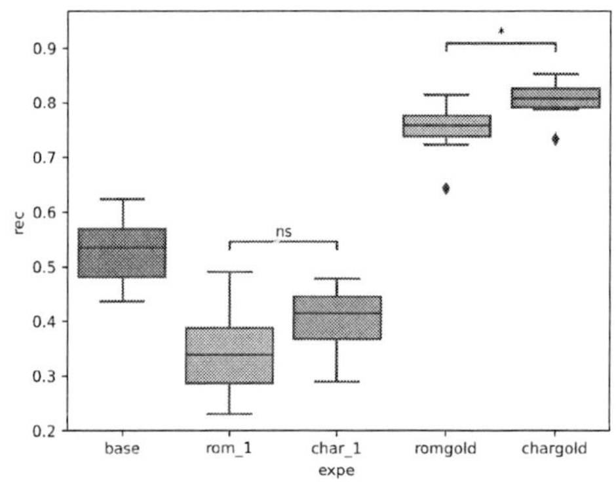

(b) Recall

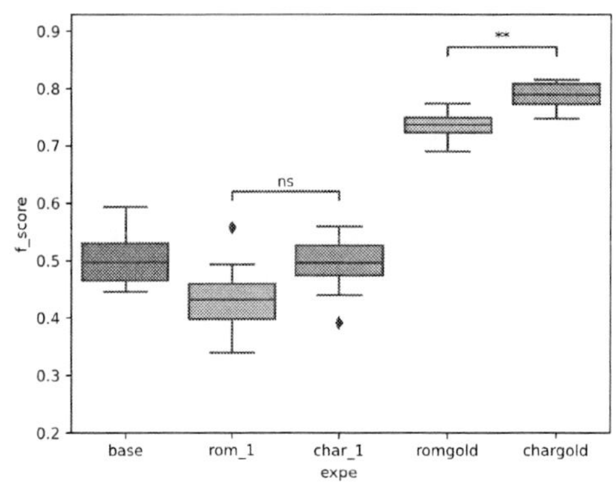

(c) F-score

Figure 4: Characters vs. Romanized. *blue: 200ms pause baseline; orange: romanized; green: characters. From left to right _1:1% training data (~700 toks), _100:~70K toks)*

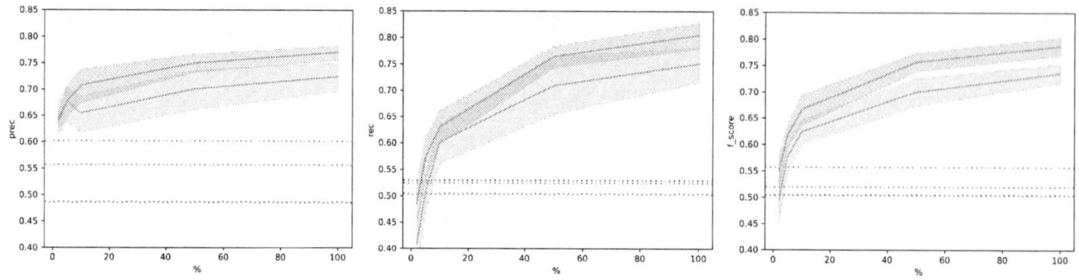

(a) Precision (b) Recall (c) F-score

Figure 5: Amount of training data. *orange: romanized corpus ; green: character version. From 1% training data (~700 toks) to 100% (~70K toks). Dotted lines, blue: baseline, green and orange : weak supervision*

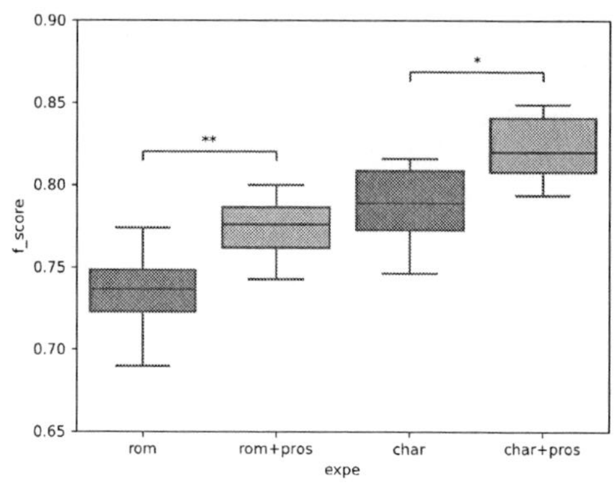

Figure 6: Adding prosody. F-score

Romanized: 72.5/75.1/73.6). It seems to be also the case when little amount of data is provided but this difference did not reach statistical significance. There also seems to be some complexities where we could expect to find a sweet spot for the romanized version (a little data for fine-tuning but not a lot, see the precision and recall with 5% and 10% of training data on figure 5) but the numbers do not allow to conclude on this result.

Potential help from prosody Prosody information used in this study had been manually added. As explained above, this prosodic annotation is however completely independent from the discourse segmentation. From a linguistic perspective, prosody should help in segmenting discourse units in speech since segmentation is one of the linguistic function of prosody (Swerts, 1997; Hirschberg and Grosz, 1992; Degand and Simon, 2009; Di Cristo, 2013). However, the recent work of (Gravellier et al., 2021), realized in a similar framework as ours, did not show the benefit of adding prosodic-acoustic cues for performing discourse segmentation. This was based however on automatic acoustic extraction. Given the data available to us, we decided to test whether "gold" prosodic segmentation would help on discourse segmentation performance. More precisely, every token in our dataset carries the information of whether it is at the beginning of a prosodic unit or not.

The base model we used did not allow for an enrichment at the token level. We therefore translated the prosodic information into a token. More precisely, for each start of labeled prosodic unit we inserted a rare character in the transcript. The figure 6 illustrates the statistically significant benefit of adding prosodic information for the characters and romanized versions of the corpus. The increase for the character version was +4.5,+2.5 and +3.5 for precision, recall and f-score respectively. These increases might seem modest but one should remember that pause duration and turn information was already taken into account before exploiting these prosodic labels.

6 Error Analysis

To further understand how our models could be improved we performed a detailed qualitative error analysis of the various models output.

(1) is an example where the model trained on gold and WS show the same segmentation error: While the gold annotation does not segment this sequence into two DUs, the models put a boundary after the sentence-final particle 'oh' and a pause. It is a representative example on the overuse of pause as a segmentation cue, especially for the WS-trained model. It also shows that the human annotator has a stronger tendency to only segment DUs with a main verb (thus 'reversely my only friend oh' is not a DU) while also neglecting potential disfluencies and false starts ('reversely is'). It

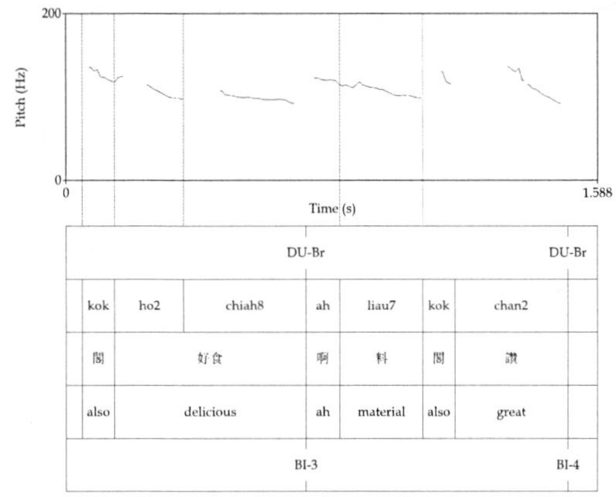

(a) DU/PU-initial 'ah'

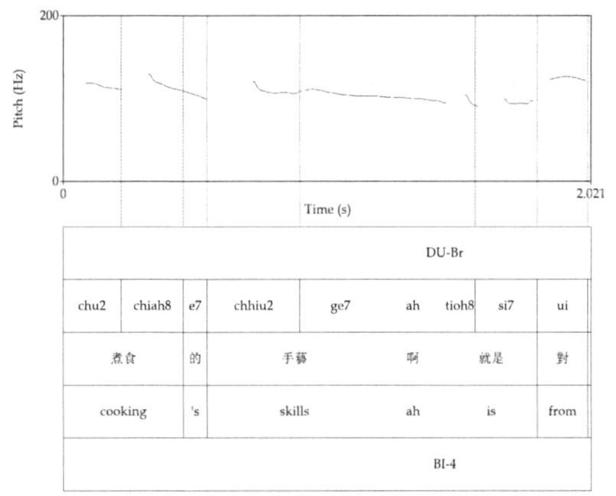

(b) DU/PU-final 'ah'

Figure 7: Illustration of prosodic help to discourse unit segmentation: (a) The particle 'ah' being used as a DU-initial marker is coincided with an intermediate phrase break (BI-3) signaled by pitch reset, i.e., higher f0 at 'ah'. (b) The particle is DU-final and exhibit lengthening and continued f0 declination with the preceding syllable, both of which are characteristics of an intonational phrase boundary (BI-4).

is worth noting that while the literal word sequence contains 'reversely is', the whole phrase has the same interpretation as 'reversely'. The presence of complex adverbs and/or discourse markers is likely another reason that this task is challenging for the models.

(1) 'On the other hand, my boyfriend oh he would still gone to see me' (GEN: genitive marker; PART: a marker similar to ba5 in Mandarin ba construction.)

   a. Gold annotation: [ah reversely is # reversely is I GEN boy friend oh # he still would go PART me see]

   b. Gold & WS-trained: [ah reversely is # reversely is I GEN boy friend oh #] [he still would go PART me see]

(2) is another example where the gold-trained model oversegmented a DU that was viewed by the human annotator as a noun and a relative clause ('The boyfriends that I had').

(2) 'The boyfriends that I had I always didn't marry them'

   a. Gold annotation (and WS-trained): [I self have GEN boy friend all all marry no success]

   b. Gold trained: [I self have GEN boy friend] [all all marry no success]

Finally, (3) shows an example of how gold-trained and WS-trained segmentation may differ from the gold annotation in distinct ways. The gold annotation has a DU boundary between the main clause and the tag question, the former containing some disfluencies. The model trained on gold annotation did not recognize the boundary with the tag question and instead put a boundary before the word 'like this' (an2-ne), which reflects the fact that an2-ne is a discourse marker that can occur in clause-initial and clause-final positions. The model trained on WS data, on the other hand, did not put a DU boundary for the entire sequence (thus having an error of under-segmentation before 'you know not'), as there was no pause nor words that have a strong tendency to start a DU in the corpus.

(3) 'At that time, walking still didn't require tiptoeing, you know?' (hyphen-connected units denote a word in TSM).

a. Gold annotation: [Then walking still does-not like this does-not require tip-toeing] [you know not]

b. Gold-trained: [Then walking still does-not] [like-this does-not require tiptoeing you know not]

c. WS-trained: [Then walking still does-not like-this does-not require tiptoeing you know not]

7 Discussion and Future Work

In this paper, we applied state-of-art techniques of discourse segmentation to a dataset of Taiwan Southern Min. We compared supervised and weakly supervised approaches. Moreover the linguistic information included in the original dataset allowed us to test some hypotheses along the way. We tested whether (i) it was easier to segment with the character-based or romanized version of the corpus ; and (ii) prosodic gold labels could help these new models of discourse segmentation.

An important overall result is that the approach employed (fine-tuning a sequence-to-sequence model) performs extremely well on this Taiwan Southern Min corpus, a language not included in the base Language Model (LLM) used. This is an important result with regard to the applicability of such approaches to low-resource languages for this task. The longer term goal of this work is to apply the best model we can build to a much larger corpus of Taiwanese interviews. The results obtained enable us to try to replicate existing studies on discourse-prosody interface in spontaneous speech, which have relied solely on manually annotated data.

Getting into the comparison of the two approaches tested, we should remind here that the scores obtained with gold annotations should be taken as a top line for the weak supervision approach. Indeed, the amount of manual gold segmentation for this corpus is substantial and does not aligh with the typical scenario for adopting a weak-supervision approach. With this consideration in mind, we observe that the weakly supervised approach failed to produce comparable results to the supervised setting. This can be attributed on the one hand to the supervised approach yielding highly competitive results through fine-tuning with only about 10% of our full amount of annotated data (corresponding $7K$ tokens, 700 discourse units); and on the other hand to the relatively low performance of our weakly supervised model. However, this does not negate the potential interest of weak supervision. Our current rules are rudimentary, primarily using simple pauses, tokens information and ambiguous POS-tags. We intend to enhance these labeling rules in several directions: (i) using a real POS-tagger that would reduce ambiguity ; (ii) developing more sophisticated labeling rules to address phenomena specific to spontaneous speech, such as disfluencies.

Regarding the comparison between the character-based and romanized versions of the corpus, the clear conclusion is that the character version consistently yields better results regardless of the amount of fine-tuning data provided. This could be attributed to both the benefit of lower ambiguities of characters over romanized version and to the presence of Mandarin data in ROBERTA.

Regarding prosody, this study has shown that, in line with linguistic predictions and previous computational models, but contrary to recent findings on this task, prosodic information can indeed help in discourse unit segmentation. The next obvious step is to automatize the extraction of relevant acoustic features that approximate efficiently the manual annotations we had in this stydy. From the primary prosodic features identified in (Shriberg et al., 2000) for English, excluding the ones already exploited by our pause and turn related rules, we identify (i) pitch differences across the discourse unit boundary, and (ii) duration of phones and rhymes preceding the decision point.

Acknowledgments

The authors would like to thank Philippe Muller and Pierre Magistry for side discussions related to the content of the paper. This study was supported by the Institute of Linguistics, Academia Sinica (LING-113-018-01), Taiwan's National Science and Technology Council (NSTC-112-2410-H-001-098-MY2) as well as by the Institut Convergence ILCB (ANR-16-CONV-0002) and the ANR-Funded project SUMM-RE (ANR-20-CE23-0017).

References

Nicholas Asher and Alex Lascarides. 2003. *Logics of conversation*. Cambridge University Press.

Antonis Botinis, Aikaterini Bakakou-Orphanou, and Charalabos Themistocleous. 2007. Mutlifactor analysis of discourse turn in greek. In *16th International Congress of Phonetic Sciences*, pages 1341–44.

Chloé Braud, Ophélie Lacroix, and Anders Søgaard. 2017. Does syntax help discourse segmentation? not so much. In *Conference on Empirical Methods in Natural Language Processing*, pages 2432–2442.

Chloé Braud, Yang Janet Liu, Eleni Metheniti, Philippe Muller, Laura Rivière, Attapol Rutherford, and Amir Zeldes. 2023. The DISRPT 2023 shared task on elementary discourse unit segmentation, connective detection, and relation classification. In *Proceedings of the 3rd Shared Task on Discourse Relation Parsing and Treebanking (DISRPT 2023)*, pages 1–21, Toronto, Canada. The Association for Computational Linguistics.

Miao-Hsia Chang. 2002. Discourse functions of anne in taiwanese southern min. *Concentric: Studies in English Literature and Linguistics*, 28(2):85–115.

Miao-Hsia Chang. 2008. Discourse and grammaticalization of contrastive markers in taiwanese southern min: A corpus-based study. *Journal of pragmatics*, 40(12):2114–2149.

Miao-Hsia Chang and Shu-Kai Hsieh. 2017. A corpus-based study of the recurrent lexical bundle ka li kong 'let (me) tell you'in taiwanese southern min conversations. *Chinese Language and Discourse*, 8(2):174–211.

Hilary Chappell. 2019. Southern min. *The mainland Southeast Asia linguistic area*, pages 176–233.

Alvin Cheng-Hsien Chen and Shu-Chuan Tseng. 2019. Prosodic encoding in mandarin spontaneous speech: Evidence for clause-based advanced planning in language production. *Journal of Phonetics*, 76:100912.

Mao-Hsu Chen. 2018. *Tone Sandhi Phenomena in Taiwan Southern Min*. University of Pennsylvania.

Liesbeth Degand and Anne Catherine Simon. 2009. On identifying basic discourse units in speech: theoretical and empirical issues. *Discours. Revue de linguistique, psycholinguistique et informatique. A journal of linguistics, psycholinguistics and computational linguistics*, (4).

Jacob Devlin, Ming-Wei Chang, Kenton Lee, and Kristina Toutanova. 2018. Bert: Pre-training of deep bidirectional transformers for language understanding. *arXiv preprint arXiv:1810.04805*.

Albert Di Cristo. 2013. *La prosodie de la parole*. De Boeck Superieur.

J Fon. 2004. A Preliminary construction of Taiwan Southern Min spontaneous speech corpus. Technical Report NSC-92-2411-H-003-050.

Roxana Suk-Yee Fung. 2000. *Final particles in standard Cantonese: semantic extension and pragmatic inference*. The Ohio State University.

J.P. Goldman. 2011. EasyAlign: an automatic phonetic alignment tool under Praat. In *Proceedings of Interspeech 2011: 12th Annual Conference of the International Speech Communication Association, Florence, Italy, August 27-31*, pages 3233–3236.

Lila Gravellier, Julie Hunter, Philippe Muller, Thomas Pellegrini, and Isabelle Ferrané. 2021. Weakly supervised discourse segmentation for multiparty oral conversations. In *Proceedings of EMNLP 2021*.

Julia Hirschberg and Barbara Grosz. 1992. Intonational features of local and global discourse structure. In *Proceedings of the DARPA workshop on Spoken Language Systems*. Association for Computational Linguistics.

Julia Hirschberg and Christine H Nakatani. 1996. A prosodic analysis of discourse segments in direction-giving monologues. In *34th Annual Meeting of the Association for Computational Linguistics*, pages 286–293.

Matthew Honnibal and Ines Montani. 2017. spacy 2: Natural language understanding with bloom embeddings, convolutional neural networks and incremental parsing. *To appear*, 7(1):411–420.

Junfei Hu and Liesbeth Degand. 2023. The conversational discourse unit: Identification and its role in conversational turn-taking management. *Dialogue & Discourse*, 14(2):83–112.

Ing Cherry Li. 1999. *Utterance-final particles in Taiwanese: A discourse-pragmatic analysis*. Crane Publishing Company.

Chinfa Lien. 1988. Taiwanese sentence-final particles. In Robert L. Cheng and Shuanfan Huang, editors, *The structure of Taiwanese: A modern synthesis*, pages 209–240. The Crane Publishing Taipei.

Pierre Lison, Jeremy Barnes, and Aliaksandr Hubin. 2021. skweak: Weak supervision made easy for nlp. *arXiv preprint arXiv:2104.09683*.

Yinhan Liu, Myle Ott, Naman Goyal, Jingfei Du, Mandar Joshi, Danqi Chen, Omer Levy, Mike Lewis, Luke Zettlemoyer, and Veselin Stoyanov. 2019. Roberta: A robustly optimized bert pretraining approach.

Eleni Metheniti, Chloé Braud, Philippe Muller, and Laura Rivière. 2023. DisCut and DiscReT: MELODI at DISRPT 2023. In *Proceedings of the 3rd Shared Task on Discourse Relation Parsing and Treebanking (DISRPT 2023)*, pages 29–42, Toronto, Canada. The Association for Computational Linguistics.

Amina Mettouchi and Martine Vanhove. 2021. Prosodic segmentation and cross-linguistic comparison in corpafroas and cortypo: Corpus-driven and corpus-based approaches.

Philippe Muller, Chloé Braud, and Mathieu Morey. 2019. Tony: Contextual embeddings for accurate multilingual discourse segmentation of full documents. In *Proceedings of the Workshop on Discourse Relation Parsing and Treebanking 2019*, pages 115–124. Association for Computational Linguistics.

Volha Petukhova, Laurent Prévot, and Harry Bunt. 2011. Multi-level discourse relations between dialogue units. In *Proceedings 6th joint ACL-ISO workshop on interoperable semantic annotation (ISA-6), Oxford*, pages 18–27.

Janet Pierrehumbert and Julia Bell Hirschberg. 1990. The meaning of intonational contours in the interpretation of discourse. In *Intentions in communication*. MIT press.

Laurent Prevot, Julie Hunter, and Philippe Muller. 2023. Comparing methods for segmenting elementary discourse units in a French conversational corpus. In *Proceedings of the 24th Nordic Conference on Computational Linguistics (NoDaLiDa)*, pages 436–446, Tórshavn, Faroe Islands. University of Tartu Library.

Laurent Prévot, Shu-Chuan Tseng, Klim Peshkov, and Alvin Chen. 2015. Processing units in conversation: A comparative study of French and Mandarin data. *Language and Linguistics*, 16(1):69–92.

Yada Pruksachatkun, Phil Yeres, Haokun Liu, Jason Phang, Phu Mon Htut, Alex Wang, Ian Tenney, and Samuel R. Bowman. 2020. jiant: A software toolkit for research on general-purpose text understanding models. In *Proceedings of the 58th Annual Meeting of the Association for Computational Linguistics: System Demonstrations*, pages 109–117, Online. Association for Computational Linguistics.

Alexander Ratner, Stephen H Bach, Henry Ehrenberg, Jason Fries, Sen Wu, and Christopher Ré. 2017. Snorkel: Rapid training data creation with weak supervision. In *Proceedings of the VLDB Endowment. International Conference on Very Large Data Bases*, volume 11, page 269. NIH Public Access.

Elizabeth Shriberg, Andreas Stolcke, Dilek Hakkani-Tür, and Gökhan Tür. 2000. Prosody-based automatic segmentation of speech into sentences and topics. *Speech communication*, 32(1-2):127–154.

Marc Swerts. 1997. Prosodic features at discourse boundaries of different strength. *The Journal of the Acoustical Society of America*, 101(1):514–521.

Sheng-Fu Wang. 2022. The interaction between predictability and pre-boundary lengthening on syllable duration in taiwan southern min. *Phonetica*, 79(4):315–352.

Sheng-Fu Wang. 2023. Boundary Strength and Predictability Effects on Durational Cues at Tone Sandhi Group Boundaries in Taiwan Southern Min. In *Proceedings of the 20th International Congress of Phonetic Sciences*.

Sheng-Fu Wang and Janice Fon. 2012. Durational cues at discourse boundaries in taiwan southern min. In *Speech Prosody 2012*.

Sheng-Fu Wang and Janice Fon. 2013. A taiwan southern min spontaneous speech corpus for discourse prosody. *The Proceedings of Tools and Resources for the Analysis of Speech Prosody, Aix-en-Provence, France*, pages 20–23.

Yizhong Wang, Sujian Li, and Jingfeng Yang. 2018. Toward fast and accurate neural discourse segmentation. In *Proceedings of the 2018 Conference on Empirical Methods in Natural Language Processing*, pages 962–967, Brussels, Belgium. Association for Computational Linguistics.

Amir Zeldes, Debopam Das, Erick Galani Maziero, Juliano Antonio, and Mikel Iruskieta. 2019. The disrpt 2019 shared task on elementary discourse unit segmentation and connective detection. In *Proceedings of the Workshop on Discourse Relation Parsing and Treebanking 2019*, pages 97–104.

Amir Zeldes, Yang Janet Liu, Mikel Iruskieta, Philippe Muller, Chloé Braud, and Sonia Badene, editors. 2021. *Proceedings of the 2nd Shared Task on Discourse Relation Parsing and Treebanking (DISRPT 2021)*. Association for Computational Linguistics, Punta Cana, Dominican Republic.

A Appendix

A.1 Global Results

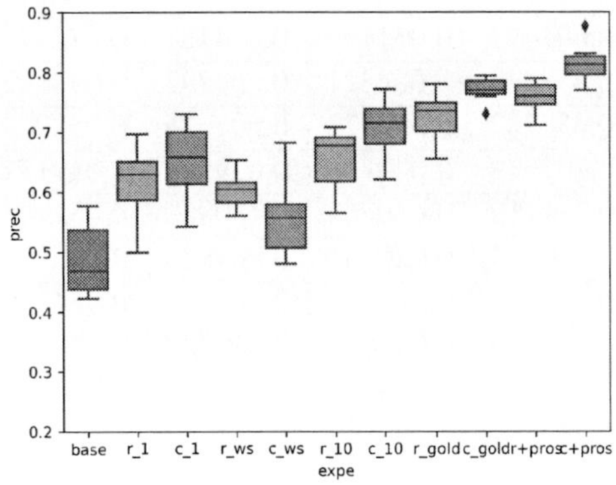

(a) Precision

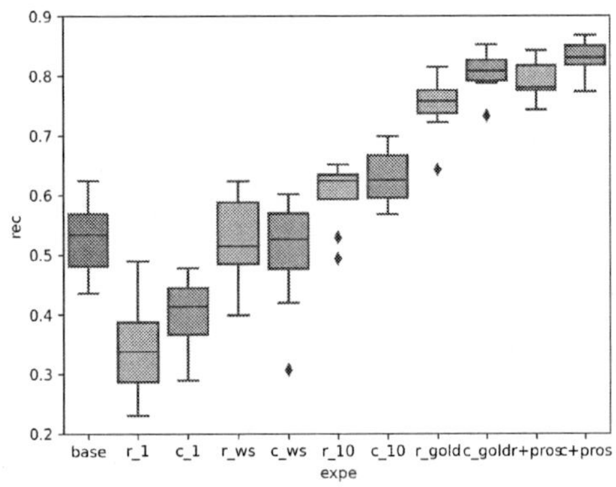

(b) Recall

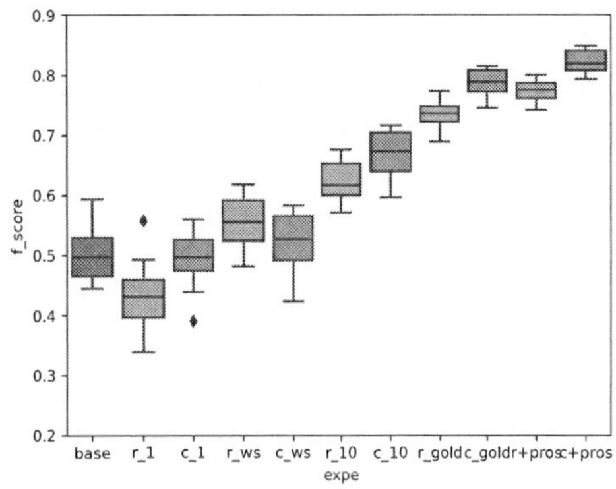

(c) F-score

Figure 8: Global Results *blue: baseline, orange: romanized corpus ; green: character version*

	prec mean	prec std	rec mean	rec std	fscore mean	fscore std
pause baseline (200ms)	0.486618	0.060169	0.529578	0.068400	0.504385	0.050271
super. rom (700 toks)	0.616545	0.061804	0.344490	0.081643	0.435640	0.067387
super. char (700 toks)	0.652257	0.063328	0.398917	0.065834	0.490842	0.053958
weakly super. rom	0.601497	0.031159	0.524181	0.077477	0.557128	0.047371
weakly super. char	0.556877	0.064321	0.503797	0.098992	0.519769	0.055981
super. rom (7K)	0.654762	0.054972	0.601636	0.058013	0.624031	0.036572
super. char (7K)	0.707989	0.049716	0.629861	0.049157	0.666265	0.046354
super. rom (70K)	0.724710	0.040760	0.750888	0.052945	0.735763	0.028225
super. char (70K)	0.770644	0.020731	0.804883	0.036518	0.787142	0.025453
super. rom (70K) + pros	0.757477	0.027094	0.792695	0.034534	0.774099	0.020699
super. char (70K) + pros	0.814579	0.031807	0.829729	0.029347	0.821556	0.020996

Table 3: Global Results

A.2 Tokens and POS lists used in the labelling rules

A.2.1 POS list

```
BEGIN_POS = ['interjection']
END_POS = ['interjection', 'onomatopoeia', 'particle']
NON_BEGIN_POS = ['interrogative', 'locative', 'numeral', 'onomatopoeia', 'quantifier']
NON_END_POS = ['adposition', 'conjunction', 'numeral', 'pronoun']
```

A.2.2 Romanized token lists

```
BEGIN_UNI_ROM = ['tan7-si7', 'li5-chhiann2', 'sou2-i2', 'henn', 'ran2m-houm']
END_UNI_ROM = ['lah', 'bo', 'mah', 'neh', 'nia5', 'm']
BEGIN_BI_ROM = ['ah chit-ma2',  'ah na7', 'henn ah', 'li2 e7', 'ah i', 'in-ui7 li2',
               'sou2-i2 gun2', 'ah ma7', 'sou2-i2 goa2', 'ah cho3', 'tan7-si7 goa2',
                'ah si7','ah m7-koh','henn goa2','oh he','ah hit-chun7','ah chiah',
                'tioh8 bo']
END_BI_ROM = ['bo5 lah', 'ni5 ah', 'u7 ah', 'e5 lah', 'ho2 chiah8', 'bo5 ah','ah lah',
              'tioh8 ah', 'si5-chun7 honn', 'lah honn', 'henn ah', 'an2-ne lah',
            'goa2 kam2-kak', 'khi3 ah', 'kam2-kak kong2', 'an2-ne nia5', 'e5 an2-ne',
             'koe3 ah', 'tioh8 lah', 'ho2 ah', 'e5 oh', 'chai-iann2 kong2', 'e5 neh',
              'kang5-khoan2 ah', 'ho2 lah', 'an2-ne honn', 'tioh8 bo']
```

B Labelling Rules

B.1 More examples

```
def very_long_pause(doc):
    for idx, token in enumerate(doc):
        if idx > 0:
            if doc[idx-1].text in PAUSE_TOK and doc[idx-1]._.dur > VERY_LONG_PAUSE:
                yield idx,idx+1,'BDU'
            else:
                yield idx,idx+1,'ABS'
        else:
            yield idx,idx+1,'BDU' #beginning of doc

def begin_pos(doc):
    for idx, token in enumerate(doc):
        if idx > 0:
            for cat in string_to_list(doc[idx]._.pos_list):
```

```
            if cat in BEGIN_POS:
                yield idx,idx+1,'BDU'
        yield idx,idx+1,'ABS'
    else:
        yield idx,idx+1,'ABS'
```

B.2 Labeling Functions profles (Romanized)

	annotator	label	conflict	precision	recall	f1
1	non_end_pos	NO	0.028	0.991	0.252	0.401
2	non_begin_pos	NO	0.112	0.970	0.070	0.130
3	cluster_rom_neg	NO	1.000	0.700	0.001	0.002
5	pause_ending_bi_rom	BDU	0.109	0.927	0.048	0.092
6	pause_begin_pos	BDU	0.112	0.888	0.082	0.151
7	begin_bi_rom	BDU	0.121	0.888	0.090	0.163
8	pause_begin_bi_rom	BDU	0.121	0.879	0.048	0.091
9	pause_endrom	BDU	0.200	0.875	0.033	0.064
10	turn	BDU	0.158	0.842	0.111	0.196
11	beginrom	BDU	0.180	0.839	0.172	0.286
12	extreme_pause	BDU	0.181	0.826	0.116	0.204
13	pause_beginrom	BDU	0.181	0.819	0.064	0.119
14	cluster_rom_pos	BDU	0.200	0.800	0.008	0.015
15	endrom	BDU	0.318	0.773	0.016	0.032
16	very_long_pause	BDU	0.263	0.741	0.144	0.241
17	long_pause	BDU	0.417	0.588	0.235	0.335
18	pause_end_pos	BDU	0.463	0.551	0.148	0.233
19	ending_bi_rom	BDU	0.490	0.530	0.101	0.170
20	conjunction	BDU	0.494	0.525	0.128	0.205
21	pause	BDU	0.490	0.514	0.336	0.406
22	short_pause	BDU	0.583	0.424	0.520	0.467
23	begin_pos	BDU	0.597	0.410	0.160	0.230

Table 4: Label Functions profiles for Romanized version

Actor Identification in Discourse: A Challenge for LLMs?

Ana Barić[*†] and **Sebastian Padó**[*] and **Sean Papay**[*]
[*]: IMS, University of Stuttgart, Stuttgart, Germany
[†]: TakeLab, FER, University of Zagreb, Croatia
{ana.baric,sebastian.pado,sean.papay}@ims.uni-stuttgart.de

Abstract

The identification of political actors who put forward claims in public debate is a crucial step in the construction of *discourse networks*, which are helpful to analyze societal debates. Actor identification is, however, rather challenging: Often, the locally mentioned speaker of a claim is only a pronoun (*"He proposed that [claim]"*), so recovering the *canonical* actor name requires discourse understanding. We compare a traditional pipeline of dedicated NLP components (similar to those applied to the related task of coreference) with a LLM, which appears a good match for this generation task. Evaluating on a corpus of German actors in newspaper reports, we find surprisingly that the LLM performs worse. Further analysis reveals that the LLM is very good at identifying the right reference, but struggles to generate the correct *canonical form*. This points to an underlying issue in LLMs with controlling generated output. Indeed, a hybrid model combining the LLM with a classifier to normalize its output substantially outperforms both initial models.

1 Introduction

Political decision-making in democracies is generally preceded by political debates taking place in parliamentary forums (committees, plenary debates) or different public spheres (e.g., newspapers, television, social media). One way in which political scientists have analyzed such processes is to adopt the framework of political claims analysis (Koopmans and Statham, 1999), identifying the *claims* (i.e., calls for or against specific courses of action) and *actors* involved in a given debate. Actors, claims, and the relations between them can then be represented as bipartite *discourse networks* (Leifeld and Haunss, 2012; Leifeld, 2016), such as shown in Figure 1. Such networks permit researchers to investigate debates on a fine-grained level, identifying, e.g., discourse coalitions, decision makers, or argumentative clusters.

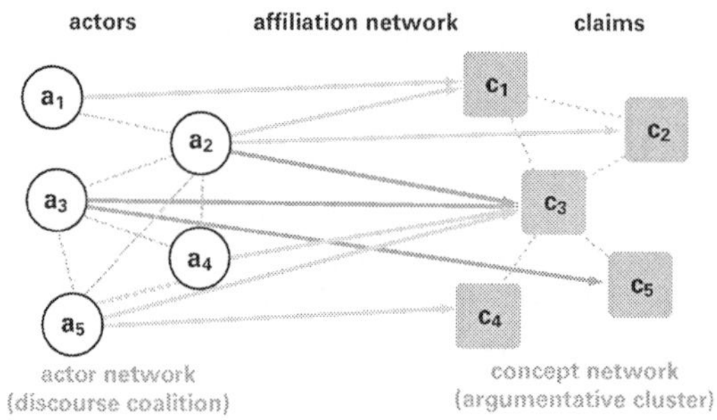

Figure 1: Discourse network with actors as circles and claims as squares (adapted from Padó et al., 2019)

While early work on discourse networks was based on manual analysis, widespread use of discourse networks requires quick, ideally automatic, methods to construct them from text. This calls for NLP methods to (1) detect instances of claims, assign them to their categories (c_i in Figure 1), and (2) identify actors for these claims in terms of some canonical representation (a_i), cf. Padó et al. (2019).

At least for newswire, there are several NLP models for claim detection and categorization (Subramanian et al., 2018; Padó et al., 2019). In contrast, there is little work on actor identification. Arguably, this is because claims are easier to handle: Both detection and categorization are sentence-level classification tasks which can be modeled based on predominantly sentence-internal features. In contrast, actor identification calls for a substantial amount of discourse understanding: models must *locally* identify an actor for the claim, but since these are often just a pronoun or a definite description (cf. Table 1), they must *globally* find a reasonable canonical representation for that actor.

This paper asks whether this situation has improved with the emergence of prompt-based LLMs (Liu et al., 2023) and their promise for text-to-text generation, which appears to be a good match for the actor identification task. We contrast an LLM-based architecture with a traditionally trained

Proceedings of the 5th Workshop on Computational Approaches to Discourse (CODI 2024), pages 64–70
March 21, 2024

	Local mention of actor	Canonical version
1	*President Joe Biden* pleaded with Republicans ...	Joe Biden
2	*Biden* signaled a willingness to make significant changes ...	Joe Biden
3	"We can't let Putin win", *he* said.	Joe Biden
4	However, *Senate Republicans* later on Wednesday blocked ...	Senate Republicans
5	A *U.S. official* said Washington had less than $1B ...	U.S. official

Table 1: Actor mentions and their canonicalizations in newswire article (`https://shorturl.at/WZ159`)

pipeline of dedicated NLP components on a German dataset with actor-claim annotation (Blokker et al., 2023). We find that, surprisingly, the traditional architecture outperforms the LLM. Our error analysis shows that the LLM often identifies the correct actor entity, but fails to generate the canonical actor name. We attribute this to the general difficulty in controling what exactly LLMs generate, a problem which has given rise to a substantial body of work (Zheng et al., 2023). In line with this interpretation, we show that combining the LLM with the traditional model (for post-processing) achieves substantially better performance on the actor identification task than either model alone.

2 Methods

2.1 Actor Identification: Task Definition

Table 1 shows mentions of actors making claims in a newswire article and the canonical actors they refer to, i.e., input–output pairs for actor mapping.

One possible approach is to treat this task as entity linking (Sevgili et al., 2022), typically realized as classification where the classes are the set of entities from a knowledge base (KB) such as Wikidata. While frequent actors (cf. lines 1–3) are mostly represented in such KBs, texts also introduce ad-hoc actors through plurals (line 4) or unspecific descriptions (line 5) which are generally not part of KBs. That rules out pure entity linking.

Instead, we formalize actor identification directly as *canonical name string prediction*: Models are presented with a claim, along with its context within an article, and are tasked with predicting a string representing that actor. For actors which commonly recur across claims, this string will be a canonical form of the actor's full name, while for singleton actors, this string will be the verbatim realization of an actor mention from the article.

While this formalization seems to ignore much of the structure of the task (after all, actor names are not fundamentally arbitrary strings), it has the benefit of allowing fair comparisons between vastly different model architectures: Text generation models can produce short strings directly, and other modeling approaches can take advantage of task structure internally, while still outputting a string. For example, we could approach the task with a coreference model, extended with a component which chooses the most canonical realization in each coreference chain from among the mentions.[1]

2.2 A Traditional Pipeline Architecture

The first method we apply to this task is a pipeline of two "traditional" NLP approaches: an entity extractor for actor mentions, and a classifier for associating mentions with canonical actor names.

Our mention extractor is a CRF-based sequence labeler. As input, we provide full articles in which the target claim has been marked and encode the input with a pretrained XLM-RoBERTa encoder (Conneau et al., 2020), which we fine-tune during training. The CRF's task is to extract mentions of the actor for the marked claim. As each claim must have at least one actor mention, we constrain (Papay et al., 2022) our CRF to always predict at least one actor mention. In order to map actor mentions to canonical forms, we employ a simple neural classifier based on the same XLM-RoBERTa encoder as above. As classes, we use the set of all canonical actor names which occur at least twice in the training partition of our data (see Section 3.1), along with a special 'verbatim' class for the remaining cases. In these cases, the string output we predict is the exact text of the actor mention.

2.3 An LLM-Based Architecture

In our LLM-based approach, we treat actor identification as an end-to-end task by combining the subtasks of actor detection and mapping within the prompt to directly predict the canonicalized actor.

[1]We do not evaluate a coreference model since full coreference is known to be a very hard task (see, e.g., Peng et al., 2015) and actor identification only requires solving a subpart.

Due to the limited availability of language-specific LLMs, we opted to experiment with the Llama 2 language model (Touvron et al., 2023) for both base- and instruction model options in all available size variants. This model family could be used on German, despite being predominantly trained on English corpora, because of the cross-lingual transferability that is shown to occur in such multilingual LLMs (Choenni et al., 2023).

We assess this task in zero- and few-shot settings, employing current best practices for robust prompt construction. These include: (1) using different instruction paraphrases for prompt templates, given the fact that 'canonical name' is not a very established concept (cf. Appendix A); (2) selecting exemplars semantically similar to the input (Margatina et al., 2023); and (3) varying exemplar quantity and order within the prompt (Lu et al., 2022). We construct the prompts by combining the English task description as prompt instruction with the preprocessed article in German (again, cf. Appendix A). Due to the context length limitation, we preprocess articles by extracting the target claim, marked with special tags, with its surrounding context at the sentence level. We use greedy decoding.

In these trials, zero-shot Llama-2-70b-chat outperforms all few-shot settings. We choose this setting for the rest of the paper.

3 Experimental Setup

3.1 Data

As gold standard for our studies we use DEbateNet (Blokker et al., 2023), a German large corpus resource for the analysis of the domestic debate on migration in Germany in 2015. After domain experts from political science developed a codebook for the policy domain, roughly 700 newspaper articles from the German left-wing quality newspaper "taz – die tageszeitung" with a total of over 550,000 tokens were annotated for actors, claims, and their relations. For each article, all claims are marked and labeled, and each claim is associated with a canonical actor (our gold standard), yielding a collection of about 1,800 actor-attributed claims. Most claims are also associated with a named entity mention from the vicinity of the claim, though this may not be the nearest mention, cf. Table 1. We use the established DEbateNet train–dev–test split, with 1383 claims in train, 220 in dev, and 207 in test.

	Evaluation	Pr	Re	F_1
LLM	exact match	42.66	43.46	43.06
	up to formatting	43.56	44.39	43.98
	up to canonic.	62.39	63.55	62.96
dedicated pipeline	exact match	48.66	59.35	53.47
	up to formatting	48.66	59.35	53.47
	up to canonic.	54.79	66.82	60.21

Table 2: Results for the LLM and traditional pipeline models in the different evaluation settings

3.2 Evaluation

Both models are evaluated and compared via F_1-score. In order to gain a more detailed understanding, we use three evaluation settings:

In the strictest *exact-match* setting, predictions are counted as correct only if they exactly match the gold-standard actor string. This setting can be performed automatically.

In our *correct-up-to-formatting* setting, predictions are counted as correct if they match the gold standard string modulo text formatting differences (e.g. whitespace differences, capitalization, punctuation). This setting tells us how often a model is "almost right" but receives no credit in the strict setting. We carry out this evaluation manually.

Finally, our *correct-up-to-canonicalization* setting counts predictions as correct if they predict the correct entity, even if a different referring expression is generated. For example, "the chancellor" or "Merkel" would be considered correct predictions for the gold-standard actor "Angela Merkel." As with before, this evaluation is performed manually.

4 Results and Analysis

Main results. Table 2 summarizes the performance of our two models under our three evaluation settings. We first consider our strictest setting, exact match. We find results in the range of 40–50 points F_1 score, in line with the assumption that actor mapping is a difficult task. Both models have somewhat higher recall than precision, and the dedicated pipeline outperforms the LLM by 10 point F_1 score. This is somewhat surprising, given LLMs' well-known capabilities in instruction-following text generation (Brown et al., 2020; Webson and Pavlick, 2022; Zhou et al., 2023).

We form two non-mutually exclusive hypotheses for this performance gap: either that the traditional model, through its supervised training, came to be more competent at predicting the *correct* political actor, or, through virtue of its inductive biases, it came to better and predicting the *exact* canonical name. We examine these hypotheses by evaluating the model with the other two settings. We also carry out a qualitative analysis of errors made by the LLM-based model (see Table 3).

One simple factor that would lead an essentially correct LLM to be inexact is formatting errors in its output – either mismatched spacing, punctuation, or capitalization, or natural language responses that could not be correctly post-processed. Such effects should show up as a difference between the 'exact match' and the 'up to formatting' setting. However, the numbers (43.06 F_1 vs. 43.98 F_1) show that these types of error account for less than one percentage point. Our qualitative error analysis (Table 3, top part) finds (few) cases of formatting errors, which often co-occur with other problems (unexpected LLM responses, gold standard errors). We conclude that such errors have a relatively minor effect on performance.

The reliance of our exact evaluation metric on gold-standard canonical forms provides another opportunity for a largely correct model to show low performance due to an inability to pick the exact canonical form required. This factor should come to the fore when we compare exact match results to the 'up-to-canonicalization' setting. Indeed, for this setting, both models show a substantial increase in performance – which implies that canonicalization represents a large part of the difficulty for this task. Interestingly, the LLM shows a much larger improvement, ultimately outperforming the traditional pipeline by about 2.5 points F_1. Our qualitative error analysis in Table 3 (center part) indicates that our LLM predictions have a hard time hitting the right level of verbosity: they are either too verbose, spuriously including government positions (e.g. [*Interior Minister*] *Thomas de Maizière*), or not verbose enough, omitting first names (e.g. [*Angela*] *Merkel*).

We take this as evidence that our LLM-based model is adept at selecting the correct actor, but struggles to select the canonical form. This is somewhat to be expected, as our LLM-based model has neither a training signal nor a strong inductive bias to prefer any particular canonical form. However, as mentioned in Section 2.3, preliminary experiments with a few-shot setting where we included canonical forms in prompts showed no improvements over our proposed model. We believe that this indicates that the task of predicting 'canonical names' remains a non-straightforward task for LLMs even in the presence of training data.

Error Type	Model output	Ground Truth
Format	Bayern The claim is	Bayern *(Bavaria)*
	EU-Kommission *(EU commission)*	EU-Kommision [*sic*]
Canonicalization	Bundesinnenminister *(federal minister of the interior)* Thomas de Maizière	Thomas de Maizière
	Kommissions-präsident *(commission president)* Jean-Claude Juncker	Jean-Claude Juncker
	Zimmermann	Klaus F. Zimmermann
	Merkel	Angela Merkel
Wrong Actor	EU-Kommission *(EU commission)*	Jean-Claude Juncker
	Germany	Thomas Bauer

Table 3: Some illustrative examples of the errors exhibited by the LLM-based actor identification model: German outputs with English translations

Finally, responses which bungled the reference completely (Table 3, bottom part) sometimes tended to be plausible, e.g. metonymyic, mistakes, such as predicting the EU commission instead of Jean-Claude Juncker, its president.

Hybrid model. The observations on the errors motivate a follow-up experiment with a hybrid approach combining both our traditional and LLM-based models. This hybrid is structurally similar to our traditional model, but it is provided the LLM's prediction in addition to its other inputs. In this way, the LLM can decide which actor made the claim, while the traditional pipeline can be responsible for predicting that actor in a canonical form. Table 4 shows that this approach has similar properties to the individual models (no effect of formatting, but a large effect of canonicalization) but that it represents, crucially, a substantial improvement

Evaluation	Pr	Re	F_1
exact match	54.33	64.49	58.97
up to formatting	54.33	64.49	58.97
up to canonic.	64.96	76.39	70.21

Table 4: Results for the hybrid model in the different evaluation settings

in terms of quality: In the strictest setting (exact match), it achieves an F_1 score of 59 points (previous best: 53 F_1), and in the laxest setting it obtains 70 points F_1 (previous best: 63 F_1).

5 Conclusion

In this work, we investigate alternative approaches to tackling the discourse-level actor identification task, comparing LLM prompting with a conventional NLP pipeline. We find that our LLM better recognize the appropriate actor entities compared to the traditional pipeline, but has a harder time controlling the exact output. This problem cannot be solved easily with tuning, as the failure of our few-shot setup shows, which is also in line with recent studies on the controllability of LLM output (Reif et al., 2022; Sun et al., 2023). Our solution is a hybrid model which integrates the LLM-generated output as a cue in the pipeline approach, resulting in a clear improvement over the individual models.

The current study is limited in several respects: It only considers one LLM, one corpus, and one evaluation. In the future, we also plan to carry out an extrinsic evaluation of our actor identifier on generating full discourse networks. In terms of future directions, we believe that actor identification is a task which could plausibly profit from retrieval-augmented generation (RAG) proposed by Lewis et al. (2020) which would give the LLM access to information beyond the current discourse.

Acknowledgements

We acknowledge funding by the Deutsche Forschungsgemeinschaft (DFG) for the project MARDY 2 (375875969) within the priority program RATIO.

References

Nico Blokker, Andre Blessing, Erenay Dayanik, Jonas Kuhn, Sebastian Padó, and Gabriella Lapesa. 2023. Between welcome culture and border fence: The European refugee crisis in German newspaper reports. *Language Resources and Evaluation* 57:121–153. https://doi.org/10.1007/s10579-023-09641-8.

Tom Brown, Benjamin Mann, Nick Ryder, Melanie Subbiah, Jared D Kaplan, Prafulla Dhariwal, Arvind Neelakantan, Pranav Shyam, Girish Sastry, Amanda Askell, Sandhini Agarwal, Ariel Herbert-Voss, Gretchen Krueger, Tom Henighan, Rewon Child, Aditya Ramesh, Daniel Ziegler, Jeffrey Wu, Clemens Winter, Chris Hesse, Mark Chen, Eric Sigler, Mateusz Litwin, Scott Gray, Benjamin Chess, Jack Clark, Christopher Berner, Sam McCandlish, Alec Radford, Ilya Sutskever, and Dario Amodei. 2020. Language models are few-shot learners. In H. Larochelle, M. Ranzato, R. Hadsell, M.F. Balcan, and H. Lin, editors, *Advances in Neural Information Processing Systems*. volume 33, pages 1877–1901. https://proceedings.neurips.cc/paper/2020/file/1457c0d6bfcb4967418bfb8ac142f64a-Paper.pdf.

Rochelle Choenni, Dan Garrette, and Ekaterina Shutova. 2023. How do languages influence each other? studying cross-lingual data sharing during llm fine-tuning.

Alexis Conneau, Kartikay Khandelwal, Naman Goyal, Vishrav Chaudhary, Guillaume Wenzek, Francisco Guzmán, Edouard Grave, Myle Ott, Luke Zettlemoyer, and Veselin Stoyanov. 2020. Unsupervised cross-lingual representation learning at scale. In Dan Jurafsky, Joyce Chai, Natalie Schluter, and Joel Tetreault, editors, *Proceedings of the 58th Annual Meeting of the Association for Computational Linguistics*. Association for Computational Linguistics, Online, pages 8440–8451. https://doi.org/10.18653/v1/2020.acl-main.747.

Ruud Koopmans and Paul Statham. 1999. Political Claims Analysis: Integrating Protest Event And Political Discourse Approaches. *Mobilization* 4(2):203–221.

Philip Leifeld. 2016. Discourse Network Analysis: Policy debates as dynamic networks. In *The Oxford Handbook of Political Networks*, Oxford University Press.

Philip Leifeld and Sebastian Haunss. 2012. Political discourse networks and the conflict over software patents in Europe. *European Journal of Political Research* 51(3):382–409.

Patrick Lewis, Ethan Perez, Aleksandra Piktus, Fabio Petroni, Vladimir Karpukhin, Naman Goyal, Heinrich Küttler, Mike Lewis, Wen tau Yih, Tim Rocktäschel, Sebastian Riedel, and Douwe Kiela. 2020. Retrieval-augmented generation for knowledge-intensive NLP tasks. In *Proceedings of the 34th Conference on Neural Information Processing Systems*. Vancouver, Canada.

Pengfei Liu, Weizhe Yuan, Jinlan Fu, Zhengbao Jiang, Hiroaki Hayashi, and Graham Neubig. 2023. Pre-train, prompt, and predict: A systematic survey of prompting methods in natural language processing. *ACM Comput. Surv.* 55(9). https://doi.org/10.1145/3560815.

Yao Lu, Max Bartolo, Alastair Moore, Sebastian Riedel, and Pontus Stenetorp. 2022. Fantastically ordered prompts and where to find them: Overcoming few-shot prompt order sensitivity. In Smaranda Muresan, Preslav Nakov, and Aline Villavicencio, editors, *Proceedings of the 60th Annual Meeting of the Association for Computational Linguistics (Volume 1: Long Papers)*. Association for Computational Linguistics, Dublin, Ireland, pages 8086–8098. https://doi.org/10.18653/v1/2022.acl-long.556.

Katerina Margatina, Timo Schick, Nikolaos Aletras, and Jane Dwivedi-Yu. 2023. Active learning principles for in-context learning with large language models. In Houda Bouamor, Juan Pino, and Kalika Bali, editors, *Findings of the Association for Computational Linguistics: EMNLP 2023*. Association for Computational Linguistics, Singapore, pages 5011–5034. https://doi.org/10.18653/v1/2023.findings-emnlp.334.

Sebastian Padó, Andre Blessing, Nico Blokker, Erenay Dayanik, Sebastian Haunss, and Jonas Kuhn. 2019. Who sides with whom? Towards computational construction of discourse networks for political debates. In *Proceedings of the 57th Annual Meeting of the Association for Computational Linguistics*. Association for Computational Linguistics, Florence, Italy, pages 2841–2847. https://doi.org/10.18653/v1/P19-1273.

Sean Papay, Roman Klinger, and Sebastian Pado. 2022. Constraining linear-chain CRFs to regular languages. In *Proceedings of the International Conference on Learning Representations*. https://openreview.net/forum?id=jbrgwbv8nD.

Haoruo Peng, Daniel Khashabi, and Dan Roth. 2015. Solving hard coreference problems. In Rada Mihalcea, Joyce Chai, and Anoop Sarkar, editors, *Proceedings of the 2015 Conference of the North American Chapter of the Association for Computational Linguistics: Human Language Technologies*. Association for Computational Linguistics, Denver, Colorado, pages 809–819. https://doi.org/10.3115/v1/N15-1082.

Emily Reif, Daphne Ippolito, Ann Yuan, Andy Coenen, Chris Callison-Burch, and Jason Wei. 2022. A recipe for arbitrary text style transfer with large language models. In Smaranda Muresan, Preslav Nakov, and Aline Villavicencio, editors, *Proceedings of the 60th Annual Meeting of the Association for Computational Linguistics (Volume 2: Short Papers)*. Association for Computational Linguistics, Dublin, Ireland, pages 837–848. https://doi.org/10.18653/v1/2022.acl-short.94.

Özge Sevgili, Artem Shelmanov, Mikhail Arkhipov, Alexander Panchenko, and Chris Biemann. 2022. Neural entity linking: A survey of models based on deep learning. *Semantic Web* 13(3).

Shivashankar Subramanian, Trevor Cohn, and Timothy Baldwin. 2018. Hierarchical structured model for fine-to-coarse manifesto text ana lysis. In *Proceedings of the 2018 Conference of the North American Chapter of the Association for Computational Linguistics: Human Language Technologies, Volume 1 (Long Papers)*. Association for Computational Linguistics, New Orleans, Louisiana, pages 1964–1974. https://doi.org/10.18653/v1/N18-1178.

Jiao Sun, Yufei Tian, Wangchunshu Zhou, Nan Xu, Qian Hu, Rahul Gupta, John Wieting, Nanyun Peng, and Xuezhe Ma. 2023. Evaluating large language models on controlled generation tasks. In Houda Bouamor, Juan Pino, and Kalika Bali, editors, *Proceedings of the 2023 Conference on Empirical Methods in Natural Language Processing*. Association for Computational Linguistics, Singapore, pages 3155–3168. https://doi.org/10.18653/v1/2023.emnlp-main.190.

Hugo Touvron, Louis Martin, Kevin Stone, Peter Albert, Amjad Almahairi, Yasmine Babaei, Nikolay Bashlykov, Soumya Batra, Prajjwal Bhargava, Shruti Bhosale, et al. 2023. Llama 2: Open foundation and fine-tuned chat models. *arXiv preprint arXiv:2307.09288* .

Albert Webson and Ellie Pavlick. 2022. Do prompt-based models really understand the meaning of their prompts? In Marine Carpuat, Marie-Catherine de Marneffe, and Ivan Vladimir Meza Ruiz, editors, *Proceedings of the 2022 Conference of the North American Chapter of the Association for Computational Linguistics: Human Language Technologies*. Association for Computational Linguistics, Seattle, United States, pages 2300–2344. https://doi.org/10.18653/v1/2022.naacl-main.167.

Carolina Zheng, Claudia Shi, Keyon Vafa, Amir Feder, and David Blei. 2023. An invariant learning characterization of controlled text generation. In Anna Rogers, Jordan Boyd-Graber, and Naoaki Okazaki, editors, *Proceedings of the 61st Annual Meeting of the Association for Computational Linguistics (Volume 1: Long Papers)*. Association for Computational Linguistics, Toronto, Canada, pages 3186–3206. https://doi.org/10.18653/v1/2023.acl-long.179.

Jeffrey Zhou, Tianjian Lu, Swaroop Mishra, Siddhartha Brahma, Sujoy Basu, Yi Luan, Denny Zhou, and Le Hou. 2023. Instruction-following evaluation for large language models. https://doi.org/10.48550/arXiv.2311.07911.

A Prompt Templates

#	Instruction templates
1	*"Extract only the entity that made the claim in the article. The claim is surrounded with <claim>and <\claim>tags. Output only the entity without any additional explanation. Article: [ARTICLE]"*
2	*"Extract and standardize only the entity that made the marked claim in the article. The claim is surrounded with <claim>and <\claim>tags. Output only the standardized entity without any additional explanation. Article: [ARTICLE]"*
3	*"Retrieve the party or parties responsible for the statement in the given article, contained within <claim>and <\claim>tags. Output only the entity without further elaboration. Article:[ARTICLE]"*
4	*"Identify and output the entity or entities that made the claim within the specified article, enclosed by <claim>and <\claim>tags. Do not include any supplementary information. Article: [ARTICLE]"*

Table 5: Prompt template instruction paraphrases used for robustness check for zero- and few-shot setting.

Quantitative metrics to the CARS model in academic discourse in biology introductions

Charles Lam
Language Centre
School of Languages, Cultures and Societies
University of Leeds
Woodhouse Lane Leeds LS2 9JT
C.Lam@leeds.ac.uk

Nonso Nnamoko
Department of Computer Science
Edge Hill University
St Helens Road, Ormskirk L39 4QP
nnamokon@edgehill.ac.uk

Abstract

Writing research articles is crucial in any academic's development and is thus an important component of the academic discourse. The *Introduction* section is often seen as a difficult task within the research article genre. This study presents two metrics of rhetorical moves in academic writing: step-n-grams and lengths of steps. While scholars agree that expert writers follow the general pattern described in the CARS model (Swales, 1990), this study complements previous studies with empirical quantitative data that highlight how writers progress from one rhetorical function to another in practice, based on 50 recent papers by expert writers. The discussion shows the significance of the results in relation to writing instructors and data-driven learning.

1 Introduction

The research article is one of the most, if not the single most, important genres in academic discourse. The *Introduction* section in the research article is often reported to be difficult to write (Flowerdew, 1999; Hsu and Kuo, 2009).

Scholars have long recognized the central role of rhetorical moves in academic writing. The widely known analysis of the structure, the "Create a Research Space" (CARS) model (Swales, 1990, 2004) is the *de facto* standard in genre studies in academic discourse, alongside with the metadiscourse model by Hyland (2005, 2018). Swales (1990)'s CARS model observes the common pattern found in academic research articles, which encompasses three rhetorical moves (that can be seen as any textual unit, often one or more sentences, that aims to fulfill a particular function for a text). Each move can be decomposed to finer steps, while some steps are "optional", and some "obligatory" or expected. In the teaching setting, these moves and steps can be used to guide novice authors in presenting the context, purpose, objectives, literature review, and overall significance of their research logically and persuasively. The moves and associated steps (in bracket) are *Establishing a Territory* (define the field, provide background information, set the context), *Establishing a Niche* (identify a gap, problem, or unanswered question), *Occupying the Niche* (clearly state the purpose, focus, and objectives), *Reviewing Previous Research* (summarize relevant literature, critically review existing research), and *Establishing the Significance of the Research* (demonstrate the importance within the broader context).

A prevalent strand of studies under this tradition focuses on the correlation between particular rhetorical moves (e.g. *Establishing a Niche* or *Occupying the Niche*) and linguistic forms (e.g. frequent words or formulaic language, such as the n-gram "the aim of the study"). Beyond the study of lexical bundles, scholars often investigate the organizational structure of various parts of research articles from a qualitative perspective, while using empirical corpus data. Our study focuses on the structure of the *Introduction* section from an annotated corpus of biology research articles written by expert writers. While previous studies have investigated the same phenomenon, few works investigate the co-occurrence or relation between moves and steps at scale. For example, Samraj (2002, 2005) adopts a qualitative and manual close reading method with a few texts) for biology texts. In some cases, the focus is on the implementation of moves in actual linguistic forms (Lu et al., 2021, 2020), and the dataset were not made publicly available to facilitate follow-up studies or replication. As such, there is no existing dataset with clear annotation of the rhetorical moves.

This study presents our analysis of a small dataset of 50 texts in biology as a proof-of-concept and proposes two quantitative metrics to conduct move-step analysis. The contribution of this paper is two-fold: First, we discuss quantitative mea-

Proceedings of the 5th Workshop on Computational Approaches to Discourse (CODI 2024), pages 71–77
March 21, 2024 ©2024 Association for Computational Linguistics

sures that allow for genre and rhetorical analysis without close reading by researchers, which is time-consuming and requires expert knowledge of genre analysis. Second, we outline our efforts in making the materials useful for writing instructors and novice learners of academic writing in higher education environments.

2 Related Work

Using corpus data to facilitate understanding of academic discourse is no novel approach. Specific to the English for Academic Purposes (EAP) community[1], there has been many corpora like the British Academic Written English (BAWE) corpus (Nesi and Gardner, 2018), Michigan Corpus of Spoken Academic English (MICASE) (Simpson et al., 2002), and the Michigan Corpus of Upper-Level Student Papers (MICUSP) (Römer and Swales, 2010). These resources have been widely used in the EAP community for analyzing academic language to facilitate materials development and instructions. The wider coverage of various disciplines means that the data are discipline-agnostic and capable of showing the overall patterns in the language of academic discourse.

To better understand rhetorical strategies through the CARS model, scholars have also employed corpus tools to investigate the use of common phrases associated with specific rhetorical moves. For example, combinations like "in this paper we present" and "it is well known that" are often found in the *Introduction* (Louvigné et al., 2014). Similarly, Jalali and Moini (2014) identify 161 common lexical bundles (i.e. frequent combinations of lexical items) in the *Introduction*. The most frequent ones in their study are often related to stating the purpose of the study, such as "The aim of the", "The objective of this", "study was to evaluate". Pérez-Llantada (2014) compares the skills in native and non-native speakers' of using formulaic combinations, using similar methods. While these findings provide solid evidence from attested examples used by writers, they are also limited in not addressing the organization of the *Introduction*, which is reported to be a common issue (Flowerdew, 1999).

Focusing on the organization and sequencing of the steps, scholars have also investigated how closely writers actually follow the CARS model in their practice. Previous studies have suggested that expert writers do not follow strictly the CARS model in their *Introductions* (Anthony, 1999; Samraj, 2002). Meanwhile, articles from different disciplines may display variations, e.g. applied linguistics (Ozturk, 2007), computer science (Orr, 1999; Maher and Milligan, 2019), engineering (Kanoksilapatham, 2015), and mathematics (McGrath and Kuteeva, 2012; Kuteeva and McGrath, 2015). Samraj (2005) discusses how introductions and abstracts of Wildlife Behavior and Conservation Biology, two closely related branches of biology, also show deviations from Swales' CARS model. Similarly, Milagros del Saz Rubio (2011) suggests that there are particular step-combinational patterns used (i.e. how rhetorical steps are assembled together) for achieving a variety of communicative purposes in agriculture.

3 Method

A total of 50 manuscripts from BioRxiv[2] were downloaded. From each of the five categories (Animal Behavior & Cognition, Biochemistry, Biophysics, Ecology, and Physiology), ten papers were randomly selected and annotated by the researcher.

The annotation is based on the original model by Swales (1990)[3], which includes three 'moves' essential to the introductory text, which can be further broken down into steps or options. In this study, each sentence is annotated with step label. The details are listed in Table 1. For simplicity, Moves are coded with 1-3, and Steps are coded with a-d, e.g. "Move 2 Step 3" is coded "2b".

4 Results

Taken the *introductions* of all the 50 articles together, the annotated small corpus contains 43,187 words and 1,297 sentences in total. Each category is represented by *introductions* of 10 articles. Table 2 shows the relevant statistics.

Figure 1 shows that Move 1 Step 3 'Reviewing previous research' is the most common type of

[1]The GENIA corpus (Kim et al., 2003), for example, was not designed for the purpose academic writing research or instruction. Rather, it was designed for knowledge mining in biology.

[2]https://www.biorxiv.org/

[3]While a revised model is proposed in Swales (2004) with the aim to better accommodate variations in response to some critiques (see e.g. Anthony (1999); Samraj (2002); Ozturk (2007)), the updates (e.g. grouping all steps in Move 1 to "Topic generalizations of increasing specificity" (Swales, 2004, 230) do not appear to generate concrete steps that can better account for variations. Rather, the updated description accommodates a wider range of variations simply by being more generic. For the practical purpose of annotation, this study uses the original scheme with more fine-grained steps.

Table 1: Steps in the CARS model (Swales, 1990)

Move/Step	Description	Code
Move 1	*Establish Research Territory*	
Step 1	Claiming centrality	1a
Step 2	Making topic generalizations	1b
Step 3	Reviewing previous research	1c
Move 2	*Establish a Niche*	
Option 1	Counter-claiming	2a
Option 2	Indicating a gap	2b
Option 3	Question-raising	2c
Option 4	Continuing a tradition	2d
Move 3	*Occupy the Niche*	
Step 1a	Outlining purposes	3a
Step 1b	Announcing present research	3b
Step 2	Announcing principal findings	3c
Step 3	Indicating article structure	3d

Table 2: Mean word counts and sentence counts per file

Category	Mean Word Count	Mean Sentence Count
Animal Behv & Cogn	714.8	20.4
Biochemistry	836.8	27.8
Biophysics	883.1	28.4
Ecology	1077.9	26.7
Physiology	806.1	26.4

sentence in the data.

4.1 Step Collocation

To better understand the sequencing of rhetorical steps, this study proposes a simple measure of step-n-grams that captures the common sequences of steps. In the data, the same steps tend to span over multiple sentences, which likely signals the same rhetorical function expressed by multiple sentences. For example, the segment[4] in Table 3 was coded as 1b-1c-2b in step-n-gram, where the repetition of 1c over three sentences is coded as one single step.

Excluding these repetition of the same steps, there are 169 attested combinations. The most common step-n-grams are listed in Table 4:

[4]https://doi.org/10.1101/2023.10.29.564363 The biology texts are not cited in this study as they are used as textual data, not academic citation.

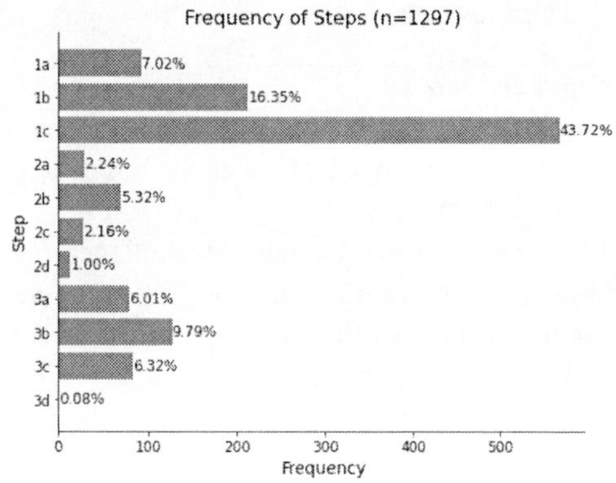

Figure 1: Frequency of steps (n=1,297)

The results in Table 4 indicate that the rhetorical progression (i.e. moving from one step to another) "1a-1b-1c" is common, occurring in 34 out of the 50 texts. For bigrams "1b-1c" (n=62) and "1a-1b" (n=51), we even observe repetition within the texts, as their frequencies are higher than the number of texts (n=50). It is not surprising that the step 1c occurs in almost all combinations, due to its central role to review previous studies and thus the high frequency. The second highest step-3-gram is "1b-1c-2b" (n=18), which can also be explained by the high frequency of step 2b "Indicating a gap", and how it connects the steps "Making topic generalizations" and "Indicating a gap", which is the most frequent option among the four in Move 2. See more in section 4.3.

4.2 Lengths of Steps

The length of step measures how many sentences the same step may span over in a contiguous manner. Table 5 shows the lengths of all the steps. Values of 0 indicate that the step can be absent in some texts. Step "1c - Reviewing previous research" is the only step that is never skipped in the attested data. The step is also the longest among all steps. Again, this is not surprising given its central role.

On the other hand, most other steps are much shorter, as indicated by their maximum lengths and mean lengths. The discussion will further defend the use of this seemingly mundane information from a pedagogical perspective for students or even novice writers.

4.3 How to "Establish a Niche" (Move 2)

The classic CARS model includes four options or approaches to implement the rhetorical move of establishing a niche. That is, scholars decide whether

Table 3: A multi-sentence step in "1b-1c-2b"

Step & Sentence
[1b]: Cancer cells grow in a microenvironment wherein they closely interact with the extracellular matrix (ECM).
[1c]: As a major ECM component, collagen composition regulates various steps of cancer progression including growth, invasion, and metastasis, partly through activation of its canonical receptor integrin to regulate cytoskeleton organization and cell motility [5–7].
[1c]: Recently, discoidin domain receptor tyrosine kinase 2 (DDR2), a non-typical collagen receptor that is dysregulated in various cancer types, has emerged as a key signaling molecule in carcinogenesis [8, 9].
[1c]: Collagen binding to DDR2 activates its tyrosine kinase activity to initiate canonical pathways such as ERK/MAPK and PI3K/AKT signaling cascades [10–12].
[2b]: Despite these studies, how DDR2 regulates cancer cell behavior is incompletely understood.

Table 4: Top 5 step-bigrams and step-trigrams

Step-Bigram	Freq	Step-Trigram	Freq
1b-1c	62	1a-1b-1c	34
1a-1b	51	1b-1c-2b	18
1c-2b	38	1b-1c-1b	17
1c-1b	29	1c-1b-1c	17
2b-1c	23	1c-2b-1c	15

they are making a counter-claim (e.g. "However, this validity may not be related to the neurobiology of depression"[5]) or to indicate a research gap (e.g. "Despite these studies, how DDR2 regulates cancer cell behavior is incompletely understood."[6]) in order to show the niche of their own study. It has been made clear that these options are not mutually exclusive, nor do they follow any particular hierarchy or ordering. Authors from our data often adopts the option of "Indicating a gap". Almost half of the 139 examples of Move 2 are from option 2 (Option 1 = 20.86%, n=29, Option 2 = 49.64%, n=69, Option 3 = 20.14%, n=28, Option 4 = 9.35%, n=13). It is, however, important to note that these options are not mutually exclusive. The same introduction may contain multiple options by both indicating a gap (option 2) and raising a question (option 3).

Table 5: Lengths of steps

Step	Min	Max	Mean
1a	0	4	1.28
1b	0	10	2.14
1c	1	16	3.97
2a	0	5	1.61
2b	0	6	1.33
2c	0	4	1.27
2d	0	3	1.44
3a	0	6	1.47
3b	0	8	1.98
3c	0	7	2.65
3d	0	1	1

5 Discussion

In the EAP community, studies on rhetorical moves are abundant, especially with the focus on the correlation between lexical bundles and particular rhetorical moves, i.e. what phrases appear in which moves/steps (Cortes, 2013; Staples et al., 2013; Moreno and Swales, 2018; Omidian et al., 2018; Appel, 2022). To complement this strand of research that focuses on language use, the present study discusses the progression of the moves and steps. By introducing quantitative measures, we have identified the distribution of specific steps, as well as how different steps may collocate with each other. Potentially, a scaled up version using similar methods will be able to identify any micro-variations across sub-disciplines, as some previous studies suggest.

Our results also confirms what Samraj (2005) argues with regard to the deviations from the classic CARS model. In our sentence-by-sentence annotation, it is often found that Move-1 Step-3 ("Reviewing previous research") is interspersed with other moves. It can be explained by the need to provide further support from previous studies, once the authors have made topic generalizations (see bigram "1b-1c": n=62) or indicated a gap (see bigram "2b-1c": n=23).

While the quantitative results from the step-*n*-gram and lengths of steps may seem mundane, novice scientific writers can use these numerical results as quick reference. The attested data in the annotated corpus will also facilitate material development. Rather than prescribing to students[7]

[5]https://doi.org/10.1101/2023.11.08.566266

[6]https://doi.org/10.1101/2023.11.03.565457

[7]In the authors' context, the students are all at the post-

that the *Introduction* must follow a certain pattern, students can see both conformity to and deviation from the standard CARS model. This allows students to gain better understanding of how expert writers may consciously depart from the CARS model.

Given the internationalization of many institutions and the increasing needs for support in academic literacy to both students and early career researchers, the findings here may also mean that instructions to discipline-specific writing should be more fine-grained. For instance, students in biodiversity would have different needs and writing models from students in molecular biology. Annotated corpus data will allow instructors to easily find attested data for various needs of students.

6 Conclusion and Future Work

This study has shown results from a small annotated corpus and how they enhance our understanding of academic discourse through the lens of the CARS model. The study bears implications on our understanding of progression in rhetorical across steps (through step collocation) and implementation of steps (through lengths of steps), which in turn benefits teaching of academic writing. In future research, it may also be interesting to investigate whether there is any significant differences between preprints (e.g. from BioRxiv as in the present study) and published research articles. While both kinds of data are supposed to be written by advanced or expert writers, there appears to be little research on the contribution of peer review and editing specific to the rhetorical quality of the articles. We acknowledge that the dataset is limited by its size and the single annotator, and intend to remedy these limitations in our ongoing work.

In future work, we aim to enhance the efficiency of the annotation process through the application of semi-supervised learning techniques. This involves leveraging the manually annotated corpus to develop an enriched corpus. For example, training a KNN model will be useful for the multi-class task that classify the sentences into the various steps. Additionally, we can also implement few-shot learning methodologies with the moves and steps being vectorised with pre-trained LLMs, such as GPT (Brown et al., 2020), on the modest "labelled" dataset to develop machine learning models that can generalise and make accurate classifications on new data samples.

graduate level of MSc in biology programs, with a mix of L1 and L2 users of English.

References

Laurence Anthony. 1999. Writing research article introductions in software engineering: How accurate is a standard model? *IEEE transactions on Professional Communication*, 42(1):38–46.

Randy Appel. 2022. Lexical bundles in l2 english academic texts: relationships with holistic assessments of writing quality. *System*, 110:102899.

Tom B. Brown, Benjamin Mann, Nick Ryder, Melanie Subbiah, Jared Kaplan, Prafulla Dhariwal, Arvind Neelakantan, Pranav Shyam, Girish Sastry, Amanda Askell, Sandhini Agarwal, Ariel Herbert-Voss, Gretchen Krueger, Tom Henighan, Rewon Child, Aditya Ramesh, Daniel M. Ziegler, Jeffrey Wu, Clemens Winter, Christopher Hesse, Mark Chen, Eric Sigler, Mateusz Litwin, Scott Gray, Benjamin Chess, Jack Clark, Christopher Berner, Sam McCandlish, Alec Radford, Ilya Sutskever, and Dario Amodei. 2020. Language models are few-shot learners.

Viviana Cortes. 2013. The purpose of this study is to: Connecting lexical bundles and moves in research article introductions. *Journal of English for academic purposes*, 12(1):33–43.

John Flowerdew. 1999. Problems in writing for scholarly publication in english: The case of hong kong. *Journal of Second Language Writing*, 8(3):243–264.

Yu-kai Hsu and Chih-Hua Kuo. 2009. Writing RA introduction: Difficulties and strategies. In *2nd International Conference on English, Discourse, and Intercultural Communication, Macau, China*. Citeseer.

Ken Hyland. 2005. *Metadiscourse*. London: Continuum.

Ken Hyland. 2018. *Metadiscourse: Exploring interaction in writing*. Bloomsbury Publishing.

Zahra Sadat Jalali and M Raouf Moini. 2014. Structure of lexical bundles in introduction section of medical research articles. *Procedia - Social and Behavioral Sciences*, 98:719–726.

Budsaba Kanoksilapatham. 2015. Distinguishing textual features characterizing structural variation in research articles across three engineering subdiscipline corpora. *English for Specific Purposes*, 37:74–86.

J-D Kim, Tomoko Ohta, Yuka Tateisi, and Jun'ichi Tsujii. 2003. GENIA corpus—a semantically annotated corpus for bio-textmining. *Bioinformatics*, 19(suppl_1):i180–i182.

Maria Kuteeva and Lisa McGrath. 2015. The theoretical research article as a reflection of disciplinary practices: The case of pure mathematics. *Applied Linguistics*, 36(2):215–235.

Sébastien Louvigné, Jie Shi, and Sonia Sharmin. 2014. A corpus-based analysis of the scientific RA genre and RA introduction. In *Proceedings of the 2014 International Conference on Advanced Mechatronic Systems*, pages 123–127.

Xiaofei Lu, J Elliott Casal, and Yingying Liu. 2020. The rhetorical functions of syntactically complex sentences in social science research article introductions. *Journal of English for Academic Purposes*, 44:100832.

Xiaofei Lu, Jungwan Yoon, Olesya Kisselev, J. Elliott Casal, Yingying Liu, Jinlei Deng, and Rui Nie. 2021. Rhetorical and phraseological features of research article introductions: Variation among five social science disciplines. *System*, 100:102543.

Paschal Maher and Simon Milligan. 2019. Teaching master thesis writing to engineers: Insights from corpus and genre analysis of introductions. *English for specific purposes*, 55:40–55.

Lisa McGrath and Maria Kuteeva. 2012. Stance and engagement in pure mathematics research articles: Linking discourse features to disciplinary practices. *English for Specific Purposes*, 31(3):161–173.

M. Milagros del Saz Rubio. 2011. A pragmatic approach to the macro-structure and metadiscoursal features of research article introductions in the field of agricultural sciences. *English for Specific Purposes*, 30(4):258–271.

Ana I Moreno and John M Swales. 2018. Strengthening move analysis methodology towards bridging the function-form gap. *English for specific purposes*, 50:40–63.

Hilary Nesi and Sheena Gardner. 2018. The BAWE corpus and genre families classification of assessed student writing. *Assessing Writing*, 38:51–55.

Taha Omidian, Hesamoddin Shahriari, and Anna Siyanova-Chanturia. 2018. A cross-disciplinary investigation of multi-word expressions in the moves of research article abstracts. *Journal of English for academic purposes*, 36:1–14.

Thomas Orr. 1999. Genre in the field of computer science and computer engineering. *IEEE Transactions on Professional Communication*, 42(1):32–37.

Ismet Ozturk. 2007. The textual organisation of research article introductions in applied linguistics: Variability within a single discipline. *English for Specific Purposes*, 26(1):25–38.

Carmen Pérez-Llantada. 2014. Formulaic language in l1 and l2 expert academic writing: Convergent and divergent usage. *Journal of English for Academic Purposes*, 14:84–94.

Ute Römer and John M Swales. 2010. The Michigan corpus of upper-level student papers (MICUSP). *Journal of English for Academic Purposes*, 9(3):249.

Betty Samraj. 2002. Introductions in research articles: Variations across disciplines. *English for specific purposes*, 21(1):1–17.

Betty Samraj. 2005. An exploration of a genre set: Research article abstracts and introductions in two disciplines. *English for specific purposes*, 24(2):141–156.

Rita Simpson, Sarah Briggs, Janine Ovens, and John M Swales. 2002. The Michigan corpus of upper-level student papers (MICUSP). http://quod.lib.umich.edu/cgi/c/corpus/corpus. Accessed: 2023-11-30.

Shelley Staples, Jesse Egbert, Douglas Biber, and Alyson McClair. 2013. Formulaic sequences and eap writing development: Lexical bundles in the toefl ibt writing section. *Journal of English for academic purposes*, 12(3):214–225.

John M Swales. 1990. *Genre analysis: English in academic and research settings*. Cambridge University press.

John M Swales. 2004. *Research genres: Explorations and applications*. Cambridge University Press.

A Appendix

Figure 2 shows the sequence of the steps in all the 50 annotated texts.

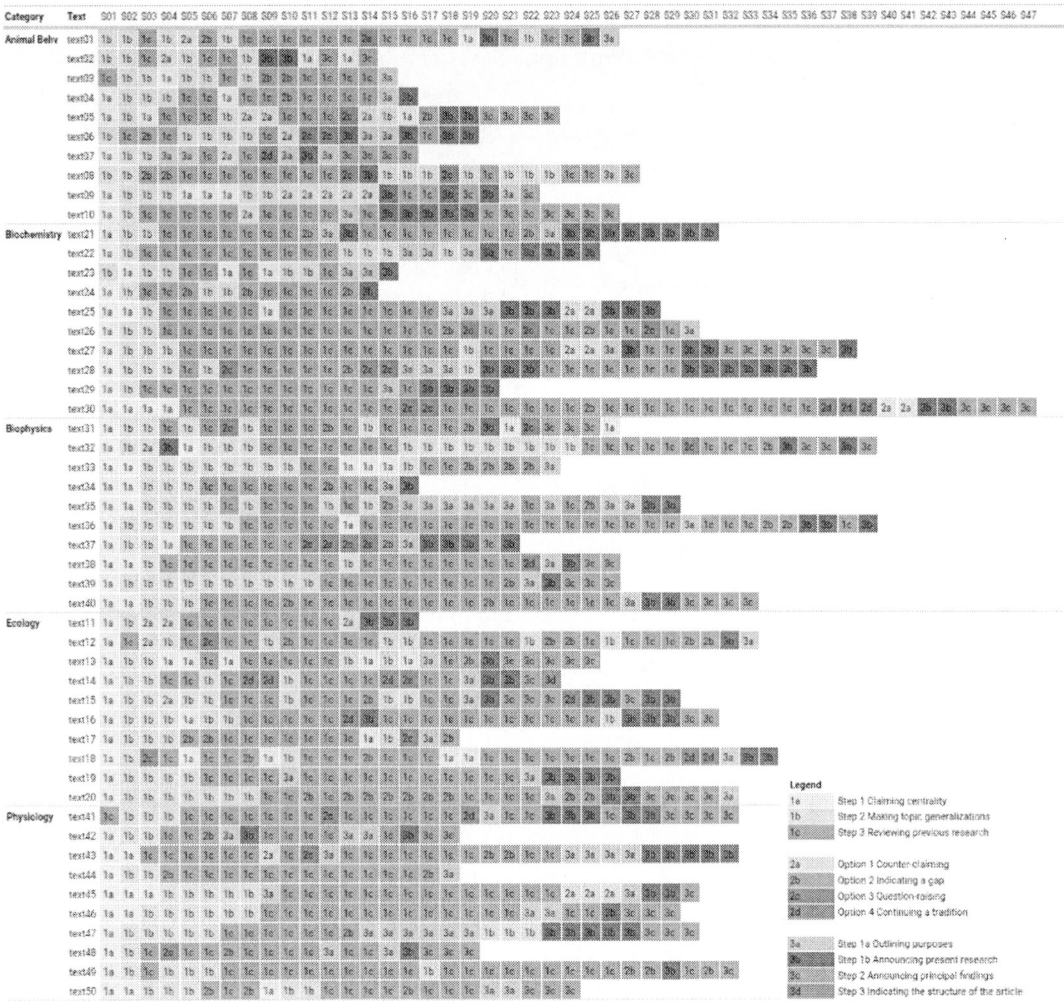

Figure 2: Sequencing of the Steps

Probing of pretrained multilingual models on the knowledge of discourse

Mary Godunova[λ] and **Ekaterina Voloshina**[ϕ]
[λ]HSE University
[ϕ]Work done at AIRI

Abstract

With the raise of large language models (LLMs), different evaluation methods, including probing methods, are gaining more attention. Probing methods are meant to evaluate LLMs on their linguistic abilities. However, most of the studies are focused on morphology and syntax, leaving discourse research out of the scope. At the same time, understanding discourse and pragmatics is crucial to building up the conversational abilities of models.

In this paper, we address the problem of probing several models of discourse knowledge in 10 languages. We present an algorithm to automatically adapt existing discourse tasks to other languages based on the Universal Dependencies (UD) annotation. We find that models perform similarly on high- and low-resourced languages. However, the overall low performance of the models' quality shows that they do not acquire discourse well enough.

1 Introduction

Various methods of evaluating language models, including probing methods (Koto et al., 2021), have recently been popular. The probing methods help to shed light on the linguistic abilities of Large Language Models (LLMs), which could be later used to improve models' qualities (Saphra, 2021). However, probing studies were mainly conducted at such language levels as morphology and syntax (Kassner and Schütze, 2020; Marvin and Linzen, 2018). While pre-trained language models have shown remarkable performance on various language tasks, there is still much to be explored regarding their ability to capture broader discourse in documents. By *discourse*, we understand a language level that operates linguistic units bigger than sentences.

It involves organizing and connecting ideas to create coherent and cohesive communication.

In this paper, we are testing models' ability to capture different aspects of discourse knowledge. Discourse probing can involve tasks such as identifying the relations between sentences within a document or the role of one sentence in the document structure, investigating main topics, discovering a suitable ending, and finding out whether one sentence belongs to a particular paragraph or not (Koto et al., 2021; Chen et al., 2019a). Such tasks shed light on the strengths and limitations of pre-trained language models in capturing the nuances of discourse structure.

Our main contribution is a new suite of probing tasks on multilingual data from ten languages. Moreover, our method can be used for other languages with data available in Universal Dependencies format (De Marneffe et al., 2021). Overall, we state our contributions as follows:

- To bridge the gap in discourse probing research, the paper introduces a probing task to interpret the ability of pretrained LMs to capture discourse relations in 10 linguistically diverse languages;
- We present a tool to generate tasks for probing discourse in any language for which there is enough data in Universal Dependencies (UD) format[1];
- The study validates the findings across different models, languages, and discourse probing tasks, providing valuable insights into the limitations of current LMs in capturing discourse knowledge.

2 Related work

Probing tasks were first introduced in Conneau et al. (2018) and described as simple classification tasks that would reveal if a model contains any linguistic knowledge. Probing involves different methods, for instance, probing classifiers (Belinkov, 2022). After training a model on a specific task, we create representations using the model and then train a separate classifier to predict a particular attribute based on these representations. If the classifier demonstrates strong performance, we conclude that the model has acquired relevant information for the attribute. However, upon further examination, it becomes clear that additional complexities are at play. Also, probing methods involve prompting: transforming a set of probing tasks into question-answer pairs and directing the model to respond to the questions with a specific prefix (Li et al., 2021). This approach essentially serves as a probe that is independent of the model. By using prompting instead of a diagnostic probe, researchers can circumvent the challenge of distinguishing

[1]Our code is available at `https://github.com/mashagodunova/discource_probing`

Proceedings of the 5th Workshop on Computational Approaches to Discourse (CODI 2024), pages 78–90
March 21, 2024 ©2024 Association for Computational Linguistics

between the content of the representations and what the probe learns. After all, one of the most developing fields in probing LLMs is task relevance which is aimed at investigating whether the information encoded in sentence representations, as discovered through a probe, is used by the model to perform its task. Task relevance is also our method of research, which will be discussed later.

Most probing studies focus on evaluating semantic knowledge, which focuses on the meaning of individual words and sentences. The probing methodology combining various annotated data is commonly used as the benchmark for language model comparison and evaluation of their generalizing ability (Conneau and Kiela, 2018). On the other hand, probing of discourse examines how linguistic units are organized and connected to form coherent texts, a crucial ability to generate long sequences. However, only some works investigate the ability of LLMs to understand discourse. Ettinger (2020) shows that BERT produces pragmatically incorrect outputs because it does not consider an extended context. Among other works, Nie et al. (2019a) evaluate models on discourse relations expressed with conjunctions. Chen et al. (2019b) propose a benchmark for model evaluation on different discourse tasks such as prediction of implicit discourse relations based on the Penn Discourse Treebank annotation (Prasad et al., 2008), discourse coherence, and others.

3 Tasks

3.1 General Description

All examples of the described tasks are presented in Appendix 7. We adapt tasks from DiscoEval (Chen et al., 2019a), a framework for discourse probing of language models. The main difference between this research and our work is that we do not concatenate vectors for separate sentences but use the sequence as an input for our models. From the described paper, we borrowed and adapted the following tasks, making them suitable for multiple languages:

Sentence Position (SP): this task tests the model's understanding of linearly-structured discourse. By randomly moving one of the five sentences to the first position, the model must be able to accurately predict the correct order within the discourse sequence based on the content of the sentences.

Binary sentence ordering (BSO): this task is to identify the correct order between the two contextually codependent sentences. BSO could be useful in testing a model's ability to capture local discourse coherence and understand the relationships between adjacent sentences in a text.

Discourse coherence (DC): having a sequence of 6 sentences that form a coherent paragraph, we need to randomly replace one sentence from the coherent sequence with a sentence from another discourse. A model needs to determine whether the resulting sequence of 6 sentences still forms a coherent document. In the DC task, the models must determine the coherence of a document in which any of the five sentences could be replaced except for the first.

Besides that paper, we adapt several tasks from (Koto et al., 2021):

Next sentence prediction: The preceding context consists of 2 to 8 sentences, while the candidates (4 sentences) for prediction are always single sentences. Nevertheless, we adopted it as a binary classification task by mixing one of the sentences in a way that researchers in (Chen et al., 2019a) did.

Sentence ordering: This task is to determine whether the order of sentences in the document is correct. Texts from 3 to 7 sentences mixed within the same sequence are presented as incorrect options.

Cloze story test: Data for this task consists of sequences with four sentences in each. A model needs to pick the best-ending sentence for all documents. We adapted the task as binary, so for incorrect pairs 'key: value', we shuffle ending sentences within all documents.

Although probing studies (Koto et al., 2021; Chen et al., 2019a; Nie et al., 2019b) in the field of discourse have already been conducted, they included a small number of languages (mostly English). They focused on a limited number of tasks in terms of content: either predicting a discourse marker, analyzing the model's understanding of the coherence of the entire text, or the connectivity between a certain number of sentences in a document. Therefore, it seems essential to conduct a general study, having compiled tasks on various aspects of discourse and choosing different languages as a training sample.

3.2 Tasks' theoretical background in terms of RST

As it was already mentioned, the main theoretical background for parsing UD documents was Rhetorical Structure Theory. We have not tried to consider individual types of relations, such as opposition or entailment. Instead, we focused on general patterns, called schemas in this theory, and the constraints they impose on the text.

There are 4 types of restrictions that must be observed in order not to violate the structure of the text:

- Completedness: The set contains one schema application that contains a set of text fragments that make up the entire text
- Connectedness: With the exception of the entire text in the form of a text fragment, each text fragment in the analysis is either a minimal unit or an integral part of another application of the analysis scheme.
- Uniqueness: Each schema application consists of a different set of area text, and within a multi-link schema, each link is applied to another a set of text areas.
- Adjacency: The text intervals of each schema application are equal to one text interval.

According to this classification, we divided all tasks into three groups. The first group included tasks in which the rules of coherence and contiguity were not observed at the same time. Among these tasks are Sentence Position and Binary sentence ordering. The difference between the tasks lies in the size of the sentences and the static part: in the first case, four out of five sentences remain static, while in the second one element moves relative to another. The similarity lies in the fact that in both tasks the order is disrupted by changing the adjacency relations, that is, the sentence changes its position in the general structure, but the new sentence, which was not originally in the discourse, is not involved.

Another group that we deduced was a group of examples in which the rules of completedness and uniqueness are violated: Discourse coherence, Next sentence prediction, Cloze story test. In this group, the desired element is removed from the discourse and replaced with an element from another discourse. Due to this general characteristic, tasks from this group can be characterized by two properties: loss of text integrity and the presence of elements that do not fit into the structure of the text.

The latter group is characterized by the absence of an important element (sentence or word form) necessary for the connectivity of the text (at the same time, nuclear part is not missing, therefore, in this sence the text is completed), therefore, only the rule of connectivity is violated in them. Among the tasks included in this category: Sentence ordering and Discourse connective prediction.

4 Methods

4.1 Data

All data for our probing tasks was taken from the UD framework (De Marneffe et al., 2021), which provides a standardized set of grammatical dependencies and syntactic relations for annotating treebanks in different languages (more than a hundred languages). One of the main tasks of our research was to create a parser that generates multilingual tasks for discourse on UD data automatically without the need for manual markup. As a result, we extracted .csv files as training samples from the UD data. The general format of such files consists of:

1. Answer in correctness rating format: 0 or 1. In this case 1 indicates that presented sentences (and discourse connective for DCP task) meet the criteria for the correctness of a specific task. For example, for the Binary sentence ordering task, two sentences will be presented; if they are in the correct order, there will be 1, otherwise - 0.

2. Data type marker: training or test

3. Sentences - each sentence is displayed in a separate column

4. Present only in the Discourse connective prediction task - discourse connective itself

This parser can be used on treebanks for any language. We frame almost all presented tasks as binary classification problems, and they involve different aspects of Rhetorical Structure Theory[2], models' understanding of which is being tested in this study. More information about the generation of tasks is presented in section A.

4.2 Models

In our study, we probe several multilingual LLMs of different architectures: mBERT (Devlin et al., 2019), XLM-XLM-RoBERTa (Yinhan et al., 2019), mGPT, and mT5. We do not fine-tune models since we aim to test the basic models in understanding the discourse. Instead, we extract [CLS] embeddings and train a Logistic regression on these representations to assess the quality of the models' performance.

4.3 Languages

Most of the languages in the sample belong to the Indo-European language family (limited to the most common language groups – Romance, Germanic, and Slavic); as for our experiments, the dataset size was essential. We also included Turkish, which treebank is one of the largest in the Universal Dependencies. In addition, Turkish is part of one of the largest language families, Altai. The sample also included the Armenian language since data for this language was massive enough to parse it, and it has never been included in any previous probing studies. The table below shows the number of examples for each task and language that were extracted from treebanks:

Most of the languages in our sample were chosen as they have been mentioned little to no in previous works. However, we also include languages often appearing in Natural Language Processing works, such as English, French, and Russian, to make our results comparable to other works.

Moreover, the difference in corpora sizes shows how models perform in best (high-resourced languages) and worst cases (low-resourced languages). It allows us to investigate further how the number of examples in a particular language determines a multilingual transformer's understanding of several idioms at once.

5 Results

5.1 Results by languages

Overall, models show some understanding of discourse structures, especially in high-resourced languages.

As for the differences in performance on different languages, as Figure 1 shows, models show better quality

[2]Rhetorical Structure Theory (Forsbom, 2005) is a framework for analyzing and understanding how texts are organized and constructed rhetorically. It focuses on the patterns and relationships between different text elements, such as the primary point or argument, supporting evidence, and rhetorical devices used

Language	BSO	CST	DC	NSP	SO	SP	DCP
Russian	15632	9385	3450	12949	5302	2790	14036
Bulgarian	17354	67142	33567	42781	18579	22152	37620
Czech	1230	18437	2143	13561	9450	7664	2089
Serbian	1389	6780	2013	4998	4356	1732	1503
Catalan	1476	47852	34701	21952	1938	9909	7605
French	1468	1201	1750	7620	2395	1042	1201
Latin	1474	51867	21602	13764	1027	1395	3047
English	1823	21770	3502	16067	3750	7438	8993
Armenian	2094	46209	29436	49673	19820	10347	28049
Turkish	15203	12064	3972	30166	1960	1704	6775

Table 1: Number of examples in each treebank. *BSO*: Binary Sentence Ordering, *CST*: Cloze Story Test, *DC*: Discource Coherence, *NSP*: Next Sentence Prediction, *SO*: Sentence Ordering, *SP*: Sentence Position, *DCP*: Discourse Connective Prediction

in the languages better presented in the training set. As can be seen, a writing system does not appear to be an essential factor, as models show better performance in Armenian than in Turkish or even French in some cases.

Armenian XLM-RoBERTa performs best in this language, although mBERT and mT5 demonstrate almost identical results. Although there are practically no studies devoted to the structure of discourse in the Armenian language, and this language is considered underresourced, it is surprising that models show results similar to results in English.

Bulgarian In this case, there is a distribution common to most tasks (and obtained by averaging the results for both tasks and languages), in which XLM-RoBERTa demonstrates the highest accuracy, mBERT performs slightly worse, followed by mT5, and the worst results are observed for mGPT.

English Results demonstrated by models for English may show the actual distribution of ratings because this language always has the largest number of examples in the training sample. We can assume that mBERT potentially has more knowledge about discourse, but it is more difficult to cope with longer sequences, or it has a smaller multilingual base.

Catalan For Catalan we observe extremely unexpected results exceeding XLM-RoBERTa, as mBERT demonstrates the best accuracy (while still lower than the average value for other languages), and mGPT is in second place. mT5 demonstrated a slightly lower average accuracy, and XLM-RoBERTa performed the worst.

Czech XLM-RoBERTa's absolute superiority may stem from the fact that the compilers of the treebank for the Czech language emphasized long-distance discourse relations in accordance with (Poláková et al., 2020), meaning that to capture a core sense of the sentence you need to 'parse' it from the beginning to an end and keep in mind all the details. As proven, one of the main advantages of XLM-RoBERTa is the ability to analyze large text sequences (Conneau et al., 2020).

French The utterance in Romance languages (compared to the linear structure of utterance in English) is distinguished by ornateness. The main idea is usually expressed at the beginning and at the end. In this vein, the accuracy of mGPT can be explained by the sparse attention mechanism, which allows each output position to focus on only a subset of input positions, selected based on predefined patterns or rules (Martins et al., 2020).

Russian For Russian, we observe the same distribution that has already been described for Bulgarian. Since the distribution was almost the same for the Czech language (the difference is that the mGPT showed slightly higher accuracy than mT5), it can be assumed that such similarity in the results is explained by the affiliation of the above languages to the same language group.

Latin In (Kroon, 2009), it is established that the structure of discourse in Latin is characterized by solid fragmentation in the sense of the distance between discursive units united by various word forms, which are also polysemic. Thus, the high average accuracy of most models in tasks with the Latin language reflects the ability to build non-trivial connections within the text and understand the general meaning.

Serbian Since Serbian discourse has not been sufficiently studied before, the only factor by which we can explain such a distribution of model performances is the small amount of data for the language under study. Regarding mBERT's superiority over XLM-RoBERTa, it can be assumed that differences in the token masking procedure explain it - in the case of mBERT, it is always a fixed set of tokens when the model is working, which may help in working with low-resource languages.

Turkish XLM-RoBERTa achieved the highest performance, surpassing mBERT, mT5, and mGPT. However, mBERT still performed better than mGPT and mT5; mT5 showed the lowest accuracy among the four models.

5.2 Results by tasks

Now, we will examine the correlation between each model's understanding of discourse and different types

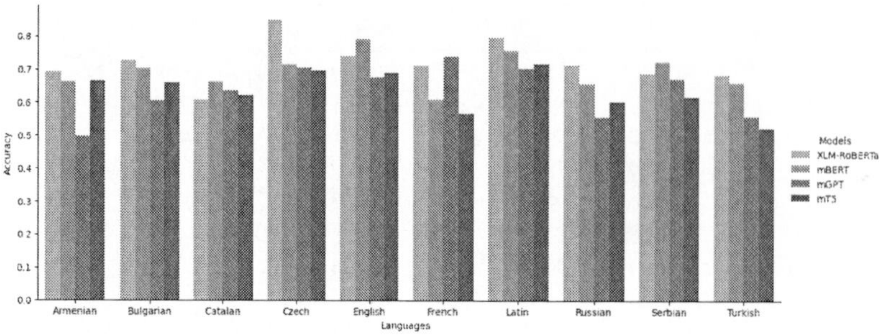

Figure 1: Average accuracy depending on the language and type of model

of tasks. As seen from Figure 5.2, the models show the best performance on *Cloze Story Test (CST)* and *Next sentence prediction* tasks. In both tasks, the focus of the prediction is the last sentence of the document. However, the accuracy on a similar task, the *Discourse coherence (DC)* task, is much lower. We can conclude that the number of sentences is not a crucial factor, as for the DC test, there was a sequence of 5 sentences provided, while for CST, all documents consisted of 4 sentences. However, the position of a shuffled sentence appears to be important.

Binary sentence ordering is the only task where mGPT copes with it best, but in all other tasks, it demonstrates the lowest accuracy rates due to obvious issues like the lack of some investigated languages in the mGPT's training data.

Cloze story test In this task XLM-RoBERTa shows the best performance. Our results replicate the results by Conneau et al. (2020) where they show that XLM-RoBERTa surpasses mBERT on cross-lingual classification, but specifically with low-resource languages used in training data. XLM-RoBERTa's superiority over mBERT can be explained not only by its overall better accuracy in most tasks but also by the phenomenon called the "generalization gap", which occurs when a language model's ability to perform well on downstream tasks exceeds its performance on the validation set during training.

Discourse coherence Even though one of the two main mBERT's objectives is Next sentence prediction, we should remember that the DC task provides the model with not two but several sentences as input to determine whether they are coherent. As shown by the results, XLM-RoBERTa copes better with long sequences because compared to mBERT, more extensive training data with lengthier sequence segments is trained. Results for this task indicate that the model's architecture type does not play a crucial role in this case. Although mBERT and XLM-RoBERTa are encoders, mGPT is a decoder, and mT5 is an encoder-decoder transformer, we can see that mT5 and mGPT-2 have shown almost the same results, which are relatively close to mBERT's accuracy.

Next sentence prediction NSP is a task of the type for which we expect high accuracy of predictions from a model whose main specificity is text generation (mGPT). Hypothetically, bidirectional self-attention is not required in this case, and it is enough to predict the output based only on the previous context. To understand why mGPT still performs the worst and mT5 shows the same results as XLM-RoBERTa (thereby neutralizing the importance of having a decoder in the architecture), we must consider the differences between generating the next sentence and a single token. Presumably, for the accurate recognition of the next sentence, the context of both the previous and the subsequent sentences plays a decisive role, the complete understanding of which is impossible without the encoder (due to the mechanism of bidirectional attention).

Sentence ordering Unexpectedly, mBERT performs better than XLM-RoBERTa, which differences in the masking procedures for XLM-RoBERTa and mBERT may have caused. In XLM-RoBERTa, the masking of 0.15 of tokens is dynamic and changes for each pre-training epoch. Our results correlate with (Rothe et al., 2020) where the authors demonstrated that mBERT performs best with sequence-splitting tasks, indicating that its understanding of sentence ordering exceeds XLM-RoBERTa's.

Sentence position In this case, XLM-RoBERTa demonstrates the best results. This task is similar to the previous one, the difference is that in SO not all proposals are mixed, but only four and another randomly selected. In contrast, in the SP all proposals for incorrect options occupy new randomly selected positions. Presumably, in this case, XLM-RoBERTa's superiority is explained by the fact that XLM-RoBERTa was trained on a much larger corpus of text data than mBERT, which allowed it to learn more complex and nuanced patterns in language. Additionally, XLM-RoBERTa was trained for longer than mBERT.

Discourse connective prediction For this task where the input consists of two sentences and transformers must predict correct connective XLM-RoBERTa unsurprisingly demonstrates the best results. This result can be attributed to the NSP loss being removed in XLM-RoBERTa's architecture and the whole input being replaced with full sentences. An obvious problem

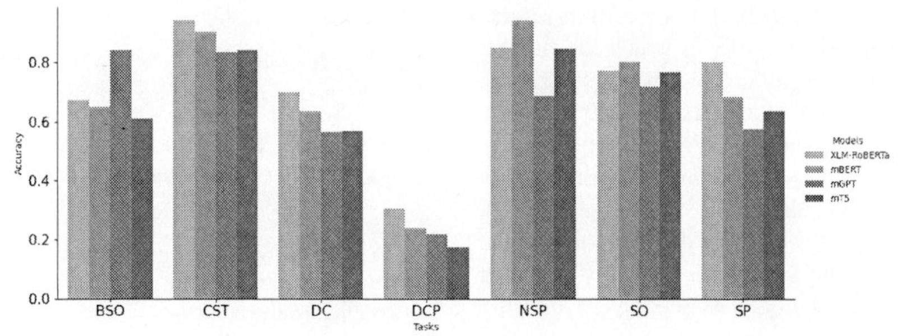

Figure 2: Average accuracy depending on the task and type model
BSO: Binary Sentence Ordering, *CST*: Cloze Story Test, *DC*: Discource Coherence, *NSP*: Next Sentence Prediction, *SO*: Sentence Ordering, *SP*: Sentence Position, *DCP*: Discourse Connective Prediction

with mGPT and mT5 in solving these kinds of tasks is their generative objective since the sample used for fine-tuning may lack the necessary connectives, in which case the correct answer simply cannot be generated by the model by definition and will eventually be read as incorrect.

6 Discussion

The influence of the discourse structure in English The so-called 'complicated simple sentences' (Dagnev et al., 2019) in Bulgarian generate heavy complementation, and that is the main difference between Bulgarian and English rhetorical structure. It can be that the model borrows discourse patterns from the language that prevails in the training sample. Thus, presumably, the fewer languages in the model and the greater the presence of English, the greater the accuracy in those languages whose discursive patterns are similar to patterns in English. The results obtained for Catalan, which is also structurally significantly different from English, display the same trend and can be explained by right-branching (right-dislocation constructions), which is not often found in English.

mGPT's sparse attention mechanism Due to mGPT's performance for French and Russian we can hardly consider that the sparse attention mechanism applied for mGPT helps to cope best with long sequences found in Russian, rather it turns out to be the best in the case when the main topic of the utterance is concentrated at the beginning and end of the text (as in French). At the same time, for Russian Kaplan (Kaplan, 2006) establishes a structure characterized by situationality, instability of discourse patterns and a constant change of focus of text, which, although in some sense similar to the ornate rhetorical structure in French (both are non-linear with respect to discourse in English), differs in the lack of integrity according to Kaplan. It can be assumed that this difference is the reason for the strong decrease in the accuracy of the mGPT for Russian compared to French.

Models performing similarly with languages belonging to the same group The hypothesis that the models act equally (in relation to each other) for languages belonging to the same language group and therefore having common discourse patterns is confirmed by the example of French and Latin. At the same time, this is still a hypothesis, since such a distribution seems to be universal in most cases and has also been recorded for most languages of the Slavic group. This assumption is contradicted by the distribution of model accuracy obtained for Serbian, but in this case it seems appropriate to refer to the lack of resources of this language.

Advantages of dynamic masking procedure In the case of Turkish, we were talking about shared arguments that occur when two distinct discourse connectives use the same text span as their argument. This can create ambiguity or confusion for the reader or listener, as it may not be immediately clear which connective governs the argument. Properly contained arguments occur when a larger text span that is the argument of one connective contains a smaller text span that is the argument of another connective. For XLM-RoBERTa, the complexity of text may be potentially overcome via dynamic masking, as in this case the number of potentially different masked versions of each sentence is not bounded like in mBERT, therefore the probability of understanding complicated structures gets bigger. At the same time, we can see that dynamic masking procedure benefits only in cases where the complicated structure of the text does not change drastically. For instance, in SO task this change could lead to a deterioration in the quality of the model's performance in this case, since the SO task assumes that for incorrect examples all sentences in a sequence are being shuffled. Accordingly, in this case, masking the fixed part of the input can serve as an advantage of mBERT.

mT5's superiority over mGPT In the NSP task we can assume that the results obtained can be explained by the fact that in mT5 the decoder typically produces two additional tokens: the class label and an end-of-sequence token, which can contribute to a better understanding of the connectivity of the final element of the sequence and the previous elements. This hypothesis can be applied to all results in which mT5 exceeds mGPT in accuracy.

How context and focus sentence position affects models' performance In tasks in which the highest accuracy of the models' performance was recorded, the focus sentence for prediction is fixed (always the last, only the size of the sequence varied). Nevertheless, context definitely affects the model's performance on the task. For example, models perform worse on a task in which it is required to determine the correctness of the order of sentences within a binary sequence (0.61) than on a task containing multiple sequences (0.77). Also, quite unexpected and contrary to hypotheses results were obtained for the task Sentence Position. In the original paper, the BERT-Large accuracy for SP was 0.538, while in our case we got an 0.8 accuracy. Such a difference in the results may indicate the importance of the first position in the sequence, the weight of which in the context of the multi-head attention method is the largest.

7 Conclusion

Our work is devoted to the study of the degree of discourse acquisition by various multilingual models. Despite the fact that many tasks and hypotheses were built on the materials of their predecessors, our research differs from them in that it involves several languages in discourse probing at once and combines completely different tasks that ultimately somehow test the understanding of the model of the whole text. Also, some of our results do not correspond to the conclusions of other researchers which analyzed English and other few languages (Chinese in most cases) and add new information about the understanding of the language by individual models. Moreover, we have come to a conclusion that models, on average, perform equally in low-resource and conventional (popular) languages with binary-classification tasks. This result may indicate the presence of certain trends associated with the assimilation of the document structure by models, which apply to all idiolects. We also identified some characteristics of tasks and training samples that affect the performance of the model, such as the size of the sequence, the number of sentences involved in shuffle, the focus of prediction (the last sentence is often easier to predict than the first) – and this factor is stronger than the significance of the size of the context. The more randomness there is in choosing proposals that will change the position in the document, the better the performance of some models, for example, XLM-RoBERTa, since its main principle is masking an unfixed set of tokens. Consequently, we have identified certain aspects of tasks that models generally do worse with, such as predicting the connective marker when there is a limited amount of resources, as well as those factors of individual model's architecture that worsen the results. We also compared the results obtained with the accuracy of the predictions of monolingual models and did not reveal a significant deterioration in the quality of transformers.

References

Barzilay, R. and Lapata, M. (2017). Modeling local coherence: An entity-based approach.

Belinkov, Y. (2022). Probing classifiers: Promises, shortcomings, and advances. *Computational Linguistics*, 48(1):207–219.

Chen, M., Chu, Z., and Gimpel, K. (2019a). Evaluation benchmarks and learning criteria for discourse-aware sentence representations.

Chen, M., Chu, Z., and Gimpel, K. (2019b). Evaluation benchmarks and learning criteria for discourse-aware sentence representations. *arXiv preprint arXiv:1909.00142*.

Conneau, A., Khandelwal, K., Goyal, N., Chaudhary, V., Wenzek, G., Guzmán, F., Grave, E., Ott, M., Zettlemoyer, L., and Stoyanov, V. (2020). Unsupervised cross-lingual representation learning at scale.

Conneau, A. and Kiela, D. (2018). SentEval: An evaluation toolkit for universal sentence representations. In *Proceedings of the Eleventh International Conference on Language Resources and Evaluation (LREC 2018)*, Miyazaki, Japan. European Language Resources Association (ELRA).

Conneau, A., Kruszewski, G., Lample, G., Barrault, L., and Baroni, M. (2018). What you can cram into a single $&!#* vector: Probing sentence embeddings for linguistic properties. In *Proceedings of the 56th Annual Meeting of the Association for Computational Linguistics (Volume 1: Long Papers)*, pages 2126–2136, Melbourne, Australia. Association for Computational Linguistics.

Dagnev, I., Mariya, Saykova, and Yaneva, M. (2019). Discourse and linguistic characteristics of rma introduction sections – a bulgarian-english comparative study.

De Marneffe, M.-C., Manning, C. D., Nivre, J., and Zeman, D. (2021). Universal dependencies. *Computational linguistics*, 47(2):255–308.

Devlin, J., Chang, M.-W., Lee, K., and Toutanova, K. (2019). Bert: Pre-training of deep bidirectional transformers for language understanding. *Proceedings of NAACL-HLT 2019*, pages 4171–4186.

Ettinger, A. (2020). What BERT is not: Lessons from a new suite of psycholinguistic diagnostics for language models. *Transactions of the Association for Computational Linguistics*, 8:34–48.

Forsbom, E. (2005). Rhetorical structure theory in natural language generation.

Kaplan, R. B. (2006). Cultural thought patterns in intercultural education. *Information from lecture delivered by M. R. Montaño-Harmon, Ph. D., Professor Emeritus, California State University, Fullerton, June, 2001, based on (1) doctoral dissertation research and (2) ongoing research in four states in the United States*, pages 1–20.

Kassner, N. and Schütze, H. (2020). Negated and misprimed probes for pretrained language models: Birds can talk, but cannot fly. *In Proceedings of the 58th Annual Meeting of the Association for Computational Linguistics*, pages 7811–7818.

Koto, F., Lau, J. H., and Baldwin, T. (2021). Discourse probing of pretrained language models. *Proceedings of the 2021 Conference of the North American Chapter of the Association for Computational Linguistics: Human Language Technologies*, pages 3849–3864.

Kroon, C. H. M. (2009). Latin linguistics between grammar and discourse: Units of analysis, levels of analysis.

Li, L., Ma, C., Yue, Y., and Hu, D. (2021). Improving encoder by auxiliary supervision tasks for table-to-text generation. In Zong, C., Xia, F., Li, W., and Navigli, R., editors, *Proceedings of the 59th Annual Meeting of the Association for Computational Linguistics and the 11th International Joint Conference on Natural Language Processing (Volume 1: Long Papers)*, pages 5979–5989, Online. Association for Computational Linguistics.

Malmi, E., Pighin, D., Krause, S., and Kozhevnikov, M. (2017). Automatic prediction of discourse connectives.

Martins, A. F. T., Farinhas, A., Treviso, M., Niculae, V., Aguiar, P. M. Q., and Figueiredo, M. A. T. (2020). Sparse and continuous attention mechanisms. *4th Conference on Neural Information Processing Systems (NeurIPS 2020), Vancouver, Canada.*

Marvin, R. and Linzen, T. (2018). Targeted syntactic evaluation of language models. *In Proceedings of the 2018 Conference on Empirical Methods in Natural Language Processing*, pages 1192–1202.

Mostafazadeh, N., Chambers, N., He, X., Devi Parikh, D. B., Vanderwende, L., Kohli, P., and Allen, J. (2016). A corpus and evaluation framework for deeper understanding of commonsense stories.

Nie, A., Bennett, E., and Goodman, N. (2019a). DisSent: Learning sentence representations from explicit discourse relations. In *Proceedings of the 57th Annual Meeting of the Association for Computational Linguistics*, pages 4497–4510.

Nie, A., Bennett, E. D., and Goodman, N. D. (2019b). Dissent: Learning sentence representations from explicit discourse relations.

Poláková, L., Mírovský, J., Nedoluzhko, A., Jínová, P., Šárka Zikánová, and Hajičová, E. (2020). Introducing the prague discourse treebank 1.0.

Prasad, R., Dinesh, N., Lee, A., Miltsakaki, E., Robaldo, L., Joshi, A. K., and Webber, B. L. (2008). The Penn Discourse TreeBank 2.0. In *LREC*.

Rishi Sharma, James Allen, O. B. N. M. (2018). Tackling the story ending biases in the story cloze test. *Proceedings of the 56th Annual Meeting of the Association for Computational Linguistics (Volume 2: Short Papers) Authors:*.

Rothe, S., Narayan, S., and Severyn, A. (2020). Leveraging pre-trained checkpoints for sequence generation tasks.

Saphra, N. (2021). Training dynamics of neural language models.

Yinhan, L., Myle, O., Naman, G., Jingfei, D., Mandar, J., Danqi, C., Omer, L., Mike, L., Luke, Z., and Veselin, S. (2019). Roberta: A robustly optimized bert pretraining approach.

A Examples of tasks' generation

The ideas for all the tasks were taken from the articles of the predecessors. At the same time, all the previous probing studies, the tasks from which we borrowed, were mainly conducted on the basis of English and they did not use multilingual models. Therefore, we needed to adapt all the borrowed tasks in such a way that they correspond to the treebanks of any language from the database. This is one of the reasons why in our study we did not test the models' understanding of segmentation into clauses: in each language the division into clauses occurs differently, therefore, we are not allowed to implement a universal code for extracting EDU. All tasks, except for the discourse connective prediction, are a binary classification problem. This approach was chosen to better evaluate the accuracy of the models. Taking into account that many of the languages in the sample are not very large and have not been studied sufficiently, their datasets are also small. As a result, if, for instance, in the case of a task for the order of sentences in a sequence, integer answers with an order were submitted to the input, not all numeric sequences would occur in the training sample. Therefore, given that all analyzed models have masking objects, correct and incorrect sequences should be generated by the models themselves. Thus, the correct sequences are marked as 1, the incorrect ones as 0.

A.1 Discourse connective prediction

Unlike previous approaches(Koto et al., 2021), we did not set a frequency threshold for accounting the connective due to the limited shapes of the data for some languages. Following the approach presented in (Malmi et al., 2017), we predict only connectives which occur in the beginning of the sentence, considering this as a base position for an explicit binding marker. This choice is explained by the fact that before testing the understanding of implicit connectives by a multilingual model, we must first pay attention to explicit ones.

$Sent_1$	$Sent_2$	Discourse Connective
Obviously because I want to vote	If anyone else has voted, what did you guys vote for?	And

Table 2: Example of a discourse connective prediction task

A.2 Sentence position

The position of a sentence within the text can provide context and help to understand the overall structure and purpose of the document. The opening sentences often provide an introduction to the topic, while the following sentences provide more detailed information and support the main idea. (Chen et al., 2019a) discovered that in the SP task, removing the surrounding sentences can make it more challenging to accurately predict the position of the target sentence, as the model has less information to work with. Due to the fact that the context plays a crucial role in a sentence position, we decided to take 5-sentence sequences for our dataset and swap the fourth of them with the other randomly chosen sentence in a sequence. This method was partly proposed by (Mostafazadeh et al., 2016), and, although in the described article researchers swap the forth sentence with the first one, we decided not to swap fixed elements of a text, and choose one of them randomly, so we complicated the task, because usually models demonstrate high results in this test.

Examples	Labels
The problem is that customers can find features between low-end camera companies. It's tough to make money branching out when your appeal is in your focus. If they continue to add features th,ey can justify their likely sky-high valuation.	1
The Greater New Orleans Fair Housing Action Center (GNOFHAC) filed a housing discrimination ast week. The complaint, filed with the United States Department of Housing and Urban Development. Thomas Housing Development residents, the City of New Orleans. VI redevelopment of St	0

Table 3: Example of a sentence position task

A.3 Binary sentence ordering

This task differs from SP in that a much smaller amount of context is supplied to the input, so this test allows us to evaluate the ability of the model to determine the relationship between the minimum context of two sentences.

A.4 Discourse coherence

In order to evaluate the ability of a model to capture local discourse coherence, it would need to be able to capture characteristics of the entity being discussed or the topic of the sentence group, and perform inference across multiple

Examples	Labels
Based on specific intelligence inputs, Army arrested Ghulam Mohiuddin Lone, a LeT man, from Doda district. During the preliminary interrogation, Lone 'confessed' his involvement in the blasts and gave several vital clues	1
Salon is clean and girls are nice. I didn't know what I was missing	0

Table 4: Example of a binary sentence ordering task

sentences to determine the coherence of the discourse. This can be a non-trivial task, as it requires the model to have a deep understanding of the underlying meaning and context of the text being analyzed. Connectivity within the document, in accordance with our research and the previous work, is determined from 6 sentences. In our case, this number is fixed. Negative examples are created by replacing one of the sentences with a sentence from another text.

Examples	Labels
This idea may seem strange if they are familiar with the King James Version's translation: "In the beginning, God created the heaven and the earth." However, as we have seen, this translation is not correct. Even so, there might seem to be room for the idea of creation made from nothing. It might appear to readers that this idea of creation from nothing is expressed or symbolized in Genesis 1:2 by the mention of "void and vacuum". These two nouns, connected by a conjunction and forming a fixed, com pound phrase, would seem to describe precisely the kind of nothingness that facilitates the concept of creation ex nihilo.	1
Genesis 1 envisions creation not simply as God making; it is as much as a process of "separation" and differentiation of elements from one another, as we will see in chapter 3. It involves a transformation from an unformed, wate1y mass into the world that sustains human existence with water.Creation is a process in which a deity makes the world as it came to be. Psalm 33:6-7 nicely expresses this transformation. Let's consider this more closely.	0

Table 5: Example of a discourse coherence task

A.5 Next sentence prediction

In the source paper there were 3 negative candidates and a single positive one for the next sentence, but we adopted it as a binary classification problem, therefore, for negative examples of sequences we shuffle the last sentence with the other sentence, but not within one document to sustain the text structure.

Examples	Labels
It was ok, but the place was old. It was clean, but just a little dumpy. Hard to get into, though.	1
Horrible customer service. I came in to get a nice gift for my wife. But thankfully there are other flowers shops around	0

Table 6: Example of a Next sentence prediction task

A.6 Sentence ordering

Originally this task was done by shuffling from 3 to 7 sentences, providing the model with the correct ordering and then predicting it. We reworked it by shuffling all the sentences for the incorrect sequences. This method allows the model to select the most consistent sequences in the dataset and further develop a coherency metric based on NLP analytics (Barzilay and Lapata, 2017).

A.7 Cloze story test

As was described earlier, in this task, the model receives a document containing 4 sentences as input and chooses the best completion for the text. We changed this task by making the answers binary and shuffling the last sentences in the sequence for negative samples. We also did not take into account text biases conducting stylistic feature analysis (Rishi Sharma, 2018) as it is harder to trace on a large language data. In (Mostafazadeh et al., 2016) it is claimed that cloze story test indeed helps to identify the model's understanding of the text coherence. If a model performs well on this task, it suggests that it has some level of understanding of the story's narrative structure and can generate coherent and logical endings based on that understanding.

Examples	Labels
This is unlike the situation last year in Asia when we evacuated US citizens from areas that were hit by the tsunami - a phenomenon that is much less predictable than the Hezbollah-provoked destruction that rained down on Lebanon. The American-Arab Discrimination Committee is suing Condoleeza Rice and Donald Rumsfeld, charging that they mismanaged the evacuation efforts	1
My favorite so far in Bellevue. They have good sushi for a good price	0

Table 7: Example of a sentence ordering task

Examples	Labels
Heh, yep, I like to wear silk chemises. Also panties even stockings with garter belt .Later on, I red somewhere that it's seakness	1
You've already asked this . Why would someone post the location of a dealer in a public place? Drop by my house, I can get you some real cheap. Give me an address or something please idk	0

Table 8: Example of a cloze story test task

B Detailed results

Task	Language	Models			
		mBERT	XLM-RoBERTa	mGPT	mT5
Cloze story test	Bulgarian	**1.0**	0.924	0.899	0.9
	Catalan	0.947	0.9	**0.948**	0.934
	English	0.838	**0.892**	0.865	0.784
	French	0.875	**0.889**	0.625	0.633
	Armenian	0.8	**0.943**	0.829	0.8
	Latin	0.906	0.969	0.903	0.906
	Russian	0.875	0.884	0.625	0.75
	Czech	1.0	1.0	0.909	0.879
	Turkish	0.833	0.917	0.708	0.792
	Serbian	0.971	1.0	0.941	0.941
Binary sentence ordering	Bulgarian	0.517	0.724	0.759	0.621
	Catalan	0.577	0.615	0.808	0.615
	English	0.759	0.552	0.793	0.586
	French	0.514	0.6	0.943	0.429
	Armenian	0.8	0.8	0.6	1.0
	Latin	0.762	0.78	0.75	0.75
	Russian	0.515	0.697	1.0	0.455
	Czech	0.77	**1.0**	0.97	0.75
	Turkish	0.529	0.588	0.971	0.5
	Serbian	0.8	0.4	0.8	0.453
Discourse coherence	Bulgarian	0.75	0.719	0.594	0.594
	Catalan	0.548	0.645	0.546	0.677
	English	0.875	0.833	0.75	0.708
	French	0.333	0.667	0.998	0.667
	Armenian	0.615	0.769	0.462	0.615
	Latin	0.75	0.75	0.45	0.55
	Russian	0.667	0.689	0.333	0.667
	Czech	0.571	**1.0**	0.857	0.571
	Turkish	0.75	0.25	0.25	0.25
	Serbian	0.5	0.7	0.4	0.4
Discourse connective prediction	Bulgarian	0.226	0.29	0.161	0.258
	Catalan	0.313	0.313	0.375	0.125
	English	0.4	0.35	0.4	0.45
	French	0.429	0.429	0.429	0.286
	Armenian	0.184	0.026	0.158	0.105
	Latin	0.077	0.154	0.031	0.077
	Russian	0.357	0.214	0.286	0.286
	Czech	0.167	0.292	0.125	0.167
	Turkish	0.051	**0.999**	0.051	0.063
	Serbian	0.25	0.03	0.25	0.033
Next sentence prediction	Bulgarian	0.758	0.788	0.576	0.727
	Catalan	0.968	0.563	0.688	0.625
	English	0.981	0.939	0.697	0.758
	French	0.936	0.733	0.7	0.733
	Armenian	0.957	0.967	0.5	0.9
	Latin	1.0	0.998	0.97	1.0
	Russian	0.922	0.742	0.452	0.903
	Czech	0.958	1.0	0.783	0.99
	Turkish	0.94	0.774	0.677	0.839
	Serbian	1.0	**0.986**	0.833	1.0

Table 9: Overall results of different models on each task in each language

Task	Language	Models			
		mBERT	XLM-RoBERTa	mGPT	mT5
Sentence ordering	Bulgarian	0.759	0.793	0.62	0.586
	Catalan	0.531	0.563	0.656	0.5
	English	0.917	0.792	0.75	0.625
	French	0.682	0.682	0.727	0.729
	Armenian	0.629	0.63	0.519	0.593
	Latin	**1.0**	0.91	0.893	1.0
	Russian	0.867	0.8	0.767	0.811
	Czech	0.923	0.934	0.962	0.808
	Turkish	0.897	0.689	0.828	0.862
	Serbian	0.833	0.867	0.852	0.7
Sentence position	Bulgarian	0.912	0.765	0.797	0.559
	Catalan	0.761	0.61	0.71	0.585
	English	0.775	0.815	0.8	0.6
	French	0.52	**1.0**	0.47	0.75
	Armenian	0.667	0.714	0.703	0.333
	Latin	0.815	0.963	0.74	852
	Russian	0.4	0.92	0.42	0.4
	Czech	0.636	0.727	0.545	0.455
	Turkish	0.667	0.556	0.444	0.431
	Serbian	0.714	0.857	0.688	0.786

Table 10: Overall results of different models on each task in each language

Feature-augmented model for multilingual discourse relation classification

[1]Eleni Metheniti and [1,2,3]Chloé Braud and [1,3]Philippe Muller
[1]UT3 - IRIT ; [2]CNRS ; [3]ANITI
firstname.lastname@irit.fr

Abstract

Discourse relation classification within a multilingual, cross-framework setting is a challenging task, and the best-performing systems so far have relied on monolingual and mono-framework approaches. In this paper, we introduce transformer-based multilingual models, trained jointly over all datasets—thus covering different languages and discourse frameworks. We demonstrate their ability to outperform single-corpus models and to overcome (to some extent) the disparity among corpora, by relying on linguistic features and generic information about the nature of the datasets. We also compare the performance of different multilingual pretrained models, as well as the encoding of the relation direction, a key component for the task. Our results on the 16 datasets of the DISRPT 2021 benchmark show improvements in accuracy in (almost) all datasets compared to the monolingual models, with at best 65.91% in average accuracy, thus corresponding to a 4% improvement over the state-of-the-art.

1 Introduction

Discourse relation classification is the process of identifying the semantic-pragmatic relations between clauses or sentences, forming the discourse structure of a document. It is considered a crucial step in building knowledge graphs (Zhang et al., 2022) and NLP downstream tasks requiring textual coherence and additional context, for example, text generation (Bosselut et al., 2018) or summarization (Xu et al., 2020), text categorization (Liu et al., 2021), and question answering (Jansen et al., 2014).

These relations, also called rhetorical relations, may be considered *explicit*, when the connection is denoted by the presence of distinct words called *connectives*, or *implicit*, i.e. relations expressed without a discourse connective. For example, the *concession* relation between the two arguments is expressed with the connective *however* in the first example below, while in the second example, the relation *manner* is implicit. Most previous studies focused on implicit discourse relation classification, which is considered a harder task than the prediction of explicit relations. However, our setting requires that the system identifies both explicit and implicit relations simultaneously, a configuration that is more realistic and includes corpora with and without annotations of explicit markers.

1. [It's best to wash adults' overalls alone, especially men's.] [*However*, it is okay to wash just a few items with them, like blue jeans.] (GUM_whow_overalls)
   Label: CONCESSION

2. [The ad would have run during the World Series tomorrow,] [replacing the debut commercial of Shearson's new ad campaign, "Leadership by Example."] (wsj_2201)
   Label: EXPANSION.MANNER

Varied typologies of discourse relations have been presented in the literature and applied to annotate several corpora in different languages. In this paper, we are presenting an approach to address multilingual, multi-framework discourse relation classification. We use as a take-off point the DISRPT Shared Task on *Discourse Relation Classification across Formalisms* and its datasets covering various languages and frameworks (Zeldes et al., 2021), and compare our results to the current state-of-the-art system on the DISRPT data, which is composed of monolingual models, DisCoDisCo (Gessler et al., 2021).

Our multilingual approach is based on joint training across all available corpora, covering varied languages and discourse frameworks. We conduct experiments over 16 corpora, covering 11 languages and 3 discourse frameworks. We jointly train a classifier with all the datasets of the Shared Task,

Proceedings of the 5th Workshop on Computational Approaches to Discourse (CODI 2024), pages 91–104
March 21, 2024 ©2024 Association for Computational Linguistics

and we compare different transformer-based multilingual pretrained models. We extend the feature-based approach proposed by Gessler et al. (2021) and Gessler et al. (2022), to investigate its effect within a multilingual, cross-domain setting. Each DisCoDisCo monolingual model used different features, hence we evaluate which features are more informative in our joint setting. We also enhance our models with features targeted to our multilingual, cross-framework setting. Moreover, we test the effect of relation direction to the classification process. We examine two methods of expressing the direction of the relation between two units, either by annotating it with new tokens (Gessler et al., 2021) or by switching the position to unify it across relations (Metheniti et al., 2023). We adhere to the use of pretrained models of base size and fine-tune them for the discourse relation classification task. This ensures reproducibility, and shorter training times and computational power required.

Overall, we observe that XLM-RoBERTa models perform better than BERT models and that, contrary to the monolingual models presented in (Gessler et al., 2021), for the multilingual, cross-framework settings, using all available features is the most beneficial for all models. For the encoding of the relation position, we observe that encoding with additional tokens is more beneficial than switching the argument position, and both approaches are better than none. Finally, we report state-of-the-art performance on discourse relation classification with a maximum of 65.91% in average accuracy over all the datasets, thus outperforming previous results by about 4%. The code for fine-tuning the classifiers can be found on GitLab[1].

2 Previous Work

Most of the existing literature on discourse relation classification has focused on *implicit* relations, since explicit ones are considered easier to predict, with already accuracy above 90% with simple models and features (Pitler and Nenkova, 2009). However, it has been shown that the task can be more difficult for different domains or languages associated with small datasets (Xue et al., 2016; Scholman et al., 2021; Johannsen and Søgaard, 2013).

Approaches for **implicit relation classification** have either made use of linguistic features (Lin et al., 2009) or the least ambiguous connectives as implicit connectives (Qin et al., 2017), or even explicit connectives (Shi et al., 2017; Kurfalı and Östling, 2021). More recently, several approaches have been proposed relying on transformer-based architectures and pre-trained language models, demonstrating their effectiveness for domain transfer (Shi and Demberg, 2019), or for learning effective representation of sentences for the task (Nie et al., 2019; Sileo et al., 2019), with also attempts relying on additional pre-training of language models (Kishimoto et al., 2020).

The **DISRPT Shared Tasks** were created to motivate research on challenging discourse analysis tasks, within a multilingual, cross-framework setting, by providing unified file formats for multiple discourse datasets. There have been two editions including the task on Discourse Relation Classification (Zeldes et al., 2021; Braud et al., 2023b): since not all datasets have annotations distinguishing between explicit and implicit relations, the focus is on predicting simultaneously all types of relations. This makes for a more realistic scenario, where the nature of the relation is not assumed to be known, and it corresponds to the task performed by a discourse parser.

In DISRPT 2021 (Zeldes et al., 2021), there were two submitted systems, for 16 datasets and 11 languages. **DisCoDisCo** (Gessler et al., 2021) is a system based on monolingual and corpus-specific classifiers based on pretrained BERT language models. The inputs were enriched with handcrafted features and direction annotations (described in detail in Section 3.2). It was the most successful system, with an average 61.82% accuracy. Meanwhile, **DisCRel** (Varachkina and Pannach, 2021) aimed for a hierarchical and multilingual approach. They used sentence-level embeddings made with Sentence-BERT (Reimers and Gurevych, 2019) and stacked random forest classifiers, to predict coarse-grained relations first and then fine-grained ones. They achieved 54.23% averaged accuracy.

In DISRPT 2023 (Braud et al., 2023a), three systems were submitted. Some datasets were updated from 2021, a new framework was added (DEP, Yang and Li, 2018), and 10 new datasets and 2 new languages were added, for a total of 26 datasets and 13 languages. **HITS** (Liu et al., 2023) was the system with the best performance for 2023. It employed a combination of framework-based, multilingual, and monolingual classifiers, based on large pretrained language models. To enhance performance, they also employed bootstrap aggregat-

[1] gitlab.irit.fr/melodi/andiamo/discret_feat

ing techniques and adversarial training. The average accuracy score was 62.36% overall. When the score is calculated by including only the corpora available in 2021, the average accuracy is 58.18% (Braud et al., 2023b), thus a lower score than DisCoDisCo.[2] In **DiscReT**, we (Metheniti et al., 2023) created multilingual classifiers trained jointly on all languages and corpora. We used pretrained multilingual BERT language models (Devlin et al., 2019) and adapters (Houlsby et al., 2019). We also incorporated modifications on the label distribution to reduce the total number of labels across all corpora (see Section 3.3); however, there were problems with fully reverting the labels for the evaluation process. The average accuracy was 54.44%. **DiscoFlan** (Anuranjana, 2023) used the Flan-T5 generative language model (Chung et al., 2022) and trained monolingual models. The prompts queried the model for the relation between the two units. They post-process the model's output to match the labels of each corpus label set (see Section 3.3). Accuracy was 31.2% on average.

3 Methodology

3.1 Dataset

For the multilingual, cross-framework motivation of our experiments, we use the datasets created for the DISRPT Shared Task (Zeldes et al., 2021) for Task 3: *Discourse Relation Classification across Formalisms*.[3] We are using the datasets of the 2021 edition so that our results can be directly compared to the results of Gessler et al. (2021). These datasets are made of 16 corpora, in 11 languages, annotated in one of the following theoretical frameworks: PDTB (Penn Discourse Treebank Prasad et al., 2004), RST (Rhetorical Structure Theory, Mann and Thompson, 1988) and SDRT (Segmented Discourse Representation Theory, Asher and Lascarides, 2003). In all datasets, despite the different frameworks, discourse relations are annotated between pairs of segments that are primarily clauses or at most sentences.

3.2 DisCoDisCo augmentation methodology

Gessler et al. (2021) was the winning system of the DISRPT 2021, and compared to the results of the 2023 models on the common corpora, it is still the most successful system on the relation classification task. The submitted system is composed of multiple models; each model is a classifier fine-tuning a monolingual pretrained BERT model trained on one dataset. They use the same monolingual pretrained model for datasets of the same language but train each dataset separately. They apply two methods of feature augmentation: handcrafted features in addition to the input sequence, and annotation of the relation direction between the two units.

DisCoDisCo features Regarding the additional features of the input sequence, Gessler et al. insert manually created features as a dense embedding before the encoder. The feature vector is added between the `[CLS]` token and the input sequence tokens, and it includes sequence-level information with categorical and numerical features. Categorical features are embedded whereas numerical features are log-scaled or binned and embedded, and the feature layer is padded for the leftover dimensions.

The authors create a total of 28 features for each input sequence. These features were created by exploiting existing annotations (e.g. GENRE from the GUM corpus, SPEAKER identities from STAC corpora), by calculating them (e.g. LENGTH, DISTANCE), with the help of the syntactic parses from the DISRPT 2021 Tasks 1-2 datasets, or with external libraries (e.g. SpaCy (Honnibal et al., 2020) to eliminate stop-words for the LEXICAL OVERLAP features). The full list of these features can be found in Table 1, which includes information from Gessler et al. (2021) and the system's source code. While they generate all features for all inputs and corpora, in their submitted system for the DISRPT 2021 Shared Task, for the discourse relation classification task, they only use a few of these features for each corpus-specific model. These decisions seemed to be geared toward optimizing performance rather than being based on language, framework, or human insights; for example, only using the features of one of the units. For our experiments, we are testing both the use of all features and the use of only the "common" features that were used for at least one dataset.

Unit direction annotation Discourse relations are annotated between pairs of text segments. Some relations can be directed, meaning that the order of the arguments of the relation is meaningful. This feature depends on the way relations are encoded,

[2]Note that the comparison is inequitable, because there have been changes in some corpora, e.g. English GUM.

[3]The datasets and their statistics can be found in github.com/disrpt/sharedtask2021.

Feature in JSON	Feature	Type	Example	Description	Used
nuc_children	Nucleus' Children	Num.	2	No. of discourse units in Unit 1	5
sat_children	Satellite's Children	Num.	2	No. of discourse units in Unit 2	8
genre	Genre	Cat.	reddit	Genre of a document (where available)	5
u1_discontinuous	Discontinuous	Cat.	`True`	Whether Unit 1's tokens are not all contiguous in the text	3
u2_discontinuous	Discontinuous	Cat.	`True`	Whether Unit 2's tokens are not all contiguous in the text	5
u1_issent	Is Sentence	Cat.	`True`	Whether Unit 1 is a whole sentence	3
u2_issent	Is Sentence	Cat.	`True`	Whether Unit 2 is a whole sentence	5
u1_length	Length	Num.	9	Length of Unit 1, in tokens	-
u2_length	Length	Num.	13	Length of Unit 2, in tokens	-
length_ratio	Length Ratio	Num.	0.3	Ratio of unit 1 and unit 2's token lengths	3
u1_speaker	Name of Speaker 1	Cat.	Rainbow	Name of Speaker (available only for STAC)	-
u2_speaker	Name of Speaker 2	Cat.	Markus	Name of Speaker (available only for STAC)	-
same_speaker	Same Speaker	Cat.	`True`	Whether the same speaker produced Unit 1 and Unit 2	2
u1_func	Unit Function	Cat.	root	Universal Dependencies Relation of Unit 1's Head to the Head of the input sequence	1
u1_pos	Part of speech & Morphological Tag	Cat.	VBN	Part of speech & Morphological tag of the Unit 1's Head	-
u1_depdir	Universal Part of speech Tag	Cat.	ROOT	Part of speech of the Unit 1's Head wrt. the Head of the input sequence	8
u2_func	Unit Function	Cat.	advcl	Universal Dependencies Relation of Unit 2's Head to the Head of the input sequence	8
u2_pos	Part of speech & Morphological Tag	Cat.	VB	Part of speech & Morphological tag of the Unit 2's Head	8
u2_depdir	Universal Part of speech Tag	Cat.	LEFT	Part of speech of the Unit 2's Head wrt. the Head of the input sequence	7
doclen	Document Length	Num.	214	Length of the document, in tokens	-
u1_position	Position	Num.	0.4	Position of Unit 1 in the document, between 0.0 and 1.0	9
u2_position	Position	Num.	0.4	Position of Unit 2 in the document, between 0.0 and 1.0	-
percent_distance	Percent of distance	Num.	0.05	No. of discourse units between Unit 1 and Unit 2 divided by sequence length	-
distance	Distance	Num.	7	No. of other discourse units between Unit 1 and Unit 2	9
lex_overlap_words	Lexical Overlap	Cat.	assets sold	List of overlapping non-stoplist words in Unit 1 and Unit 2	-
lex_overlap_length	Lexical Overlap	Num.	3	No. of overlapping non-stoplist words in Unit 1 and Unit 2	1
unit1_case	Uppercased letter	Cat.	cap_initial	Whether the unit starts with a capital letter or not	1
unit2_case	Uppercased letter	Cat.	other	Whether the unit starts with a capital letter or not	1

Table 1: List of all features generated by the DisCoDisCo system, in the preprocessing stage, with descriptions. "Type" refers to whether the feature is categorical or numerical. With "No. Used" we note how many corpus-specific DisCoDisCo models used said feature (out of 16 models in total).

we could have different labels with the arguments following the order of the text (e.g. *cause vs result*), or one unique label where the first argument has always the same role compared to the second regarding the semantics of the relation. All existing studies focusing on discourse relation identification consider this information as given: they present to the learning model the arguments in the order given by the annotation, thus first, then second argument of the relation. It is not the case when one performs full discourse parsing: the parser knows that two segments are attached, but not in which order, and the segments are presented in the order of the text. In order to better understand this important aspect of the task, we investigate different encodings of this information within a transformer architecture.

In the DISRPT datasets, the pairs of segments are presented in the linear order of the text, but an additional column indicates the order of the arguments for the annotated relation. Gessler et al. introduced two pseudo-tokens (not as BERT special tokens) in order to encode the direction between the two units:

- If the direction of the relation follows the linear order of the text, a case annotated as (1>2) in DISRPT data, the } token is added after the `[CLS]` token and before Unit 1 and the > token before Unit 2.
- If the direction of the relation is reversed, a case annotated as (1<2) in DISRPT data, the < token is added after Unit 1 and the { token after Unit 2.

3.3 Proposed additional augmentation

Corpus-specific features Previous approaches to training multilingual, cross-framework classifiers with all corpora and languages reported results lower than monolingual systems. We assumed that one issue was the lack of guidance of the model, where it was hard for the model to make correlations between datasets. In order to tackle this issue, we add at the start of each sequence some additional tokens that characterize the dataset and should help the model to link samples from the same language or framework. We add as additional tokens, after the `[CLS]` token and before the input sequence tokens, the following tokens:

- Language: the language of the corpus in English (e.g. English, French, German, etc.);[4]
- Corpus: the name of the dataset in the DISRPT 2021 data (e.g. `deu.rst.pcc`, `eng.rst.rstdt`, `fra.sdrt.annodis`, etc);
- Framework: the framework name (e.g. rst, pdtb, sdrt, dep).

Feature embedding as tokens Instead of creating a dense embedding as Gessler et al. did, we are adding the additional features in the input sequence as tokens. Each feature value (numerical, categorical, and Boolean) is added to the vocabulary, in order not to be split into subwords by the tokenizer. Only the value of the feature is added, not its key, to not create an excessive amount of new tokens (e.g. all numbers encoded separately for each numerical feature). For example, the new token `0.1` does not refer to a number in the text but may refer to the feature **u1_position** or **length_ratio**, depending on its order in the input sequence. This extends the size of the vocabulary and, therefore, extends the size of the token embedding matrix of the model to match the embedding matrix of the tokenizer. This technique stays close to the process of concatenating the feature vector with the token vector while assuring reproducibility with the HuggingFace models (Wolf et al., 2020).

Unit direction unification In addition to implementing the relation direction annotation of the DisCoDisCo system (i.e. additional tokens), we are also testing the effectiveness of unifying the direction by switching unit positions. In Metheniti et al. (2023), we proposed to reorder the two units in the input sequence, to follow the order of the arguments of the relation, instead of the linear order of the text as encoded in DISRPT files. If the arguments are in the same order as in the text (1>2), then the input is unchanged, but if they are in reverse order (1<2), the units have their position switched in the input sequence of the model.

Label merging The joint training set of the 16 corpora of the DISRPT 2021 Shared Task contains 126 labels, making for a complex learning problem. These labels come from three different annotation frameworks, and sometimes overlap; for example, the labels *Expansion.Correction* in `tur.pdtb.tdb` (Turkish, PDTB) and *correction* in `eng.sdrt.stac` (English, SDRT) point to the same relation. Suggestions for unified label sets are limited to specific frameworks or do not cover all relations present in corpora (Benamara and Taboada, 2015; Braud et al., 2017; Varachkina and Pannach, 2021). We adapt the label harmonization that we proposed for the DISRPT 2023 Shared Task datasets, which implements minimal substitutions to less-frequent labels, and lower-casing (Metheniti et al., 2023). The number of our labels was reduced from 126 originally to 102 labels.

Label Filtering Multilingual, multi-framework classification models provide a probability distribution of every label included in the training set, regardless of the target language and framework. We took inspiration from the strategy of Anuranjana (2023) who addressed the problem of generating annotations that may not match the labels of the training set by filtering the output of their generative model so that it converts them to existing labels. We are also post-processing our classification model label outputs, and we keep in the predictions only labels coming from the target corpus' framework. Thus a label that is present in the combined training corpus but not in the target framework label set will not be returned, even if it were assigned a higher probability by the model.

3.4 Classification models

We fine-tune multilingual classifiers built on pretrained multilingual transformer-based models. Fine-tuning is performed with all training sets of all languages and datasets jointly, while evaluation is performed on the evaluation and test sets of each dataset individually. We used PyTorch (Paszke et al., 2019) and the HuggingFace libraries to build our classifiers, with

[4]Preliminary experiments with the language token in the corpus' original language (e.g. English, Français, Deutsch, etc.) showed the same performance as with the language token in English since the models we are using contain multilingual embeddings.

Model	DisCoDisCo 2021 (BERT)	mBERT	DistilmBERT	XLM	mBERT	DistilmBERT	XLM
Relation direction	Add. tokens		Add. tokens			Switching units	
No features	60.41	59.54	56.81	62.09	58.36	55.69	60.52
Common DisCoDisCo features	61.82	62.56	60.92	64.86	59.75	57.24	61.14
All DisCoDisCo features	-	63.09	60.28	64.50	62.33	59.08	**63.95**
Language, Corpus, Framework (LCF)	-	61.76	59.17	64.13	58.34	55.69	60.52
LCF + Common	-	63.46	**62.01**	**65.91**	61.12	57.75	62.88
LCF + All	-	**63.67**	61.92	65.53	**63.89**	**59.65**	63.51

Table 2: Average accuracies of the models, reported on the test set. We report the results of the DisCoDisCo system with individual models trained with or without their specific features and the DisCoDisCo relation annotation. For our multilingual models, we report models trained with the DisCoDisCo direction annotation ("Add. tokens") or the DiscReT direction normalization ("Switching units"). The models were trained with different sets of features or without. In bold are the best scores for each column, so for model and direction fixed.

the models: `bert-base-multilingual-cased`,[5] `distilbert-base-multilingual-cased`,[6] and `xlm-roberta-base`.[7] Each classification model is trained for 10 epochs, keeping the best result out of the 10 epochs, based on the development set. The fine-tuning process for these models, per epoch, was around 1 hour for DistilmBERT, 2 hours for mBERT, and 2 hours 10 minutes for XLM-RoBERTa, on a GPU cluster with 4 Nvidia Geforce GTX 1080TI graphics cards.

Multilingual BERT (mBERT) (Devlin et al., 2019) is a pretrained model based on BERT. It has been trained on Wikipedia data of the top 104 languages, with masked language modeling (MLM) and next-sentence prediction objectives. The base and cased version of the model contains 12 layers, 12 heads, and 177M parameters. We selected it, in order to compare it with the DisCoDisCo models that were built on monolingual BERT-base architectures. DistilmBERT (Sanh et al., 2019) is a multilingual distilled version of mBERT with the same training set and objectives. The base and cased model has 6 layers, 12 heads, and 134M parameters. As a lighter version of BERT, it would be interesting to compare a BERT-based model with fewer parameters. XLM-RoBERTa (Conneau et al., 2020) is a multilingual pretrained model based on RoBERTa. It is pretrained on 2.5TB of filtered CommonCrawl data in 100 languages. The base version of the model has 12 layers and 279M parameters. RoBERTa models have outperformed BERT in several datasets in the Shared Task (Liu et al., 2023), therefore we decided to include them in our experiments.

[5]huggingface.co/bert-base-multilingual-cased
[6]huggingface.co/distilbert-base-multilingual-cased
[7]huggingface.co/xlm-roberta-base

4 Results

In Table 2 we present the average accuracy for all the multilingual classification models we trained, with different pretrained models, with different combinations of features, and with different handling of relation annotation. We report the results of DisCoDisCo (Gessler et al., 2021) in the second column, and the results obtained by our system in the others. The second row indicates how the direction of the relation is encoded, based on unit direction annotation ("Add. tokens") as in Gessler et al. or by unit direction modification ("Switching units") as in Metheniti et al. In the Appendix, the results for individual test sets can be found: in Table 4 for models trained with features and direction annotation based on additional tokens, in Table 5 for models trained with features and direction unification based on switching units, and in Table 6 for models trained without features, with different direction handling (including no encoding of the direction at all).

Overall, our models outperform the state-of-the-art system DisCoDisCo in several settings, when linguistic features (i.e. "Common/All DisCoDisCo features") and/or dataset information ("LCF", Language, Corpus, Framework) are used, with at best 65.91% in average accuracy, against 61.82% for DisCoDisCo. This demonstrates that single multilingual, cross-framework models are able to leverage correlations between the different datasets, and thus take advantage of a larger amount of data if fed with additional information.

For the models most similar to DisCoDisCo, i.e. using mBERT with annotations of direction ("Add. Tokens"), our results are very close to theirs: 60.41% *vs* 59.54% ("No features") and 61.82% *vs* 62.56% ("Common features"). XLM-RoBERTa models performed better than the mBERT-based models and also surpassed the lightweight DistilmBERT models. They were the ones that steadily surpassed the DisCoDisCo system, with 62.09% and 64.86% respectively for the same configurations. Moreover, the mBERT models also performed better than the DisCoDisCo baseline, when they were provided with the LCF tokens, either when limited to "Common features" (63.46%), or when using "All features" (63.67%).

Observing the different sets of features that we used, the addition of any features improves the accuracy of multilingual classification, and the best configuration was, in most cases, the features used by Gessler et al. (2021), with the addition of corpus-specific features. When we used additional tokens to encode the direction of the relation, the most beneficial set of features for all the models was the "common" features, i.e. only the features used by at least one model in the DisCoDisCo 2021 system. We notice that the model with the highest accuracy of all is the XLM-RoBERTa model, using this encoding of the direction and the common DisCoDisCo and LCF features. However, using all features in this setting leads to very similar results (-0.4%). When the direction is encoded by switching the units, the situation is reversed: results are better when using all the features rather than only the common ones. The addition of the LCF tokens, alongside the DisCoDisCo features, showed an increase in accuracy as well. For the XLM-RoBERTa models, the presence of all features was also most beneficial, but not necessarily the presence of the LCF features.

Looking at individual datasets, our models outperformed the DisCoDisCo 2021 system in all but one dataset, the Basque `eus.rst.ert` (by 0.15%, Table 4). For some datasets, the improvement was significant (with XLM-RoBERTa models), for example up to 15.72% for `spa.rst.sctb` (Spanish) and over 8% for `fas.rst.prstc` (Farsi) and `zho.rst.sctb` (Chinese). The mBERT models trailed not far behind the XLM-RoBERTa ones, however, there was an instance where an mBERT model was more successful, mBERT with all DisCoDisCo and LCF features for `fra.sdrt.annodis` (French). Also, models with all features were more successful for the French, Portuguese, and Spanish datasets.

Comparing the performance between the two ways of handling the direction of the relation, the direction annotation based on additional tokens was the better option for most datasets when the DisCoDisCo features were used. However, for the Dutch `nld.rst.nldt` and Portuguese `por.rst.cstn` datasets, the performance was identical with either setting. Observing the effect of the direction handling without the addition of features, we note that, while the method based on additional tokens performed better overall, there were instances where switching the arguments was better (English `eng.rst.rstdt`, `eng.sdrt.stac`, Spanish `spa.rst.rststb`), and one dataset for which no change was marginally better (Portuguese `por.rst.cstn`), see Tables 4, 5 and 6 in Appendix.

5 Discussion

Our multilingual approach outperformed the monolingual approach of DisCoDisCo (Gessler et al., 2021) in all but one dataset, the Basque one. Our initial assumption was that the use of the multilingual setting would be beneficial since the use of more data is favorable to the models and the instances of less frequent labels would be higher. Indeed, for the very small datasets `spa.rst.sctb` (Spanish, 326 train sentences) and `zho.rst.sctb` (Chinese, 361 train sentences), the improvement was elevated with all models. For the largest datasets (`eng.pdtb.pdtb`, English, 44.5K train sentences; `rus.rst.rrt`, Russian, 19K train sentences; `tur.pdtb.tdb`, Turkish, 25K train sentences) there was also an improvement of $3 - 4\%$. In the case of `eus.rst.ert` (Basque) with 1.6K train sentences, we observed the label distribution; it has 25 unique labels and similar distributions to `spa.rst.rststb`, `spa.rst.sctb`, and `zho.rst.sctb`. We observe the classification report results (Pedregosa et al., 2011) for the most successful model in Table 3. In the 2021 edition of the data, there were a few labels in this dataset with misspellings (*motibation* instead of *motivation*), which were corrected in the 2023 edition. These labels were not changed by the DiscReT mappings and were not corrected in order to stay true to the 2021 data. Even with these errors, however, this is not the smallest, most complex, or relation-rich dataset. Therefore, the failure of the Basque dataset may be related to the language's typological dif-

	precision	recall	f1-score	support
motibation	0	0	0	2
summary	0	0	0	3
concession	0.58	0.65	0.61	17
purpose	0.87	0.80	0.83	50
joint	0	0	0	1
causation	0.51	0.51	0.51	37
interpretation	0.50	0.08	0.13	13
circumstance	0.76	0.67	0.71	48
expansion.conjunction	0.28	0.48	0.35	25
unconditional	0.50	0.25	0.33	4
evaluation	0.30	0.56	0.39	16
anthitesis	0	0	0	5
unless	0.59	0.62	0.60	21
solution-hood	0	0	0	8
result	0.50	0.53	0.51	34
background	0.52	0.76	0.62	29
means	0.69	0.68	0.68	37
conditional	1.00	0.33	0.50	9
preparation	0.90	0.85	0.87	73
elaboration	0.66	0.69	0.67	140
list	0.63	0.44	0.52	54
evidence	0.40	0.25	0.31	8
sequence	0.37	0.48	0.42	23
justify	0.42	0.62	0.50	8
restatement	0.60	0.23	0.33	13
accuracy			0.60	678
macro avg	0.41	0.37	0.37	678
weighted avg	0.62	0.60	0.60	678

Table 3: Classification report for the `eus.rst.ert` (Basque) test set, with the XLM-RoBERTa model with Common and LCF features (epoch 8).

ference from the rest, as it benefits less from the multilingual pretrained language models.

Comparing the use of different models, we observe that the XLM-RoBERTa base models are more successful, probably because of their larger number of parameters. For the original DisCoDisCo model, the use of BERT-based models was obligatory for most languages, as at the time there were fewer options available, especially for less common languages. The mBERT base models were not far less successful than the XLM-RoBERTa, with the help of features. The DistilmBERT models are far too optimized and lightweight, missing parameters that were, as is shown, necessary for the classification process.

Overall, the addition of features, even as simple as additional tokens in the input sequence, improved classification accuracy significantly. In the monolingual setting, it was possible to test different feature sets to configure which was the best, but for the multilingual setting, selecting features is not straightforward, as different corpora contain different annotations (e.g. the GUM and STAC corpora are the only ones with the SPEAKER information). The small differences in accuracy between using all features and only the ones used for the DisCoDisCo 2021 system are produced because, in a multilingual setting with all the datasets used jointly, some features that are informative for some corpora will not be for others, if the annotation does not exist. The addition of the language, framework, and corpus name was also beneficial, in order to annotate the presence of corpus-specific features, even if the information of language is not directly accessible to the model.

Finally, regarding the relation direction, human intuition is different than the way models process input. The proposal to unify all relation directions by switching the arguments (Metheniti et al., 2023) sounds beneficial in theory, especially when the same relation can be initiated in either unit. However, transformer-based models are not necessarily sensitive to word order; even though positional information is injected in them, some research suggests that they are not sensitive to permutations (Pham et al., 2021; Gupta et al., 2021). However, other research supports that not all permutations are processed equally (Sinha et al., 2021) and that the models learn structural information (Wang and Chen, 2020; Papadimitriou et al., 2022). It is, therefore, understandable that the presence of additional tokens noting the direction as in (Gessler et al., 2021) may communicate more information about the relation direction to the models, than switching unit positions. However, there was also a smaller improvement with the unification of the direction; this points to the models either being capable of constructing a rudimentary structure of the two arguments or the models not being completely insensible to word order.

6 Conclusion

In this paper, we reprised the DISRPT 2021 Shared Task on Relation Classification across Formalisms and revisited the most successful model of the last two editions, DisCoDisCo (Gessler et al., 2021). We adapted DisCoDisCo methodologies to multilingual relation classification models, with the addition of techniques and suggestions from other participating teams of the 2023 edition (Metheniti et al., 2023; Anuranjana, 2023).

We found that XLM-RoBERTa models outperform BERT models, in the multilingual setting, especially with the presence of DisCoDisCo's handcrafted features. The most successful model was trained only with the features used by DisCoDisCo models, as opposed to all features created in the preprocessing stage—but this success was only marginal to the use of all features, and was not true for all architectures. The addition of corpus-specific tokens (language, corpus name, framework) was also beneficial in the multilingual setting. Finally, annotating the relation direction with additional tokens was more successful than unifying the position of the two arguments, due to the make of transformer-based models. It should be noted that this information proved crucial and that further studies are needed on this aspect, in particular on the possibility of predicting direction and on the heterogeneity of existing corpora with regard to its encoding.

As a future direction, we are considering using our approach on the updated DISRPT 2023 benchmark, which includes modified corpora, additional corpora in more languages, and some small validation datasets that allow for testing out-of-domain performance.

Acknowledgements

This work is supported by the AnDiaMO project (ANR-21-CE23-0020). Our work has benefited from the AI Interdisciplinary Institute ANITI. ANITI is funded by the French "Investing for the Future – PIA3" program under the Grant agreement n°ANR-19-PI3A-0004. This work is also partially supported by the SLANT project (ANR-19-CE23-0025). Chloé Braud and Philippe Muller are part of the program DesCartes and are also supported by the National Research Foundation, Prime Minister's Office, Singapore under its Campus for Research Excellence and Technological Enterprise (CREATE) program. The work was also supported by the ANR grant SUMM-RE (ANR-20-CE23-0017).

References

Kaveri Anuranjana. 2023. DiscoFlan: Instruction fine-tuning and refined text generation for discourse relation label classification. In *Proceedings of the 3rd Shared Task on Discourse Relation Parsing and Treebanking (DISRPT 2023)*, pages 22–28, Toronto, Canada. The Association for Computational Linguistics.

Nicholas Asher and Alex Lascarides. 2003. *Logics of Conversation*. Cambridge University Press.

Farah Benamara and Maite Taboada. 2015. Mapping different rhetorical relation annotations: A proposal. In *Proceedings of the Fourth Joint Conference on Lexical and Computational Semantics*, pages 147–152, Denver, Colorado. Association for Computational Linguistics.

Antoine Bosselut, Asli Celikyilmaz, Xiaodong He, Jianfeng Gao, Po-Sen Huang, and Yejin Choi. 2018. Discourse-aware neural rewards for coherent text generation. In *Proceedings of the 2018 Conference of the North American Chapter of the Association for Computational Linguistics: Human Language Technologies, Volume 1 (Long Papers)*, pages 173–184, New Orleans, Louisiana. Association for Computational Linguistics.

Chloé Braud, Maximin Coavoux, and Anders Søgaard. 2017. Cross-lingual RST discourse parsing. In *Proceedings of the 15th Conference of the European Chapter of the Association for Computational Linguistics: Volume 1, Long Papers*, pages 292–304, Valencia, Spain. Association for Computational Linguistics.

Chloé Braud, Yang Janet Liu, Eleni Metheniti, Philippe Muller, Laura Rivière, Attapol Rutherford, and Amir Zeldes. 2023a. The DISRPT 2023 shared task on elementary discourse unit segmentation, connective detection, and relation classification. In *Proceedings of the 3rd Shared Task on Discourse Relation Parsing and Treebanking (DISRPT 2023)*, pages 1–21, Toronto, Canada. The Association for Computational Linguistics.

Chloé Braud, Yang Janet Liu, Eleni Metheniti, Philippe Muller, Laura Rivière, Attapol Rutherford, and Amir Zeldes, editors. 2023b. *Proceedings of the 3rd Shared Task on Discourse Relation Parsing and Treebanking (DISRPT 2023)*. The Association for Computational Linguistics, Toronto, Canada.

Hyung Won Chung, Le Hou, Shayne Longpre, Barret Zoph, Yi Tay, William Fedus, Eric Li, Xuezhi Wang, Mostafa Dehghani, Siddhartha Brahma, et al. 2022. Scaling instruction-finetuned language models. *arXiv preprint arXiv:2210.11416*.

Alexis Conneau, Kartikay Khandelwal, Naman Goyal, Vishrav Chaudhary, Guillaume Wenzek, Francisco Guzmán, Edouard Grave, Myle Ott, Luke Zettlemoyer, and Veselin Stoyanov. 2020. Unsupervised cross-lingual representation learning at scale. In *Proceedings of the 58th Annual Meeting of the Association for Computational Linguistics*, pages 8440–8451, Online. Association for Computational Linguistics.

Jacob Devlin, Ming-Wei Chang, Kenton Lee, and Kristina Toutanova. 2019. BERT: Pre-training of deep bidirectional transformers for language understanding. In *Proceedings of the 2019 Conference of the North American Chapter of the Association for Computational Linguistics: Human Language Technologies, Volume 1 (Long and Short Papers)*, pages 4171–4186, Minneapolis, Minnesota. Association for Computational Linguistics.

Luke Gessler, Shabnam Behzad, Yang Janet Liu, Siyao Peng, Yilun Zhu, and Amir Zeldes. 2021. DisCoDisCo at the DISRPT2021 shared task: A system for discourse segmentation, classification, and connective detection. In *Proceedings of the 2nd Shared Task on Discourse Relation Parsing and Treebanking (DISRPT 2021)*, pages 51–62, Punta Cana, Dominican Republic. Association for Computational Linguistics.

Luke Gessler, Lauren Levine, and Amir Zeldes. 2022. Midas loop: A prioritized human-in-the-loop annotation for large scale multilayer data. In *Proceedings of the 16th Linguistic Annotation Workshop (LAW-XVI) within LREC2022*, pages 103–110, Marseille, France. European Language Resources Association.

Ashim Gupta, Giorgi Kvernadze, and Vivek Srikumar. 2021. Bert & family eat word salad: Experiments with text understanding. In *Proceedings of the AAAI Conference on Artificial Intelligence*, volume 35, pages 12946–12954.

Matthew Honnibal, Ines Montani, Sofie Van Landeghem, and Adriane Boyd. 2020. spaCy: Industrial-strength Natural Language Processing in Python. Technical report, Zenodo.

Neil Houlsby, Andrei Giurgiu, Stanislaw Jastrzebski, Bruna Morrone, Quentin De Laroussilhe, Andrea Gesmundo, Mona Attariyan, and Sylvain Gelly. 2019. Parameter-efficient transfer learning for NLP. In *International Conference on Machine Learning*, pages 2790–2799. PMLR.

Peter Jansen, Mihai Surdeanu, and Peter Clark. 2014. Discourse complements lexical semantics for non-factoid answer reranking. In *Proceedings of the 52nd Annual Meeting of the Association for Computational Linguistics (Volume 1: Long Papers)*, pages 977–986, Baltimore, Maryland. Association for Computational Linguistics.

Anders Johannsen and Anders Søgaard. 2013. Disambiguating explicit discourse connectives without oracles. In *Proceedings of the Sixth International Joint Conference on Natural Language Processing*, pages 997–1001, Nagoya, Japan. Asian Federation of Natural Language Processing.

Yudai Kishimoto, Yugo Murawaki, and Sadao Kurohashi. 2020. Adapting BERT to implicit discourse relation classification with a focus on discourse connectives. In *Proceedings of the Twelfth Language Resources and Evaluation Conference*, pages 1152–1158, Marseille, France. European Language Resources Association.

Murathan Kurfalı and Robert Östling. 2021. Let's be explicit about that: Distant supervision for implicit discourse relation classification via connective prediction. In *Proceedings of the 1st Workshop on Understanding Implicit and Underspecified Language*, pages 1–10, Online. Association for Computational Linguistics.

Ziheng Lin, Min-Yen Kan, and Hwee Tou Ng. 2009. Recognizing implicit discourse relations in the Penn Discourse Treebank. In *Proceedings of the 2009 Conference on Empirical Methods in Natural Language Processing*, pages 343–351, Singapore. Association for Computational Linguistics.

Wei Liu, Yi Fan, and Michael Strube. 2023. HITS at DISRPT 2023: Discourse segmentation, connective detection, and relation classification. In *Proceedings of the 3rd Shared Task on Discourse Relation Parsing and Treebanking (DISRPT 2023)*, pages 43–49, Toronto, Canada. The Association for Computational Linguistics.

Xin Liu, Jiefu Ou, Yangqiu Song, and Xin Jiang. 2021. Exploring discourse structures for argument impact classification. In *Proceedings of the 59th Annual Meeting of the Association for Computational Linguistics and the 11th International Joint Conference on Natural Language Processing (Volume 1: Long Papers)*, pages 3958–3969, Online. Association for Computational Linguistics.

William C. Mann and Sandra A. Thompson. 1988. Rhetorical Structure Theory: Toward a functional theory of text organization. *Text*, 8:243–281.

Eleni Metheniti, Chloé Braud, Philippe Muller, and Laura Rivière. 2023. DisCut and DiscReT: MELODI at DISRPT 2023. In *Proceedings of the 3rd Shared Task on Discourse Relation Parsing and Treebanking (DISRPT 2023)*, pages 29–42, Toronto, Canada. The Association for Computational Linguistics.

Allen Nie, Erin Bennett, and Noah Goodman. 2019. DisSent: Learning sentence representations from explicit discourse relations. In *Proceedings of the 57th Annual Meeting of the Association for Computational Linguistics*, pages 4497–4510, Florence, Italy. Association for Computational Linguistics.

Isabel Papadimitriou, Richard Futrell, and Kyle Mahowald. 2022. When classifying arguments, BERT doesn't care about word order...except when it matters. In *Proceedings of the Society for Computation in Linguistics 2022*, pages 203–205, online. Association for Computational Linguistics.

Adam Paszke, Sam Gross, Francisco Massa, Adam Lerer, James Bradbury, Gregory Chanan, Trevor Killeen, Zeming Lin, Natalia Gimelshein, Luca Antiga, Alban Desmaison, Andreas Kopf, Edward Yang, Zachary DeVito, Martin Raison, Alykhan Tejani, Sasank Chilamkurthy, Benoit Steiner, Lu Fang, Junjie Bai, and Soumith Chintala. 2019. Pytorch: An imperative style, high-performance deep learning library. In *Advances in Neural Information Processing Systems 32*, pages 8024–8035. Curran Associates, Inc.

F. Pedregosa, G. Varoquaux, A. Gramfort, V. Michel, B. Thirion, O. Grisel, M. Blondel, P. Prettenhofer, R. Weiss, V. Dubourg, J. Vanderplas, A. Passos, D. Cournapeau, M. Brucher, M. Perrot, and E. Duchesnay. 2011. Scikit-learn: Machine learning in

Python. *Journal of Machine Learning Research*, 12:2825–2830.

Thang Pham, Trung Bui, Long Mai, and Anh Nguyen. 2021. Out of order: How important is the sequential order of words in a sentence in natural language understanding tasks? In *Findings of the Association for Computational Linguistics: ACL-IJCNLP 2021*, pages 1145–1160, Online. Association for Computational Linguistics.

Emily Pitler and Ani Nenkova. 2009. Using syntax to disambiguate explicit discourse connectives in text. In *Proceedings of the ACL-IJCNLP 2009 Conference Short Papers*, pages 13–16, Suntec, Singapore. Association for Computational Linguistics.

Rashmi Prasad, Eleni Miltsakaki, Aravind Joshi, and Bonnie Webber. 2004. Annotation and data mining of the Penn Discourse TreeBank. In *Proceedings of the Workshop on Discourse Annotation*, pages 88–95, Barcelona, Spain. Association for Computational Linguistics.

Lianhui Qin, Zhisong Zhang, Hai Zhao, Zhiting Hu, and Eric Xing. 2017. Adversarial connective-exploiting networks for implicit discourse relation classification. In *Proceedings of the 55th Annual Meeting of the Association for Computational Linguistics (Volume 1: Long Papers)*, pages 1006–1017, Vancouver, Canada. Association for Computational Linguistics.

Nils Reimers and Iryna Gurevych. 2019. Sentence-BERT: Sentence embeddings using Siamese BERT-networks. In *Proceedings of the 2019 Conference on Empirical Methods in Natural Language Processing and the 9th International Joint Conference on Natural Language Processing (EMNLP-IJCNLP)*, pages 3982–3992, Hong Kong, China. Association for Computational Linguistics.

Victor Sanh, Thomas Wolf, and Sebastian Ruder. 2019. A hierarchical multi-task approach for learning embeddings from semantic tasks. In *Proceedings of the AAAI Conference on Artificial Intelligence*, volume 33, pages 6949–6956.

Merel Scholman, Tianai Dong, Frances Yung, and Vera Demberg. 2021. Comparison of methods for explicit discourse connective identification across various domains. In *Proceedings of the 2nd Workshop on Computational Approaches to Discourse*, pages 95–106, Punta Cana, Dominican Republic and Online. Association for Computational Linguistics.

Wei Shi and Vera Demberg. 2019. Learning to explicitate connectives with Seq2Seq network for implicit discourse relation classification. In *Proceedings of the 13th International Conference on Computational Semantics - Long Papers*, pages 188–199, Gothenburg, Sweden. Association for Computational Linguistics.

Wei Shi, Frances Yung, Raphael Rubino, and Vera Demberg. 2017. Using explicit discourse connectives in translation for implicit discourse relation classification. In *Proceedings of the Eighth International Joint Conference on Natural Language Processing (Volume 1: Long Papers)*, pages 484–495, Taipei, Taiwan. Asian Federation of Natural Language Processing.

Damien Sileo, Tim Van De Cruys, Camille Pradel, and Philippe Muller. 2019. Mining discourse markers for unsupervised sentence representation learning. In *Proceedings of the 2019 Conference of the North American Chapter of the Association for Computational Linguistics: Human Language Technologies, Volume 1 (Long and Short Papers)*, pages 3477–3486, Minneapolis, Minnesota. Association for Computational Linguistics.

Koustuv Sinha, Prasanna Parthasarathi, Joelle Pineau, and Adina Williams. 2021. UnNatural Language Inference. In *Proceedings of the 59th Annual Meeting of the Association for Computational Linguistics and the 11th International Joint Conference on Natural Language Processing (Volume 1: Long Papers)*, pages 7329–7346, Online. Association for Computational Linguistics.

Hanna Varachkina and Franziska Pannach. 2021. A unified approach to discourse relation classification in nine languages. In *Proceedings of the 2nd Shared Task on Discourse Relation Parsing and Treebanking (DISRPT 2021)*, pages 46–50, Punta Cana, Dominican Republic. Association for Computational Linguistics.

Yu-An Wang and Yun-Nung Chen. 2020. What do position embeddings learn? an empirical study of pre-trained language model positional encoding. In *Proceedings of the 2020 Conference on Empirical Methods in Natural Language Processing (EMNLP)*, pages 6840–6849, Online. Association for Computational Linguistics.

Thomas Wolf, Lysandre Debut, Victor Sanh, Julien Chaumond, Clement Delangue, Anthony Moi, Pierric Cistac, Tim Rault, Remi Louf, Morgan Funtowicz, Joe Davison, Sam Shleifer, Patrick von Platen, Clara Ma, Yacine Jernite, Julien Plu, Canwen Xu, Teven Le Scao, Sylvain Gugger, Mariama Drame, Quentin Lhoest, and Alexander Rush. 2020. Transformers: State-of-the-art natural language processing. In *Proceedings of the 2020 Conference on Empirical Methods in Natural Language Processing: System Demonstrations*, pages 38–45, Online. Association for Computational Linguistics.

Jiacheng Xu, Zhe Gan, Yu Cheng, and Jingjing Liu. 2020. Discourse-aware neural extractive text summarization. In *Proceedings of the 58th Annual Meeting of the Association for Computational Linguistics*, pages 5021–5031, Online. Association for Computational Linguistics.

Nianwen Xue, Hwee Tou Ng, Sameer Pradhan, Attapol Rutherford, Bonnie Webber, Chuan Wang, and Hongmin Wang. 2016. CoNLL 2016 shared task on multilingual shallow discourse parsing. In *Proceedings of the CoNLL-16 shared task*, pages 1–19, Berlin, Germany. Association for Computational Linguistics.

An Yang and Sujian Li. 2018. SciDTB: Discourse dependency TreeBank for scientific abstracts. In *Proceedings of the 56th Annual Meeting of the Association for Computational Linguistics (Volume 2: Short Papers)*, pages 444–449, Melbourne, Australia. Association for Computational Linguistics.

Amir Zeldes, Yang Janet Liu, Mikel Iruskieta, Philippe Muller, Chloé Braud, and Sonia Badene. 2021. The DISRPT 2021 shared task on elementary discourse unit segmentation, connective detection, and relation classification. In *Proceedings of the 2nd Shared Task on Discourse Relation Parsing and Treebanking (DISRPT 2021)*, pages 1–12, Punta Cana, Dominican Republic. Association for Computational Linguistics.

Hongming Zhang, Xin Liu, Haojie Pan, Haowen Ke, Jiefu Ou, Tianqing Fang, and Yangqiu Song. 2022. ASER: Towards large-scale commonsense knowledge acquisition via higher-order selectional preference over eventualities. *Artificial Intelligence*, 309:103740.

A Appendix: Full classification results

Model	Control	m	d	x	m	d	x	m	d	x	m	d	x	m	d	x
Features		Common Features			All Features			LCF			LCF + Common Features			LCF + All Features		
deu.rst.pcc	39.23	41.54	38.46	45.00	42.69	37.69	**48.85**	36.92	31.15	40.00	41.92	41.15	44.23	40.38	39.62	43.08
eng.pdtb.pdtb	74.44	73.64	70.71	74.48	73.68	70.14	74.97	74.61	72.66	76.83	74.48	72.18	**77.45**	74.39	72.35	76.25
eng.rst.gum	66.76	66.43	64.61	68.15	67.29	65.76	68.05	63.18	61.98	67.43	67.34	65.57	67.96	67.05	65.04	**68.87**
eng.rst.rstdt	67.10	61.48	59.49	63.48	58.75	56.52	59.95	68.26	67.66	69.98	69.10	68.17	**70.44**	69.88	67.94	68.96
eng.sdrt.stac	65.03	62.78	63.18	65.83	64.04	63.18	65.23	58.81	59.40	62.25	63.58	61.92	**66.16**	62.85	61.92	65.50
eus.rst.ert	**60.62**	56.93	56.49	57.23	58.26	56.78	56.93	55.31	54.28	57.37	57.23	58.55	60.47	56.78	56.49	57.82
fas.rst.prstc	52.53	58.11	56.08	60.64	57.26	56.08	59.97	55.91	53.72	59.80	58.11	56.25	**60.98**	58.45	55.07	58.11
fra.sdrt.annodis	46.40	50.56	45.44	48.96	**51.52**	44.16	47.20	48.80	43.20	49.28	49.28	44.48	49.28	51.36	44.48	47.84
nld.rst.nldt	55.21	51.84	51.53	57.67	53.07	52.45	**58.59**	48.16	46.01	56.75	54.29	49.39	**58.59**	54.60	51.84	57.06
por.rst.cstn	64.34	67.28	68.01	**69.85**	68.75	66.54	68.38	68.38	63.97	68.38	68.75	69.12	69.49	**69.85**	66.54	68.75
rus.rst.rrt	66.44	68.91	67.25	71.02	68.73	66.48	**71.30**	65.04	63.74	67.71	68.66	67.39	71.19	69.47	68.34	70.59
spa.rst.rststb	54.23	55.16	51.64	57.75	55.4	51.64	54.93	53.99	50.47	56.57	56.81	54.69	55.16	56.81	54.93	**59.39**
spa.rst.sctb	66.04	71.70	75.47	76.10	75.47	72.33	75.47	74.84	74.84	74.84	73.58	78.62	78.62	73.58	79.25	**81.76**
tur.pdtb.tdb	60.09	58.53	54.27	62.80	58.77	54.27	62.32	57.11	54.50	63.51	57.35	55.69	62.80	56.87	57.58	**64.22**
zho.pdtb.cdtb	86.49	87.47	85.36	**89.58**	87.86	85.62	88.79	87.73	84.30	88.65	88.13	84.83	89.45	88.52	85.22	88.52
zho.rst.sctb	64.15	68.55	66.67	69.18	67.92	64.78	71.07	71.07	64.78	66.67	66.67	64.15	**72.33**	67.92	64.15	71.70
AVERAGE	61.82	62.56	60.92	64.86	63.09	60.28	64.50	61.76	59.17	64.13	63.46	62.01	**65.91**	63.67	61.92	65.53

Table 4: Results of models with features and direction normalization based on additional tokens as in Gessler et al. (2021), for all datasets. The models are: DisCoDisCo 2021 System with features (Control), mBERT (m), DistilmBERT (d), and XLM-RoBERTa (x).

Model	Control	m	d	x	m	d	x	m	d	x	m	d	x	m	d	x
Features		Common Features			All Features			LCF			LCF + Common Features			LCF + All Features		
deu.rst.pcc	39.23	33.08	33.46	41.92	39.62	35.77	43.08	31.92	26.15	35.00	37.31	33.08	40.77	40.38	35.77	**43.46**
eng.pdtb.pdtb	74.44	70.98	68.37	71.78	72.66	69.34	73.37	72.44	70.05	73.90	73.55	70.45	74.52	75.01	71.42	**75.45**
eng.rst.gum	66.76	63.46	61.65	64.04	**67.53**	61.65	67.38	58.54	56.10	61.50	64.71	62.41	64.99	66.38	63.89	66.52
eng.rst.rstdt	67.10	60.56	59.54	60.70	59.63	58.42	61.21	65.89	63.62	66.73	67.80	66.87	67.89	68.82	67.70	**69.28**
eng.sdrt.stac	65.03	64.17	62.58	66.62	64.37	62.32	**67.09**	59.54	58.68	61.79	63.05	62.78	64.83	64.17	62.45	66.49
eus.rst.ert	**60.62**	53.54	52.65	53.98	57.52	56.19	57.82	50.44	45.43	51.62	54.57	51.18	53.39	59.59	53.39	56.49
fas.rst.prstc	52.53	53.21	51.18	55.24	57.43	53.38	**59.12**	50.68	49.16	53.89	53.38	51.18	56.93	58.95	55.24	57.60
fra.sdrt.annodis	46.40	48.16	42.72	47.84	48.64	40.96	48.16	47.84	43.20	48.48	**49.44**	42.24	46.88	48.96	38.24	45.28
nld.rst.nldt	55.21	50.92	45.40	51.53	53.37	48.77	**58.90**	45.40	41.72	51.23	51.23	43.87	55.21	55.21	51.53	53.68
por.rst.cstn	64.34	68.01	65.44	68.38	68.75	66.54	**70.59**	66.54	67.28	68.38	66.91	64.71	68.01	67.28	63.60	67.65
rus.rst.rrt	66.44	66.51	64.69	67.82	68.87	67.18	**70.10**	62.26	58.78	63.00	66.41	63.74	66.94	68.62	66.76	69.26
spa.rst.rststb	54.23	54.93	52.82	55.16	54.93	51.41	56.34	54.69	50.94	53.99	55.63	51.41	55.87	**56.57**	53.05	55.40
spa.rst.sctb	66.04	71.07	66.67	71.07	72.96	71.07	72.33	69.18	67.30	72.33	74.21	70.44	**79.25**	78.62	69.81	74.84
tur.pdtb.tdb	60.09	50.24	48.34	54.74	56.64	54.03	**61.61**	50.24	49.76	57.11	50.00	49.76	56.87	57.58	55.45	60.19
zho.pdtb.cdtb	86.49	84.30	83.11	85.22	86.41	84.70	87.60	84.30	81.93	86.54	84.96	83.25	85.88	**87.60**	83.91	87.20
zho.rst.sctb	64.15	62.89	57.23	62.26	67.92	63.52	**68.55**	63.52	61.01	62.89	64.78	56.60	67.92	68.55	62.26	67.30
AVERAGE	61.82	59.75	57.24	61.14	62.33	59.08	**63.95**	58.34	55.69	60.52	61.12	57.75	62.88	63.89	59.65	63.51

Table 5: Results of models with features and direction normalization based on switching units as in Metheniti et al. (2023), for all datasets. The models are: DisCoDisCo 2021 System with features (Control), mBERT (m), DistilmBERT (d), and XLM-RoBERTa (x).

Model	**Control**	**m**	**d**	**x**	**m**	**d**	**x**	**m**	**d**	**x**
Direction		**No change**			**Switching units**			**Add. tokens**		
deu.rst.pcc	33.85	31.15	28.46	35.77	31.92	26.15	35.00	38.46	33.08	**42.31**
eng.pdtb.pdtb	**75.63**	65.22	63.89	68.68	71.95	70.05	73.90	72.35	69.87	73.99
eng.rst.gum	**62.65**	51.08	47.97	54.95	60.21	56.10	61.50	57.29	53.18	60.26
eng.rst.rstdt	66.45	49.42	48.40	50.95	64.73	63.62	**66.73**	52.44	51.14	55.45
eng.sdrt.stac	59.67	53.64	53.58	57.28	57.62	58.68	**61.79**	54.70	55.30	57.62
eus.rst.ert	**59.59**	49.85	46.31	50.44	50.74	45.43	51.62	57.52	51.03	57.08
fas.rst.prstc	51.18	51.86	48.82	54.90	50.84	49.16	53.89	56.42	53.38	**58.45**
fra.sdrt.annodis	48.32	48.64	42.88	48.80	47.68	43.20	48.48	**49.28**	44.16	48.80
nld.rst.nldt	52.15	47.55	42.33	51.84	45.40	41.72	51.23	48.16	46.01	**57.98**
por.rst.cstn	67.28	66.18	64.71	**69.49**	68.01	67.28	68.38	67.65	64.34	69.12
rus.rst.rrt	65.46	59.69	57.72	62.50	62.29	58.78	63.00	65.67	63.67	**67.39**
spa.rst.rststb	54.23	52.82	51.17	51.41	52.35	50.94	53.99	53.99	50.47	**57.04**
spa.rst.sctb	61.01	60.38	63.52	59.75	71.70	67.30	**72.33**	69.81	71.07	71.07
tur.pdtb.tdb	57.58	51.66	47.87	59.48	50.71	49.76	57.11	58.06	53.79	**61.37**
zho.pdtb.cdtb	87.34	80.87	78.89	82.85	82.85	81.93	86.54	84.17	84.30	**88.13**
zho.rst.sctb	64.15	56.6	49.69	55.35	64.78	61.01	62.89	66.67	64.15	**67.30**
AVERAGE	60.41	54.79	52.26	57.15	58.36	55.69	60.52	59.54	56.81	**62.09**

Table 6: Results of models without features and different direction handling, for all datasets. The models are: DisCoDisCo 2021 System with features (Control), mBERT (m), DistilmBERT (d), and XLM-RoBERTa (x).

Complex question generation using discourse-based data augmentation

Kushnur Binte Jahangir
UT3 - IRIT
khushnur@cse.uiu.ac.bd

Philippe Muller
UT3 - IRIT ; ANITI
philippe.muller@irit.fr

Chloé Braud
UT3 - IRIT ; CNRS ; ANITI
chloe.braud@irit.fr

Abstract

Question Generation (QG), the process of generating meaningful questions from a given context, has proven to be useful for several tasks such as question answering or FAQ generation. While most existing QG techniques generate simple, fact-based questions, this research aims to generate questions that can have complex answers (e.g. "why" questions). We propose a data augmentation method that uses discourse relations to create such questions, and experiment on existing English data. Our approach generates questions based solely on the context without answer supervision, in order to enhance question diversity and complexity. We use an encoder-decoder trained on the augmented dataset to generate either one question or multiple questions at a time, and show that the latter improves over the baseline model when doing a human quality evaluation, without degrading performance according to standard automated metrics.

1 Introduction

Question generation is the task of automatically producing varied questions about a document or a set of documents. It is used to facilitate matching real users' questions looking for information contained in those documents, for instance in the context of Customer Relationship Management or producing FAQs (Mass et al., 2020), in dialogue systems to improve interaction with users (Li et al., 2017), to develop interactive learning for educational purposes (Yao et al., 2022; Scharpf et al., 2022; CH and Saha, 2023; Eo et al., 2023) or as auxiliary tasks for e.g. summarization (Pagnoni et al., 2023). More generically, it can help question-answering (QA) systems by augmenting the amount of instances available for training, as in (Duan et al., 2017) where automatically generated questions are integrated within a text-based QA system, or in (Bartolo et al., 2021) where they are used as adversarial data to improve robustness.

As pointed out in e.g. (Sultan et al., 2020; Eo et al., 2023), question diversity is crucial, meaning that a QG system should be able to produce different types of questions, with varied lexical content and associated explicit and implicit answers. However, the majority of the current research techniques in QG have primarily focused on factoid and multiple-choice questions, where the systems are designed to retrieve factual information or require short-span answers. Since they rely more on reasoning, complex questions might help the user to gain deeper and multiple perspectives on a topic. This makes them especially useful in learning environments, complex dialogue systems, and applications that call for a better understanding of text.

On the other hand, generating complex questions is a challenging task, as the system must have a grasp of underlying semantic relationships between different parts of the text. This is where discourse relations can play an important role: discourse, or rhetorical, relations are the semantic-pragmatic links between sentences or clauses within a text, describing e.g. causal, temporal or manner connections. We assume that including discourse relations into the generation process could help the system to produce complicated questions that accurately represent the depth and complexity of the text while also being contextually relevant. For instance, recognizing a "cause-effect" discourse relation can inspire "why" questions that aim to go deeper into the reasons behind a certain occurrence or circumstance addressed in the text.

In this paper, we present an answer-agnostic QG system, based on a Transformer-driven model fine-tuned specifically for question generation. The emphasis of our QG system is on generating complex questions using discourse relations, with a particular focus on causality related questions to enhance contextual understanding. Our approach relies on data augmentation: the system is fine-

Proceedings of the 5th Workshop on Computational Approaches to Discourse (CODI 2024), pages 105–119
March 21, 2024 ©2024 Association for Computational Linguistics

tuned on reference datasets for QA that are reversed to perform the QG task, and augmented with "why" questions that are automatically built from discourse annotated data using simple heuristics. By using gold annotated data for discourse, we ensure the quality of our synthetic data. We use several datasets, the Stanford Question Answering Dataset or SQuAD (Rajpurkar et al., 2016) and Explain Like I'm Five, or ELI5 (Fan et al., 2019) for training a generator, and the Penn Discourse Treebank 2.0 (Prasad et al., 2008) for data augmentation. We evaluate the results using both automatic evaluation metrics comparing generated questions to existing reference questions about the same paragraphs, and a human assessment of the quality of the generated questions, since automated metrics do not account well for the variety of outputs from answer-agnostic models.

2 Related work

Question generation aims at producing relevant questions from documents, that could be a single text or a collection, or other types of inputs such as knowledge bases or images. In this paper, we focus on generating questions from a single document, using datasets in which each source text (i.e. context) is associated to question-answer pairs. In this context, many annotated datasets, primilarly built for QA, have been used for QG with two different settings: answer-aware systems provide the context and the targeted answer to generate the question, while answer-agnostic ones only rely on contexts.

First systems for QG were rule-based: Heilman and Smith (2010) proposed to apply syntactic modifications to generate question from declarative sentences, while Dhole and Manning (2020) refined generating patterns using semantic resources. Interestingly, Agarwal et al. (2011) demonstrated the importance of discourse connections for QG by designing patterns also relying on discourse connectives, i.e. specific expressions that can trigger discourse relations (e.g. *because, but, as a result...*), and that also constrain the type of the question to be generated. We also rely on syntactic templates and discourse information, but we significantly extend this line of work by using gold discourse annotations and by also including implicit relations.

Current approaches rely on neural architectures, either RNNs (Duan et al., 2017; Liu, 2020) or Transformers (Scialom et al., 2019; Lopez et al., 2020; Grover et al., 2021). As in our work, Scialom et al. (2019); Lopez et al. (2020) proposed an answer-agnostic QG system based on a Transformer architecture but only evaluated on SQuAD, where complex questions are almost nonexistent. Within the same setting, Grover et al. (2021) demonstrated the ability of a T5-model to generate relevant and natural questions, but the authors highlighted the challenge of evaluating generated questions using SQuAD: while the answer-agnostic setting encourages diversity, the generated questions could be far from the reference ones, an issue we address through human evaluation (see Section 8).

While these studies successfully applied transformer models such as T5 to QG, they primarily focuses on generic, simple questions, leaving complex questions less explored. Beside (Agarwal et al., 2011), discourse information was also leveraged in Stasaski et al. (2021) where rules are used to extract cause-effect relations in SQuAD: a language model then generates questions on both the cause and effect aspects, and the synthetic questions are evaluated via a QA task. Contrary to this work, we use causal relations that are manually annotated to create synthetic data to augment a generic QG model. In addition, relevant to our work is the approach introduced in (Lal et al., 2021): the authors propose simple transformations based on syntactic templates to create a corpus of "why" questions. Our heuristics to generate questions are inspired by this work, but our evaluation is not done directly on these synthetic, possibly noisy questions, but on a natural, classic benchmark (e.g. SQuAD).

Also using data augmentation, Ashok Kumar et al. (2023) rely on prompting an LLM using context-answer-question triplets to generate a set of new questions, using varied decoding strategies with the aim of increasing diversity. These questions are then ranked, based on perplexity or on a separate model, and the best ranked is added to the training set of a Flan-T5 model fine-tuned on FairytaleQA (Xu et al., 2022a) to generate questions given context-answer pairs. The evaluation demonstrates that the approach allows to generate questions for which the answer is implicit, i.e. no directly present as text span but need to be inferred. Our approach is much simpler, relying on heuristics to generate questions, with a focus on difficult, complex questions while their approach aims at producing generic diversity, with no insight on the

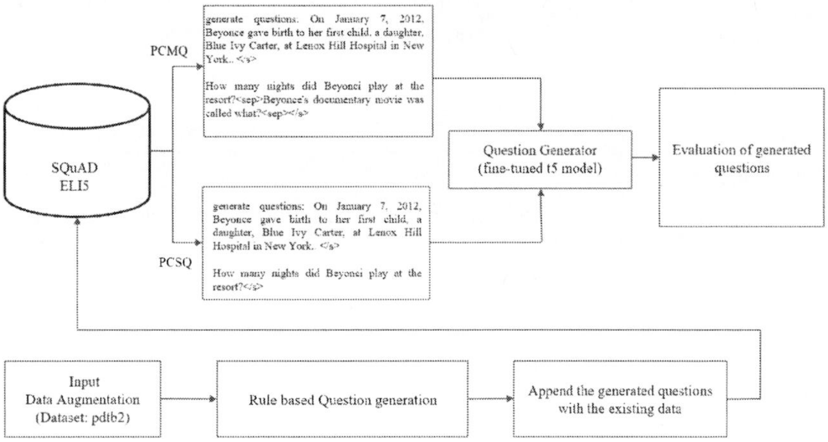

Figure 1: Proposed Pipeline For Complex Question Generation Task.

types of questions generated.

3 Methodology

The pipeline for our question generation task is illustrated in Figure 1 and consists of the following elements:

- Two primary datasets, namely SQuAD, and ELI5, serve as a basis for training a model. Since we want to create an answer-agnostic model we only use the context paragraphs and the associated questions as input (ignoring information about the answer).

- The primary datasets are augmented using discourse annotated data, namely the PDTB2 dataset. We extract sentences with specific relations annotated (causal relations).

- We apply a manual rule-based approach to derive why-questions from these extracted sentences, relying on their syntactic structures, and add them to the primary datasets, with the original sentences from PDTB2 as context paragraphs.

- The augmented dataset is then used as an input for fine-tuning an encoder-decoder model from the T5 family, with two different setups:
  - PCSQ (Per Context Single Question), in which each training instance includes a context paragraph and a corresponding single question associated with it. The context and question together serve as a 'training instance' for the T5 model during the fine-tuning process. A paragraph can thus appear several times with different questions associated.
  - PCMQ (Per Context Multiple Questions), in which each training instance contains a context and all the questions associated with this context.

PCMQ makes for a more complex decoding, but is supposed to encourage question diversity and avoid redundant generations. This setup is made possible because the reference answer for each question is ignored, and so a given paragraph is associated to several different questions in SQuAD.

Given the scarcity of complex questions in existing datasets, we aim to expand our training examples by integrating more "why" based questions. We thus use the PDTB2 dataset which contains documents annotated with discourse relations, including causality relations. These can be signaled by discourse markers, such as "because", "as", and "since", or be *implicit*, and the annotation consists of a typical marker that could be inserted.

We take the sentences from the PDTB2 dataset for both implicit and explicit relations that represent causal relations and produce questions based on some predefined rule-based templates. The rules operate on the syntactic structure of a sentence to identify the main verb and auxiliary, and transform it to produce a grammatically correct interrogative sentence, in a manner similar to how data was produced in the dataset of (Lal et al., 2021). Table 1 contains some example questions produced by this procedure. More sample of questions generated based on discourse relations is displayed in

Sentence/Arg1	Tense	Question Template	Generated Question
[jaguar was *shocked by mr. ridley's decision]*$_{ARG1}$ because *[...]*$_{ARG2}$	Past	**Why**{aux}*{rest_arg1}*?	**Why** was *jaguar shocked by mr. ridley's decision*?
the beebes' symptoms were not *related to the carpeting*	Past	**Why**{aux}{neg} *{rest_arg1}*?	**Why** were not *the beebes' symptoms related to the carpeting*?
frequently, clients express *interest in paintings but do not end up bidding*	Present	**Why** *do {rest_arg1}*?	***Why** does *frequently, clients express interest in paintings but do not end up bidding* ?

Table 1: Questions generated based on the question templates. Discourse relations link two spans of text ARG1 and ARG2 (explicitly with a marker or implicitly). Except for the first example, we only show the first argument of the causal relation (ARG1) as it is the only part used to create the question. Underlined text in the Sentence/ARG1 column represents verbs, auxiliary verbs, or negation particles extracted from the original sentence. Text in bold in the Question Template column represents fixed elements used in creating the question templates. The generated question column showcases the final questions formed using the respective templates, and incorrect question formations are marked with a star.

Appendix A.

4 Datasets

There are numerous datasets available for question generation tasks, including but not limited to NewsQA (Trischler et al., 2017), MS MARCO (Nguyen et al., 2016), Natural Questions (Kwiatkowski et al., 2019), FairytaleQA (Xu et al., 2022b), SQuAD (Rajpurkar et al., 2016), and ELI5 (Fan et al., 2019). Initially, these datasets were designed for question-answering tasks, yet they are now also broadly used in question generation research. For the present work we rely on two datasets, namely SQuAD and ELI5, to perform question generation from a given text.

SQuAD is chosen for its diverse range of source paragraphs and questions from Wikipedia, it is commonly used as a reliable benchmark for both QA and QG. The dataset was produced by Stanford University academics and contains a sizable number of paragraphs that were taken from Wikipedia articles (Rajpurkar et al., 2016). For our experiment, we use the training and development datasets from SQuAD v2.0, which were created by Rajpurkar et al. (Rajpurkar et al., 2018) in 2018.[1] However, SQuAD focuses mostly on simple factoid questions, so the ELI5 dataset, consisting of more complex questions, is incorporated.

ELI5 which stands for "Explain Like I'm Five", is another popular benchmark dataset used for tasks like QA, QG, and other NLP tasks. It is sourced from the subreddit r/explainlikeimfive. It provides long-form answers and is available from the Hugging Face website.[2] In the ELI5 dataset, each instance consists of a question and user-provided answers on reddit. In our context, we consider the answer as the source paragraph and the questions as our system's input.

PDTB2.0: Additionaly, we use the Penn Discourse Treebank Version 2.0 (PDTB2) (Prasad et al., 2008) that provides discourse annotated texts. The PDTB2 is used here to leverage discourse marker-based annotations and produce additional data to augment the training set. Other corpora exist for discourse annotations, but the PDTB is the largest annotated dataset for English including annotations for discourse relations (e.g. *cause, result, manner*), both explicit – that is triggered by a discourse connective (e.g. *because, as a result, then...*) –, and implicit – no lexical marker. Of particular interest, the PDTB2 has annotations of causal relations that we use to create "why" questions. We use the version provided from the CoNLL 2016 Shared Task (Xue et al., 2016), with level-2 annotations (15 different relation types).

5 Experiments

Our experiments aim at evaluating the influence of the training data composition, the model size, and the generating procedure as outlined in Section 3.

PCSQ *vs* PCMQ: We build the training set differently for the PCSQ and PCMQ setups: for PCSQ – i.e. one question per paragraph –, we select paragraphs and all questions about them to generate one instance per paragraph-question pair ; for PCMQ,

[1]Retrieved from the GitHub page `https://rajpurkar.github.io/SQuAD-explorer/`.

[2]`https://huggingface.co/datasets/eli5`.

Input: Many locals and tourists frequent the southern California coast for its popular beaches, and the desert city of Palm Springs is popular for its resort feel and nearby open spaces.
Reference Question: Other than the desert city why do many locals and tourists frequent southern California?
Baseline: How many locals and tourists frequent the southern California coast? **SQuAD+ELI5:** What city has a beach? **+ELI5+PDTB (Exp):** Why do many locals and tourists frequent the southern California coast? **+ELI5+PDTB (Exp+Imp):** Why do many locals and tourists frequent the southern California coast?

Table 2: Example of generated questions by different models in PCMQ approach for SQuAD test data.

all questions about a paragraph are concatenated in the same instance.

Training data composition: For the training data, we use SQuAD data as a baseline, and vary the training set by adding either (i) ELI5 data only, or (ii) ELI5 and the generated questions from the explicit examples of the PDTB, or (iii) ELI5 and the generated questions from both the implicit and explicit examples of the PDTB.

For the baseline dataset (SQuAD) we keep approximately 50k instances for the PCSQ setup, and compare to similarly-sized datasets, by having 20k instances from SQuAD and 30k instances from ELI5. The additional augmentation from the PDTB is much smaller, with about $1,600$ instances generated from explicit relations, and $1,550$ from implicit relations.

For the PCMQ setup we cannot hold the number of instances constant without restraining SQuAD too much (there are only 19k paragraphs in total), so we chose to start from a baseline including all of SQuAD + 30k ELI5 instances (note that there are much less questions per paragraph in ELI5). We kept the SQuAD-only setup for comprehensiveness, but the PCMQ setup is not entirely fair to this dataset compared to the others.

While the training and development sets of SQuAD are publicly available, the test set is not accessible to the public. So we divided the development set evenly, allocating 50% for validation and the remaining 50% for testing.

Models The experiments are conducted using the T5-base model, which is available in the Hugging Face transformers library.[3] The code, written in Python, uses the PyTorch library for fine-tuning the model. This experiment was conducted in a Google Colab Pro environment. The T5 base model has 220 million parameters. The T5 tokenizer handled data preprocessing, limiting input sequences to 512 tokens and target sequences to 64 tokens. The training involves a batch size of 4, a gradient accumulation size of 32, and 3 epochs, employing the Adam optimizer with a learning rate of 1e-4.

Decoding and post-processing To ensure diversity and comprehensiveness in questions, we keep a generation beam of four results for each test paragraph. In the case of PCSQ this ensures we have more than one question to match to the several references in SQuAD. In the PCMQ approach, the model independently generates varying lengths of questions per set, offering a greater variety compared to PCSQ. We need some post-processing to remove duplicate questions and some not well-formed ones, lacking a '?' mark (incomplete generations), and this impacts the final count of questions obtained for each input text. Examples of questions generated by different models are shown in Table 2. In Table 9 in Appendix C, we provide a more complete example of a question generated by the "+ELI5+PDTB (Exp+Imp)" model in the PCMQ setup.

6 Automated evaluation

We generated questions in both approaches on the SQuAD left-out paragraphs and evaluated against the corresponding reference questions using automated evaluation metrics: BLEU (Bilingual Evaluation Understudy) (Papineni et al., 2002), METEOR (Metric for Evaluation of Translation with Explicit ORdering) (Lavie and Denkowski, 2009), and ROUGE-L (Recall-Oriented Understudy for Gisting Evaluation-longest common subsequences or LCS) (Lin, 2004). These metrics are widely adopted in the literature for evaluating question generation. The evaluation tasks involved the use of the following library packages: the Natural Language Toolkit (NLTK), ROUGE, and METEOR

[3] https://huggingface.co/docs/transformers/index

Approach	Training	BLEU-1	BLEU-2	BLEU-3	BLEU-4	ROUGE-L	METEOR
PCSQ	SQuAD Baseline	**37.51**	**25.25**	**18.54**	**13.81**	**45.57**	**46.13**
	+ELI5	36.77	24.41	17.75	12.99	45.07	45.24
	+ELI5+P-E	37.10	24.74	18.09	13.40	45.18	45.18
	+ELI5+P-(E+I)	**37.51**	25.11	18.36	13.56	45.53	45.53
PCMQ	SQuAD alone	33.48	21.94	15.86	11.60	41.27	40.34
	SQuAD+ELI5	33.55	22.14	16.12	11.86	41.52	40.36
	+ELI5+P-E	33.78	22.39	16.32	12.03	**41.63**	40.77
	+ELI5+P-(E+I)	**33.89**	**22.45**	**16.34**	**12.07**	**41.63**	**40.91**

Table 3: Comparative performance of PCSQ and PCMQ approaches with different models. The scores are given in percentages. The highest scores in each metric and approach are highlighted in bold. Here, the baseline model is trained on the SQuAD dataset only. The results are presented for t5-base models. P-E and I stand for PDTB explicit and implicit relations respectively. Note that PCMQ/SQuAD alone is here for reference but not comparable to the other PCMQ setups.

in calculating BLEU (1 to 4), Rouge-L, and METEOR scores. Note that those measures, relying on common ngrams or subsquences between reference and system outputs, are moderately appropriate to our setup, where we try to generate more diverse questions than are present in the reference, without a target answer. We address this problem with a human evaluation in Section 8.

A total of 500 paragraphs were chosen from the SQuAD test dataset to assess the question-generation capability of our model. These paragraphs consist of multiple reference questions, and correspondingly, our model generates multiple questions for each paragraph. To accommodate the presence of multiple references and generated questions per paragraph in the SQuAD dataset, we implemented a mapping approach to find out which reference and generated question pairs are more relevant to each other for the evaluation, especially focusing on one-to-one match between reference and generated questions. For both PCSQ and PCMQ approaches, we combined questions generated for each context's four outputs from the beam. Using automatic evaluation metrics such as BLEU, ROUGE-L, or METEOR, we then calculated scores for each pair of matched generated and reference questions. This filtering resulted in a one-to-one matching between generated and reference questions, ensuring meaningful evaluation of our model's question-generation accuracy. Given the decoding procedure, the average number of non-duplicate generated questions was about 3.9 for PCSQ, and 9.5 for PCQM (with small variations depending on the training data).

7 Results

The results presented in Table 3 provide insights into the impact of data augmentation and the effectiveness of PCSQ and PCMQ approaches. For PCSQ, the model trained solely on SQuAD slightly outperforms augmented models in all mentioned evaluation metrics, highlighting the effectiveness of focused training on a single dataset. On the other hand, PCMQ, when using everything from SQuAD, ELI5, and the PDTB2 augmentation, outperforms slightly the baseline in BLEU (1 to 4), ROUGE-L, and METEOR.

When train with PDTB derived instances, the number of "why" question is higher (+38% when using explicit and implicit with PCMQ wrt the baseline, +24% with only explicit). In PCSQ, the increase in "why" questions is limited (going from 0 for the baseline to 10 for the full training data), reflecting its lower effectiveness in generating this question type. Questions in "how" do not seem positively affected (each system generates almost the same amount), but we did not distinguish simple "how" questions (asking for quantities, i.e "how much/many") and more complex ones. We just observed that some generated "how" questions were causal in nature, but more manual analysis is needed to evaluate this precisely.

Thus, aligned with our objective, our augmentation techniques effectively increased the number of generated "why" questions, particularly within the PCMQ models, without detrimentally affecting the quality of the questions generated as a whole, at least according to the automated metrics.

This is notable since our models are not trained

on example answers, meaning they can generate questions about any aspect of the chosen paragraph, for which it is likely the reference does not include any question-answer pair.

This is why it is important to have a separate, more fine-grained evaluation of the quality of the generated answers, and this is the subject of the following section.

Model	how	why
SQuAD alone	**866**	63
SQuAD+ELI5	747	64
+ELI5+P-E	781	78
+ELI5+P-(E+I)	772	**87**

Table 4: The table presents the number of "why" and "how" questions generated by various models in PCMQ approach. The results are presented for T5-base models. Here, the baseline model is trained on the SQuAD dataset only. P-E and I stand for PDTB explicit and implicit relations respectively.

8 Human evaluation

Model	Bad	$\approx$ ok	Good
Baseline	39.29	10.71	50.00
All+P-E	40.43	2.13	57.45
All+P-(E+I)	26.15	3.08	**70.77**

Table 5: Human quality assessment of generated questions in % according to the data that was used to train the generation model (PCMQ setup). Baseline means T5 was only fine-tuned on SQuAD.

We conducted a human evaluation to assess the quality of questions generated in PCMQ approach by three models: Baseline model, +ELI5+PDTB (Exp), and +ELI5+PDTB (Exp+Imp), all fine-tuned from the T5-base model. Two of the authors annotated a subset of randomly selected questions and their context from the SQuAD test dataset using a set of 7 predetermined categories that included subcategories for incorrect questions (more details are provided in Appendix 12); the selection was done by a third author, who kept hidden the system that produced each question. There were 137 annotated questions, some generated by more than one system. Adjudications of annotations were done by the two annotators. It turned out some of the error subcategories were quite similar, and the final categories were restricted to three cases: (1) the generated question is good: fluent, and can be answered from the source paragraph, (2) the generated question is almost good: minor disfluency and the answer is in the paragraph, (3) the question is either impossible to understand or too vague, or the paragraph does not contain an answer to the question.

Cohen's kappa (κ) was 0.48 on the 7 original categories, indicating a moderate level of inter-annotator agreement, but was 0.74 when only distinguishing between good questions and all the rest.

Table 5 presents the model-wise percentage distribution of the final adjudicated categories, providing insights into the quality assessment of generated questions. The +ELI5+PDTB (Exp+Imp) model exhibits fewer "bad" questions and a substantial increase in "good" questions compared to the baseline, presenting improved question quality with explicit and implicit relation augmentations.

Moreover, from the annotated questions, we determined the distribution of good, almost okay, and bad questions for each question type (e.g., what, why, etc.), see Table 6. We can see for instance that implicit examples help generating more why questions (32), but with a cost on the average quality of the questions (61% of good questions), while using only explicit examples has a much higher quality (79% of good questions, vs 55% for the baseline) with less why questions generated (12). This is done on a small sample of "why questions" so must be taken with a grain of salt.

9 Conclusion

We presented an approach based on discourse relation annotations to augment a question generation training set, in the case of a general answer-agnostic question generation system, and with a focus on causal questions. Our experiments show that with a small set of additional instances we can make the system generate more causal questions with a good quality, as evaluated by human annotators, and with almost no difference with respect to classic automated metrics for question generation. This is only preliminary, as the results would need to be tested on different base question-answer corpora, and more human evaluation would be precious to better separate the roles of the different factors at play here. It would also be interesting to investigate the impact of including other discourse relation types to generate different kinds of questions (e.g. "how" questions with relations of the type "goal" or "manner").

Type	Model	% correct	nb
How	ELI5+Exp	58.33	12
	ELI5+Exp+Imp	80.95	21
	Baseline	50.00	18
Others	ELI5+Exp	0.00	1
What	ELI5+Exp	43.75	16
	ELI5+Exp+Imp	70.00	5
	Baseline	61.36	22
When	ELI5+Exp	75.00	4
	ELI5+Exp+Imp	100.00	4
	Baseline	33.33	3
Where	ELI5+Exp	0.00	1
	Baseline	75.00	2
Who	ELI5+Exp	100.00	1
	ELI5+Exp+Imp	100.00	3
Why	ELI5+Exp	79.17	12
	ELI5+Exp+Imp	60.94	32
	Baseline	54.55	11

Table 6: Breakdown of the number of questions in the human evaluation by type, with the % of correct questions and the number of generated questions.

10 Limitations

The proposed approach augments existing datasets and thus depends on the quality and diversity of this basis. We are also reliant on existing annotated discourse data, which is costly to produce, and exist only in various quantities for some languages. As mentioned in the conclusion, the results would need to be tested on different base question-answer corpora and other languages, and more human evaluation is needed to better separate the roles of the different factors at play here. A limitation of our evaluation is the use of automated metrics, which are already known not to be very adequate to compare semantically equivalent questions if they have lexical differences, but are even more inappropriate with the goal to produce diverse questions not tied to existing answers.

Acknowledgements

This work is supported by the Quantum project (ANR-19-CE23-0022). Our work has benefited from the AI Interdisciplinary Institute ANITI. ANITI is funded by the French "Investing for the Future – PIA3" program under the Grant agreement n°ANR-19-PI3A-0004. This work is also partially supported by the AnDiaMO project (ANR-21-CE23-0020). Chloé Braud and Philippe Muller are part of the program DesCartes and are also supported by the National Research Foundation, Prime Minister's Office, Singapore under its Campus for Research Excellence and Technological Enterprise (CREATE) program.

References

Manish Agarwal, Rakshit Shah, and Prashanth Mannem. 2011. Automatic question generation using discourse cues. In *Proceedings of the Sixth Workshop on Innovative Use of NLP for Building Educational Applications*, pages 1–9.

Nischal Ashok Kumar, Nigel Fernandez, Zichao Wang, and Andrew Lan. 2023. Improving reading comprehension question generation with data augmentation and overgenerate-and-rank. In *Proceedings of the 18th Workshop on Innovative Use of NLP for Building Educational Applications (BEA 2023)*, pages 247–259, Toronto, Canada. Association for Computational Linguistics.

Max Bartolo, Tristan Thrush, Robin Jia, Sebastian Riedel, Pontus Stenetorp, and Douwe Kiela. 2021. Improving question answering model robustness with synthetic adversarial data generation. In *Proceedings of the 2021 Conference on Empirical Methods in Natural Language Processing*, pages 8830–8848, Online and Punta Cana, Dominican Republic. Association for Computational Linguistics.

Dhawaleswar Rao CH and Sujan Kumar Saha. 2023. Generation of multiple-choice questions from textbook contents of school-level subjects. volume 16, pages 40–52.

Kaustubh D Dhole and Christopher D Manning. 2020. Syn-qg: Syntactic and shallow semantic rules for question generation. *arXiv preprint arXiv:2004.08694*.

Nan Duan, Duyu Tang, Peng Chen, and Ming Zhou. 2017. Question generation for question answering. In *Proceedings of the 2017 Conference on Empirical Methods in Natural Language Processing*, pages 866–874, Copenhagen, Denmark. Association for Computational Linguistics.

Sugyeong Eo, Hyeonseok Moon, Jinsung Kim, Yuna Hur, Jeongwook Kim, SongEun Lee,

Changwoo Chun, Sungsoo Park, and Heuiseok Lim. 2023. Towards diverse and effective question-answer pair generation from children storybooks. In *Findings of the Association for Computational Linguistics: ACL 2023*, pages 6100–6115, Toronto, Canada. Association for Computational Linguistics.

Angela Fan, Yacine Jernite, Ethan Perez, David Grangier, Jason Weston, and Michael Auli. 2019. ELI5: Long form question answering. In *Proceedings of the 57th Annual Meeting of the Association for Computational Linguistics*, pages 3558–3567, Florence, Italy. Association for Computational Linguistics.

Khushnuma Grover, Katinder Kaur, Kartikey Tiwari, Rupali, and Parteek Kumar. 2021. Deep learning based question generation using t5 transformer. In *Advanced Computing: 10th International Conference, IACC 2020, Panaji, Goa, India, December 5–6, 2020, Revised Selected Papers, Part I 10*, pages 243–255. Springer.

Michael Heilman and Noah A. Smith. 2010. Good question! statistical ranking for question generation. In *Human Language Technologies: The 2010 Annual Conference of the North American Chapter of the Association for Computational Linguistics*, pages 609–617, Los Angeles, California. Association for Computational Linguistics.

Tom Kwiatkowski, Jennimaria Palomaki, Olivia Redfield, Michael Collins, Ankur Parikh, Chris Alberti, Danielle Epstein, Illia Polosukhin, Jacob Devlin, Kenton Lee, et al. 2019. Natural questions: a benchmark for question answering research. *Transactions of the Association for Computational Linguistics*, 7:453–466.

Yash Kumar Lal, Nathanael Chambers, Raymond Mooney, and Niranjan Balasubramanian. 2021. TellMeWhy: A dataset for answering why-questions in narratives. In *Findings of the Association for Computational Linguistics: ACL-IJCNLP 2021*, pages 596–610, Online. Association for Computational Linguistics.

Alon Lavie and Michael J Denkowski. 2009. The meteor metric for automatic evaluation of machine translation. *Machine translation*, 23:105–115.

Jiwei Li, Alexander H. Miller, Sumit Chopra, Marc'Aurelio Ranzato, and Jason Weston. 2017. Learning through dialogue interactions by asking questions. Publisher Copyright: © ICLR 2019 - Conference Track Proceedings. All rights reserved.; 5th International Conference on Learning Representations, ICLR 2017 ; Conference date: 24-04-2017 Through 26-04-2017.

Chin-Yew Lin. 2004. ROUGE: A package for automatic evaluation of summaries. In *Text Summarization Branches Out*, pages 74–81, Barcelona, Spain. Association for Computational Linguistics.

Bingran Liu. 2020. Neural question generation based on seq2seq. In *Proceedings of the 2020 5th International Conference on Mathematics and Artificial Intelligence*, pages 119–123.

Luis Enrico Lopez, Diane Kathryn Cruz, Jan Christian Blaise Cruz, and Charibeth Cheng. 2020. Transformer-based end-to-end question generation. *arXiv preprint arXiv:2005.01107*, 4.

Yosi Mass, Boaz Carmeli, Haggai Roitman, and David Konopnicki. 2020. Unsupervised FAQ retrieval with question generation and BERT. In *Proceedings of the 58th Annual Meeting of the Association for Computational Linguistics*, pages 807–812, Online. Association for Computational Linguistics.

Tri Nguyen, Mir Rosenberg, Xia Song, Jianfeng Gao, Saurabh Tiwary, Rangan Majumder, and Li Deng. 2016. MS MARCO: A human generated machine reading comprehension dataset. In *Proceedings of the Workshop on Cognitive Computation: Integrating neural and symbolic approaches 2016 co-located with the 30th Annual Conference on Neural Information Processing Systems (NIPS 2016), Barcelona, Spain, December 9, 2016*, volume 1773 of *CEUR Workshop Proceedings*. CEUR-WS.org.

Artidoro Pagnoni, Alex Fabbri, Wojciech Kryscinski, and Chien-Sheng Wu. 2023. Socratic pretraining: Question-driven pretraining for controllable summarization. In *Proceedings of the 61st Annual Meeting of the Association for Computational Linguistics (Volume 1: Long Papers)*, pages 12737–12755, Toronto, Canada. Association for Computational Linguistics.

Kishore Papineni, Salim Roukos, Todd Ward, and Wei-Jing Zhu. 2002. Bleu: a method for automatic evaluation of machine translation. In *Proceedings of the 40th Annual Meeting of the Association for Computational Linguistics*, pages 311–318, Philadelphia, Pennsylvania, USA. Association for Computational Linguistics.

Rashmi Prasad, Nikhil Dinesh, Alan Lee, Eleni Miltsakaki, Livio Robaldo, Aravind Joshi, and Bonnie Webber. 2008. The Penn Discourse TreeBank 2.0. In *Proceedings of the Sixth International Conference on Language Resources and Evaluation (LREC'08)*, Marrakech, Morocco. European Language Resources Association (ELRA).

Pranav Rajpurkar, Robin Jia, and Percy Liang. 2018. Know what you don't know: Unanswerable questions for SQuAD. In *Proceedings of the 56th Annual Meeting of the Association for Computational Linguistics (Volume 2: Short Papers)*, pages 784–789, Melbourne, Australia. Association for Computational Linguistics.

Pranav Rajpurkar, Jian Zhang, Konstantin Lopyrev, and Percy Liang. 2016. SQuAD: 100,000+ questions for machine comprehension of text. In *Proceedings of the 2016 Conference on Empirical Methods in Natural Language Processing*, pages 2383–2392, Austin, Texas. Association for Computational Linguistics.

Philipp Scharpf, Moritz Schubotz, Andreas Spitz, André Greiner-Petter, and Bela Gipp. 2022. Collaborative and ai-aided exam question generation using wikidata in education. In *Workshop Proceedings*, page 18568.

Thomas Scialom, Benjamin Piwowarski, and Jacopo Staiano. 2019. Self-attention architectures for answer-agnostic neural question generation. In *Proceedings of the 57th Annual Meeting of the Association for Computational Linguistics*, pages 6027–6032, Florence, Italy. Association for Computational Linguistics.

Katherine Stasaski, Manav Rathod, Tony Tu, Yunfang Xiao, and Marti A. Hearst. 2021. Automatically generating cause-and-effect questions from passages. In *Proceedings of the 16th Workshop on Innovative Use of NLP for Building Educational Applications*, pages 158–170, Online. Association for Computational Linguistics.

Md Arafat Sultan, Shubham Chandel, Ramón Fernandez Astudillo, and Vittorio Castelli. 2020. On the importance of diversity in question generation for QA. In *Proceedings of the 58th Annual Meeting of the Association for Computational Linguistics*, pages 5651–5656, Online. Association for Computational Linguistics.

Adam Trischler, Tong Wang, Xingdi Yuan, Justin Harris, Alessandro Sordoni, Philip Bachman, and Kaheer Suleman. 2017. NewsQA: A machine comprehension dataset. In *Proceedings of the 2nd Workshop on Representation Learning for NLP*, pages 191–200, Vancouver, Canada. Association for Computational Linguistics.

Ying Xu, Dakuo Wang, Mo Yu, Daniel Ritchie, Bingsheng Yao, Tongshuang Wu, Zheng Zhang, Toby Li, Nora Bradford, Branda Sun, Tran Hoang, Yisi Sang, Yufang Hou, Xiaojuan Ma, Diyi Yang, Nanyun Peng, Zhou Yu, and Mark Warschauer. 2022a. Fantastic questions and where to find them: FairytaleQA – an authentic dataset for narrative comprehension. In *Proceedings of the 60th Annual Meeting of the Association for Computational Linguistics (Volume 1: Long Papers)*, pages 447–460, Dublin, Ireland. Association for Computational Linguistics.

Ying Xu, Dakuo Wang, Mo Yu, Daniel Ritchie, Bingsheng Yao, Tongshuang Wu, Zheng Zhang, Toby Jia-Jun Li, Nora Bradford, Branda Sun, Tran Bao Hoang, Yisi Sang, Yufang Hou, Xiaojuan Ma, Diyi Yang, Nanyun Peng, Zhou Yu, and Mark Warschauer. 2022b. Fantastic questions and where to find them: FairytaleQA – an authentic dataset for narrative comprehension. Association for Computational Linguistics.

Nianwen Xue, Hwee Tou Ng, Sameer Pradhan, Attapol Rutherford, Bonnie Webber, Chuan Wang, and Hongmin Wang. 2016. CoNLL 2016 shared task on multilingual shallow discourse parsing. In *Proceedings of the CoNLL-16 shared task*, pages 1–19, Berlin, Germany. Association for Computational Linguistics.

Bingsheng Yao, Dakuo Wang, Tongshuang Wu, Zheng Zhang, Toby Li, Mo Yu, and Ying Xu. 2022. It is AI's turn to ask humans a question: Question-answer pair generation for children's story books. In *Proceedings of the 60th Annual Meeting of the Association for Computational*

Linguistics (Volume 1: Long Papers), pages 731–744, Dublin, Ireland. Association for Computational Linguistics.

Paragraph	Generated Questions
Due to the heavy rain, the soccer match was canceled[1], and as a result, the players were disappointed[3]. Since the field was waterlogged, it was unsafe to play[6]. The organizers made the decision to cancel the match[7], and consequently, the players had to wait for another opportunity to showcase their skills[4]. Additionally, the spectators were also disappointed[5] because they were eagerly looking forward to the game. The cancellation of the match, due to the inclement weather, not only affected the players' morale but also dampened the overall excitement surrounding the event.	1. Why was the soccer match canceled? 2. Why was the soccer match canceled due to heavy rain? **(Incorrect Question)** 3. What caused the players to be disappointed? 4. What caused players to wait for another opportunity to showcase their skills? 5. Why were spectators disappointed? 6. Why was it unsafe to play? 7. Who made the decision to cancel the match?

Table 7: Example of generation from one paragraph. The table presents a text passage along with a set of generated questions intended to reflect cause-effect relationships described within the text. Corresponding answers within the text passage are color-coded to match their respective questions, and annotated with superscripts denoting question numbers for clear cross-referencing. The question is generated by +ELI5+PDTB (Exp) model in PCMQ approach.

A Sample of Generated Questions from Data Augmentation

The questions generated from the PDTB2 dataset, along with the corresponding discourse relation and discourse connective used in their formulation, are presented in Table 8.

Sentence: jaguar was shocked by mr. ridley's decision because management had believed the government wouldn't lift the golden share without consulting the company first. **(Explicit Relation)** **Connective** : because **Arg1:** jaguar was shocked by mr. ridley's decision **Question:** Why was jaguar shocked by mr. ridley's decision?
Sentence: jeastern airlines' creditors have begun exploring alternative approaches to a chapter 11 reorganization , they are unhappy with the carrier's latest proposal. **(Implicit Relation)** **Connective** : None **Arg1:** jeastern airlines' creditors have begun exploring alternative approaches to a chapter 11 reorganization **Question:** Why have eastern airlines' creditors begun exploring alternative approaches to a chapter 11 reorganization?

Table 8: Examples of generated questions for both explicit and implicit relation from PDTB2 dataset.

B Sample of Generated Questions

We have included some samples of generated questions from the fine-tuned models on test dataset in Table 9 and 10. In Table 9, for a given input paragraph, the augmented model in PCMQ approaches generated 4 set of questions where each question set may contain various length questions.

C Human Annotation

C.1 Sample of Annotated Questions

We have provided some sample questions that have been annotated by the annotators. The annotated questions can be found in Table 11.

Input: The Normans (Norman: Nourmands; French: Normands; Latin: Normanni) were the people who in the 10th and 11th centuries gave their name to Normandy, a region in France. They were descended from Norse ("Norman" comes from "Norseman") raiders and pirates from Denmark, Iceland and Norway who, under their leader Rollo, agreed to swear fealty to King Charles III of West Francia. Through generations of assimilation and mixing with the native Frankish and Roman-Gaulish populations, their descendants would gradually merge with the Carolingian-based cultures of West Francia. The distinct cultural and ethnic identity of the Normans emerged initially in the first half of the 10th century, and it continued to evolve over the succeeding centuries.

Generated Questions:

1. Who gave their name to Normandy? What was the name of the region in France? Who did the Normans swear fealty to? When did the distinct cultural and ethnic identity of the Norman people emerge?
2. What was the name of the Normans in the 10th and 11th centuries? What was Normandy? Who did the Norman people swear fealty to? When did the distinct cultural and ethnic identity of the people emerge?
3. What was the name of the Normans in the 10th and 11th centuries? What was Normandy? Who did the Norman people swear fealty to?When did the distinct cultural and ethnic identity of the people emerge? How did the people of Normand
4. Who gave their name to Normandy? Who did the Normans swear fealty to?What did the people of Normands mix with? When did the distinct cultural and ethnic identity of the Norman people emerge?

Table 9: Example of input text and generated questions in PCMQ format for SQuAD test set. The question is generated by "+ELI5+PDTB2(Exp+Imp)". The incorrect questions are red-colored and the yellow-highlighted text present an incomplete question.

Input: Price controls exacerbated the crisis in the US. The system limited the price of "old oil" (that which had already been discovered) while allowing newly discovered oil to be sold at a higher price to encourage investment. Predictably, old oil was withdrawn from the market, creating greater scarcity. The rule also discouraged development of alternative energies. The rule had been intended to promote oil exploration. Scarcity was addressed by rationing (as in many countries). Motorists faced long lines at gas stations beginning in summer 1972 and increasing by summer 1973.
Reference Question: Why was old oil withdrawn from the market?
Baseline: What was withdrawn from the market? **SQuAD+ELI5:** What did the price control limit? **+ELI5+PDTB (Exp):** Old oil was withdrawn from the market creating what? **+ELI5+PDTB (Exp+Imp):** Why was old oil withdrawn from the market?

Table 10: Example of generated questions by different models in PCMQ approach for SQuAD test data.

Input Text	Generated Questions	Category
Price controls exacerbated the crisis in the US. The system limited the price of "old oil" (that which had already been discovered) while allowing newly discovered oil to be sold at a higher price to encourage investment. Predictably, old oil was withdrawn from the market, creating greater scarcity. The rule also discouraged development of alternative energies. The rule had been intended to promote oil exploration. Scarcity was addressed by rationing (as in many countries). Motorists faced long lines at gas stations beginning in summer 1972 and increasing by summer 1973.	Why was old oil withdrawn from the market?	Good question. Answer is present in the text.
Highly concentrated sources of oxygen promote rapid combustion. Fire and explosion hazards exist when concentrated oxidants and fuels are brought into close proximity; an ignition event, such as heat or a spark, is needed to trigger combustion. Oxygen is the oxidant, not the fuel, but nevertheless the source of most of the chemical energy released in combustion. Combustion hazards also apply to compounds of oxygen with a high oxidative potential, such as peroxides, chlorates, nitrates, perchlorates, and dichromates because they can donate oxygen to a fire.	How do compounds with oxidation potential contribute oxygen to?	Incorrect question but with relevant words from the input.
As indigenous territories continue to be destroyed by deforestation and ecocide, such as in the Peruvian Amazon indigenous peoples' rainforest communities continue to disappear, while others, like the Urarina continue to struggle to fight for their cultural survival and the fate of their forested territories. Meanwhile, the relationship between non-human primates in the subsistence and symbolism of indigenous lowland South American peoples has gained increased attention, as have ethno-biology and community-based conservation efforts.	Why do indigenous territories continue to be destroyed by deforestation and ecocide?	Grammatically correct but the answer doesn't exist.

Table 11: Sample of Annotated Questions by the Annotators. Red-colored text represents the answer texts for the question within the paragraph. The input paragraph is from SQuAD test dataset.

Question Category	Description
Good question. Answer is present in the text.	The answer to the generated question exists in the given sentence/paragraph.
Incorrect question but with relevant words from the input.	The generated question contains some words/phrases from the input, but the question is not grammatically correct and/or does not make sense.
Question and answer are mixed	The generated question contains some part of the answer.
Grammatical mistake	The generated question is grammatically incorrect.
Grammatically correct but the answer doesn't exist	The generated question is grammatically correct, but the answer to the question does not exist in the input context.
Completely vague	The generated question is not meaningful, too vague.
Two valid questions are mixed	The generated question contains two questions from different parts of the input.

Table 12: Description of different category set for question evaluation

C.2 Question Category for Annotations

The annotators assigned each question to one of the seven predetermined categories. Details of each category are provided in Table 12.

Exploring Soft-Label Training for Implicit Discourse Relation Recognition

Nelson Filipe Costa and **Leila Kosseim**
Computational Linguistics at Concordia (CLaC) Laboratory
Department of Computer Science and Software Engineering
Concordia University, Montréal, Québec, Canada
nelsonfilipe.costa@mail.concordia.ca
leila.kosseim@concordia.ca

Abstract

This paper proposes a classification model for single label implicit discourse relation recognition trained on soft-label distributions. It follows the PDTB 3.0 framework and it was trained and tested on the DiscoGeM corpus, where it achieves an F1-score of 51.38 on third-level sense classification of implicit discourse relations. We argue that training on soft-label distributions allows the model to better discern between more ambiguous discourse relations.

1 Introduction

The Penn Discourse Treebank (PDTB) framework (Miltsakaki et al., 2004; Prasad et al., 2008) defines 36 discourse relation senses organized hierarchically according to three levels of sense granularity (Prasad et al., 2019). Being able to correctly recognize these discourse relations in a text is of great importance for many downstream NLP tasks.

While current explicit discourse relation recognition (EDRR) models can already obtain F1-scores of 90.22 (Xue et al., 2016) when considering the second-level sense, the task of implicit discourse relation recognition (IDRR) remains arguably the hardest task in discourse analysis with state-of-the-art models reaching F1-scores of 55.26 (Liu and Strube, 2023) at the second-level sense. The gap in performance between the two tasks stems from the inherently subjective nature of IDRR, where even trained expert human annotators find it difficult to agree on the sense annotation of implicit discourse relations (Rohde et al., 2016; Hoek et al., 2021).

The difficulty in IDRR is evidenced by the inter-annotator agreement on different corpora. While we do not have access to the inter-annotator agreement of the last version of the PDTB 3.0 corpus (Prasad et al., 2019), the agreement at the third-level sense of PDTB 2.0 (Prasad et al., 2008) was of 80% - which also includes the easier to annotate explicit relations (45.6% of the entire corpus). Moreover, 1,075 (4.93%) of the 21,827 implicit discourse relations on the PDTB 3.0 corpus were annotated with two senses since the annotators could not agree on a single sense. This difficulty is also highlighted in the DiscoGeM corpus (Scholman et al., 2022a), where the inter-annotator agreement at the implicit third-level sense was 60%. However, if we allow implicit relations to convey multiple senses depending on the interpretation of the reader, disagreements do not necessarily indicate inaccuracies in labeling (Aroyo and Welty, 2013; Pavlick and Kwiatkowski, 2019; Jiang and de Marneffe, 2022). In fact, it might be helpful in downstream NLP applications to have a distribution of multiple interpretations for ambiguous texts (Basile et al., 2021; Pyatkin et al., 2023).

In this paper, we propose a single label implicit discourse relation recognition model trained on soft-label distributions. The model follows the annotation guidelines of PDTB 3.0 (Prasad et al., 2019) and was trained and tested on the DiscoGeM corpus (Scholman et al., 2022a). We argue that training on soft-label distributions allows the IDRR model to better generalize and discern between the possible multiple interpretations of more ambiguous texts. Our model reaches an F1-score of 51.38 on third-level sense classification of implicit discourse relations in the DiscoGeM corpus (Scholman et al., 2022a) while state-of-the-art IDRR models (Liu and Strube, 2023) achieve an F1-score of 55.26 on second-level sense classification in the PDTB 3.0 corpus (Prasad et al., 2019).

2 Previous Work

In recent years, different models have tried to leverage the power of language models either through fine-tuning (Long and Webber, 2022; Liu and Strube, 2023) or prompt-tuning (Zhao et al., 2023; Chan et al., 2023) to face the challenging task of IDRR. So far, these efforts have relied on the prin-

Proceedings of the 5th Workshop on Computational Approaches to Discourse (CODI 2024), pages 120–126
March 21, 2024

ciple that there should be a single sense in the interpretation of implicit discourse relations. However, IDRR is an inherently ambiguous task even for expert human annotators (Pavlick and Kwiatkowski, 2019; Jiang and de Marneffe, 2022).

Acknowledging the importance of including sources of ambiguity in human inference in the evaluation of natural language processing tasks led to a recent paradigm shift in discourse annotation. Rather than relying on expert annotators to find a single label for each implicit relation, recent annotation efforts (Yung et al., 2019; Pyatkin et al., 2020; Scholman et al., 2022a,b; Pyatkin et al., 2023) have crowdsourced this task to multiple workers in order to capture the possible multiple interpretations of more ambiguous relations.

The idea that discourse annotation can often be ambiguous is not new (Stede, 2008) and had already been highlighted by Huber et al. (2021) at the nuclear level of the RST framework (Mann and Thompson, 1988). In their work, Huber et al. (2021) proposed a weighted approach to the annotation of nuclearity in discourse relations following the RST framework where, similarly to the PDTB framework, a consensual annotation is hard to obtain (Demberg et al., 2019; Costa et al., 2023).

3 Dataset

In this work we used the DiscoGeM corpus (Scholman et al., 2022a) to train and test our IDRR classification model. The corpus contains 6,505 intersentential implicit discourse relations following the PDTB 3.0 annotation guidelines distributed across three different genres: 2,800 implicit discourse relations in political texts, 3,060 in literary texts and 645 in encyclopedic texts.

Rather than relying on a few trained annotators to find a sense label for each implicit discourse relation, the DiscoGeM corpus crowdsourced the annotation of each relation to multiple participants which allowed to capture a distribution of labels for each relation. Participants were asked to insert a discourse connective between the two arguments of each relation and the authors then inferred the associated sense label from the third-level senses in the PDTB 3.0 (Prasad et al., 2019). Through this method, Scholman et al. (2022a) were able to collect 65,863 annotations from 199 participants for a total of 6,505 implicit discourse relations.

3.1 Data Preparation

We generated two datasets based on the DiscoGeM corpus (Scholman et al., 2022a): one containing the arguments and the sense distribution of each discourse relation and one containing the arguments as well as their context (the adjacent text before and after each argument). We used the arguments (with or without context) as the input of our model and the sense distribution as the target values to calculate the soft cross-entropy loss. Figure 1 shows the character length distribution of both datasets.

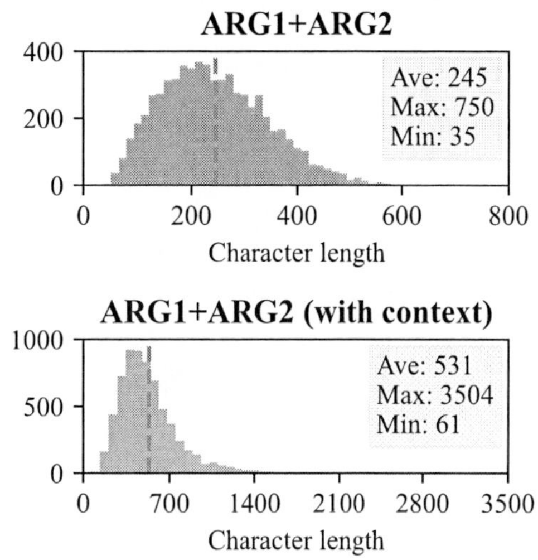

Figure 1: Distribution of character length size of the arguments of the discourse relations in the DiscoGeM corpus with and without additional textual context.

The dataset containing only the arguments (ARG1+ARG2) has an average length of 245 characters and the dataset including the context of the arguments (ARG1+ARG2 with context) has an average length of 531 characters. To ensure a balanced distribution of senses in the training and evaluation of our model, we determined the sense with the highest score for each discourse relation and then split both datasets equally while preserving the same distribution of majority-senses in training and testing. Figure 2 shows the majority-sense distribution of both datasets, after splitting 80% (5,204) of the 6,505 implicit discourse relations for training and 20% (1,301) for testing.

Note that the DiscoGeM corpus (Scholman et al., 2022a) was annotated only with 27 of the 36 third-level senses in the PDTB 3.0 (Prasad et al., 2019). The BELIEF and SPEECHACT senses were not included in the annotation process. However, as Fig-

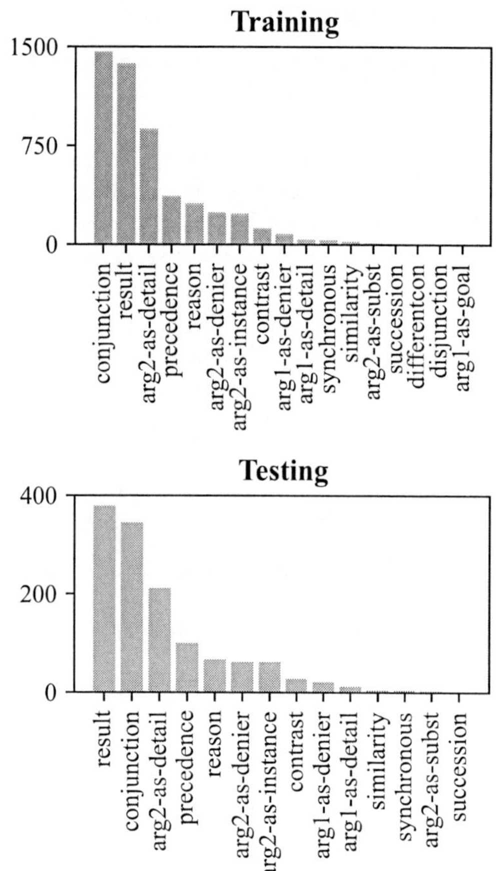

Figure 2: Distribution of the majority-sense labels in the training and testing splits of both our datasets.

ure 2 shows, not all of the 27 senses occurred in the annotated texts.

4 Classification Model

Similarly to the current state-of-the-art model in IDRR (Liu and Strube, 2023), we based our classification model on the bidirectional RoBERTa-base (Liu et al., 2019) language model. We fine-tuned the sequence classification model from Hugging Face[1] with a single classification layer using a soft cross-entropy loss with a mean reduction over batches to allow training with soft-label distributions and we optimized our model using the Adam method (Kingma and Ba, 2015). We then inferred the single label sense of each discourse relation at the evaluation stage from the element with the highest score at the output of the model. All of the code used in this paper can be found on GitHub[2].

4.1 Fine-Tuning

To optimize our model for the present task, we conducted a series of experiments with different hyperparameters to determine the configuration which yielded better results. We did not, however, experiment with different values for the beta terms in the Adam optimizer. Instead, we used the recommended values for fine-tuning RoBERTa (Liu et al., 2019): $\beta_1 = 0.9$ and $\beta_2 = 0.98$. Table 1 shows the impact of training the model with different epochs (EP) and batch sizes (BS), while keeping a constant learning rate ($\gamma = 1e^{-5}$) and no decay ($\lambda = 0$). In these experiments we considered only the dataset made of the arguments of the discourse relations (see ARG1+ARG2 in Figure 1).

Hyperparameters	F1	Precision	Recall
EP: 10 / BS: 16	49.98	49.55	51.35
EP: 10 / BS: 32	50.91	50.62	51.58
EP: 10 / BS: 64	**51.38**	**51.54**	**52.19**
EP: 20 / BS: 64	50.59	50.67	51.04

Table 1: Evaluation of our model with different epochs (EP) and batch sizes (BS), while keeping a constant learning rate ($\gamma = 1e^{-5}$) and no decay ($\lambda = 0$).

The values highlighted in bold in Table 1 show the best configuration on the test split: $EP = 10$ and $BS = 64$. For smaller batch sizes and higher epochs, the model performed better in training but worst in testing. Given the relatively small dataset, these configurations might have been more prone to over-fitting. Keeping the optimal number of epochs and batch size, in Table 2 we studied the influence of different learning rates (γ) and the impact of introducing a linear decay (λ) in the performance of the model.

The values highlighted in bold in Table 2 show the best configuration on the test split: $\gamma = 1e^{-5}$ and $\lambda = 0$. Similarly to the number of epochs and batch sizes, higher learning rates led to better results in training but worst in testing. The same phenomenon occurred with the introduction of the linear decay rate. This hints at the susceptibility of the model to over-fitting and emphasizes the importance of carefully selecting hyperparameters to ensure better generalization.

[1]https://huggingface.co/docs/transformers/model_doc/roberta

[2]https://github.com/CLaC-Lab/Implicit-Discourse-Relation-Recognition

Hyperparameters	F1	Precision	Recall
γ: 5e^{-5} / λ: 0.0	48.77	49.91	49.42
γ: 2e^{-5} / λ: 0.0	49.43	49.64	50.88
γ: 1e^{-5} / λ: 0.0	**51.38**	**51.54**	**52.19**
γ: 1e^{-5} / λ: 0.1	49.67	50.78	50.73

Table 2: Evaluation of our model with different learning rates (γ) and with decay (λ), for 10 epochs and a batch size of 64.

5 Results and Analysis

Having selected the optimal hyperparameter configuration ($EP = 10$, $BS = 64$, $\gamma = 1e^{-5}$ and $\lambda = 0$), we applied our classification model to the task of IDRR under two different settings. In the first setting we considered only the arguments of the discourse relations as input to our model, while in the second setting we also took into consideration their adjacent textual context. In both settings, the model outputs a soft-label distribution over the possible third-level senses in the PDTB 3.0 (Prasad et al., 2019), from which the sense with the highest score is selected and evaluated against the respective majority-sense from the DiscoGeM corpus (Scholman et al., 2022a). Table 3 presents the results of our model under both settings.

Input	F1	Precision	Recall
ARG1+ARG2	**51.38**	**51.54**	**52.19**
ARG1+ARG2 (with context)	43.67	43.22	45.43

Table 3: Results of third-level sense classification of implicit discourse relations considering the arguments without and with additional textual context.

As indicated in Section 3.1, our model is based on the RoBERTa (Liu et al., 2019) language model, whose maximum input length size is 512. However, the average length of the input with context is 531 characters, while the average length of the input without context is 245 characters (see Figure 1). The results in Table 3 indicate that the extra contextual information gain does not outweigh the information lost to truncation, as we obtain higher scores on all metrics for the shorter inputs without context. We include the confusion matrix of the output of our model without context in Table 4 of Appendix A.

Although we did not test our model directly on the PDTB 3.0 corpus (Prasad et al., 2019), our results suggest the benefits of training IDRR classification models on soft-label distributions. Our model obtained an F1-score of 51.38 on a subset of the DiscoGeM corpus (Scholman et al., 2022a), while the current best model in IDRR (Liu and Strube, 2023) obtained an F1-score of 55.26 on a subset of the PDTB 3.0 corpus (Prasad et al., 2019). In their work, Pyatkin et al. (2023) obtained an accuracy of 41% on a subset of the PDTB 3.0 corpus when training their model on the union of the DiscoGeM and the QADiscourse (Pyatkin et al., 2020) corpora.

6 Conclusion

In this paper we proposed a single label implicit discourse relation recognition model trained on soft-label distributions from the DiscoGeM corpus and evaluated it on single label classification to allow an easier comparison against existing state-of-the-art IDRR models. We obtained an F1-score of 51.38 on third-level sense classification of implicit discourse relations on the DiscoGeM corpus following the PDTB 3.0 annotation guidelines. Our results hint at the possible benefits of training IDRR classification models on soft-label distributions to help generalize and discern between possible multiple interpretations of ambiguous texts.

7 Limitations and Future Work

In this work we trained and evaluated our model using only the DiscoGeM corpus. Although the training was done using soft-labels, the evaluation considered only single labels. We would now like to evaluate the performance of our model also on the soft-label prediction task itself using soft evaluation metrics. In addition, since most state-of-the-art IDRR models are trained and evaluated on the PDTB 3.0 corpus, we would also like to evaluate the performance of our model on single label classification using the PDTB 3.0 corpus. This would allow us to draw a direct comparison between our approach and other existing IDRR models.

Finally, our proposed classification model consists of a rather simple configuration of the RoBERTa-base model with a sequential classification layer on top. In future work, we would like to explore more elaborate model configurations. We would also like to train our model on the traditional single label IDRR classification task and use it as a baseline to evaluate the true potential of training our model on soft-labels.

Acknowledgements

The authors would like to thank the anonymous reviewers for their feedback on the previous version of this paper. They would also like to thank the Linguistics Data Consortium (LDC) for providing access to the PDTB 3.0 corpus and the authors of the DiscoGeM corpus for providing free access to their corpus. This work was financially supported by the Natural Sciences and Engineering Research Council of Canada (NSERC).

References

Lora Aroyo and Chris Welty. 2013. Crowd Truth: Harnessing disagreement in crowdsourcing a relation extraction gold standard. In *Proceedings of the 5th Annual Association for Computing Machinery Web Science Conference (WebSci'13)*, Paris, France. Association for Computing Machinery (ACM).

Valerio Basile, Michael Fell, Tommaso Fornaciari, Dirk Hovy, Silviu Paun, Barbara Plank, Massimo Poesio, and Alexandra Uma. 2021. We Need to Consider Disagreement in Evaluation. In *Proceedings of the 1st Workshop on Benchmarking: Past, Present and Future*, pages 15–21, Online. Association for Computational Linguistics (ACL).

Chunkit Chan, Xin Liu, Jiayang Cheng, Zihan Li, Yangqiu Song, Ginny Y Wong, and Simon See. 2023. DiscoPrompt: Path Prediction Prompt Tuning for Implicit Discourse Relation Recognition. In *Proceedings of the 61st Annual Meeting of the Association for Computational Linguistics (ACL'23)*, pages 35–57, Toronto, Ontario, Canada. Association for Computational Linguistics (ACL).

Nelson Filipe Costa, Nadia Sheikh, and Leila Kosseim. 2023. Mapping Explicit and Implicit Discourse Relations between the RST-DT and the PDTB 3.0. In *Proceedings of the 14th International Conference on Recent Advances in Natural Language Processing (RANLP'23)*, pages 344–352, Varna, Bulgaria.

Vera Demberg, Merel CJ Scholman, and Fatemeh Torabi Asr. 2019. How compatible are our discourse annotation frameworks? Insights from mapping RST-DT and PDTB annotations. *Dialogue & Discourse*, 10(1):87–135.

Jet Hoek, Merel C.J. Scholman, and Ted J.M. Sanders. 2021. Is there less annotator agreement when the discourse relation is underspecified? In *Proceedings of the 1st Workshop on Integrating Perspectives on Discourse Annotation*, pages 1–6, Tübingen, Germany. Association for Computational Linguistics (ACL).

Patrick Huber, Wen Xiao, and Giuseppe Carenini. 2021. W-RST: Towards a Weighted RST-style Discourse Framework. In *Proceedings of the 59th Annual Meeting of the Association for Computational Linguistics and the 11th International Joint Conference on Natural Language Processing (ACL-IJCNLP'21)*, pages 3908–3918, Online. Association for Computational Linguistics (ACL).

Nan-Jiang Jiang and Marie-Catherine de Marneffe. 2022. Investigating Reasons for Disagreement in Natural Language Inference. *Transactions of the Association for Computational Linguistics (TACL)*, 10:1357–1374.

Diederik P. Kingma and Jimmy Ba. 2015. Adam: A Method for Stochastic Optimization. In *Proceedings of the 3rd International Conference on Learning Representations (ICLR'15)*, pages 1–15, San Diego, California, USA.

Wei Liu and Michael Strube. 2023. Annotation-Inspired Implicit Discourse Relation Classification with Auxiliary Discourse Connective Generation. In *Proceedings of the 61st Annual Meeting of the Association for Computational Linguistics (ACL'23)*, pages 15696–15712, Toronto, Ontario, Canada. Association for Computational Linguistics (ACL).

Yinhan Liu, Myle Ott, Naman Goyal, Jingfei Du, Mandar Joshi, Danqi Chen, Omer Levy, Mike Lewis, Luke Zettlemoyer, and Veselin Stoyanov. 2019. RoBERTa: A Robustly Optimized BERT Pretraining Approach.

Wanqiu Long and Bonnie Webber. 2022. Facilitating Contrastive Learning of Discourse Relational Senses by Exploiting the Hierarchy of Sense Relations. In *Proceedings of the 2022 Conference on Empirical Methods in Natural Language Processing (EMNLP'22)*, pages 10704–10716, Abu Dhabi, United Arab Emirates. Association for Computational Linguistics (ACL).

William C Mann and Sandra A Thompson. 1988. Rhetorical Structure Theory: Toward a functional theory of text organization. *Text-interdisciplinary Journal for the Study of Discourse*, 8(3):243–281.

Eleni Miltsakaki, Rashmi Prasad, Aravind Joshi, and Bonnie Webber. 2004. The Penn Discourse Treebank. In *Proceedings of the Fourth International Conference on Language Resources and Evaluation (LREC'04)*, pages 2237–2240, Lisbon, Portugal. European Language Resources Association (ELRA).

Ellie Pavlick and Tom Kwiatkowski. 2019. Inherent Disagreements in Human Textual Inferences. *Transactions of the Association for Computational Linguistics (TACL)*, 7:677–694.

Rashmi Prasad, Nikhil Dinesh, Alan Lee, Eleni Miltsakaki, Livio Robaldo, Aravind Joshi, and Bonnie Webber. 2008. The Penn Discourse TreeBank 2.0. In *Proceedings of the Sixth International Conference on Language Resources and Evaluation (LREC'08)*, pages 2961–2968, Marrakech, Morocco. European Language Resources Association (ELRA).

Rashmi Prasad, Bonnie Webber, Alan Lee, and Aravind Joshi. 2019. Penn Discourse Treebank Version 3.0. LDC2019T05. Web Download. Philadelphia: Linguistic Data Consortium.

Valentina Pyatkin, Ayal Klein, Reut Tsarfaty, and Ido Dagan. 2020. QADiscourse - Discourse Relations as QA Pairs: Representation, Crowdsourcing and Baselines. In *Proceedings of the 2020 Conference on Empirical Methods in Natural Language Processing (EMNLP'20)*, pages 2804–2819, Online. Association for Computational Linguistics.

Valentina Pyatkin, Frances Yung, Merel C. J. Scholman, Reut Tsarfaty, Ido Dagan, and Vera Demberg. 2023. Design Choices for Crowdsourcing Implicit Discourse Relations: Revealing the Biases Introduced by Task Design. *Transactions of the Association for Computational Linguistics (TACL)*, 11:1014–1032.

Hannah Rohde, Anna Dickinson, Nathan Schneider, Christopher N. L. Clark, Annie Louis, and Bonnie Webber. 2016. Filling in the Blanks in Understanding Discourse Adverbials: Consistency, Conflict, and Context-Dependence in a Crowdsourced Elicitation Task. In *Proceedings of the 10th Linguistic Annotation Workshop (LAW'16)*, pages 49–58, Berlin, Germany. Association for Computational Linguistics.

Merel Scholman, Tianai Dong, Frances Yung, and Vera Demberg. 2022a. DiscoGeM: A Crowdsourced Corpus of Genre-Mixed Implicit Discourse Relations. In *Proceedings of the Thirteenth Language Resources and Evaluation Conference (LREC'22)*, pages 3281–3290, Marseille, France. European Language Resources Association (ELRA).

Merel Scholman, Valentina Pyatkin, Frances Yung, Ido Dagan, Reut Tsarfaty, and Vera Demberg. 2022b. Design Choices in Crowdsourcing Discourse Relation Annotations: The Effect of Worker Selection and Training. In *Proceedings of the Thirteenth Language Resources and Evaluation Conference (LREC'22)*, pages 2148–2156, Marseille, France. European Language Resources Association (ELRA).

Manfred Stede. 2008. Disambiguating Rhetorical Structure. *Research on Language and Computation*, 6(3):311–332.

Nianwen Xue, Hwee Tou Ng, Sameer Pradhan, Attapol Rutherford, Bonnie Webber, Chuan Wang, and Hongmin Wang. 2016. CoNLL 2016 Shared Task on Multilingual Shallow Discourse Parsing. In *Proceedings of the CoNLL-16 shared task*, pages 1–19, Berlin, Germany. Association for Computational Linguistics (ACL).

Frances Yung, Vera Demberg, and Merel Scholman. 2019. Crowdsourcing Discourse Relation Annotations by a Two-Step Connective Insertion Task. In *Proceedings of the 13th Linguistic Annotation Workshop*, pages 16–25, Florence, Italy. Association for Computational Linguistics (ACL).

Haodong Zhao, Ruifang He, Mengnan Xiao, and Jing Xu. 2023. Infusing Hierarchical Guidance into Prompt Tuning: A Parameter-Efficient Framework for Multi-level Implicit Discourse Relation Recognition. In *Proceedings of the 61st Annual Meeting of the Association for Computational Linguistics (ACL'23)*, pages 6477–6492, Toronto, Ontario, Canada. Association for Computational Linguistics (ACL).

A Appendix - Confusion Matrix

Targets \ Predictions	Synchronous	Precedence	Succession	Reason	Result	Arg1-as-Cond	Arg2-as-Cond	Arg1-as-NegCond	Arg2-as-NegCond	Arg1-as-Goal	Arg2-as-Goal	Arg1-as-Denier	Arg2-as-Denier	Contrast	Similarity	Conjunction	Disjunction	Arg1-as-Instance	Arg2-as-Instance	Arg1-as-Detail	Arg2-as-Detail	Equivalence	Arg1-as-Manner	Arg2-as-Manner	Arg1-as-Exception	Arg2-as-Exception	Arg2-as-Substitution	Different-Conn	NoRel
Synchronous	0	2	0	0	1	0	0	0	0	0	0	0	1	0	0	6	0	0	0	0	0	0	0	0	0	0	0	0	0
Precedence	2	66	0	1	20	0	0	0	0	0	0	0	0	0	0	13	0	0	0	0	8	0	0	0	0	0	0	0	0
Succession	0	0	0	1	0	0	0	0	0	0	0	0	0	0	0	1	0	0	0	0	0	0	0	0	0	0	0	0	0
Reason	0	0	0	48	11	0	0	0	0	0	0	0	2	3	0	12	0	0	1	0	12	0	0	0	0	0	0	0	0
Result	0	22	0	20	245	0	0	0	0	0	0	0	0	23	2	0	63	0	0	8	0	31	0	0	0	0	0	0	0
Arg1-as-Cond	0	0	0	0	0	0	0	0	0	0	0	0	0	0	0	0	0	0	0	0	0	0	0	0	0	0	0	0	0
Arg2-as-Cond	0	0	0	0	0	0	0	0	0	0	0	0	0	0	0	0	0	0	0	0	0	0	0	0	0	0	0	0	0
Arg1-as-NegCond	0	0	0	0	0	0	0	0	0	0	0	0	0	0	0	0	0	0	0	0	0	0	0	0	0	0	0	0	0
Arg2-as-NegCond	0	0	0	0	0	0	0	0	0	0	0	0	0	0	0	0	0	0	0	0	0	0	0	0	0	0	0	0	0
Arg1-as-Goal	0	0	0	0	0	0	0	0	0	0	0	0	0	0	0	0	0	0	0	0	0	0	0	0	0	0	0	0	0
Arg2-as-Goal	0	0	0	0	0	0	0	0	0	0	0	0	0	0	0	0	0	0	0	0	0	0	0	0	0	0	0	0	0
Arg1-as-Denier	0	0	0	3	2	0	0	0	0	0	0	2	3	0	0	6	0	0	0	4	0	0	0	0	0	0	0	0	0
Arg2-as-Denier	0	0	0	1	11	0	0	0	0	0	0	1	19	1	0	12	0	0	1	0	3	0	0	0	0	0	0	0	0
Contrast	0	1	0	6	4	0	0	0	0	0	0	1	2	3	0	10	0	0	0	0	1	0	0	0	0	0	0	0	0
Similarity	0	0	0	0	2	0	0	0	0	0	0	0	0	0	0	7	0	0	0	0	1	0	0	0	0	0	0	0	0
Conjunction	0	17	0	24	46	0	0	0	0	0	0	3	11	1	0	187	0	0	5	0	31	0	0	0	0	0	0	0	0
Disjunction	0	0	0	0	0	0	0	0	0	0	0	0	0	0	0	0	0	0	0	0	0	0	0	0	0	0	0	0	0
Arg1-as-Instance	0	0	0	0	0	0	0	0	0	0	0	0	0	0	0	0	0	0	0	0	0	0	0	0	0	0	0	0	0
Arg2-as-Instance	0	2	0	6	4	0	0	0	0	0	0	0	0	0	0	11	0	0	21	0	11	0	0	0	0	0	0	0	0
Arg1-as-Detail	0	0	0	3	3	0	0	0	0	0	0	0	1	0	0	0	0	0	0	0	2	0	0	0	0	0	0	0	0
Arg2-as-Detail	0	1	0	21	16	0	0	0	0	0	0	1	1	0	0	37	0	0	5	0	88	0	0	0	0	0	0	0	0
Equivalence	0	0	0	0	0	0	0	0	0	0	0	0	0	0	0	0	0	0	0	0	0	0	0	0	0	0	0	0	0
Arg1-as-Manner	0	0	0	0	0	0	0	0	0	0	0	0	0	0	0	0	0	0	0	0	0	0	0	0	0	0	0	0	0
Arg2-as-Manner	0	0	0	0	0	0	0	0	0	0	0	0	0	0	0	0	0	0	0	0	0	0	0	0	0	0	0	0	0
Arg1-as-Exception	0	0	0	0	0	0	0	0	0	0	0	0	0	0	0	0	0	0	0	0	0	0	0	0	0	0	0	0	0
Arg2-as-Exception	0	0	0	0	0	0	0	0	0	0	0	0	0	0	0	0	0	0	0	0	0	0	0	0	0	0	0	0	0
Arg2-as-Substitution	0	0	0	0	2	0	0	0	0	0	0	0	0	0	0	0	0	0	0	0	0	0	0	0	0	0	0	0	0
Different-Conn	0	1	0	2	2	0	0	0	0	0	0	0	0	0	0	2	0	0	0	0	1	0	0	0	0	0	0	0	0
NoRel	0	0	0	0	0	0	0	0	0	0	0	0	0	0	0	0	0	0	0	0	0	0	0	0	0	0	0	0	0

Table 4: Confusion matrix for the majority third-level sense classification of implicit discourse relations considering only the arguments without the context of the relation as input. Color gradients are calculated at the target level (row-wise).

The ARRAU 3.0 Corpus

Massimo Poesio[1], Maris Camilleri[1], Paloma Carretero Garcia[1], Juntao Yu[1], Mark-Christoph Müller[2]
[1]Queen Mary Univ., UK [2]Leibniz-Institut für Deutsche Sprache
{m.poesio,m.camilleri,p.carreterogarcia,juntao.yu}@qmul.ac.uk
mark-christoph.mueller@ids-mannheim.de

Abstract

ARRAU is an anaphorically annotated corpus designed to cover a variety of aspects of anaphoric reference in a variety of genres, including both written text and spoken language. The objective of this annotation project is to push forward the state of the art in anaphoric annotation, by overcoming the limitations of current annotation practice and the scope of current models of anaphoric interpretation, which in turn may reveal other issues. The resulting corpus is still therefore very much a work in progress almost twenty years after the project started. In this paper, we discuss the issues identified with the coding scheme used for the previous release, ARRAU 2, and through the use of this corpus for three shared tasks; the proposed solutions to these issues; and the resulting corpus, ARRAU 3.

1 Introduction

Although the scope and ambition of anaphoric annotation projects has enormously increased in the last twenty years (Poesio, 2004; Hinrichs et al., 2004; Pradhan et al., 2007, 2012; Poesio and Artstein, 2008; Uryupina et al., 2020; Recasens and Martí, 2010; Rahman and Ng, 2012; Nedoluzhko, 2013; Muzerelle et al., 2014; Cohen et al., 2017; Zeldes, 2017; Webster et al., 2018; Bamman et al., 2020; Sakaguchi et al., 2020; Khosla et al., 2021; Yu et al., 2022a; Nedoluzhko et al., 2022) a number of open questions about anaphoric annotation remain, and many if not most of the existing corpora have limitations either in size or coverage.

The ARRAU annotation (Poesio and Artstein, 2008; Uryupina et al., 2020; Poesio et al., 2018) is a long-term project to expand the range of anaphoric annotation by creating an anaphorically annotated corpus covering a wide variety of aspects of anaphoric reference (Poesio, 2016). The annotation project started in 2004 as the result of a series of studies of the reliability of 'difficult' aspects of anaphoric annotation (Poesio, 2004; Poesio and Artstein, 2005b,a; Artstein and Poesio, 2006, 2008) and the first release was primarily focused on anaphoric reference in dialogue (Poesio and Artstein, 2008). The scope of the annotation then broadened both in terms of linguistic aspects that were annotated and in terms of genres, resulting in a second release in 2013 (Uryupina et al., 2020). This second release was then used as the core dataset for the 2018 CRAC Shared Task (Poesio et al., 2018), the first shared task for anaphora resolution covering also identification of non-referring expressions, bridging reference and discourse deixis; and as additional material for the 2021 and 2022 CODI-CRAC shared tasks on anaphora resolution in dialogues (Khosla et al., 2021; Yu et al., 2022a). These shared tasks highlighted the need to revise the annotation guidelines for a range of phenomena including discourse deixis and genericity and reference in dialogues. They also revealed a number of issues with tokenization and markup. We therefore started an extensive reannotation and cleaning up, resulting in a third, substantially revised release of the corpus.

In this paper we discuss the issues identified with the previous annotation, the revised annotation scheme and guidelines, the cleaning up procedure, and the new corpus resulting from this effort.

2 Anaphoric Annotation

We review in this Section the aspects of anaphoric interpretation captured in the ARRAU annotation.

Identity Anaphora Most modern anaphoric annotation projects cover identity anaphora as in (1).

(1) [Mary]$_i$ bought [a new dress]$_j$ but [it]$_j$ didn't fit [her]$_i$.

However, many other types of identity anaphora exist, as well as other types of anaphoric relations, discussed below.

Proceedings of the 5th Workshop on Computational Approaches to Discourse (CODI 2024), pages 127–138
March 21, 2024 ©2024 Association for Computational Linguistics

Split-antecedent anaphora In most corpora, plural reference is only marked when the antecedent is mentioned by a single noun phrase. But in **split-antecedent anaphors** (Eschenbach et al., 1989; Kamp and Reyle, 1993) such as (2), plural pronoun *they* refers to a set composed of two entities introduced by separate noun phrases.

(2) $[\text{John}]_1$ met $[\text{Mary}]_2$. $[\text{He}]_1$ greeted $[\text{her}]_2$. $[\text{They}]_{1,2}$ went to the movies.

Such references are not annotated in many corpora, or *They* is treated as a bridging reference.

The semantic function of noun phrases The nominal expressions in (1) are examples of **referring** noun phrases, which either introduce new entities in a discourse (first mention of Mary and the new dress) or link to previously introduced entities (pronouns *it* and *her*). But NPs can serve different functions. **Quantificational** NPs such as *No one* in *No one would put the blame on him/herself* (Partee, 1972) do not refer to an individual or set of individuals, but can still participate in anaphoric relations even though anaphoric reference to quantifiers has distinctive properties (Partee, 1972) and is subject to semantic constraints (Karttunen, 1976). **Predicative** noun phrases express properties of objects: for instance, in sentence (3), the NP *a busy place* does not introduce a new discourse entity or refer back to an existing discourse entity, but expresses a property. Finally, in languages like English, forms like *it* and *there* can also be used to express semantically vacuous **expletives** as well as pronouns, like the *it* in *It is four o'clock.* Distinguishing referring from non-referring nominals is a part of the task of interpreting anaphoric expressions which cannot be evaluated in corpora where non-referring expressions are not annotated.

(3) [This] seems to be [a busy place]

Discourse deixis The term 'anaphoric reference' covers a wide variety of phenomena, not all of which are annotated in all corpora. **Event anaphora** is the type of anaphoric reference exemplified by *that* in (4), which does not refer to an entity introduced by a nominal, but to the event of a white rabbit with pink ears running past Alice.

(4) ... when suddenly a White Rabbit with pink eyes ran close by her. There was nothing so VERY remarkable in [that]; nor did Alice think it so VERY much out of the way to hear the Rabbit say to itself, 'Oh dear! Oh dear! I shall be late!' (when she thought it over afterwards, it occurred to her that she ought to have wondered at [this], but at the time it all seemed quite natural); ....

Event anaphora is a subtype of the more complex phenomenon of **discourse deixis** (Webber, 1991; Kolhatkar et al., 2018) which also includes references like *this* in (4), which refers to the fact that the Rabbit was able to talk. Not many corpora attempt to cover the entire range of discourse deixis.

Bridging references and other non-identity anaphora Possibly the most studied type of non-identity anaphora is **bridging reference** or **associative anaphora** (Clark, 1977; Hawkins, 1978; Prince, 1981) as in (5), where bridging reference *the roof* refers to an object which is related to / associated with, but not identical to, the *hall*.

(5) There was not a moment to be lost: away went Alice like the wind, and was just in time to hear it say, as it turned a corner, 'Oh my ears and whiskers, how late it's getting!' She was close behind it when she turned the corner, but the Rabbit was no longer to be seen: she found herself in [a long, low hall, which was lit up by a row of lamps hanging from [the roof]].

Other types of non-identity anaphora also exist, besides bridging references. Examples include *other* anaphora like *the other* in (6), as well as **identity of sense** anaphora such as *a blue one* in (7) (Poesio, 2016).

(6) John gave one book to Mary, and [the other] to Bill.

(7) John bought a red ball, and Mary [a blue one].

The interplay between anaphora and other semantic properties of nominals Often, whether two mentions corefer depends on how they get semantically interpreted in other respects. In (8), for instance, whether the mention *bananas* in 40.2 is interpreted as coreferring with mention *bananas* in 37.8 depends on whether these bare plurals are taken to be references to the generic kind **bananas** (Carlson and Pelletier, 1995). If those mentions are interpreted as non-generic, they would not corefer. Some anaphoric corpora therefore include an annotation of noun phrases' genericity (Uryupina et al., 2020; Nedoluzhko, 2013).

	37.1	M:	all right
	37.2	:	and then at the same time
			...
	37.5	:	E2 was zipping over to Bath to pick up a boxcar
	37.6	:	heading down to Avon
	37.7	:	to
	37.8	:	collect [bananas]$_i$
	37.9	:	and then shipping [em]$_i$ back to Corning
(8)	37.10	:	shortest route
			...
	38.1	S:	okay so
	38.2	:	E2
	38.3	:	goes to Corning
	38.4	:	then
	38.5	:	on to Bath
	38.6	:	and gets a boxcar
	39.1	M:	m hm
	40.1	S:	then on to Avon
	40.2	:	load [bananas]$_?$

Anaphoric reference in dialogue Anaphora resolution in dialogue requires systems to handle grammatically incorrect language suffering from disfluencies and mentions jointly created across utterances (Poesio and Rieser, 2010) or whose function is to establish common ground rather than refer (Clark and Brennan, 1990; Heeman and Hirst, 1995). Dialogue contains more deictic reference, vaguer anaphoric and discourse deictic reference, or speaker grounding of pronouns. These complexities are normally absent from news or Wikipedia articles, which form the bulk of current datasets for coreference resolution (Poesio et al., 2016). There has been some research on coreference in dialogue in English (Byron, 2002; Eckert and Strube, 2001; Müller, 2008), but very limited in scope (primarily pronominal interpretation), due to the lack of suitable corpora, although the situation is better for other languages (Muzerelle et al., 2014; Grobol, 2020).

3 ARRAU 1 and 2

3.1 Genres

The ARRAU corpus[1] (Poesio and Artstein, 2008; Uryupina et al., 2020) was designed to cover a variety of genres. Initially, the corpus was meant to focus on anaphoric reference in dialogue and spoken language (Poesio and Artstein, 2008). Its TRAINS sub-corpus includes all the task-oriented dialogues in the TRAINS-93 corpus[2] (Heeman and Allen, 1995) already used in Byron's work on pronominal reference in dialogue (Byron and Allen, 1998; Byron, 2002) as well as the pilot dialogues in the so-called TRAINS-91 corpus. The PEAR sub-corpus consists of the complete collection of spoken narratives in the Pear Stories that provided some of the early evidence on salience and anaphoric reference (Chafe, 1980).[3] Subsequently, the corpus was extended to cover a substantial amount of written text, including news text in a sub-corpus called RST, consisting of the entire subset of the Penn Treebank (Marcus et al., 1993) that was annotated in the RST treebank (Carlson et al., 2003).[4] The GNOME sub-corpus covers documents from the medical and art history genres covered by the GNOME corpus (Poesio, 2004).

3.2 Annotation scheme

The same coding scheme was used for all sub-corpora, but separate guidelines were written for the spoken dialogue and written language sub-corpora. The original annotation scheme used for Release 1 (Poesio and Artstein, 2008), focused on dialogue, is distributed with the dataset and is also available from the ARRAU corpus page. For the second release (Uryupina et al., 2020), the guidelines for bridging were extended and genericity was also annotated using the GNOME guidelines, but a complete new manual was not produced. However, a fairly extensive description can be found in Uryupina et al. (2020).

Markable definition Many older anaphorically annotated corpora impose syntactic, semantic or discourse-based restrictions on markables. For instance, in ONTONOTES neither expletives nor singletons are annotated (Poesio et al., 2016). By contrast, in ARRAU *all* NPs are considered as markables, including non-referring expressions (e.g., expletives such as *it* or predicative NPs such as *a busy place*) in (3), and expressions do not corefer with any other markable ('singletons'). Moreover, in ARRAU non-referring markables are manually subclassified into expletives, predicative, and quantifiers. In addition, all generic references are marked, including premodifiers when the entity referred to is mentioned again, e.g., in the case of the proper name *US* in (9), and premodifiers that refer to a kind, like *exchange-rate* in (10).

(9) ...The Treasury Department said that the [US]$_1$ trade deficit may worsen next year

[1] http://www.arrauproject.org/corpus

[2] http://www.ldc.upenn.edu/Catalog/catalogEntry.jsp?catalogId=LDC95S25

[3] https://www.linguistics.ucsb.edu/research/pear-film

[4] https://catalog.ldc.upenn.edu/LDC2002T07

after two years of significant improvement... The statement was the [US]$_1$'s government first acknowledgment...

(10) The Treasury report, which is required annually by a provision of the 1988 trade act, again took South Korea to task for its [exchange-rate]$_1$ policies. "We believe there have continued to be indications of [exchange-rate]$_1$ manipulation...

A distinctive feature of ARRAU's definition of markables is that, due to its initial focus on dialogue, it also allows **discontinuous** markables such as the collaborative constructed *three ... loaded boxcars* in (11), building on (Müller, 2008) and leveraging MMAX2's support for such markables.

(11)
S: okay um if you can only pull three loaded boxcars
U: [three]^1
S: yeah [loaded boxcars]^1

Referential status A markable can be marked as semantically non-referring (an expletive, a predicate, a quantifier, a coordination, an idiom, or incomplete) or referring (either `discourse new` or `discourse old`). Discourse new mentions introduce new entities and thus are not marked as being coreferent with an entity already introduced (**antecedent**). For discourse-old markables, the annotation of different types of anaphoric relations is supported. The antecedent of discourse-old mentions can be either of type `phrase` (if the antecedent was introduced using a nominal markable) or `segment` (not introduced by a nominal markable, for **discourse deixis**).[5] In addition, referring NPs can be marked as **related** to a previously mentioned discourse entity to identify them as examples of associative (**bridging**) anaphora.

Bridging references Annotating — indeed, even identifying — bridging references in a reliable way is difficult, which is one of the reasons why so few large-scale corpora for anaphora include this type of annotation (Poesio et al., 2016; Kobayashi and Ng, 2020). The ARRAU guidelines for bridging anaphora are based on experiments that ran from (Poesio and Vieira, 1998) to (Poesio, 2004). The ARRAU Release 1 and 2 guidelines followed the GNOME guidelines, but with an extension and a simplification. Annotators were asked to mark a markable as `related` to a particular antecedent if it stood to that antecedent in one of the GNOME relations or in the two additional relations

- `other`, for *other* NPs, broadly following the guidelines in Modjeska (2003);
- an `undersp-rel` relation for 'obvious cases of bridging that didn't fit any other category'.

However, the actual relations were not marked in ARRAU 1. Relation annotation started with ARRAU 2, but only for the RST portion. One of the objectives for ARRAU 3 was to annotate the relations underlying bridging reference for all sub-corpora.

Discourse deixis Discourse deixis in its full form is a very complex form of reference, both to annotate and to resolve (Kolhatkar et al., 2018) . Very few anaphoric annotation projects have attempted to annotate discourse deixis in its entirety (Kolhatkar et al., 2018). More typical is a partial annotation, as in (Byron and Allen, 1998; Navarretta, 2000), who annotated pronominal reference to abstract objects; in ONTONOTES, where event anaphora was marked (Pradhan et al., 2007); and in (Kolhatkar and Hirst, 2014), which focused on so-called shell nouns. In ARRAU, a coder specifying that a referring expression is discourse-old is asked whether its antecedent was introduced using a `phrase` (markable) or a `segment` (discourse segment). Coders who choose `segment` have to mark a sequence of *predefined* clauses as antecedent.

Genericity ARRAU is not a multi-layer corpus like ANCORA, GUM, ONTONOTES or the Prague Dependency Treebank, meaning that other linguistic information relevant for the study of anaphora (morphosyntax, dependency structure, semantics) also has to be annotated within the anaphoric layer. We only discuss in this paper genericity, as it's the one among these attributes for which the guidelines changed in ARRAU 3.

The ARRAU scheme and guidelines for genericity build on the studies of genericity reliability carried out as part of the GNOME annotation (Poesio et al., 2004). This scheme is based on a generalised notion of scopal dependence for nominals covering both genericity and scopal dependence on a range of operators including conditionals, quantifiers, and temporal adverbials. More specifically, according to the guidelines used for ARRAU 1 and 2, the annotation of the `generic` attribute is carried out following a decision tree going from the

[5] Identity anaphora also includes split antecedent plural anaphoric reference.

easiest cases to the more complex ones. Coders are first asked to check whether the nominal is in the syntactic scope of an *explicit* operator such as a conditional like *if* (as in (12)) or an individual quantifier such as *every* or *most* (iquant) In these cases, the nominal is *not* marked as generic, but as being in the scope of the appropriate operator. If no such explicit quantifier/operator is present, coders are asked to check whether the nominal refers to semantic objects whose genericity is left underspecified, such as substances (e.g., *gold*), as in (13) Finally, the annotator is asked whether the sentence in which the markable occurs is generic, and in this case, to mark the nominal as generic-yes if it refers generically, as in (14), or generic-no otherwise. With these instructions, reasonable intercoder agreement was achieved ($\kappa = .82$) (Poesio, 2004).

(12) New York State Comptroller Edward Regan predicts a \$ 1.3 billion budget gap for the city 's next fiscal year, a gap that could grow if there is [a recession]$^{operator-conditional}$. "

(13) Not that [oil]$^{undersp-substance}$ suddenly is a sure thing again .

(14) In its report to Congress on [international economic policies]$^{generic-yes}$, the Treasury said that any improvement in the broadest measures of trade, known as the current account.

3.3 Annotation procedure

ARRAU 1 and 2 were annotated using MMAX2 (Müller and Strube, 2006). All annotation was carried out by trained (computational) linguists. ARRAU 1 was primarily annotated at the University of Essex between 2004 and 2007 under the direction of Ron Artstein, who also designed the MMAX2 style, and in collaboration with Mark-Christoph Müller. The initial annotation was then extended and checked as part of the Johns Hopkins 2007 Workshop on Entity Disambiguation (ELERFED).

ARRAU 2 was annotated at the University of Trento between 2008 and 2016 under the coordination of Kepa Rodriguez, Francesca Delogu, Federica Cavicchio, and Olga Uryupina. Most of the annotation was carried out by Antonella Bristot.

3.4 Use in shared tasks

In recent years, ARRAU was used for three shared tasks: the CRAC 2018 shared task on anaphora resolution with the ARRAU corpus (Poesio et al., 2018), and the 2021 and 2022 CODI-CRAC shared tasks on anaphora resolution in dialogue (Khosla et al., 2021; Yu et al., 2022a).

The use of the corpus for such tasks was enabled by two improvements brought about by the Universal Anaphora initiative.[6] The first of these was the development of a tabular markup format extending the CONLL-U tabular format used for the CONLL 2011 and 2012 shared tasks on coreference (Pradhan et al., 2012) with ways to represent the additional types of anaphoric information encoded in ARRAU, but consistent with it so that modellers would understand it better. And second, the development of scorers extending the Coreference Reference scorer (Pradhan et al., 2014) with ways of scoring the interpretation of these additional phenomena (Poesio et al., 2018; Yu et al., 2022b).

4 ARRAU 3: Summary of the Revisions

The CRAC 2018 shared task revealed a number of issues with the ARRAU 2 annotation - first of all with the annotation of bridging references and discourse deixis- that prompted a first round of revisions to the annotation scheme and the annotation guidelines. More issues about the annotation of anaphoric reference in dialogue were revealed when the data were used for the CODI-CRAC 2021 shared task, resulting in a second round of revisions. During the CODI-CRAC shared task we also discovered issues with tokenization and with the way the RST portion had been converted. As a result, we started revising the corpus by: (i) revising annotation schemee and guidelines (ii) fixing the issues with tokenization and with conversion. In the following two sections, we discuss each of these revisions in detail.

5 Revised Guidelines and Re-annotation

5.1 Revised annotation scheme and guidelines

The changes to the annotation scheme and guidelines between ARRAU 2 and ARRAU 3 can be summarized as follows: (i) alternative schemes especially for the more complex aspects of the annotation (e.g., bridging reference, genericity, discourse deixis) were carefully analyzed and the annotation scheme and guidelines for these aspects were (partially) revised at the light of the solutions proposed in this work; (ii) a more *semantic* approach was adopted for the annotation of certain aspects that

[6] http://www.universalanaphora.org

had been previously annotated following purely syntactic guidelines (e.g., predication, genericity); (iii) for the dialogue sub-corpora, more attention was paid to aspects of reference in dialogue that previously had not been sufficiently considered (e.g., deictic first and second person pronouns, or the use of referring expressions for grounding purposes).

Predicative NPs The ARRAU 2 guidelines for predicative NPs were not very explicit and essentially relied on syntactic information, marking as predicates object NPs in copular clauses (*Antonio Conte was [an Italian prime minister]*) and clauses with verbs such as *become* (*Antonio Conte became [the Italian prime minister]* as well as appositions (*Antonio Conte, [the Italian prime minister], arrived in London for talks today*).

However, the decision whether an NP is predicative cannot always be made on syntactic grounds alone (Zeldes, 2022). For instance, in *[The Italian prime minister, [Antonio Conte]], arrived in London for meetings today*, it is the NP in appositive position (*Antonio Conte*) that acts as term-denoting, whereas the outside NP has a predicative function. In so-called **specificational** copular clauses, it is the subject that is predicative, whereas the object is generally taken to be referential:

(15) [The director of Anatomy of a Murder] is Otto Preminger

Whereas in so-called **identificational** copular clauses, both the subject and object are generally taken to be referring:

(16) [That woman] is [Sylvia]

Some of these cases were covered in the previous guidelines, but not systematically. The annotation guidelines were therefore thoroughly revised, to make the decision about whether a clause is predicative depend more on semantic criteria.

Non-identity anaphora The first objective of the revision of the bridging reference annotation for ARRAU 3 was to add information about the semantic relation for all subcorpora.

Equally importantly, however, we intended to produce much more explicit guidance. One issue was highlighted by the CRAC 2018 shared task (Poesio et al., 2018). Following her participation to the shared task, in which she found that the approach proposed by Hou et al (Hou et al., 2014, 2018) for the ISNOTES corpus (Markert et al., 2012) achieved very poor results on ARRAU (Roesiger, 2018), Ina Rösiger et al carried out a detailed analysis of the difference between the annotation of bridging references in the two corpora (Roesiger et al., 2018), concluding that very different notions of 'bridging' were used. In ISNOTES, only what they called **referential** bridging references were annotated, such as *the door* in (17)–cases where the anaphoric expression contains an implicit anaphoric argument (*the door [of the house]*). (We think the term 'referential' is misleading, so we will call these bridging references **implicitly anaphoric**, or IA.) In ARRAU, in addition to implicitly anaphoric bridging references, a second category of referring expressions was also annotated as bridging references, that Rösiger et al called **lexical** bridging references. One example is *Dubrovnik* in (18): the NP is not implicitly anaphoric, but it establishes entity coherence with its anchor *Croatia* through shared knowledge. (We will call this category of bridging references **coherence-establishing**, or CE.) Rösiger et al disagreed with this broader definition of bridging reference, but also pointed out that several examples of both IA and CE bridging references were not actually annotated in ARRAU 2.

(17) John walked towards the house. [The door] was open.

(18) Croatis's tourism industry has been booming. The number of yearly visitors to [Dubrovnik] grew to over 2 million by 2019.

Following that discussion, the annotation guidelines for bridging were expanded to provide more explicit information about these types of bridging references. Explicit instructions were also added to mark split-antecedent plurals not as bridging references, but using the separate multiple antecedent mechanism offered by MMAX2. Furthermore, explicit instructions about identity of sense anaphora weree added. Further instructions were also added requiring attributes to be marked as bridging (e.g., *income* in *Kellogg reported its financial results for the year yesterday. [Income] grew to ....*).

Genericity Another issue observed while running the shared tasks was that the guidelines for genericity followed in ARRAU 1 and 2 has resulted in an excessively syntactic interpretation of scope in general and genericity in particular. Consider for instance the contrast between (19) and (20), from the TRAINS corpus. We consider instructions as introducing an implicit modal operator, and our guidelines therefore required to annotate NPs in such utterances as `operator-instruction`. This is appropriate for both *a boxcar from Elmira* and *oranges* in (19). However, not all such NPs are in fact in the scope of the implicit modal operator–for instance, *the boxcar from Elmira* refers deictically to an entity in the visual scence (the TRAINS world map). As a result, we changed the guidelines to only annotate NPs in utterances containing implicit or explicit operators when they were actually in the *semantic* scope of the operator.

(19) take [a boxcar from Elmira]$_i$ and load [it]$_i$ with [oranges]

(20) take [the boxcar from Elmira]$_i$ and load [it]$_i$ with [oranges]

Reference in dialogue One issue with the previous guidelines that emerged in particular from the annotation for the CODI-CRAC dataset was that many aspects of reference in dialogue were not covered, or covered only in part.

The first such issue was the annotation of **first and second person pronouns**. Such pronouns were not annotated in the TRAINS sub-corpora in ARRAU 1 and 2, based on the belief that they were all deictic and referring to one or the other speaker, such as the instance of *you* in (21).

(21) S: hello how can I help [you]

However, this belief proved incorrect; first and second person pronouns are used in a number of other ways. E.g., in (22) the two instances of *you* in the first utterance are most likely interpreted *generically*–U is asking about what is possible in the task. We revised the guidelines providing directions for distinguishing between the uses.

(22) U: an [you] do can [you] do things simultaneously here or do they have to be done like can I have the same time having it the engine

Another issue that had not been sufficiently considered in previous releases was the relation between a wh-NP like *how long* in (23) and the answer to the question, *eight hours*. Clearly, this is not a case of coreference. However, even though wh-NP are annotated as quantifiers in ARRAU, it's not a case of bound anaphora either (as in *[No student]$_i$ forgot [their]$_i$ passport*). In the end, we decided to mark such cases as cases of associative references of type `element`, given that it may be argued that the wh-NP denotes a set (the set of possible answers) of which the answer is an element; but this decision may be reconsidered in the future.

(23)
U : so [how long] will it take if I take the two boxcars
...
S [eight hours]
U eight hours

A new manual A revised version of the annotation guidelines was produced.[7] These new guidelines were also used for the annotation of the documents included in the CODI-CRAC dataset used for the 2021 and 2022 shared tasks.

5.2 Re-Annotation

The revision proceeded in two passes. In the first pass we checked the more settled aspects of the annotation: the attributes encoding morphosyntactic information, referentiality (non referring / referring), identity anaphora, and bridging references (including e.g., checking split antecedent anaphora). The second pass was devoted to the more complex forms of annotation, including in particular genericity, ambiguity, and discourse deixis. In this second pass, we also reconsidered the annotation of the dialogue corpora at the light of the experience with the CODI-CRAC annotation. In both passes all documents were checked and possibly corrected; and each document was completely checked by each annotator.

6 Correcting tokenization and conversion errors

ARRAU 3 fixes a couple of errors and inconsistencies in the markup in previous versions. If the corrections resulted in modifications to the underlying text (the *basedata* in MMAX2 parlance), existing annotations were adapted such that they were still valid. Depending on the complexity of the corrections, they were performed in a fully or semi-automatic manner (based on scripts using pyMMAX2 (Müller, 2020)), with manual checks afterwards.

6.1 Tokenization

Tokenization, i.e. splitting of text into basedata elements, was improved for all sub-corpora by using a more fine-grained splitting scheme than the previous one, which was only sensitive to white space

[7] https://github.com/arrauproject/data/blob/main/ARRAU_3_Annotation_Manual_1.0.pdf

and punctuation. Most notably, basedata is split at word-internal non-word characters, including hyphens. As a result, hyphenated words (e.g. noun compounds and other hyphenated multi-word expressions) will be separated into several contiguous basedata elements, allowing for more fine-grained annotation. At the same time, tokenization keeps track of the original input string composition, including white space, and stores, for every basedata element, the number of leading white space characters. This way, the original text appearance can be reproduced in the the annotation tool MMAX2, allowing for a better-to-read, more natural and less distracting rendering of the display.

6.2 PRD Conversion Errors

Some errors were found in the RST portion of the dataset. The RST portion was originally converted from the Penn Treebank PRD format. During the first round of checks, we discovered that this conversion had introduced a couple of errors. NPs for numbers which contained commas as separators (Example (24), from WSJ_0012) were incorrectly truncated, resulting in only the first number (*4* in the example) to be imported into the ARRAU data.

(24)
```
...
(NP (NP average circulation)
    (PP of
    (NP (NP 4,393,237))))
...
```

Sentence annotations, which are instrumental for structuring the annotation tool display by adding sentence-final line breaks, are derived from the PRDs top-level S-bracketings. In previous versions of ARRAU, sentence annotations frequently left out trailing punctuations, causing both sentence-final markables to be incomplete, and the display to be incorrect. Yet another class of errors in previous versions of ARRAU were caused by imperfect creation of the PRD files from the original raw files, in cases where the original text contained slashes. Example (25), from WSJ_0207, shows the rendering in the PRD file (which is also used in ARRAU. In the original file, however, which is also distributed with ARRAU, the actual text reads "11 1/2 minutes".

(25)
```
...
(VP lasts
 (NP-TMP (QP 11 1) minutes))
...
```

While none of these issues are critical, correcting them may also help a future integration in the corpus of other types of annotation available for the RST subset, in particular discourse structure but also for instance PropBank information.

7 ARRAU3: Statistics and Availability

Basic Statistics Table 1 compares the three releases of ARRAU in terms of total number of documents, tokens, and markables. ARRAU3 is only slightly larger than ARRAU 2 in terms of documents (**DC**) (558 vs 552) tokens (**TK**) (359,500 vs 348,072) and markables (**MK**) (106,700 vs 99,582). The number of non-referring expressions and discontinuous markables in ARRAU 3 is also similar to that in ARRAU 2, suggesting that this aspect of the annotation is by now fairly stable.

Complex forms of anaphoric reference Table 2 shows that the difference between ARRAU 3 and ARRAU 2 is much more substantial when considering more complex cases of anaphoric reference. The figures for discourse deixis (**DD**) and split-antecedent plurals (**SP**) didn't change much - suggesting again that these annotations are fairly stable. However, the number of generic markables (**GE**), bridging references (**BG**) and markables identified as ambiguous (**AMB**) are much higher.

Formats The corpus is available in the native MMAX XML format as well as in the Universal Anaphora format.

Availability Like the previous version, all of ARRAU 3 will be available through LDC, whereas the copyright-free subcorpora (GNOME, PEAR, and TRAINS-91) will also be available through the Universal Anaphora repository.

8 Conclusion and Future Work

ARRAU is a long-term project to push forward the state of the art in anaphoric annotation. During each phase of the annotation we discovered new issues that were then corrected in the subsequent version. So while we think the newest release is much improved over ARRAU 2, a number of issues were identified in the last round of annotation, that we hope to correct in future releases. They include in particular several issues related to reference in dialogue (e.g., how to annotate repairs) as well as more complex forms of discourse deixis.

		ARRAU1			ARRAU2			ARRAU3		
		DC	**TK**	**MK**	**DC**	**TK**	**MK**	**DC**	**TK**	**MK**
RST	train				335	182031	57686	333	182424	57489
	dev				18	12845	3986	18	12845	3962
	test				60	33225	10341	60	33225	10319
	overall	204	146512	45990	413	228901	72013	411	228494	71770
TRAINS	91				16	14496	2884	16	14496	3706
	93				98	69158	14115	98	69158	17262
	overall	35	25783	5198	114	83654	16999	114	83654	20968
PEAR		20	14059	3881	20	14059	4008	20	14059	4023
GNOME	2	5	21599	6215	5	21458	6562	5	21458	6571
	2001							8	11835	3368
	overall	5	21599	6215	5	21458	6562	13	33293	9939
Total		264	184,748	60884	552	348,072	99582	558	359,500	106,700

Table 1: Size comparison between ARRAU 3 and previous releases in terms of documents (DC), tokens (TK), and markables (MK)

		ARRAU2					ARRAU3				
		GE	**BG**	**DD**	**SP**	**AMB**	**GE**	**BG**	**DD**	**SP**	**AMB**
RST	train	753	2797	496	346	68	5149	5398	578	353	430
	dev	198	277	36	27	0	814	431	49	26	38
	test	487	703	99	63	14	907	966	98	69	110
	overall	1438	3777	631	436	82	6870	6795	725	448	578
TRAINS	91	98	74	154	48	22	107	176	163	59	168
	93	635	636	708	182	99	651	1007	725	257	245
	overall	733	710	862	230	121	758	1183	888	316	413
PEAR		74	333	67	30	31	175	346	71	32	63
GNOME	2	12	692	73	43	16	814	737	74	53	78
	2001						800	396	9	0	11
	overall	12	692	73	43	16	1614	1133	83	53	89
Total		2257	5512	1633	739	250	9417	9457	1767	849	1143

Table 2: Complex types of anaphora in ARRAU 3 and the previous release ARRAU 2. GE=generic, BG=bridging, DD=discourse deixis, SP=split-antecedent plurals, AMB=ambiguous.

Bibliographical References

References

Ron Artstein and Massimo Poesio. 2006. Identifying reference to abstract objects in dialogue. In *Proc. of BRANDIAL*, Potsdam.

Ron Artstein and Massimo Poesio. 2008. Inter-coder agreement for computational linguistics. *Computational Linguistics*, 34(4):555–596.

David Bamman, Olivia Lewke, and Anya Mansoor. 2020. An annotated dataset of coreference in english literature. In *Proc. of LREC*. European Language Resources Association (ELRA), Association for Computational Linguistics (ACL).

Donna Byron. 2002. Resolving pronominal references to abstract entities. In *Proc. of the ACL*, pages 80–87.

Donna Byron and James Allen. 1998. Resolving demonstrative anaphora in the TRAINS-93 corpus. In *Proc. of the Second Colloquium on Discourse, Anaphora and Reference Resolution*. University of Lancaster.

Greg N. Carlson and Francis J. Pelletier, editors. 1995. *The Generic Book*. University of Chicago Press.

Lynn Carlson, Daniel Marcu, and Mary Ellen Okurowski. 2003. Building a discourse-tagged corpus in the framework of rhetorical structure theory. In J. Kuppevelt and R. Smith, editors, *Current Directions in Discourse and Dialogue*, pages 85–112. Kluwer.

Wallace L. Chafe. 1980. *The Pear Stories: Cognitive, Cultural and Linguistic Aspects of Narrative Production*. Ablex, Norwood, NJ.

Herbert H. Clark. 1977. Bridging. In P. N. Johnson-Laird and P.C. Wason, editors, *Thinking: Readings in Cognitive Science*, pages 411–420. Cambridge University Press, London and New York.

Herbert H. Clark and Susan E. Brennan. 1990. Grounding in communication. In L. B. Resnick, J. Levine, and S. D. Behrend, editors, *Perspectives on Socially Shared Cognition*. APA.

Kevin Bretonnel Cohen, Arrick Lanfranchi, Miji Joo-young Choi, Michael Bada, William A. Baumgartner Jr., Natalya Panteleyeva, Karin Verspoor, Martha Palmer, and Lawrence E. Hunter. 2017. Coreference annotation and resolution in the Colorado Richly Annotated Full Text (CRAFT) corpus of biomedical journal articles. *BMC Bioinformatics*, 18(372).

Miriam Eckert and Michael Strube. 2001. Dialogue acts, synchronising units and anaphora resolution. *Journal of Semantics*.

Carola Eschenbach, Christopher Habel, Michael Herweg, and Klaus Rehkämper. 1989. Remarks on plural anaphora. In *Proceedings of the fourth conference on European chapter of the Association for Computational Linguistics*, pages 161–167. Association for Computational Linguistics.

Loïc Grobol. 2020. *Coreference resolution for spoken French*. Ph.D. thesis, Université Sorbonne Nouvelle.

John A. Hawkins. 1978. *Definiteness and Indefiniteness*. Croom Helm, London.

Peter A. Heeman and James F. Allen. 1995. The TRAINS-93 dialogues. TRAINS Technical Note TN 94-2, University of Rochester, Dept. of Computer Science, Rochester, NY.

Peter A. Heeman and Graeme Hirst. 1995. Collaborating on referring expressions. *Computational Linguistics*, 21(3):351–382.

Erhard W. Hinrichs, Sandra Kübler, Karin Naumann, Heike Telljohann, and Julia Trushkin. 2004. Recent developments in linguistic annotations of the TüBa-D/Z treebank. In *Proceedings of the Third Workshop on Treebanks and Linguistic Theories*, Tübingen, Germany.

Yufang Hou, Katja Markert, and Michael Strube. 2014. A rule-based system for unrestricted bridging resolution: Recognizing bridging anaphora and finding links to antecedents. In *Proceedings of the 2014 Conference on Empirical Methods in Natural Language Processing (EMNLP)*, pages 2082–2093, Doha, Qatar. Association for Computational Linguistics.

Yufang Hou, Katja Markert, and Michael Strube. 2018. Unrestricted bridging resolution. *Computational Linguistics*, 44(2):237–284.

Hans Kamp and Uwe Reyle. 1993. *From Discourse to Logic*. D. Reidel, Dordrecht.

Lauri Karttunen. 1976. Discourse referents. In J. McCawley, editor, *Syntax and Semantics 7 - Notes from the Linguistic Underground*, pages 363–385. Academic Press, New York.

Sopan Khosla, Juntao Yu, Ramesh Manuvinakurike, Vincent Ng, Massimo Poesio, Michael Strube, and Carolyn Rosé. 2021. The codi-crac 2021 shared task on anaphora, bridging, and discourse deixis in dialogue. In *Proc. of the CODI/CRAC Shared Task Workshop*.

Hideo Kobayashi and Vincent Ng. 2020. Bridging resolution: A survey of the state of the art. In *Proceedings of the 28th International Conference on Computational Linguistics*, pages 3708–3721, Barcelona, Spain (Online). International Committee on Computational Linguistics.

Varada Kolhatkar and Graeme Hirst. 2014. Resolving shell nouns. In *Proc. of EMNLP*, pages 499–510, Doha, Qatar.

Varada Kolhatkar, Adam Roussel, Stefanie Dipper, and Heike Zinsmeister. 2018. Anaphora with non-nominal antecedents in computational linguistics: a Survey. *Computational Linguistics*, 44(3):547–612.

Mitchell P. Marcus, Beatrice Santorini, and Mary Ann Marcinkiewicz. 1993. Building a large annotated corpus of english: the Penn Treebank. *Computational Linguistics*, 19(2):313–330.

Katja Markert, Yufang Hou, and Michael Strube. 2012. Collective classification for fine-grained information status. In *Proc. of the ACL*, Juju island, Korea.

Natalia N. Modjeska. 2003. *Resolving other anaphors*. Ph.D. thesis, University of Edinburgh.

Mark-Christoph Müller. 2008. *Fully Automatic Resolution of It, This And That in Unrestricted Multy-Party Dialog*. Ph.D. thesis, Universität Tübingen.

Mark-Christoph Müller. 2020. pyMMAX2: Deep access to MMAX2 projects from python. In *Proceedings of the 14th Linguistic Annotation Workshop*, pages 167–173, Barcelona, Spain. Association for Computational Linguistics.

Mark-Christoph Müller and Michael Strube. 2006. Multi-level annotation of linguistic data with MMAX2. In S. Braun, K. Kohn, and J. Mukherjee, editors, *Corpus Technology and Language Pedagogy. New Resources, New Tools, New Methods*, volume 3 of *English Corpus Linguistics*, pages 197–214. Peter Lang.

Judith Muzerelle, Anaïs Lefeuvre, Emmanuel Schang, Jean-Yves Antoine, Aurore Pelletier, Denis Maurel, Iris Eshkol, and Jeanne Villaneau. 2014. Ancor_centre, a large free spoken french coreference corpus. In *Proc. of LREC*.

Costanza Navarretta. 2000. Abstract anaphora resolution in Danish. In *Proc. of the 1st SIGdial Workshop on Discourse and Dialogue*, pages 56–65. ACL.

Anna Nedoluzhko. 2013. Generic noun phrases and annotation of coreference and bridging relations in the prague dependency treebank. In *Proc. of LAW*, pages 103–111.

Anna Nedoluzhko, Michal Novák, Martin Popel, Zdeněk Žabokrtský, Amir Zeldes, and Daniel Zeman. 2022. Corefud 1.0: Coreference meets universal dependencies. In *Proceedings of the Thirteenth Language Resources and Evaluation Conference (LREC)*, page 4859–4872. European Language Resources Association.

Barbara Hall Partee. 1972. Opacity, coreference, and pronouns. In D. Davidson and G. Harman, editors, *Semantics for Natural Language*, pages 415–441. D. Reidel, Dordrecht, Holland.

Massimo Poesio. 2004. Discourse annotation and semantic annotation in the GNOME corpus. In *Proc. of the ACL Workshop on Discourse Annotation*, pages 72–79, Barcelona.

Massimo Poesio. 2016. Linguistic and cognitive evidence about anaphora. In M. Poesio, R. Stuckardt, and Y. Versley, editors, *Anaphora Resolution: Algorithms, Resources and Applications*, chapter 2. Springer.

Massimo Poesio and Ron Artstein. 2005a. Annotating (anaphoric) ambiguity. In *Proc. of the Corpus Linguistics Conference*, Birmingham.

Massimo Poesio and Ron Artstein. 2005b. The reliability of anaphoric annotation, reconsidered: Taking ambiguity into account. In *Proc. of ACL Workshop on Frontiers in Corpus Annotation*, pages 76–83.

Massimo Poesio and Ron Artstein. 2008. Anaphoric annotation in the ARRAU corpus. In *Proc. of LREC*, Marrakesh.

Massimo Poesio, Yulia Grishina, Varada Kolhatkar, Nafise Moosavi, Ina Roesiger, Adam Roussel, Fabian Simonjetz, Alexandra Uma, Olga Uryupina, Juntao Yu, and Heike Zinsmeister. 2018. Anaphora resolution with the ARRAU corpus. In *Proceedings of the First Workshop on Computational Models of Reference, Anaphora and Coreference*, pages 11–22, New Orleans, Louisiana. Association for Computational Linguistics.

Massimo Poesio, Rahul Mehta, Alex Maroudas, and Janet Hitzeman. 2004. Learning to solve bridging references. In *Proc. of ACL*, pages 143–150, Barcelona.

Massimo Poesio, Sameer Pradhan, Marta Recasens, Kepa Rodriguez, and Yannick Versley. 2016. Annotated corpora and annotation tools. In M. Poesio, R. Stuckardt, and Y. Versley, editors, *Anaphora Resolution: Algorithms, Resources and Applications*, chapter 4. Springer.

Massimo Poesio and Hannes Rieser. 2010. Completions, coordination, and alignment in dialogue. *Dialogue and Discourse*, 1(1):1–89.

Massimo Poesio and Renata Vieira. 1998. A corpus-based investigation of definite description use. *Computational Linguistics*, 24(2):183–216.

Sameer Pradhan, Xiaoqiang Luo, Marta Recasens, Eduard Hovy, Vincent Ng, and Michael Strube. 2014. Scoring coreference partitions of predicted mentions: A reference implementation. In *Proceedings of the 52nd Annual Meeting of the Association for Computational Linguistics (Volume 2: Short Papers)*, pages 30–35, Baltimore, Maryland. Association for Computational Linguistics.

Sameer Pradhan, Alessandro Moschitti, Nianwen Xue, Olga Uryupina, and Yuchen Zhang. 2012. CoNLL-2012 shared task: Modeling multilingual unrestricted coreference in OntoNotes. In *Proceedings of the Sixteenth Conference on Computational Natural Language Learning (CoNLL 2012)*, Jeju, Korea.

Sameer S. Pradhan, Lance Ramshaw, Ralph Weischedel, Jessica MacBride, and Linnea Micciulla. 2007. Unrestricted coreference: Indentifying entities and events in ontonotes. In *Proc. IEEE International Conference on Semantic Computing (ICSC)*, Irvine, CA.

Ellen F. Prince. 1981. Toward a taxonomy of given-new information. In P. Cole, editor, *Radical Pragmatics*, pages 223–256. Academic Press, New York.

Altaf Rahman and Vincent Ng. 2012. Resolving complex cases of definite pronouns: The Winograd schema challenge. In *Proceedings of the 2012 Joint Conference on Empirical Methods in Natural Language Processing and Computational Natural Language Learning*, pages 777–789, Jeju Island, Korea. Association for Computational Linguistics.

Marta Recasens and M. Antònia Martí. 2010. AnCora-CO: Coreferentially annotated corpora for Spanish and Catalan. *Language Resources and Evaluation*, 44(4):315–345.

Ina Roesiger. 2018. Rule- and learning-based methods for bridging resolution in the ARRAU corpus. In *Proc. of CRAC*.

Ina Roesiger, Arndt Riester, and Jonas Kuhn. 2018. Bridging resolution: Task definition, corpus resources and rule-based experiments. In *Proceedings of the 27th International Conference on Computational Linguistics*, pages 3516–3528, Santa Fe, New Mexico, USA. Association for Computational Linguistics.

Keisuke Sakaguchi, Ronan Le Bras, Chandra Bhagavatula, and Yejin Choi. 2020. Winogrande: An adversarial winograd schema challenge at scale. *Proceedings of the AAAI Conference on Artificial Intelligence*, 34:8732–8740.

Olga Uryupina, Ron Artstein, Antonella Bristot, Federica Cavicchio, Francesca Delogu, Kepa J. Rodriguez, and Massimo Poesio. 2020. Annotating a broad range of anaphoric phenomena, in a variety of genres: the ARRAU corpus. *Journal of Natural Language Engineering*.

Bonnie L. Webber. 1991. Structure and ostension in the interpretation of discourse deixis. *Language and Cognitive Processes*, 6(2):107–135.

Kellie Webster, Marta Recasens, Vera Axelrod, and Jason Baldridge. 2018. Mind the GAP: A balanced corpus of gendered ambiguous pronouns. *Transactions of the Association for Computational Linguistics*, 6:605–617.

Juntao Yu, Sopan Khosla, Ramesh Manuvinakurike, Lori Levin, Vincent Ng, Massimo Poesio, Michael Strube, and Massimo Poesio. 2022a. The CODI/CRAC 2022 shared task on anaphora resolution, bridging and discourse deixis in dialogue. In *Proc. of CODI/CRAC Shared Task*.

Juntao Yu, Sopan Khosla, Nafise Moosavi, Silviu Paun, Sameer Pradhan, and Massimo Poesio. 2022b. The universal anaphora scorer 1.0. In *Proc. of LREC*.

Amir Zeldes. 2017. The GUM corpus: Creating multilayer resources in the classroom. *Language Resources and Evaluation*, 51(3):581–612.

Amir Zeldes. 2022. Can we fix the scope for coreference? *Dialogue and Discourse*, 13(1):41–62.

Signals as Features: Predicting Error/Success in Rhetorical Structure Parsing

Martial Pastor
Centre for Language Studies,
Radboud University,
The Netherlands
martial.pastor@ru.nl

Nelleke Oostdijk
Centre for Language Studies,
Radboud University,
The Netherlands
nelleke.oostdijk@ru.nl

Abstract

This study introduces an approach for evaluating the importance of signals proposed by Das and Taboada in discourse parsing. Previous studies using other signals indicate that discourse markers (DMs) are not consistently reliable cues and can act as distractors, complicating relations recognition. The study explores the effectiveness of alternative signal types, such as syntactic and genre-related signals, revealing their efficacy even when not predominant for specific relations. An experiment incorporating RST signals as features for a parser error / success prediction model demonstrates their relevance and provides insights into signal combinations that prevents (or facilitates) accurate relation recognition. The observations also identify challenges and potential confusion posed by specific signals. This study resulted in producing publicly available code and data, contributing to an accessible resources for research on RST signals in discourse parsing.

1 Introduction

Discourse parsing has sparked significant interest in recent NLP applications. This task goes beyond the conventional scope of sentences and may extend to encompass the identification of Coherence Relations (relations between segments of text) at the discourse level. One of the most popular formalisms for representing coherence relations is Rhetorical Structure Theory (RST; Mann and Thompson, 1988), which has spurred the construction of various datasets that are now used for hierarchical discourse parsing. This last task is challenging and discourse parsers have not achieved the same level of success as other tasks at the sentence level. Moreover, analyzing failure cases, especially in deep learning-oriented parsers, proves difficult.

Concurrently, research on Coherence Relations has also been struggling with identifying the exact linguistic elements that signal them. At the discourse level, a diverse array of signals may occur, making it challenging to discern typical signals for specific relations and their underlying motivation. This has been addressed in the work of Das (2014), where the author provides a comprehensive overview of signals present in the RST-DT dataset (Carlson et al., 2001) and subsequently annotate the signals at play for every relation in this corpus. This process ultimately has resulted in the development of the RST Signaling corpus (Das and Taboada, 2018a). See the Appendix for a comprehensive list of individual signals and signal types for all relations in this corpus.

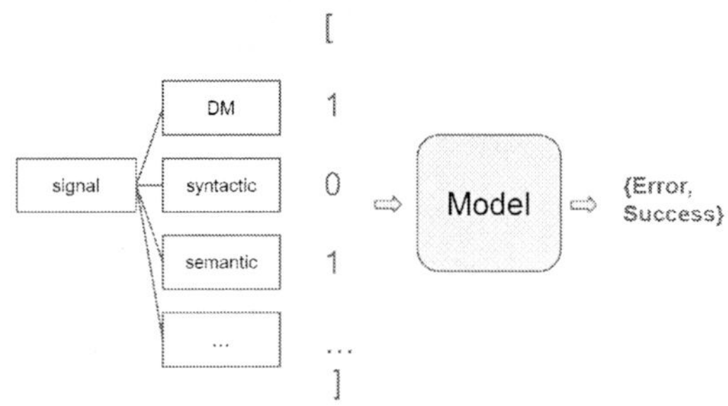

Figure 1: Flow diagram for the predictive model for error / success analysis of the DMRST parser. The predicted labels are SUCCESS for a successful parse while ERROR is where the parser fails. The features here are the signals from Das and Taboada's Signaling Corpus (Das and Taboada, 2018a). They are encoded in a binary feature vector.

In the present paper, our aim is to assess the relevance of Das and Taboada's signals in RST discourse parsing and understand how they contribute to the errors or success of a state-of-the-art parser.

We first describe an experimental set up where we replicate Liu et al.'s DMRST discourse parser (Liu et al., 2021) which achieves state-of-the-art results for coherence relation recognition and then

Proceedings of the 5th Workshop on Computational Approaches to Discourse (CODI 2024), pages 139–148
March 21, 2024 ©2024 Association for Computational Linguistics

align the results with the RST Signaling corpus. We then show that although discourse markers (DMs) are prevalent in various sorts of relations, they are not necessarily effective signals (see, for example, the DM *when* for the TEMPORAL relation in example (1)) , unlike other types of signal such as syntactic signals (for example, the *nominal modifier* in example (2)) or genre signals.[1]

(1) "[representing investor clubs from around the U.S were attending] $\xleftarrow[\text{gold:temporal}]{\text{pred:background}}$ [when the market started to slide Friday.]" **wsj_2686**

(2) "[Negotiable, bank-backed business credit instruments] $\xleftarrow[\text{gold:elaboration}]{\text{pred:elaboration}}$ [typically financing an import order.]" **wsj_0602**

Next, we validate the initial analysis by incorporating these signals into a model, using them as features for a predictive model that distinguishes between errors and successes of the DMRST parser (see the flow diagram in Figure 1). We first observe that these signals could serve as relevant features in the context of Discourse Parsing before delving into a more detailed analysis of the signals influencing the parser's predictions of errors or success.

2 Related Work

2.1 Discourse Markers and beyond

In the broader context of literature focusing on text comprehension and cognitive linguistics, investigations into the cognitive aspects of coherence relations reveal that the presence of discourse markers (DMs), or connectives as they are sometimes referred to, tends to facilitate the processing of textual information (Gaddy et al., 2001). This particular line of research has primarily delved into recognizing and categorizing coherence relations using DMs. However, a limitation of this approach is its failure to address relations that seem unmarked due to the absence of DMs.

While DMs are commonly considered the most effective indicators for identifying coherence relations, studies on signaling show that a significant proportion of relations occurs in text without the presence of DMs (Das, 2014). Das and Taboada (2018b) explore the nature of relations traditionally considered implicit or unmarked. They reveal that relations exclusively signaled by DMs constitute only 18.21% of the RST Signaling corpus. This suggests that the signaling of coherence relations is more intricate than previously perceived. The researchers then propose their own taxonomy of various signals, ultimately contributing to the development of the RST Signaling corpus (Das and Taboada, 2018a), which we use for the experiments presented in this article.

2.2 Signals and Discourse Parsers

In early studies researching the effectiveness of linguistic elements for Discourse Parsing, several investigations have explored the importance of DMs (Pitler et al., 2008). For instance, the DM *if* in example (3) is usually considered to make the CONDITION relation easy to identify.

(3) "[If I sell now,] $\xrightarrow[\text{gold:condition}]{\text{pred:condition}}$ [I'll take a big loss.]" **wsj_2386**

The role of DMs has been emphasized, particularly in the context of shallow discourse parsing with the Penn Discourse Treebank (PDTB; Prasad et al., 2008). Previous studies suggest that in a shallow parsing context, which is distinct from RST as it focuses solely on local relations in text and disregards paragraph-level structures, explicit relations are the most straightforward to recognize. Moreover, there is a widely held consensus that the sole signals involved in explicit relations are discourse markers (DMs). Studies, such as the one conducted by Knaebel (2021), demonstrate the efficacy of neural shallow parsers utilizing contextualized embeddings in identifying relations explicitly marked by DMs, achieving an F1 score of 62.75% for explicit and 40.71% for implicit relations on Section 23 of PDTB v2 (Prasad et al., 2014). Additionally, the best performing system in the relation classification task in the shared initiative established by Zeldes et al. (2021) reported a mean accuracy of 79.32% for explicit relations and 50.86% for implicit relations in the 2023 edition (Braud et al., 2023).

Although certain corpus linguistics investigations have examined DMs in the RST dataset (Das and Taboada, 2018b; Stede and Neumann, 2014), only the work conducted by Liu et al. (2023) delves into the particular role of DMs in RST parsing and begins to question their pervasiveness as effective signals. After examining both the RST-DT corpus and the GUM dataset (Zeldes, 2017) which have

[1] pred here corresponds to the predicted label by the DMRST parser presented in section 3.2 and gold corresponds to the label annotated in the gold RST-DT dataset.

been annotated with DMs and other signals, they found that, although DMs have a notable impact, their significance is overshadowed by certain intra-sentential characteristics when predicting relation labels. While this confirms the relatively easier classification of explicit relations, the subsequent analysis by the authors indicates that explicitness is not confined exclusively to discourse markers; it also extends to other intra-sentential elements. This emphasizes the need for additional research into textual elements that explicitly signal coherence relations.

2.3 Predicting Parsing Errors

When it comes to constructing models to understand parsing performance, our reference is primarily Liu et al.'s investigation, which focuses on the prediction of parsing errors (Liu et al., 2023). Liu et al. replicate several parsers and given a coherence relations and its signals they predict the number of parsers that make errors. These parsers serve the purpose of detecting those cases in which the relation label assignment is likely or potentially at fault. Following an analysis of the essential features in their predictive model for error analysis, they note the significance of syntactic signals. This underscores the importance of determining whether an Elementary Discourse Unit (EDU) holds a typical intra-sentential role, such as nominal modifier or adjunct, as such roles are more likely to be predicted accurately. Additional influential features include EDU length, with shorter EDUs more likely to have comparable instances in the training data compared to longer ones, and genre, as certain genres present greater difficulty in parsing.

3 Experimental Setup

3.1 Datasets

Our current study uses two RST corpora. One is the RST-DT dataset (Carlson et al., 2001) which is widely used for English RST parsing and has been a standard choice for evaluating RST parsers. Additionally, we here incorporate the RST Signaling corpus by Das and Taboada (2018a), which is essentially an extension of the original RST-DT dataset. The signaling dataset contains additional annotations pertaining to the linguistic elements that signal coherence relations within the original RST corpus.

3.1.1 RST Discourse Treebank

The RST-DT is known for its hierarchical tree structures and was initially annotated with 76 coherence relations. The relations investigated here come from the RST-DT test set, which contains a total of 38 documents. As for the relations labels, we currently employ the harmonized set of 18 labels as described by Braud et al. (2017).

3.1.2 RST Signaling Corpus

In the RST Signaling corpus, every single relation in the RST-DT has been annotated for the linguistic element(s) that signal the relation. In this corpus, a total of 50 different signals are identified (Das and Taboada, 2019). The authors distinguish between three main classes, viz. single, combined and unsure. The single signals belong to one of the following types: DM, reference, lexical, semantic, syntactic, graphic, genre, and numerical. With combined signals multiple (single) signals co-occur. "unsure" is used a signal label with those relations where the annotators were either unsure or were unable to identify any specific signal .

Regarding Liu et al.'s remarks about difficulties exploiting data from the RST signaling corpus, it is important to note that the data indeed offers an alignment of the annotations with specific tokens. However, an error in the calculation of token positions in the annotations scheme was identified and subsequently rectified. Following the recalculation of positions, we are now able to align the RST signals from Das and Taboada 2018a with the RST-DT test set.[2]

3.2 DMRST Discourse Parser

The experimental setup first replicates the DMRST parser developed by Liu et al. (2021). This parser, based on XLM-RoBERTa-base (Conneau et al., 2020), is a top-down multilingual system that concurrently handles EDU segmentation and RST tree parsing. Its suitability for our purposes lies in its state-of-the-art performance in relation label prediction. The authors have provided access to a well-trained model through a readily available model checkpoint optimized for inference. This particular model underwent training on a multilingual collection of RST discourse treebanks, offering native support for six languages: English, Portuguese, Spanish, German, Dutch, and Basque.

[2]The code for aligning RST signals and for the experiments can be found here: https://github.com/metaboolean5/signals-as-features

We use this model to predict the labels of the 2306 relations in the RST-DT test set and obtain an accuracy of 0.67 using the RST-Parseval metrics (Marcu, 2000).

It is worth noting that, although the parser can predict tree structure and discourse relations directly from raw text, our study opts to utilize gold EDU segmentation. In our experimental configuration, we input both the raw text from the original RST-DT test set and the segment breaks based on gold EDU segmentation.

4 Analysis

4.1 Preliminary Analysis of RST Signals

Here, we present an initial analysis of the signal distribution across the RST-DT test set. While we previously delved into Das and Taboada's analysis in the related works section, we now wish to underscore additional aspects of their signal annotation work. Notably, a significant disparity exists among various types of relations and their corresponding signals. For example, the ATTRIBUTION relation, the most successfully recognized relation by the DMRST parser, has only one relation which is signaled by a DM out of 343 relations. The ELABORATION relation, accounting for 796 instances in the test set, is signaled by a diverse array of signals (29 different signals), with only 24 cases attributed to a DM. Additionally, the SAME-UNIT relation is exclusively indicated by a singular syntactic signal, namely the *interrupted matrix clause* (127 cases).

Nonetheless, DMs continue to serve as the main signal type for certain relations. In the case of CONTRAST relations within the RST-DT test set, a DM is used to signal 112 out of 144 instances. Additionally, for CONDITION relations, 41 DMs are used in 48 cases, and for TEMPORAL relations, 47 DMs in 73 cases.

4.2 Signal Analysis of Discourse Parser Performance

4.2.1 DMs

In this section, we examine the specific performance of the DMRST parser for certain relations. The complete statistics for this section are available in the Appendix.

In cases where the relation is signaled by a DM, the DMs prove helpful for some relations: for example, 83% of the CONDITION relations signaled by DMs were correctly predicted. However, they do not necessarily make the identification easier. For CONTRAST, 73% of the relations signalled by DMs are successfully predicted and only 33% for TEMPORAL.

As for BACKGROUND relations, where DMs are still predominant but not as overwhelmingly so (53 relations signalled by DMs out of 111 cases), the parser correctly predicts 53% of them. We also observe that for the 796 ELABORATION relations, which the parser usually gets right (79% of them being successfully predicted), only 50% of relations indicated by a DM (12 out of 24 cases) are correctly predicted. The most effective signals here being syntactic.

We also note here, that 9 of the 12 cases which were not predicted correctly for this relation were either JOINT (5) or CONTRAST (4) which are relations where DMs are widely present. The confusion induced by specific DMs can offer valuable insights into the nature of distractors, a concern addressed in Liu et al. (2023). An example is the DM *and* which is typical of JOINT relations, and which might function as a distractor despite its intended role as a signal for ELABORATION. A similar kind of confusion arises with the discourse marker *when* in example (1), frequently causing the parser to misclassify temporal relations as background relations and vice versa. Similarly, we also observe that the DM *but*, while predominant in the CONTRAST relation, is also present with lower frequency in various other relations such as BACKGROUND, JOINT, ELABORATION, or CAUSE and causes comparable confusions.

(4) "[Yet another political scandal is racking Japan.] $\xrightarrow[\text{gold:cause}]{\text{pred:contrast}}$ [But this time it's hurting opposition as well as ruling-party members.]" **wsj_1189**

What emerges from this picture, is that in cases where DMs are typical of certain relations (CONDITION and CONTRAST), the model picks up on these DMs and they do play a role in correct relation label recognition. However, this is not observed for TEMPORAL relations, where DMs offer little or no assistance. Then again, TEMPORAL relations are generally hard to predict. Finally, when it comes to other relations where DMs are involved, we observe that they are not very reliable as signals and that they tend to create confusion with other relations typically signaled by DMs as seen in examples (1) and (4).

4.2.2 Other signals

Consistent with Liu et al. prior findings, our utilization of the RST signaling dataset demonstrates the effectiveness of syntactic signals for the majority of relations successfully predicted by the DMSRT parser. Similar to observations with DMs, relations typically signaled by specific syntactic cues exemplify this pattern. Notably, ATTRIBUTION, with a parser accuracy of 97%, shows 337 out of 343 relations indicated by the *reported speech* signal. ENABLEMENT follows, where 40 out of 46 relations are signaled by the *infinitival clause*, with the parser achieving 85% accuracy. The final noteworthy example is SAME-UNIT relations (127 cases), exclusively signaled by an *interrupted matrix clause*, predicted by the parser with 95% accuracy.

In the case of relations such as JOINT or ELABORATION, which are signaled by a variety of signals, syntactic ones, while not dominant, contribute to the parser's accuracy. For instance, with ELABORATION relations, those signaled by a *relative clause* (142 cases out of 796) show a 99% success rate in parser predictions.

(5) "[he hoped for unanimous support for a resolution] $\xleftarrow[\text{gold:elaboration}]{\text{pred:elaboration}}$ [he plans to offer tomorrow]"
wsj_1189

Similarly, in JOINT relations, 80% of accurately predicted *parallel syntactic constructions* (representing 30 out of 212 relations for this label) demonstrate a comparable pattern.

This implies that, unlike DMs, syntactic signals remain reliable even when not predominant. This is attributable to the specificity of syntactic structures, which are closely tied to individual relations and are not as ambiguous as DMs. Of note, we see that syntactic specificity cannot just be explained by the fact that syntactic signals, unlike DMs, belong to a set of repeated sequences or lexicalized forms. Though that may be the case for the *reported speech* signal with verba dicendi (verbs like 'say', 'report', and 'declare'), we can see that even when the relative pronoun *that* is dropped in example (5), the relation is still systematically correctly predicted.

In a similar manner, although not prominently featured in the entire RST-DT signaling corpus, the *genre* category stands out as an effective signal for various types of relationship Notably, 83% of the relations signaled by this category are accurately predicted.

5 Predictive Model for Success/Error Analysis

In this section we aim to provide a deeper insight of the previous analysis by building an error / success prediction model. Our goal here is to utilize signals from Das and Taboada's Signaling corpus to predict whether the DMRST parser will encounter an error or not. This approach enables us to assess the utility of signals in Discourse Parsing and determine if the presence or absence of these signals is linked to errors or successful parsing outcomes.

The implementation of our predictive model for error/success analysis is based on the XGBoost algorithm (Chen and Guestrin, 2016). This ensemble gradient boosting approach is renowned for its high accuracy. It has the capability to capture arbitrary interactions among features and is well-regularized to avoid overfitting.

The present experiment consists in training an XGBoost model to predict the DMRST parsing errors, the predicted label set being {1,0} where 1 is a correctly predicted error or successful parse and where 0 is where our model fails. The signals from the Signaling Corpus are encoded in a binary feature vector. With this configuration we train XGBoost on the 2306 relations outputs by the DMRST parser and get an 0.78 accuracy for a randomly selected 761 relations test set. Figure 2 presents an analysis of feature importance using classification gain which is often used to estimate feature importance (Shang et al., 2019).

Table 1 gives an overview of the distribution of the coherence relations in the test set, while Table 2 presents the distribution of the signal classes and types. Table 3 details the predicted error/success rate for specific signal types.

5.1 Observations

The most reliable of single signals overall are syntactic ones (91.6% correct+1), genre (83.3% correct+1), graphical (82.8%) and DM (59.0% correct+1). Here we note that (specific) syntactic signals are used with specific coherence relations: in the case of ATTRIBUTION we find *reported speech*, with ELABORATION we find mostly *relative clauses* and *nominal modifiers* and with SAME UNIT it is the *interrupted clause* that is used predominantly to signal the relation. Genre (*inverted*

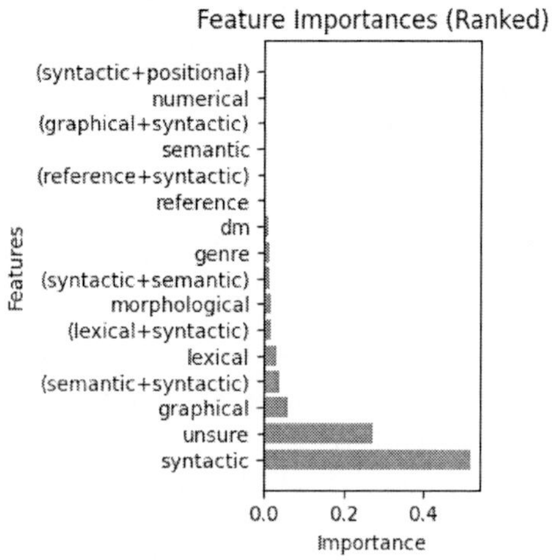

Figure 2: The relative importance of signals as features. Feature importance is based on classification gain which is often used to estimate feature importance (Shang et al., 2019).

pyramid scheme) is almost exclusively (17/18 correct+1) used with ELABORATION. Graphical signals, especially *colon* and *dash* are used with ELABORATION, while graphical - *items in sequence* are typically used with JOINT. DMs are effective in signaling the CONTRAST, JOINT and CONDITION relations. The most used DMs here are *but* for CONTRAST, *and* for JOINT, and *if* for CONDITION. With BACKGROUND, CAUSE and TEMPORAL DMs perform really poorly.

As for signals that appear effective in predicting errors in relation label assignment, there were three specifically that stood out. Thus *indicative word* was encountered as a signal with a total of 26 cases out of which 15 cases of EVALUATION were predicted as true error (error+1). *lexical chain* was found with a total of 37 cases out of which 20 cases appear as error+1 (mostly EXPLANATION, CAUSE, and ELABORATION). Finally, *unsure* proved to be a good predictor for error+1. It occurred as a 'signal' with a total of 78 cases, 66 (84.6%, Table3) of which were found to be erroneous which was correctly predicted by our predictive model. *unsure* occurred most frequently with CAUSE (14/33 cases), EXPLANATION (16/36 cases), and ELABORATION (11/279 cases).

6 Conclusion

We have presented an approach for assessing the importance of Das and Taboada's signals within the context of discourse parsing. Our initial observations reveal distinct patterns in the performance of a discourse parser when graphed for specific signals, leading to various implications.

Relation	abs. frq. (N)	rel. frq. (%)
attribution	106	13.9
background	36	4.7
cause	33	4.3
comparison	5	0.7
condition	12	1.6
contrast	46	6.0
elaboration	279	36.7
enablement	13	1.7
evaluation	26	3.4
explanation	36	4.7
joint	67	8.8
manner-means	8	1.1
same unit	39	5.1
summary	13	1.7
temporal	26	3.4
textual organization	4	0.5
topic-change	2	0.3
topic-comment	10	1.3
ALL	761	100.0

Table 1: Frequency distribution of coherence relations in the 761 relations test set.

Sign. class	signal type	abs. frq. (N)	rel. frq. (%)
single	DM	144	16.9
	reference	8	1.1
	lexical	26	3.4
	semantic	61	8.0
	morph.	8	1.1
	syntactic	275	36.1
	graphical	58	7.6
	genre	24	3.2
	numerical	0	0.0
combined	sem.+syn.	32	4.2
	lex.+syn.	6	0.8
	syn.+sem.	11	1.4
	syn.+pos.	0	0.0
	grap.+syn.	12	1.6
unsure	unsure	78	10.2
	ALL	761	100.0

Table 2: Signal classes and types in the 761 relations test set.

Initially, it is noted that DMs are not consistently reliable signals for all relationships; in fact, they can be viewed as *distractors*, causing confusion between relations signaled by the same DMs. Subsequently, an examination of the effectiveness of alternative signal types, including syntactic, semantic, and genre-related signals, is conducted. The findings demonstrate that, despite certain syntactic signals not being predominant for specific relations, they still prove to be effective.

Subsequently, we conduct an experiment incorporating the modeling of RST signals as features for an parser error or parser success prediction model. The results demonstrate the relevance of

Signal	corr.+1	corr.+0	err.+1	err.+0
DM	**59.0**	3.5	3.5	34.0
reference	0.0	25.0	37.5	37.5
lexical	0.0	15.4	**84.6**	0.0
semantic	11.5	37.7	**44.3**	6.6
morph.	0.0	0.0	100	0.0
syntactic	**91.6**	0.4	0.0	8.0
graphical	**82.8**	1.7	3.4	12.1
genre	**83.8**	0.0	0.0	16.7
numerical	0.0	0.0	0.0	0.0
ref.+syn.	0.0	**50.0**	33.3	16.7
sem.+syn.	**56.3**	0.0	0.0	43.8
lex.+syn.	**100.0**	0.0	0.0	0.0
syn.+sem.	**72.7**	0.0	0.0	27.3
syn.+pos.	0.0	0.0	0.0	0.0
grap.+syn.	16.7	33.3	0.0	**50.0**
unsure	0.0	15.4	**84.6**	0.0

Table 3: Predicted error/success rate (%) for specific signal types used to signal coherence relations. Correct/Error denotes whether the relation label assigned by the DMRST parser was correct, while 1/0 indicates whether the Predictive model was able to predict the accuracy (1=yes, 0=no).

utilizing signals as features, providing valuable insights into the signals (or combination of signals), that facilitate relation recognition. Moreover, our observations also shed light on scenarios where the presence of specific signals might pose challenges or lead to confusion, making it difficult for the parser to accurately discern certain relations.

Finally, we plan on sharing both our code and data, providing a readily accessible resource for research on RST signals within the context of discourse parsing.

7 Limitations

Initially, the examination of imbalances in characteristics constituted a challenge because of the multilingual composition of the training dataset. Furthermore, depending on a single model checkpoint for experimentation introduces the potential for errors influenced by coincidental variations in training. Additionally, we highlight that the corpus is restricted to newswire data, and exploring data from different genres is likely to provide additional insights.

It is also important to mention that in the current study, we specifically examined only those instances of potential signals that were identified as relevant for labeling coherence relations. This approach thus excluded what Liu et al. (2023) refer to as *distractors*.

8 Acknowledgements

This paper was produced as part of the HYBRIDS project, a Marie Skłodowoska-Curie Doctoral Netword funded by the European Union under grant no. 101073351 and the UK Research and Innovation (UKRI) Horizon Funding Guarantee.

We express our gratitude to the reviewers for their valuable feedback. Their feedback has helped us addressing key points of interest and implications arising from the current study.

References

Chloé Braud, Maximin Coavoux, and Anders Søgaard. 2017. Cross-lingual RST discourse parsing. In *Proceedings of the 15th Conference of the European Chapter of the Association for Computational Linguistics: Volume 1, Long Papers*, pages 292–304, Valencia, Spain. Association for Computational Linguistics.

Chloé Braud, Yang Janet Liu, Eleni Metheniti, Philippe Muller, Laura Rivière, Attapol Rutherford, and Amir Zeldes. 2023. The DISRPT 2023 shared task on elementary discourse unit segmentation, connective detection, and relation classification. In *Proceedings of the 3rd Shared Task on Discourse Relation Parsing and Treebanking (DISRPT 2023)*, pages 1–21, Toronto, Canada. The Association for Computational Linguistics.

Lynn Carlson, Daniel Marcu, and Mary Ellen Okurovsky. 2001. Building a discourse-tagged corpus in the framework of Rhetorical Structure Theory. In *Proceedings of the Second SIGdial Workshop on Discourse and Dialogue*.

Tianqi Chen and Carlos Guestrin. 2016. Xgboost: A scalable tree boosting system. In *Proceedings of the 22nd acm sigkdd international conference on knowledge discovery and data mining*, pages 785–794.

Alexis Conneau, Kartikay Khandelwal, Naman Goyal, Vishrav Chaudhary, Guillaume Wenzek, Francisco Guzmán, Edouard Grave, Myle Ott, Luke Zettlemoyer, and Veselin Stoyanov. 2020. Unsupervised cross-lingual representation learning at scale. In *Proceedings of the 58th Annual Meeting of the Association for Computational Linguistics*, pages 8440–8451, Online. Association for Computational Linguistics.

Debopam Das. 2014. *Signalling of coherence relations in discourse*. Ph.D. thesis.

Debopam Das and Maite Taboada. 2018a. Rst signalling corpus: a corpus of signals of coherence relations. *Language Resources and Evaluation*, 52.

Debopam Das and Maite Taboada. 2018b. Signalling of coherence relations in discourse, beyond discourse markers. *Discourse Processes*, 55(8):743–770.

Debopam Das and Maite Taboada. 2019. Multiple signals of coherence relations. *Discours. Revue de linguistique, psycholinguistique et informatique. A journal of linguistics, psycholinguistics and computational linguistics*, (24).

Michelle L Gaddy, Paul van den Broek, and Yung-Chi Sung. 2001. The inxuence of text cues on the allocation of attention during reading. *Text representation: Linguistic and psycholinguistic aspects*, 8:89.

René Knaebel. 2021. Discopy: A neural system for shallow discourse parsing. In *Proceedings of the 2nd Workshop on Computational Approaches to Discourse*, pages 128–133, Punta Cana, Dominican Republic and Online. Association for Computational Linguistics.

Yang Janet Liu, Tatsuya Aoyama, and Amir Zeldes. 2023. What's hard in English RST parsing? predictive models for error analysis. In *Proceedings of the 24th Meeting of the Special Interest Group on Discourse and Dialogue*, pages 31–42, Prague, Czechia. Association for Computational Linguistics.

Zhengyuan Liu, Ke Shi, and Nancy Chen. 2021. DMRST: A joint framework for document-level multilingual RST discourse segmentation and parsing. In *Proceedings of the 2nd Workshop on Computational Approaches to Discourse*, pages 154–164, Punta Cana, Dominican Republic and Online. Association for Computational Linguistics.

William C Mann and Sandra A Thompson. 1988. Rhetorical structure theory: Toward a functional theory of text organization. *Text-interdisciplinary Journal for the Study of Discourse*, 8(3):243–281.

Daniel Marcu. 2000. The rhetorical parsing of unrestricted texts: A surface-based approach. *Computational Linguistics*, 26(3):395–448.

Emily Pitler, Mridhula Raghupathy, Hena Mehta, Ani Nenkova, Alan Lee, and Aravind Joshi. 2008. Easily identifiable discourse relations. In *Coling 2008: Companion volume: Posters*, pages 87–90, Manchester, UK. Coling 2008 Organizing Committee.

Rashmi Prasad, Nikhil Dinesh, Alan Lee, Eleni Miltsakaki, Livio Robaldo, Aravind Joshi, and Bonnie Webber. 2008. The Penn Discourse TreeBank 2.0. In *Proceedings of the Sixth International Conference on Language Resources and Evaluation (LREC'08)*, Marrakech, Morocco. European Language Resources Association (ELRA).

Rashmi Prasad, Bonnie Webber, and Aravind Joshi. 2014. Reflections on the Penn Discourse TreeBank, comparable corpora, and complementary annotation. *Computational Linguistics*, 40(4):921–950.

Erbo Shang, Xiaohua Liu, Hailong Wang, Yangfeng Rong, and Yuerong Liu. 2019. Research on the application of artificial intelligence and distributed parallel computing in archives classification. In *2019 IEEE 4th Advanced Information Technology, Electronic and Automation Control Conference (IAEAC)*, pages 1267–1271.

Manfred Stede and Arne Neumann. 2014. Potsdam commentary corpus 2.0: Annotation for discourse research. In *Proceedings of the Ninth International Conference on Language Resources and Evaluation (LREC'14)*, pages 925–929, Reykjavik, Iceland. European Language Resources Association (ELRA).

Amir Zeldes. 2017. The gum corpus: Creating multilayer resources in the classroom. *Language Resources and Evaluation*, 51:581–612.

Amir Zeldes, Yang Janet Liu, Mikel Iruskieta, Philippe Muller, Chloé Braud, and Sonia Badene. 2021. The DISRPT 2021 shared task on elementary discourse unit segmentation, connective detection, and relation classification. In *Proceedings of the 2nd Shared Task on Discourse Relation Parsing and Treebanking (DISRPT 2021)*, pages 1–12, Punta Cana, Dominican Republic. Association for Computational Linguistics.

Appendix: Summary of the DMRST parser's performance for all signals and relations

Relation	Signal Type	Signal	Correct	Error	Total N
Attribution	DM	DM	0.00	**1.00**	1
	Syntactic	Reported Speech	**0.98**	0.02	337
	Graphical	Colon	0.00	**1.00**	1
	Genre	Newspaper Style Attr.	**0.75**	0.25	4
Background	DM	DM	**0.53**	0.47	53
	Lexical	Indicative Word	0.11	**0.89**	9
	Syntactic	Past Part. Clause	0.00	**1.00**	1
		Present Part. Clause	0.40	**0.60**	5
		Relative Clause	0.33	**0.67**	3
	Morphological	Tense	0.04	**0.96**	23
	Synt.+Positional	Present Part. Clause+Beginning	0.50	0.50	2
	Unsure	Unsure	0.00	**1.00**	16
Cause	DM	DM	0.15	**0.85**	27
	Reference	Reference	0.00	**1.00**	1
		Comparative Reference	0.00	**1.00**	1
	Lexical	Alternative Expression	0.00	**1.00**	1
		Indicative Word	0.00	**1.00**	3
	Semantic	Lexical Chain	0.27	**0.73**	11
	Morphological	Tense	0.00	**1.00**	3
	Syntactic	Infinitival Clause	0.00	**1.00**	2
		Present Part. Clause	**0.75**	0.25	4
	Graphical+Synt.	Comma+Present Part. Clause	**0.75**	0.25	4
	Unsure	Unsure	0.00	**1.00**	29
Comparison	DM	DM	0.36	**0.64**	11
	Reference	Reference	0.33	**0.67**	3
		Comparative Reference	0.33	**0.67**	3
	Lexical	Indicative Word	0.50	0.50	4
	Semantic	Lexical Chain	0.14	**0.86**	7
	Syntactic	Parallel Synt. Constr.	**1.00**	0.00	1
	Synt.+Semantic	Parallel Synt. Constr.+Lex. Chain	**1.00**	0.00	1
	Unsure	Unsure	0.25	**0.75**	4
Condition	DM	DM	**0.83**	0.17	41
	Unsure	Unsure	0.14	**0.86**	7
Contrast	DM	DM	**0.73**	0.27	112
	Semantic	Lex. Chain	0.25	**0.75**	12
	Syntactic	Parallel Synt. Constr.	0.40	**0.60**	5
	Synt.+Semantic	Parallel Synt. Constr.+Lex. Chain	0.40	**0.60**	5
	Unsure	Unsure	0.05	**0.95**	20
Elaboration	DM	DM	0.50	0.50	24
	Reference	Personal Reference	0.44	**0.56**	68
		Propositional Reference	0.00	**1.00**	3
	Lexical	Indicative Word	**0.67**	0.33	3
	Semantic	Meronymy	**0.80**	0.11	18
		Repetition	**0.75**	0.25	61
		Synonymy	**1.00**	0.00	2
	Syntactic	Nominal Modifier	**0.91**	0.09	180
		Adj Modifier	0.00	**1.00**	2
		Infinitival Clause	0.00	**1.00**	4
		Present Part. Clause	**0.62**	0.38	8
		Relative Clause	**0.99**	0.01	142
	Graphical	Colon	**0.89**	0.11	36
		Dash	**0.95**	0.05	41
		Items in Sequence	0.00	**1.00**	2
		Parentheses	**1.00**	0.00	15
	Genre	Inverted Pyramid Scheme	**0.85**	0.15	47
	Graphical+Synt.	Comma+Present Part. Clause	0.57	0.43	7
	Lexical+Synt.	Lexical Chain+Subject NP	**0.78**	0.22	45
	Semantic+Synt.	General Word+Subject NP	0.50	0.50	2
		Meronymy+Subject NP	**0.87**	0.13	15
		Repetition+Subject NP	**0.77**	0.23	48
		Synonymy+Subject NP	**1.00**	0.00	2
	Ref.+Synt.	Personal Ref.+Subject NP	0.46	**0.54**	57
		Proposit. Ref.+Subject NP	0.00	**1.00**	2
	Unsure	Unsure	0.45	**0.55**	33

Relation	Signal Type	Signal	Correct	Error	Total N
Enablement	DM	DM	0.00	**1.00**	1
	Syntactic	Infinitival Clause	**0.85**	0.15	40
	Unsure	Unsure	0.20	**0.80**	5
Evaluation	DM	DM	0.25	**0.75**	8
	Lexical	Alternative Expression	0.00	**1.00**	5
		Indicative Word	0.10	**0.90**	50
	Graphical	Parentheses	0.00	**1.00**	4
	Unsure	Unsure	0.15	**0.85**	13
Explanation	DM	DM	0.25	**0.75**	8
	Lexical	Alternative Expression	0.5	0.5	4
		Indicative Word	0.00	**1.00**	1
	Semantic	Lexical Chain	0.09	**0.91**	34
	Syntactic	Infinitival Clause	0.00	**1.00**	1
	Unsure	Unsure	0.18	**0.82**	44
Joint	DM	DM	**0.83**	0.17	76
	Lexical	Indicative Word	0.38	**0.62**	8
	Semantic	Lexical Chain	**0.73**	0.27	60
	Syntactic	Parallel Synt. Constr.	**0.80**	0.20	30
	Graphical	Items in Sequence	**0.98**	0.02	41
	Synt+Lexical	Parallel Synt. Constr.+Lex. Chain	**0.85**	0.15	20
	Unsure	Unsure	0.41	**0.59**	17
Manner-Means	DM	DM	0.00	**1.0**	1
	Lexical	Indicative Word	**0.80**	0.20	15
	Syntactic	Present Part. Clause	0.00	**1.00**	4
	Graph.+Synt.	Comma+Present Participle Clause	0.00	**1.00**	2
	Lexical+Synt.	Indicative Word+Part. Clause	**0.86**	0.14	14
	Unsure	Unsure	0.00	**1.00**	7
Same-Unit	Syntactic	Interrupted Matrix Clause	**0.95**	0.05	127
Summary	DM	DM	0.00	**1.00**	1
	Semantic	Lexical Chain	0.00	**1.00**	1
		Repetition	0.00	**1.00**	2
	Graphical	Parentheses	**0.67**	0.33	15
		Colon	0.00	**1.00**	2
		Dash	0.00	**1.00**	1
	Genre	Inverted Pyramid Scheme	0.00	**1.00**	3
	Lexical+Synt.	Lexical Chain+Subject NP	0.00	**1.00**	1
	Semantic+Synt.	Repetition+Subject NP	0.00	**1.00**	1
	Unsure	Unsure	0.00	**1.00**	7
Temporal	DM	DM	0.30	**0.70**	47
	Lexical	Indicative Word	**0.75**	0.25	4
	Semantic	Indicative Word Pair	**1.00**	0.00	1
		Lexical Chain	0.20	**0.80**	5
	Morphological	Tense	0.00	**1.00**	2
	Syntactic	Relative Clause	0.25	**0.75**	4
	Unsure	Unsure	0.18	**0.82**	11
Textual Org.	Genre	Newspaper Layout	**0.78**	0.22	9
Topic-Change	DM	DM	0.00	**1.00**	3
	Genre	Newspaper Layout	**0.80**	0.20	5
	Unsure	Unsure	0.00	**1.00**	5
Topic-Comment	DM	DM	0.00	**1.00**	3
	Lexical	Alternative expression	0.00	**1.00**	1
		Indicative word	0.00	**0.00**	1
	Semantic	Lexical chain	0.00	**1.00**	4
	Unsure	Unsure	0.00	**1.00**	15

GroundHog: Dialogue Generation using Multi-Grained Linguistic Input

Alexander Chernyavskiy[1], **Lidiia Ostyakova**[1,2], **and Dmitry Ilvovsky**[1]
[1] HSE University, Russia
[2] Moscow Institute of Physics and Technology, Russia
alschernyavskiy@gmail.com, ostyakova.ln@gmail.com
dilvovsky@hse.ru

Abstract

Recent language models have significantly boosted conversational AI by enabling fast and cost-effective response generation in dialogue systems. However, dialogue systems based on neural generative approaches often lack truthfulness, reliability, and the ability to analyze the dialogue flow needed for smooth and consistent conversations with users. To address these issues, we introduce GroundHog, a modified BART architecture, to capture long multi-grained inputs gathered from various factual and linguistic sources, such as Abstract Meaning Representation, discourse relations, sentiment, and grounding information. For experiments, we present an automatically collected dataset from Reddit that includes multi-party conversations devoted to movies and TV series. The evaluation encompasses both automatic evaluation metrics and human evaluation. The obtained results demonstrate that using several linguistic inputs has the potential to enhance dialogue consistency, meaningfulness, and overall generation quality, even for automatically annotated data. We also provide an analysis that highlights the importance of individual linguistic features in interpreting the observed enhancements.

1 Introduction

Text generation methods, particularly for conversational systems, have become increasingly popular in recent years. The conversational systems play a crucial role in enhancing the effectiveness of user-agent interactions (Young et al., 2018; Gu et al., 2019; Le et al., 2019). Dialogue systems are used for human-machine conversations on various topics. Some systems are built as question-answering systems or personal assistants, focusing on specific domains or general inquiries.

Despite showing impressive response generation capabilities, language models, even ones like GPT-4, have shortcomings in terms of truthfulness (OpenAI, 2023). Consequently, researchers are exploring methods to combine generative and extractive approaches in order to make the responses of dialogue systems more logical and reliable. Here, the primary objective is to incorporate external knowledge, resources, or databases into the response generation process. The previous studies have demonstrated a substantial enhancement in the quality of generation by incorporating grounding, which improves the factual accuracy of the responses (Feng et al., 2020). Grounding input is commonly integrated into dialogue generation models along with the context of a particular utterance (Zhao et al., 2020) or a preceding part of the dialogue that represents the conversational history (Rashkin et al., 2021).

Furthermore, previous works have explored leveraging grounding in combination with other features, including commonsense and named entities (Varshney et al., 2022; Wu et al., 2022), dialogue acts (Hedayatnia et al., 2020), topic shifts (Wu and Zhou, 2021), discourse annotation (Khalid et al., 2020), to improve dialogue generation. Despite the fact that additional linguistic features are frequently used to improve the consistency of generated dialogues (Ji et al., 2016; Harrison et al., 2019), previous studies focused on individual and superficial examination of linguistic features. In our research, we conducted a more comprehensive analysis, evaluating the relative significance of each of them and the overall contribution.

We primarily investigate the impact of various linguistic features on response generation in a multi-grained input framework. Specifically, we analyze the effects of semantic relations derived from Abstract Meaning Representation (AMR) (Banarescu et al., 2013), dialogue acts extracted from dialogue discourse trees (Stone et al., 2013; Zhang et al., 2017), and utterance-based sentiment representation.

Proceedings of the 5th Workshop on Computational Approaches to Discourse (CODI 2024), pages 149–160
March 21, 2024 ©2024 Association for Computational Linguistics

Experiments on response generation are generally conducted using open-source sequence-to-sequence models (Raffel et al., 2020; Rashkin et al., 2021). Among these models, the BART architecture (Lewis et al., 2020) has gained significant popularity due to its state-of-the-art performance in various text generation tasks. Due to its efficiency in processing linearized inputs, it is often utilized in graph2text tasks (Ribeiro et al., 2020). Moreover, this capability can be further extended to analyze conversation graphs. However, the length of input texts can often present challenges for Transformer-based models. In this study, we introduce GroundHog, an approach that uses multiple input encoders to preserve input information effectively.

Our contributions can be summarized as follows:

- We present a novel dataset consisting of open-domain conversations for dialogue system training. This dataset is augmented with linguistic features and grounding, enhancing its potential for training high-quality models.

- We propose the use of grounding and linguistic features for response generation in dialogue systems. An ablation study is conducted to analyze their individual contributions.

- A modification to the BART architecture is suggested to effectively capture long multi-grained inputs.

- We perform an analysis to interpret the improvements and discuss our findings.

2 Dataset

The most popular datasets, including open-domain conversations grounded in Wikipedia information, are *Wizard of Wikipedia* (Dinan et al., 2018) and *CMU DoG* (Zhou et al., 2018). To narrow the scope of this study and facilitate the language model training, CMU DoG was used as a starting point. This dataset contains 4112 grounded conversations devoted to the discussion of Wikipedia articles about popular movies. To extend the dataset, we collected Reddit[1] conversations on the same topic in English. Specifically, we parsed conversations from the 25 most popular subreddits related to films, series, and TV shows. These subreddits provided discussions that were tied to specific topics or comments. Additionally, we gathered comments that mentioned key phrases such as "movie" and "film".

[1] https://www.reddit.com/

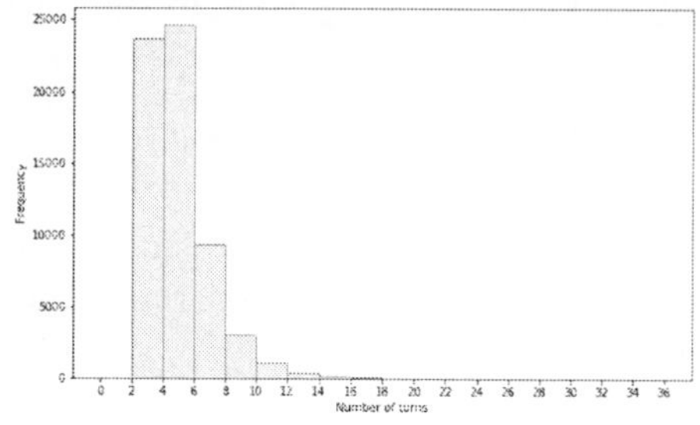

Figure 1: Distribution of dialogue lengths in collected dataset

The dataset preprocessing stage involved removing images, extra symbols, and emojis, as these were not considered in our research. In total, our collected dataset consists of approximately 62,500 multi-party dialogues, with an average of 5 turns per conversation (see Figure1). The length of extracted Reddit conversations is significantly shorter compared to CMU DoG dialogues, which have an average of 21.43 turns per conversation.

The dataset contains conversations collected along with linguistic annotations, grounding, and meta information related to each extracted dialogue. Specifically, automatically retrieved linguistic features for each turn in the dataset are presented in the following format:

- discourse annotation is represented as identifiers of connected turns with a discourse class describing the relation between them;

- sentiment class of a turn, accompanied by its probability;

- AMR graph is provided in simplified form for each turn.

The process of annotating data is described in detail in Section 3.1. Our final dataset is publicly available at the link: https://huggingface.co/datasets/alexchern5757/groundhog_reddit.

It should be emphasized that all datasets containing open-domain dialogues share the same limitations related to grounding. Casual conversations are distinguished by the absence of rigid topic boundaries, stylistic ambiguity, and a strong reliance on context. Evaluative information in these dialogues is often presented as facts, which can result in inaccurate grounding extraction.

3 Methods

3.1 Dialogue Features

In order to generate coherent and truthful responses, we incorporate grounding and several linguistic features that describe the current dialogue state as model inputs.

Discourse Discourse can be represented in various ways, with one of the most widely used approaches being Rhetorical Structure Theory (RST) for plain texts (Mann and Thompson, 1988). RST employs elementary discourse units to analyze the structure of the text, whereas in dialogue analysis, trees are constructed over utterances. Dialogue discourse graphs, as introduced by Stone et al. (2013), extend the concept of standard dialogue graphs by including discourse labels for each utterance indicating the specific function or pragmatic purpose of the utterance (e.g., Disagreement, Appreciation, Question). An example is provided in Appendix A.

The application of discourse annotation, combined with grounding techniques, has demonstrated the potential for generating media dialogues that are more consistent and truthful (Majumder et al., 2020; Chernyavskiy and Ilvovsky, 2023). This integration of linguistic features and grounding methods has shown promise in enhancing the quality of such tasks.

In order to achieve automatic discourse annotation, we implemented and trained the parser model suggested by Shi and Huang (2019). The training process was started from scratch and utilized the Coarse Discourse Sequence Corpus (CDSC) (Zhang et al., 2017), which is the largest manually annotated dataset of discourse acts in online discussions.

Abstract Meaning Representation (AMR) Abstract Meaning Representation is based on directed acyclic graphs and provides a structured semantic representation of language, including semantic role annotations consisting of arguments and values (Banarescu et al., 2013). Given that incorporating AMR graphs enhances task-oriented dialogue generation (Yang et al., 2023) and the promising prospects of integrating AMR with pragmatic intents (Bonial et al., 2020), we use these graphs as one of the linguistically motivated inputs in the experiments.

In our dataset, an AMR graph was generated for each sentence within an utterance, and then these subgraphs were combined into a single graph. To reduce the complexity of the representation, we truncated vertices at a depth beyond a specified constant. A more detailed description of the AMR graphs is provided in Appendix A. We adopt a similar method to linearize AMR graphs, as proposed by Ribeiro et al. (2020).

Sentiment The sentiment labels assigned to each utterance in the dataset indicate the polarity of the sentiment expressed, using a 3-point scale: Positive, Negative, or Neutral. The RoBERTa model, which was trained on tweets, was utilized for the corresponding labeling task (Barbieri et al., 2020). To incorporate information about sentiment, special tokens were integrated into linearized representations of the dialogues.

Grounding Grounding is an important aspect of model input as it serves to mitigate the issues associated with hallucinations in language models. Generally, when the utterance does not pertain to an opinion, the main fact can be derived from the provided grounding.

There are several approaches to fact-control realization for overcoming hallucinations within a dialogue system. One of them is the use of external memory, which was proposed in RETRO (Borgeaud et al., 2022) and KELM (Lu et al., 2021) models when the relevant parts of the training texts are passed to the cross-attention mechanism at the stage of next response generation. An alternative method is to extract grounding text from external databases, for instance, by using web mining like in the Sparrow (Glaese et al., 2022) approach. LaMDA (Thoppilan et al., 2022) proposes an approach combining structured factual grounding from an external knowledge base (Google Search API) and dialogue context both in the training and inference stages.

In this paper, we focus on the Sparrow approach and explore the importance of using grounding for generating consistent open-domain dialogues. We use the MediaWiki API[2] to conduct searches for two types of queries: movie titles and entire Reddit thread titles. A restriction was imposed to retrieve a maximum of five documents for each query. Subsequently, a summarized version of these documents was created, consisting of five sentences. These summaries were then combined into a single grounding text.

[2]https://github.com/goldsmith/Wikipedia

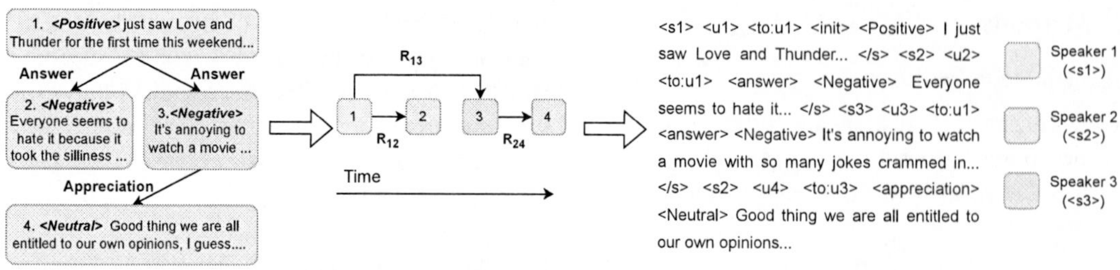

Figure 2: Example of the discursively annotated conversation linearization process. Firstly, all nodes are ordered temporally, forming a chain. Then, it is transformed into text representation using special tokens to display meta information: $\langle u_i \rangle$ are used for utterance ids; $\langle s_i \rangle$ are tokens for speaker ids (are signified by colors); $\langle \text{to:}u_i \rangle$ are used for addressees; and $\langle R_{ij} \rangle$ are used for relations. Additionally, an $\langle \text{init} \rangle$ token is introduced due to the fact that the first replica does not have an addressee.

3.2 Dialogue Linearization

The linearization of dialogue graphs plays a crucial role in our approach. Hoyle et al. (2021) demonstrated that Transformers exhibit invariance to the specific method employed for linearization. Therefore, we employ discourse and AMR graphs for dialogue modeling, followed by a thoughtful linearization process.

Our linearization procedure is implemented in the following way. Firstly, all utterances are arranged in chronological order to establish a linear sequence. Secondly, each utterance is linearized independently, taking into account its own characteristics as well as the attributes of the connecting edge to its addressee. To achieve this, each utterance is assigned a unique identifier, the current speaker is indicated, and the addressee statement to which the utterance responds is specified. Thirdly, the appropriate response strategy is determined, as indicated by a discourse relation and sentiment tokens. Finally, the text of the subsequent utterance is incorporated. We utilize special tokens to identify speakers, utterances, and addressees, namely $\{\langle s_i \rangle\}$, $\{\langle u_i \rangle\}$ and $\{\langle \text{to:}u_i \rangle\}$ respectively. As an example, a linearized i-th utterance written by the j-th speaker in response to the k-th utterance has the following form: "$\langle s_j \rangle$ $\langle u_i \rangle$ $\langle \text{to:}u_k \rangle$ $\langle \text{relation} \rangle$ $\langle \text{sentim.} \rangle$ text".

We employ a separation token to combine individual utterances and create a full representation of the dialogue state. Figure 2 provides an example of the conversation linearization procedure. By eliminating all text and sentiment tokens, the linearized representation can be conveniently converted into a raw linear discourse representation.

3.3 GroundHog Model

We suggest the GroundHog model as an effective neural approach for encoding diverse types of input information. It incorporates multiple Transformer-based encoders to capture multiple levels of granularity in the input data. Unlike previous approaches such as Longformers (Beltagy et al., 2020), our focus is on the attention mechanism within each input rather than utilizing global attention. In addition, we reduce the size of the attention matrices compared to Longformers.

The architecture is based on the customized BART, as illustrated in Figure 3. Our approach involves the utilization of multiple texts as input, on which it does not formally impose restrictions. The first input text should contain the primary information, whereas the others should provide supplementary information. In our case, the inputs are the following: (1) a dialogue history that has been enriched with discourse and sentiment tokens; (2) a raw, linearized representation of a discourse dialogue graph; and (3) an addressee's utterance and a part of its AMR graph.

Each input is first processed through a common tokenizer and then encoded separately using its own BART encoder. In order to create a more universal approach, embeddings from *all* inputs could be aggregated through convolution. However, this would substantially change the standard input format of the pre-trained BART decoder, making the training process more challenging without a large dataset for additional pre-training. Therefore, we divide the inputs into two categories: the main text and the supplementary texts.

The model does not modify the embedding of the main text before the decoder, and it retains the attention mask for this text. The other inputs are

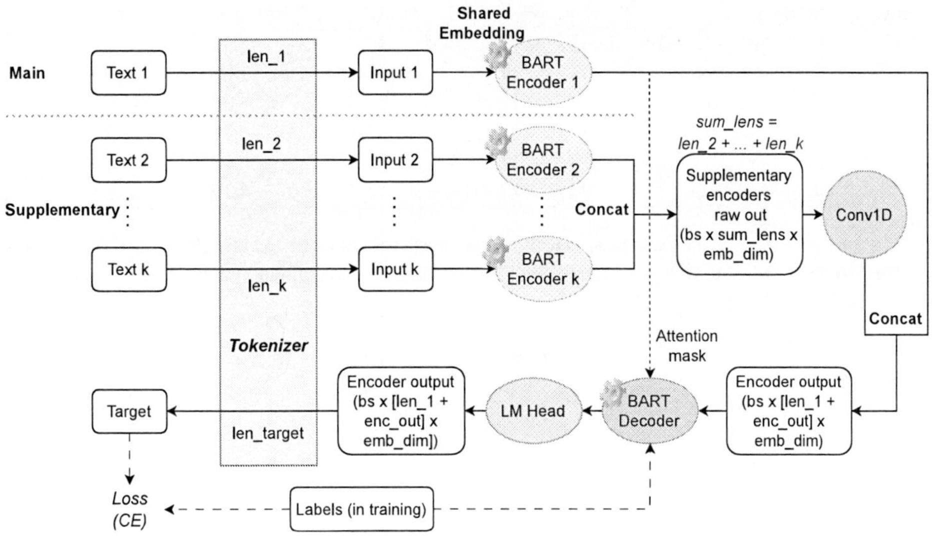

Figure 3: GroundHog architecture. The GroundHog architecture comprises individual BART encoders for each input text, which are subsequently aggregated and used as input for the BART decoder. To reduce the dimensionality of the inputs, a 1D convolutional layer is applied to all inputs except the main input. The shared embedding layer is denoted by the gear icon. In addition, intermediate tensor dimensions are indicated (batchsize is denoted as bs).

combined using concatenation and a convolutional layer. However, this approach may introduce some disruption to the token order, and consequently, the attention masks from the encoder for these inputs are not utilized in the decoder input. In this research, we conducted experiments using different aggregation methods and determined that the one-dimensional convolutional layer yielded the most favorable results.

As in the base model, the language modeling head is utilized after the decoder. We use the same tokenizers and shared embedding layer for all encoders and the decoder. As is common in language modeling decoder-based approaches, we employ a standard cross-entropy loss.

4 Experiments

4.1 Implementation Details

We fine-tuned the base-sized BART (139M parameters) model and the GroundHog models based on it. We used various lengths for different inputs but the maximum was 1024 tokens. The models were trained on batches of size 2, with a learning rate of 2e-5, for 5 epochs. For all other hyper-parameters, we used the default values.

All parsers and datasets used have the open source MIT license.

Each model was trained on the GPU Tesla V100 32G for approximately 10 hours.

4.2 Automatic Evaluation

In order to conduct a more comprehensive analysis of the generation of complex responses, we divided the dataset into two subsets: dialogues with long last responses (consisting of at least two sentences) and dialogues with short responses.

We conducted experiments using both the BART and GroundHog models for the several configurations of the dataset used for fine-tuning:

- In $\mathcal{B}$, we fine-tuned the base BART model using the concatenation of the dialogue history, thread title, and grounding as the input.
- In $\mathcal{G}_1$, we trained the GroundHog model using the concatenation of the dialogue histories and thread titles.
- In $\mathcal{G}_2$, we extended input from $\mathcal{G}_1$ by adding grounding.
- In $\mathcal{G}_3$, we enriched the dialogue history from $\mathcal{G}_2$ by discourse linguistic tokens.
- In $\mathcal{G}_4$, we added separate linguistic inputs associated with AMR: (1) AMR for the full dialogue history (concatenated representations of single utterances); (2) AMR for the addressee.
- In $\mathcal{G}_5$, we extended the input from $\mathcal{G}_4$ by adding sentiment tokens.

In all cases where grounding was utilized, it was concatenated with the main text input. This was necessary to ensure that the attention mechanism

Model	Setting	ROUGE-1	ROUGE-2	ROUGE-L	BLEU-1	BLEU-2
BART	$\mathcal{B}$ [history; title; grounding]	17.71	3.69	15.95	17.2	2.86
GroundHog	$\mathcal{G}_1$ [history; title]	17.79	3.71	16.05	16.99	2.88
	$\mathcal{G}_2$ [+grounding]	17.86	3.85	16.08	**17.32**	3.00
	$\mathcal{G}_3$ [+discourse]	17.88	3.87	16.09	17.15	3.04
	$\mathcal{G}_4$ [+AMR]	17.88	3.80	16.17	17.26	2.94
	$\mathcal{G}_5$ [+sentiment]	**17.91**	**3.93**	**16.19**	17.25	**3.09**

Table 1: Model performance on the test set (**long responses**) for different model input settings. $\mathcal{B}_i$ and $\mathcal{G}_i$ are related to the BART and GroundHog models trained using different combinations of inputs. Here, the standard deviation is less than 0.007 in all cases.

Model	Setting	ROUGE-1	ROUGE-2	ROUGE-L	BLEU-1	BLEU-2
BART	$\mathcal{B}$ [history; title; grounding]	9.86	2.10	8.98	9.18	1.65
GroundHog	$\mathcal{G}_1$ [history; title]	9.66	1.88	8.77	8.90	1.40
	$\mathcal{G}_2$ [+grounding]	9.85	2.16	8.98	9.20	1.70
	$\mathcal{G}_3$ [+discourse]	10.11	2.37	9.21	9.46	1.90
	$\mathcal{G}_4$ [+AMR]	9.82	2.06	8.93	9.12	1.56
	$\mathcal{G}_5$ [+sentiment]	**10.23**	**2.47**	**9.32**	**9.52**	**1.98**

Table 2: Model performance on the test set (**short responses**) for different model input settings.

adequately considered the specific components of grounding. Simultaneously, grounding was treated as a distinct input due to its voluminous nature, which may necessitate its truncation.

For automatic evaluation of generated responses, we calculated the ROUGE-based[3] (Lin, 2004) and BLEU-based[4] (Papineni et al., 2002) scores using target texts cleared of special tokens (raw texts). The obtained scores (mean F1 over three runs) are presented in Table 1 for the long texts.

The GroundHog model ($\mathcal{G}_2$) exhibited superior performance compared to BART across all metrics when provided with the same inputs. This suggests that longer inputs are more effectively processed when handled separately. However, it is important to note that one limitation of the GroundHog model is that its decoder requires substantial amounts of training data to learn effectively from scratch. With sufficient pretraning, these results can be improved. Also, triggered by this limitation, we conducted a grid search and determined that setting the embedding size after the 1D convolutional layer in GroundHog to 256 would prevent an unnecessary increase in the decoder's hidden state.

The results demonstrate that grounding has a positive impact on the ROUGE and BLEU scores. This can be attributed to the fact that the generated responses exhibit a higher level of accuracy in terms of factual information. However, the observed difference is not statistically significant. It can be attributed to the subjective nature of most of the generated responses, which often involve personal evaluations. Additionally, the quality of the extracted grounding is not optimal, as it is extracted based on the full dialogues.

It was observed that the inclusion of linguistic features in the model led to improved performance compared to a model trained without these features. Specifically, the model that utilized all linguistic inputs ($\mathcal{G}_5$) achieved the highest scores. The incremental addition of linguistic features resulted in a monotonic improvement in the ROUGE-L metric as well as an overall improvement in other scores.

Furthermore, the experiments indicated that the use of AMR may not be as promising as dialogue acts or sentiment. This finding can be attributed to the complexity of the AMR structure.

Results for the short target responses are presented in Table 2. The overall conclusions drawn from the analysis are consistent with the findings discussed earlier, with the exception of the monotonous growth of metrics. However, a noteworthy observation is that even for short responses, the GroundHog model exhibits superior performance compared to the base BART model.

4.3 Human Evaluation

A human evaluation was conducted to enhance the assessment process and account for aspects that cannot be evaluated using automated metrics. The main objective of this evaluation was to compare

[3]https://pypi.org/project/rouge/

[4]https://www.nltk.org/_modules/nltk/translate/bleu_score.html

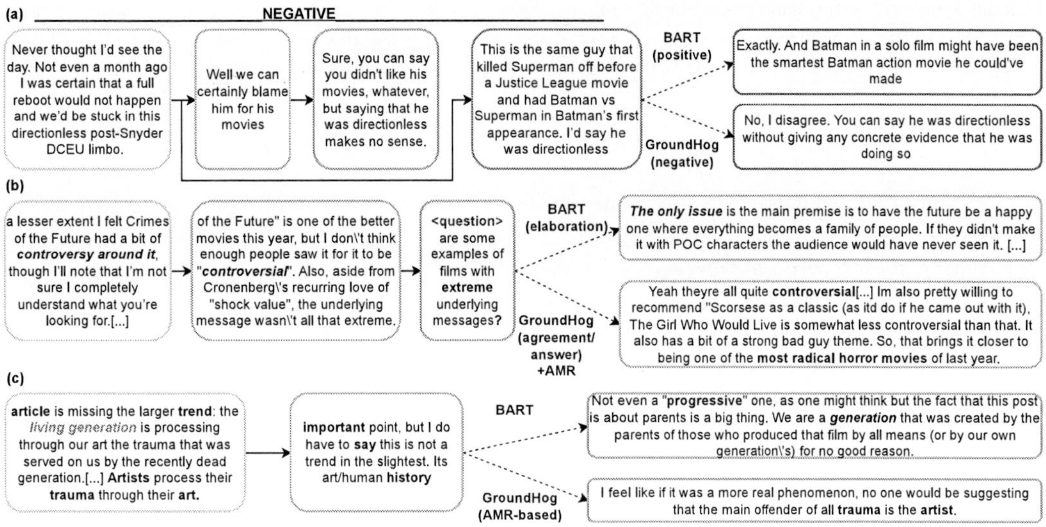

Figure 4: Examples of response generation by the base BART model and the GroundHog model fine-tuned with linguistic inputs. Each color represents a different speaker. The task was to generate text in the last utterance.

the texts generated by the BART model ($\mathcal{B}$) with those of the GroundHog model employing linguistic features ($\mathcal{G}_5$). Experts were tasked with determining the preferable option for continuing the conversation, or whether the alternatives were equal. Also, each option was evaluated on a 3-point scale based on coherence (utterance-based), meaningfulness, and consistency (dialogue-based) criteria.

Dialogue consistency assessed the connection between the current utterance and the addressee, as well as the overall logical progression of the dialogue. Meaningfulness assessed the semantic load of the utterance within its general context. Utterance-based coherence was assessed by evaluating the internal coherence of the utterance.

To ensure reliability in the evaluation process, the three scales were rated on a scale ranging from 0 to 2 (0 for poor prediction, 2 for good prediction). To minimize any potential bias, the options for rating were presented in a random order.

Table 3 presents the evaluation results obtained from 250 randomly selected dialogues from the test dataset. The linguistic approach, as observed, generates responses that are preferred in a larger number of cases. Additionally, these responses are more coherent, suitable for continuing the conversation, and formulated with better semantic appropriateness. While the overall improvement is not sizeable, there is notable progress in the generation of consistent conversations.

	# better	Coherence	Meaning.	Consist.
$\mathcal{B}$	79	1.48	1.27	1.38
$\mathcal{G}_5$	**101**	**1.53**	**1.38**	**1.40**

Table 3: Human evaluation results on the random test subset of 250 dialogues.

5 Discussion

In this section, our major objective is to gain a deeper understanding of the linguistic features that contribute to the improved quality of GroundHog. To this end, we conduct a comparative analysis of the texts generated by BART ($\mathcal{B}$) and the texts generated by GroundHog ($\mathcal{G}_5$).

Regarding the interpretation of grounding, its incorporation enhances the factual component of generation. However, the qualitative aspects of grounding in our dataset are not very robust, and it can be a direction for further research.

Sentiment We started our investigation with the analysis of sentiment due to its ease of interpretation. To assess the sentiment in the generated texts, we utilized the same classifier that was applied to the training dataset. The results yielded an overall accuracy of 0.43 for the BART model and 0.44 for the GroundHog model, with no sizeable difference observed. It is worth noting that the majority of texts in the dataset were negative or neutral, as users generally tend to criticize films or actors. Specifically, there were 1525 negative utterances, 1374 neutral utterances, and 841 positive ut-

Model	answer	elaboration	agreement	other	disagreement	appreciation	question	negative	humor
$\mathcal{B}$	1491	**1231**	446	211	158	107	80	15	1
$\mathcal{G}_5$	1508	1174	**454**	223	159	101	**97**	**22**	2

Table 4: Statistics of dialogue acts in texts generated by the base BART and GroundHog models.

terances within the test dataset. Consequently, the focus should be shifted to generating more accurate negative responses. In terms of these responses, the base BART model achieved an F1-macro score of 0.461, while the GroundHog model achieved an F1-macro score of 0.487. This improvement is particularly noteworthy as it leads to an overall enhancement in language modeling.

Figure 4 (a) presents an illustrative MPC example. It is observed that all input utterances within the dialogue are negative in nature. Consequently, the subsequent utterance should also embody a negative sentiment, either by aligning with the general criticism of the film director or by critiquing the statements expressed by other participants. In this context, it can be inferred that GroundHog has produced an appropriate response. Conversely, the response generated by the base BART model is positive in sentiment and considered inappropriate.

Discourse Dialogue acts contribute to dialogue-based consistency and, to some extent, utterance-based coherence. Since existing models do not explicitly generate dialogue acts, we utilized a trained discourse parser to label these acts for comparison with the original responses. The GroundHog model had a higher accuracy score of 0.551 compared to 0.538 for the base model. The confusion matrices showed similar patterns, but there was a slight difference in the distribution of dialogue acts (see Table 4). Specifically, the base model exhibited a higher frequency of "Elaboration", while the GroundHog model generated less common relations such as "Question" and "Agreement". This indicates that the linguistic model's responses are more diverse without compromising their quality.

In the conversation depicted in Figure 4 (b), it can be observed that the custom model response exhibits better consistency. The most correct target response should include the Answer or Agreement relations rather than Elaboration. Unlike the BART model, which lacks information about the previous response being a question, the GroundHog model incorporates this knowledge in order to generate a response that is discursively consistent. Moreover, GroundHog aims to incorporate the main AMR entities, such as the concept of "controversial."

AMR Interpreting the impact of AMR representations is challenging due to their inherent complexity. Generally, AMR has a direct influence on the semantic aspect, specifically the representation of entities and their relations. In this regard, human evaluation has shown that the scores for the criterion of "meaningfulness" are higher for GroundHog texts compared to BART texts.

Figure 4 (c) provides a concrete example illustrating a discussion where each participant expresses their opinion about some statement. Here, both generative models produced thematically correct answers. However, the GroundHog model used more appropriate words, resulting in a response that was more consistent with the dialogue history. We hypothesize that this can be attributed primarily to the AMR input. For the first utterance, the AMR representation is as follows:

(miss :ARG0 (article) :ARG1 (trend :ARG1 (and) :ARG1-of (have-degree))) ... (process :ARG0 (artist) :ARG1 (trauma :poss a) :instrument (art :poss a))

Therefore, the main entities are "article", "trend", "artists", "trauma", and "art". The GroundHog model primarily relies on these words, whereas BART's response is primarily influenced by the word "generation". However, the frequent occurrence of "generation" does not capture the underlying meaning of the text.

General View We have determined that linguistic features individually demonstrate utility and yield interpretive results. There is also the potential for uncovering valuable hidden insights through their combination. Nevertheless, our research represents a step towards achieving a coherent and meaningful generation.

It is worth considering that linguistic features can also be manually specified when the current context is insufficient for parsers to accurately perform their tasks. Such manual specifications can facilitate dialogue management.

6 Conclusion and Future Work

In this paper, we investigated the efficacy of incorporating grounding and multi-grained linguistic information for multi-party conversation generation. To address the challenge of handling lengthy input texts, we proposed the GroundHog model, which leverages both grounding and linguistic features.

For evaluation, we collected a novel Reddit-based dataset designed for training dialogue systems. This dataset was augmented with linguistic features, including semantic and discourse information, as well as sentiment. Experiments involving both automatic metrics and human evaluation have shown that generated texts using linguistic inputs were more preferable. In our supplementary analysis, we interpreted the obtained results.

Further research directions include the investigation of other linguistic inputs as well as other representations of inputs. Also, we plan to experiment with the recent LLMs to analyze their possibilities of leveraging linguistic features.

Limitations

Our approach is not constrained by language and has the potential for universal application. At the same time, we introduce a novel Transformer architecture that ideally requires pre-training on a large dataset. Furthermore, the effectiveness of the methodology is constrained by the accuracy and reliability of the parsers used to extract linguistic features, as well as the performance of the grounding extraction model.

Ethics and Broader Impact

The use of large Transformer models for training has been linked to contributing to climate change. However, it is important to highlight that our research did not involve training these models from scratch. Instead, we conducted a fine-tuning process on pre-existing models.

As is the case with any generative model, it is not possible to ensure flawless quality in the generated output. At the same time, we do not make our model publicly available. We mitigate the risks associated with generation by filtering the dataset and making business logic modifications.

The presented dataset was collected from Reddit for the purpose of scientific research and subsequent analysis. It may exhibit certain inherent biases due to its specific origin, and we suggest using it for scientific purposes only.

Acknowledgements

The article was prepared within the framework of the HSE University Basic Research Program. It was also supported in part through the computational resources of HPC facilities at NRU HSE.

The publication was also supported by the grant for research centers in the field of AI provided by the Analytical Center for the Government of the Russian Federation (ACRF) in accordance with the agreement on the provision of subsidies (identifier of the agreement 000000D730321P5Q0002) and the agreement with HSE University No. 70-2021-00139.

References

Laura Banarescu, Claire Bonial, Shu Cai, Madalina Georgescu, Kira Griffitt, Ulf Hermjakob, Kevin Knight, Philipp Koehn, Martha Palmer, and Nathan Schneider. 2013. Abstract meaning representation for sembanking. In *Proceedings of the 7th Linguistic Annotation Workshop and Interoperability with Discourse, LAW-ID@ACL 2013, August 8-9, 2013, Sofia, Bulgaria*, pages 178–186. The Association for Computer Linguistics.

Francesco Barbieri, José Camacho-Collados, Luis Espinosa Anke, and Leonardo Neves. 2020. Tweeteval: Unified benchmark and comparative evaluation for tweet classification. In *Findings of the Association for Computational Linguistics: EMNLP 2020, Online Event, 16-20 November 2020*, volume EMNLP 2020 of *Findings of ACL*, pages 1644–1650. Association for Computational Linguistics.

Iz Beltagy, Matthew E. Peters, and Arman Cohan. 2020. Longformer: The long-document transformer. *CoRR*, abs/2004.05150.

Claire Bonial, Lucia Donatelli, Mitchell Abrams, Stephanie Lukin, Stephen Tratz, Matthew Marge, Ron Artstein, David Traum, and Clare Voss. 2020. Dialogue-amr: abstract meaning representation for dialogue. In *Proceedings of the Twelfth Language Resources and Evaluation Conference*, pages 684–695.

Sebastian Borgeaud, Arthur Mensch, Jordan Hoffmann, Trevor Cai, Eliza Rutherford, Katie Millican, George van den Driessche, Jean-Baptiste Lespiau, Bogdan Damoc, Aidan Clark, Diego de Las Casas, Aurelia Guy, Jacob Menick, Roman Ring, Tom Hennigan, Saffron Huang, Loren Maggiore, Chris Jones, Albin Cassirer, Andy Brock, Michela Paganini, Geoffrey Irving, Oriol Vinyals, Simon Osindero, Karen Simonyan, Jack W. Rae, Erich Elsen, and Laurent Sifre. 2022. Improving language models by retrieving from trillions of tokens. In *International Conference on Machine Learning, ICML 2022, 17-23 July 2022, Baltimore, Maryland, USA*, volume 162 of *Proceedings of Machine Learning Research*, pages 2206–2240. PMLR.

Alexander Chernyavskiy and Dmitry Ilvovsky. 2023. Transformer-based multi-party conversation generation using dialogue discourse acts planning. In *Proceedings of the 24th Annual Meeting of the Special Interest Group on Discourse and Dialogue*, pages 519–529, Prague, Czechia. Association for Computational Linguistics.

Emily Dinan, Stephen Roller, Kurt Shuster, Angela Fan, Michael Auli, and Jason Weston. 2018. Wizard of wikipedia: Knowledge-powered conversational agents. *arXiv preprint arXiv:1811.01241*.

Song Feng, Hui Wan, Chulaka Gunasekara, Siva Sankalp Patel, Sachindra Joshi, and Luis A Lastras. 2020. doc2dial: A goal-oriented document-grounded dialogue dataset. *arXiv preprint arXiv:2011.06623*.

Amelia Glaese, Nat McAleese, Maja Trebacz, John Aslanides, Vlad Firoiu, Timo Ewalds, Maribeth Rauh, Laura Weidinger, Martin Chadwick, Phoebe Thacker, Lucy Campbell-Gillingham, Jonathan Uesato, Po-Sen Huang, Ramona Comanescu, Fan Yang, Abigail See, Sumanth Dathathri, Rory Greig, Charlie Chen, Doug Fritz, Jaume Sanchez Elias, Richard Green, Sona Mokrá, Nicholas Fernando, Boxi Wu, Rachel Foley, Susannah Young, Iason Gabriel, William Isaac, John Mellor, Demis Hassabis, Koray Kavukcuoglu, Lisa Anne Hendricks, and Geoffrey Irving. 2022. Improving alignment of dialogue agents via targeted human judgements. *CoRR*, abs/2209.14375.

Jia-Chen Gu, Zhen-Hua Ling, and Quan Liu. 2019. Interactive matching network for multi-turn response selection in retrieval-based chatbots. In *Proceedings of the 28th ACM International Conference on Information and Knowledge Management, CIKM 2019, Beijing, China, November 3-7, 2019*, pages 2321–2324. ACM.

Vrindavan Harrison, Lena Reed, Shereen Oraby, and Marilyn A. Walker. 2019. Maximizing stylistic control and semantic accuracy in NLG: personality variation and discourse contrast. *CoRR*, abs/1907.09527.

Behnam Hedayatnia, Karthik Gopalakrishnan, Seokhwan Kim, Yang Liu, Mihail Eric, and Dilek Hakkani-Tur. 2020. Policy-driven neural response generation for knowledge-grounded dialogue systems. *arXiv preprint arXiv:2005.12529*.

Alexander Miserlis Hoyle, Ana Marasovic, and Noah A. Smith. 2021. Promoting graph awareness in linearized graph-to-text generation. In *Findings of the Association for Computational Linguistics: ACL/IJCNLP 2021, Online Event, August 1-6, 2021*, volume ACL/IJCNLP 2021 of *Findings of ACL*, pages 944–956. Association for Computational Linguistics.

Yangfeng Ji, Gholamreza Haffari, and Jacob Eisenstein. 2016. A latent variable recurrent neural network for discourse relation language models. *CoRR*, abs/1603.01913.

Baber Khalid, Malihe Alikhani, Michael Fellner, Brian McMahan, and Matthew Stone. 2020. Discourse coherence, reference grounding and goal oriented dialogue. *arXiv preprint arXiv:2007.04428*.

Ran Le, Wenpeng Hu, Mingyue Shang, Zhenjun You, Lidong Bing, Dongyan Zhao, and Rui Yan. 2019. Who is speaking to whom? learning to identify utterance addressee in multi-party conversations. In *Proceedings of the 2019 Conference on Empirical Methods in Natural Language Processing and the 9th International Joint Conference on Natural Language Processing, EMNLP-IJCNLP 2019, Hong Kong, China, November 3-7, 2019*, pages 1909–1919. Association for Computational Linguistics.

Mike Lewis, Yinhan Liu, Naman Goyal, Marjan Ghazvininejad, Abdelrahman Mohamed, Omer Levy, Veselin Stoyanov, and Luke Zettlemoyer. 2020. BART: denoising sequence-to-sequence pre-training for natural language generation, translation, and comprehension. In *Proceedings of the 58th Annual Meeting of the Association for Computational Linguistics, ACL 2020, Online, July 5-10, 2020*, pages 7871–7880. Association for Computational Linguistics.

Chin-Yew Lin. 2004. Rouge: A package for automatic evaluation of summaries. In *ACL 2004*.

Yinquan Lu, Haonan Lu, Guirong Fu, and Qun Liu. 2021. KELM: knowledge enhanced pre-trained language representations with message passing on hierarchical relational graphs. *CoRR*, abs/2109.04223.

Bodhisattwa Prasad Majumder, Shuyang Li, Jianmo Ni, and Julian McAuley. 2020. Interview: Large-scale modeling of media dialog with discourse patterns and knowledge grounding. In *Proceedings of the 2020 Conference on Empirical Methods in Natural Language Processing (EMNLP)*, pages 8129–8141.

William C. Mann and Sandra A. Thompson. 1988. Rhetorical structure theory: Toward a functional theory of text organization. *Text & Talk*, 8:243 – 281.

OpenAI. 2023. Gpt-4 technical report.

Kishore Papineni, Salim Roukos, Todd Ward, and Wei-Jing Zhu. 2002. Bleu: a method for automatic evaluation of machine translation. In *Proceedings of the 40th Annual Meeting of the Association for Computational Linguistics, July 6-12, 2002, Philadelphia, PA, USA*, pages 311–318. ACL.

Colin Raffel, Noam Shazeer, Adam Roberts, Katherine Lee, Sharan Narang, Michael Matena, Yanqi Zhou, Wei Li, and Peter J. Liu. 2020. Exploring the limits of transfer learning with a unified text-to-text transformer. *Journal of Machine Learning Research*, 21(140):1–67.

Hannah Rashkin, David Reitter, Gaurav Singh Tomar, and Dipanjan Das. 2021. Increasing faithfulness in knowledge-grounded dialogue with controllable features. *arXiv preprint arXiv:2107.06963*.

Leonardo F. R. Ribeiro, Martin Schmitt, Hinrich Schütze, and Iryna Gurevych. 2020. Investigating pretrained language models for graph-to-text generation. *CoRR*, abs/2007.08426.

Zhouxing Shi and Minlie Huang. 2019. A deep sequential model for discourse parsing on multi-party dialogues. In *AAAI*.

Matthew Stone, Una Stojnic, and Ernest Lepore. 2013. Situated utterances and discourse relations. In *Proceedings of the 10th International Conference on Computational Semantics, IWCS 2013, March 19-22, 2013, University of Potsdam, Potsdam, Germany*, pages 390–396. The Association for Computer Linguistics.

Romal Thoppilan, Daniel De Freitas, Jamie Hall, Noam Shazeer, Apoorv Kulshreshtha, Heng-Tze Cheng, Alicia Jin, Taylor Bos, Leslie Baker, Yu Du, YaGuang Li, Hongrae Lee, Huaixiu Steven Zheng, Amin Ghafouri, Marcelo Menegali, Yanping Huang, Maxim Krikun, Dmitry Lepikhin, James Qin, Dehao Chen, Yuanzhong Xu, Zhifeng Chen, Adam Roberts, Maarten Bosma, Yanqi Zhou, Chung-Ching Chang, Igor Krivokon, Will Rusch, Marc Pickett, Kathleen S. Meier-Hellstern, Meredith Ringel Morris, Tulsee Doshi, Renelito Delos Santos, Toju Duke, Johnny Soraker, Ben Zevenbergen, Vinodkumar Prabhakaran, Mark Diaz, Ben Hutchinson, Kristen Olson, Alejandra Molina, Erin Hoffman-John, Josh Lee, Lora Aroyo, Ravi Rajakumar, Alena Butryna, Matthew Lamm, Viktoriya Kuzmina, Joe Fenton, Aaron Cohen, Rachel Bernstein, Ray Kurzweil, Blaise Aguera-Arcas, Claire Cui, Marian Croak, Ed H. Chi, and Quoc Le. 2022. Lamda: Language models for dialog applications. *CoRR*, abs/2201.08239.

Deeksha Varshney, Akshara Prabhakar, and Asif Ekbal. 2022. Commonsense and named entity aware knowledge grounded dialogue generation. In *Proceedings of the 2022 Conference of the North American Chapter of the Association for Computational Linguistics: Human Language Technologies*, pages 1322–1335, Seattle, United States. Association for Computational Linguistics.

Junjie Wu and Hao Zhou. 2021. Augmenting topic aware knowledge-grounded conversations with dynamic built knowledge graphs. In *Proceedings of Deep Learning Inside Out (DeeLIO): The 2nd Workshop on Knowledge Extraction and Integration for Deep Learning Architectures*, pages 31–39.

Sixing Wu, Ying Li, Ping Xue, Dawei Zhang, and Zhonghai Wu. 2022. Section-aware commonsense knowledge-grounded dialogue generation with pre-trained language model. In *Proceedings of the 29th International Conference on Computational Linguistics*, pages 521–531.

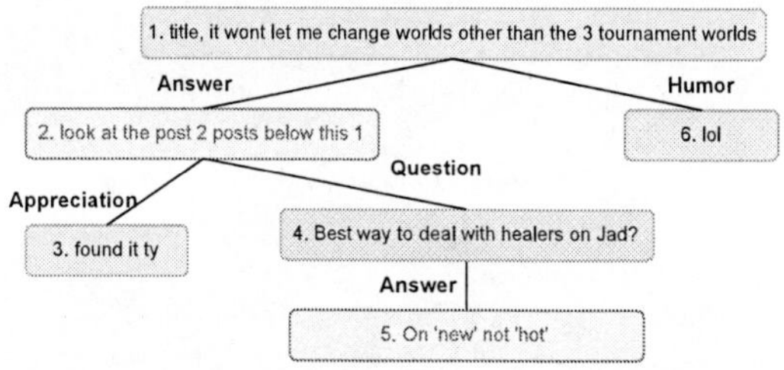

Figure 5: A manually annotated discourse tree for the multi-party dialogue. The color identifies the speaker, and edges indicate dialogue acts.

Bohao Yang, Chen Tang, and Chenghua Lin. 2023. Improving medical dialogue generation with abstract meaning representations. *arXiv preprint arXiv:2309.10608*.

Tom Young, Erik Cambria, Iti Chaturvedi, Hao Zhou, Subham Biswas, and Minlie Huang. 2018. Augmenting end-to-end dialogue systems with commonsense knowledge. In *Proceedings of the Thirty-Second AAAI Conference on Artificial Intelligence, (AAAI-18), the 30th innovative Applications of Artificial Intelligence (IAAI-18), and the 8th AAAI Symposium on Educational Advances in Artificial Intelligence (EAAI-18), New Orleans, Louisiana, USA, February 2-7, 2018*, pages 4970–4977. AAAI Press.

Amy X Zhang, Bryan Culbertson, and Praveen Paritosh. 2017. Characterizing online discussion using coarse discourse sequences. In *Eleventh International AAAI Conference on Web and Social Media*.

Xueliang Zhao, Wei Wu, Can Xu, Chongyang Tao, Dongyan Zhao, and Rui Yan. 2020. Knowledge-grounded dialogue generation with pre-trained language models. *arXiv preprint arXiv:2010.08824*.

Kangyan Zhou, Shrimai Prabhumoye, and Alan W. Black. 2018. A dataset for document grounded conversations. In *Proceedings of the 2018 Conference on Empirical Methods in Natural Language Processing, Brussels, Belgium, October 31 - November 4, 2018*, pages 708–713. Association for Computational Linguistics.

A Linguistic Representations

Dialogue Acts Figure 5 illustrates an example of a multi-party conversation that has been annotated with dialogue acts. In this figure, each node in the graph represents an utterance in the conversation and includes attributes such as the speaker's identifier (represented by colors) and the utterance text. The edges connecting the nodes indicate the flow of conversation and include attributes such as the addressee, representing the recipient of the utterance, and the dialogue act, representing the specific function or purpose of the utterance.

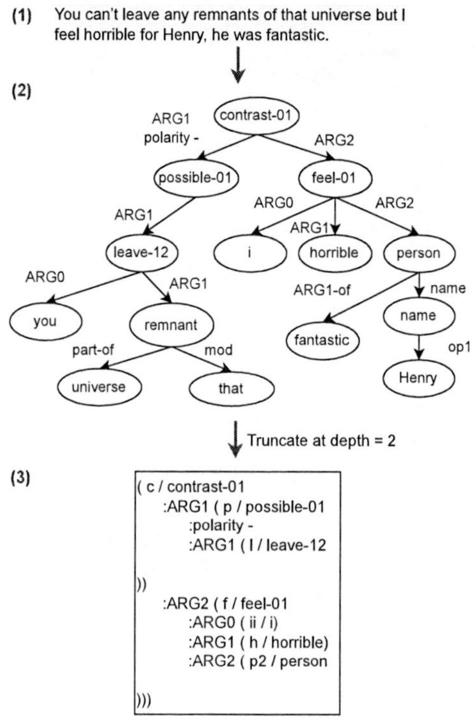

Figure 6: AMR representation for a single utterance and its truncated (by the first two levels) linearized representation. Here, (1) is the input text, (2) is the corresponding AMR graph, and (3) is the truncated plain graph2text representation.

Abstract Meaning Representation Figure 6 illustrates the representation of an utterance and its linearization using Abstract Meaning Representation (AMR). In this representation, words from the utterance are depicted as nodes in a graph, with edges representing the semantic relations between them. Higher-level vertices closer to the root of the graph capture the overall meaning, while lower-level vertices offer more specific details. In the given example, the core concept of contradiction is conveyed through the first two levels of the AMR graph. To enhance the efficiency of processing and reduce the length of the linearized representation, we only truncate the first levels of these graphs.

Discourse Relation Prediction and Discourse Parsing in Dialogues with Minimal Supervision

Chuyuan Li[1], Chloé Braud[2], Maxime Amblard[3], Giuseppe Carenini[1]
[1] University of British Columbia, V6T 1Z4, Vancouver, BC, Canada
[2] UT3 - IRIT, CNRS, ANITI, Toulouse, France
[3] Université de Lorraine, CNRS, Inria, LORIA, F-54000 Nancy, France
[1]{cli2711, carenini}@cs.ubc.ca, [2]chloe.braud@irit.fr,
[3]maxime.amblard@univ-lorraine.fr

Abstract

Discourse analysis plays a crucial role in Natural Language Processing, with discourse relation prediction arguably being the most difficult task in discourse parsing. Previous studies have generally focused on explicit or implicit discourse relation classification in monologues, leaving dialogue an under-explored domain. Facing the data scarcity issue, we propose to leverage self-training strategies based on a Transformer backbone. Moreover, we design the first semi-supervised pipeline that sequentially predicts discourse structures and relations. Using 50 examples, our relation prediction module achieves 58.4 in accuracy on the STAC corpus, close to supervised state-of-the-art. Full parsing results show notable improvements compared to the supervised models both in-domain (gaming) and cross-domain (technical chat), with better stability.

1 Introduction

Discourse analysis aims at uncovering the inherent structure of documents, where spans of text – known as Elementary Discourse Units (EDUs) – are linked by semantic-pragmatic relations such as *Explanation, Acknowledgment, Contrast, etc.* Discursive information is useful in various downstream applications, from sentiment analysis or fake news detection (Bhatia et al., 2015; Karimi and Tang, 2019), to summarization or machine translation (Chen and Yang, 2021; Chen et al., 2020). Current data-driven methods for discourse parsing have predominantly been applied to monologues, leading to limited availability and generalizability of discourse parsers for dialogues. As dialogue data soared in all kinds of forms, the need for automatic analysis systems has rapidly increased. Here, we propose to tackle the crucial problem of discourse relation identification in dialogues, and show performance of a full discourse parser that could enhance these applications.

Discourse relation classification labels the arcs in a discourse graph and is considered the most difficult part in discourse parsing: it is a multi-way classification task involving class imbalance and information at varied levels, from morpho-syntactics, to semantics, pragmatics and world knowledge. Discourse relations are often split into explicit – triggered by connectives (e.g. *because, while...)* thus allegedly easier to classify –, and implicit, without such markers. However, this distinction is not annotated in dialogue corpora. We thus cast the task as identifying all relations, which also makes for a more practical scenario as in DISRPT shared task (Zeldes et al., 2021).

One of the main hurdles in developing high-functioning parsing models is the scarcity of annotated data, along with limitations of supervised approaches in cross-domain scenarios (Liu and Chen, 2021). Strategic Conversations corpus (STAC) (Asher et al., 2016) – the most commonly used dialogue dataset annotated using the Segmented Discourse Representation Theory (SDRT) (Asher et al., 2003) – contains merely 1000 short documents. The labeling effort being expensive in terms of time and labor costs, it appears unlikely to create new large-scale expert-annotated datasets. Semi-supervised strategies are thus appealing. A few studies proposed weak or distant supervision for naked structure building (Badene et al., 2019; Li et al., 2023) while missing the important relation information. Remarkably, despite recent powerful Large Language Models (LLMs) such as ChatGPT excel in many NLP tasks, discourse parsing remains a significant challenge, given their poor performance (Chan et al., 2023a).

In this paper, we extend the bootstrapping approach to dialogues with even less annotated data, by relying on self-training (Yarowsky, 1995) where a model is used to produce pseudo labels and increase training data, a simple method shown as effective (Rosenberg et al., 2005). Using the BERT

Proceedings of the 5th Workshop on Computational Approaches to Discourse (CODI 2024), pages 161–176
March 21, 2024 ©2024 Association for Computational Linguistics

model (Devlin et al., 2019) as a base classifier and applying self-training, we achieve competitive results on a 16-way classification on STAC using only 50 dialogues for initial training. We also build a pipeline upon Li et al. (2023)'s work to perform full parsing, where we assign discourse relations on established structures, giving important extensions on semi-supervised approaches for dialogues until now limited to naked structures. Our pipeline yields 38.6 micro-F_1 score with gold EDUs and 32.8 with predicted EDUs: representing strong baselines for discourse parsing in dialogues with minimal supervision. This pipeline, or *structure-then-relation* approach, allows for a flexible architecture and greater generalizability. We further conduct cross-domain experiments by testing on a re-annotated subset of Molweni (Li et al., 2020) – a Ubuntu dataset. Despite the domain difference, our pipeline shows remarkable performances (link 75.6, link and relation 31.2), outperforming supervised SOTA models by a large margin[1].

To summarize: we propose (1) a simple and effective method that requires minimal supervision for discourse relation prediction; (2) a flexible discourse parsing pipeline that sequentially handles all tasks and exhibits strong generalizability; (3) a comprehensive comparison and in-depth exploration across in-domain and cross-domain scenarios; and (4) a small human-annotated discourse dataset in the technical chat domain which we will make public and support cross-domain evaluation.

2 Related Work

Discourse relation prediction as an individual task receives rich attention, mostly conducted on the Penn Discourse Treebank (PDTB) (Webber et al., 2019). Semi-supervised models have been mostly limited to implicit relation identification relying on synthetic data (Xu et al., 2018) or translations (Shi et al., 2019). These methods create pseudo-labeled data by using expert-composed rules or convenient linguistic resources: both in short for dialogues. The more recent effort utilizes Pre-trained Language Models (PLMs) (Shi and Demberg, 2019; Arslan et al., 2021) as backbones as they show superior performance for many classification tasks. PLMs have also been used as reliable classifiers to produce pseudo labels in self-training scenarios (Meng et al., 2020; Yu et al., 2021). Through prompt adaptation, Chan et al. (2023b) reveal that implicit relation prediction is still a tricky task, even for ChatGPT.

In recent years, there has been an increasing interest in discourse parsing in dialogues. A range of discourse parsers has emerged, including classic statistical models (Afantenos et al., 2015; Perret et al., 2016) and neural architecture models (Shi and Huang, 2019; Wang et al., 2021; Chi and Rudnicky, 2022), some are trained within multi-task learning framework (Yang et al., 2021; Fan et al., 2022). Although these supervised models achieve good performance on STAC corpus, they face limitations when applied to cross-domain scenarios (Liu and Chen, 2021). To address the challenge of data scarcity, researchers turn to weakly and semi-supervised methods (Badene et al., 2019; Li et al., 2023; Li, 2023). Nishida and Matsumoto (2022) show that co-training can considerably increase cross-domain performance on monologues, but they benefit from a larger amount of annotated data than we do for dialogues. Despite the revolutionary achievements offered by LLMs (Ouyang et al., 2022; Touvron et al., 2023), they remain notably behind fully and semi-supervised benchmarks in discourse parsing. Chan et al. (2023a) illustrate that ChatGPT struggles on STAC with 50% F_1 gap from supervised models. Fan and Jiang (2023) find that ChatGPT tends to establish discourse structures in a linear fashion. While in-context learning methods are helpful, their enhancement is limited.

3 Discourse Parsing Pipeline

A standard full discourse parsing involves three tasks: EDU segmentation, link attachment, and relation prediction (Figure 1). Most previous work applies a *structure-then-relation* approach (Afantenos et al., 2015; Shi and Huang, 2019; Liu and Chen, 2021). We follow the pipeline by providing relations on the established discourse structures.

3.1 Preliminary: Structure Construction

Our work is founded on Li et al. (2023) which entails the extraction of discourse structures from the attention matrices in PLMs. In that work, the original BART model (Lewis et al., 2020) is fine-tuned with dialogue-tailored Sentence Ordering task to better encode dialogue structures. In each attention head, the attention values among EDUs can be seen as edge weights. Thus, by using a Maximum Spanning Tree algorithm, they obtain discourse

[1]Our code and re-annotated dataset are available at https://github.com/chuyuanli/DisRel-w-selftraining

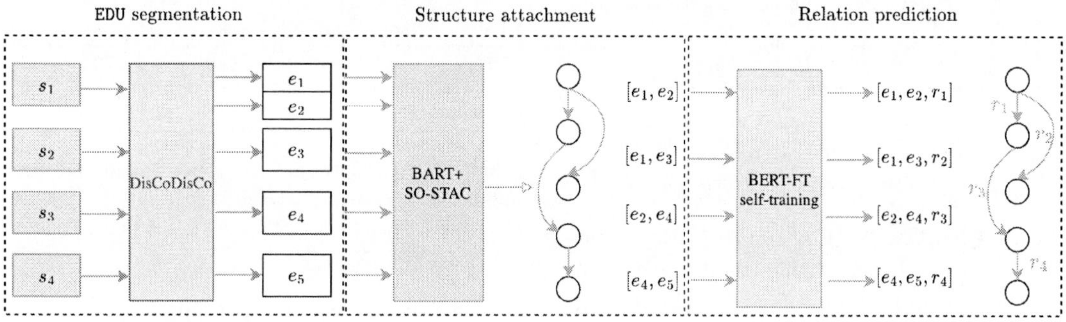

Figure 1: Semi-supervised discourse parsing pipeline proposition. s are utterances; e are EDUs; r are rhetorical relations. DisCoDisCo model is proposed in Gessler et al. (2021). BART+SO-STAC is BART model fine-tuned on Sentence Ordering task (Li et al., 2023). BERT-FT is BERT fine-tuned with self-training for relation prediction.

tree structures. That work proves that with just 50 examples, the optimal attention head can be consistently located. The extracted structures on STAC are found to be non-trivial, achieving 59.3 F_1 score.

Although most previous work begins with gold EDUs, we consider it crucial to evaluate in a deployed scenario where the parser performs EDU segmentation first. We thus integrate DisCoDisCo (Gessler et al., 2021), a straightforward sequence tagging model pre-trained on a random sample of 50 STAC dialogues, into the complete pipeline.

3.2 Relation Prediction Module

Following the setup in DISRPT shared tasks[2], we regard relation identification as multi-way classification where we classify every pair of head and dependent EDUs individually. EDU pairs reflect local coherence. A model trained in this setting is easily applicable to other discourse frameworks.

Self-Training: Our relation prediction module contains a classifier $\mathcal{M}$, a small amount of labeled data $\mathcal{L}$, and a large amount of unannotated data $\mathcal{U}$. The training process is as follow: $\mathcal{M}$ is trained on $\mathcal{L}$ to provide predictions (pseudo labels) on $\mathcal{U}$; then, under pre-defined selection criteria, a subset $\mathcal{S} \subset \mathcal{U}$ is sampled and merged with $\mathcal{L}$ for a new round of re-training. $\mathcal{M}$ can be re-trained for many rounds until a stopping criterion is met.

Classifier $\mathcal{M}$: Our classifier is an uncased BERT base model appended with a linear projection and softmax layer to produce relation probabilities. BERT has shown superior performance in discourse-related tasks (Chen et al., 2019; Atwell et al., 2021) and is the language backbone of current SOTA model for relation on STAC (Gessler et al., 2021). We prepare the input relation pairs by following the Next Sentence Prediction pattern as in Shi and Demberg (2019): a [CLS] token begins the sequence, followed by the first EDU, [SEP], and the second EDU. As additional feature, we only add the speaker marker at the beginning of the EDUs since it is the only feature we found decisive among the ones used in Gessler et al. (2021).[3]

Sample Selection Criteria: At each round, $\mathcal{M}$ gives pseudo labels on $\mathcal{U}$. The key challenges are how to measure the confidence of predictions and how to select a reliable subset $\mathcal{S}$. We loosely translate the output probabilities in $\mathcal{M}$ as its predictive confidence, enabling sorting predicted pairs. We then define two selection criteria inspired by Steedman et al. (2003); Du et al. (2021), either focusing on the confidence or combining it with class variety: (a) **Top-k**: select the top k pseudo-labeled data. k starts at 800 and increments up 7800, with an interval of 1000. This range corresponds to the top $N \times k'$ where $k' \in [0.0, 0.1]$ criterion in Nishida and Matsumoto (2022); (b) **Top-class-k**: select the most confident pseudo-labeled data in each class and together results in k examples. The label ratio is maintained between $\mathcal{L}$ and the augmented set $\mathcal{S}$. k has the same value as in Top-k.

4 Molweni Re-Annotation

To evaluate the cross-domain adaptability of our parsing pipeline, we release a newly annotated dataset, "Molweni-clean", sourced from the Molweni corpus (Li et al., 2020). Molweni contains $10,000$ SDRT-annotated documents from the

[2]https://github.com/disrpt/sharedtask2023/.

[3]Our supervised model gives 64.9 versus feature-enhanced DisCoDisCo 65.0 (Gessler et al., 2021).

	Avg branch	Avg depth	%leaf	Arc length
Molweni	1.63	6.0	0.39	0.23
∼-clean	1.29	6.8	0.28	0.19

Table 1: Tree properties in original Molweni test set and Molweni-clean. Arc length is normalized.

Dataset	#Doc train	dev	test	#Turn /doc	#Tok /doc	#Spk /doc	#Rel type
STAC	947	105	109	11.0	48.4	3.0	16
Molweni	9000	500	500	8.8	104.7	3.5	16
∼-clean	-	-	50	8.5	91.1	3.2	16

Table 2: STAC, Molweni, and Molweni-clean statistics: number of documents, averaged speech turns, tokens, and speakers per document (turn/doc, tok/doc, spk/doc).

Ubuntu Chat Corpus (Lowe et al., 2015). However, it presents heavily redundant documents and inconsistent annotations (Li et al., 2023), making the results less reliable. Therefore, we revised the annotation of a subset of Molweni to ensure a more robust evaluation (test only).

4.1 Molweni-clean Construction

Molweni test set comprises 500 documents that can be grouped into 105 clusters. Each cluster consists of highly similar dialogues, with only one or two differing utterances (Li et al., 2023). As the first step of our re-annotation process, we extract a single document from each cluster, ensuring that the selected subset contains no duplicates.

The re-annotation is carried out by 3 Ph.D. students who are fluent in English, specialized in semantics and discourse and are familiar with SDRT. We pre-selected 105 documents from the test set with no duplicates as our annotation candidates. A set of 8 documents is used for training the annotators who then annotate 10 documents in common, and 20 more separately, leading to a final subset of 50 dialogues[4]. The inter-annotator agreement (Cohen's Kappa) is strong (80.6%) for link attachment and moderate (57.0%) for full structure, similar to the scores in STAC (Asher et al., 2016), with details in Appendix B.1.

4.2 Molweni-clean Statistics

Structural Difference: More adjacent links are presented in Molweni-clean (76% vs. 68%). Intuitively, these are simpler structures. The trees in Molweni-clean are "taller" and "thinner", namely, with smaller branch sizes and larger tree depths. On average, Molweni-clean trees are one step deeper than the originally annotated ones, as shown in Table 1. Additionally, we find 3 documents in the original annotation that contain multiple roots, resulting in *forest* structures instead of trees.

Relation Distribution: Although the class distribution appears to be alike in the two annotations (details in Appendix B.2), the partition between the same (intra-) and different (inter-) speakers differs greatly. In Molweni-clean, we observe a much higher percentage of intra-speaker relations (14.7% vs. 3.8%). Certain relations, like *Continuation* and *Elaboration* — which, according to the annotation guideline, should typically occur more frequently within the same speaker — show a contrasting distribution in the original annotation. We present a case study in Appendix B.3.

5 Experimental Setup

Datasets: For the in-domain scenario (gaming), we utilize STAC, a corpus comprising of online conversations that occur during the *Settlers of Catan* game. It contains in total 12,679 relation pairs in 1161 documents. We follow the split in Shi and Huang (2019). We randomly select a small part (700 pairs from 50 documents) of the train set as labeled data $\mathcal{L}$ and the remaining examples as raw data $\mathcal{U}$. A subset from the development set (664 pairs from 50 documents) is used for validation. All 1128 pairs (109 documents) in the test set are reserved for testing. The relation distribution is highly unbalanced, see Appendix A. For the cross-domain scenario (gaming to technical chat), we use documents from STAC as the labeled training data, and the 50 Molweni-clean documents as testing data. Table 2 shows the statistics.

Evaluation Metrics: For the relation prediction module, we report accuracy. For the full parsing pipeline, we employ the traditional evaluation metrics, namely, the micro-averaged F_1 scores for unlabeled attachment (link), relation prediction (rel), and labeled attachment (full).

Full Parsing Baselines: We compare against the state-of-art parsing model Structured-Joint (SJ) (Chi and Rudnicky, 2022). Since we work with small-data setup, we also compare with a simpler graph-based Arc-Factored dependency parser (McDonald et al., 2005), by following the implementation in Nishida and Matsumoto (2022). Further-

[4]These annotations are publicly available at URL.

more, to gain insights from the latest LLMs, we show results from ChatGPT[5] (gpt-3.5-turbo model) using zero-shot and few-shot in-context learning (Chan et al., 2023a).

Implementation Details: In the relation prediction module, we use the BERT model from Huggingface (Wolf et al., 2020) and fine-tune for 10 epochs with batch of size 2, learning rate at $2e-5$, AdamW optimizers with a weight decay at 0.01. For self-training, we give maximum 20 epochs with early stopping at 5, based on the performance on the validation set. We choose 5 groups of labeled examples for initial training and report average accuracy with the standard deviation. The full pipeline is trained using 50 random documents from STAC training set and is executed 10 times.

6 Relation Prediction Module

6.1 Self-Training Results

Results for relation prediction are presented in Table 3. As baselines, we report scores of majority class *Question answer pair* (*QA pair*), the original frozen BERT base model and the fine-tuned BERT, both trained with 700 gold pairs. Using this latter model as a starting point, we present results for self-training (second part of Table 3) using two sample selection criteria: top-k and top-class-k. Both selection strategies show improved performances with self-training. When $k = 5800$, both strategies achieve their best scores. This value echos the selection strategy rank-above-$k\prime$ with $k\prime = 0.6$ in Nishida and Matsumoto (2022). For top-k selection, when k is small ($k < 2800$), the number and variety of selected pseudo-labeled data are small, resulting in lower accuracy than BERT-ft. When k is relaxed, the coverage of different classes of data increases, and the performance hits the highest point at 58.1. The accuracy then decreases, probably due to the noise of inaccurate pseudo-labeled data. In comparison, the top-class-k strategy consistently brings improvement over the initial BERT-ft model. It also exhibits an upward trend as k increases, reaching its peak at the optimal value of 5800, followed by a slight decline.

With a significant amount of unlabelled data, the self-training process can be repeated multiple times. However, limited by the data size in STAC, we can only test iterative learning with few values, $k \in [800, 1800, 2800]$. We define a stopping criterion at 3 and proceed with top-class-k selection strategy. We observe (two rightmost columns) additional improvements compared to the first loop, reaching 58.4 at best. We speculate that the model is re-trained slowly (smaller amount of data), but steadily (more reliable examples). We anticipate a better performance with more in-domain raw data.

Majority class				27.1
BERT (base 700)				$40.1_{0.8}$
BERT-ft (base 700)				$56.6_{1.0}$
Self-training	Top-k	Top-class-k		
#Pair	loop1	loop1	loop2	loop3
+ 800	$54.1_{3.0}$	$57.7_{1.1}$	$55.9_{1.1}$	$\mathbf{58.1_{1.2}}$
+ 1800	$53.6_{3.6}$	$57.3_{1.6}$	$\mathbf{58.4_{1.0}}$	$57.4_{2.1}$
+ 2800	$55.7_{1.9}$	$57.6_{0.3}$	$57.5_{1.5}$	$58.1_{2.2}$
+ 3800	$56.6_{2.1}$	$57.6_{1.6}$	-	-
+ 4800	$56.8_{0.5}$	$57.8_{1.2}$	-	-
+ 5800	$\mathbf{58.1_{0.8}}$	$\mathbf{58.0_{0.7}}$	-	-
+ 6800	$57.8_{1.0}$	$57.9_{0.9}$	-	-
+ 7800	$57.8_{0.7}$	$57.0_{2.3}$	-	-

Table 3: Baselines and BERT-ft model self-training results with Top-k and Top-class-k selection criteria. Scores are avg accuracy over 5 runs with standard deviation. Best score per row (resp. per column) is underlined (resp. bold). - not applicable due to data limitation.

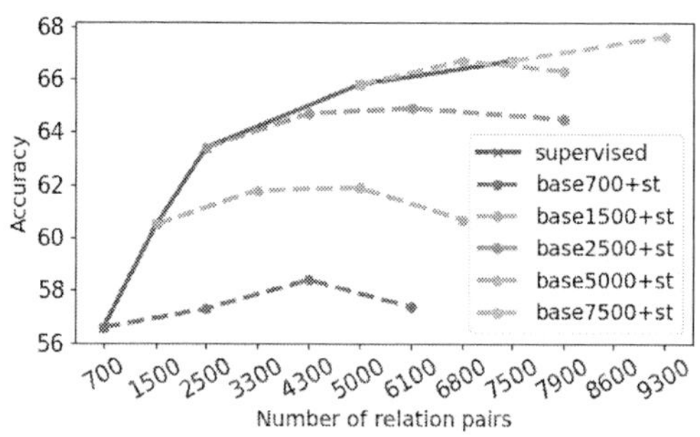

Figure 2: Accuracy of fully supervised model (solid line) and semi-supervised model with {700, 1500, 2500, 5000, 7500} base training data (dashed lines). x-axis: #relation pairs; y-axis: model accuracy on STAC.

6.2 Analysis: Model Calibration

One key challenge in self-training is to select error-free and high-coverage subsets from the pseudo-labeled data. Top-class-k selection considers the coverage aspect and less prone to overfitting. However, good coverage does not imply reliable prediction. The model could fall short in some classes and bring in noise. In this section, we study the correlation between the model's predicted probabilities

[5] https://openai.com/blog/chatgpt.

and the probabilities of correctness, also known as the calibration property (Brier, 1950; Jiang et al., 2021). We start by showing this property of base BERT-ft model (details in Appendix C.1): frequent relations (e.g. *QA pair* and *Comment*) present positive correlation while infrequent ones (e.g. *Alternation* and *Correction*) do not and have lower confidence. This shows the advantage of top-class-k strategy by adding these less confident but reliable examples. However, it also implies that the base model is not well-calibrated. We investigate two factors that may influence the model's calibration: enhancing the classifier's accuracy by training on more base data and employing iterative training.

Base Model Accuracy: We experimentally observe that with more base training data, the model performance continuously increases (e.g.: from 700 to 2500, accuracy increases by 7%). In particular, we test different sizes of base data: {700, 1500, 2500, 5000, 7500} of relation pairs and re-train the model using top-class-k ($k = 1800$) selection criterion. The results are displayed in Figure 2. With larger base volume, the gap between self-trained model and fully supervised model keeps decreasing. Interestingly, when the base data hits 5000, self-trained model achieves comparable performance as 7500 fully supervised model (66.7%), indicating that 5000 relation pairs ($\approx$ 350 documents) is a threshold where self-trained model surpasses its supervised counterpart.

Iterative Training: The concept of multi-loop self-training aims to enhance the model's performance by incorporating additional training examples for the *infrequent* classes, thereby mitigating the under-fitting issue. We investigate the correlation evolution with three loops for the less-frequent labels (details in Appendix C.2). Tellingly, the confidence scores for less and non-frequent relations such as *Alternation* and *Contrast* increase from $[0.2, 0.3]$ to $[0.7, 1.0]$, coupled with higher prediction accuracy (+ 20% $\sim$ 40%), as displayed in the confusion matrix in Figure 9.

7 Full Discourse Parsing

7.1 In-Domain Evaluation and Analysis

In-domain performance is evaluated on the STAC test set, with results in Table 4 (left part).

Baselines: We replicate the SOTA supervised model Structured-Joint (SJ) (Chi and Rudnicky, 2022) which uses RoBERTa-base model (Liu et al., 2019) as backbone and employs 3-dimension attention to encode links and relations jointly. SJ includes a dummy root in each document for training, but the link between this node and the first EDU is counted in the evaluation which artificially inflates the scores. We replicate SJ with 947 and 50 training data and evaluate with and without dummy root, the latter matching our own fairer evaluation setting. Table 4 shows our replicated scores without dummy root (detailed comparison in Appendix D). We also compare with a simpler dependency parser Arc-Factored (AF) (McDonald et al., 2005). AF parser finds the globally optimal dependency structure using dynamic programming which can be decoded using Maximum Spanning Tree algorithms such as Eisner (Eisner, 1996). Lastly, we report the performance of unsupervised LLM ChatGPT-3.5.

Parsing Results: Our pipeline consists of an EDU segmenter (Gessler et al., 2021), a link attachment module (Li et al., 2023) which we replicate the experiments and obtain predicted links, and a pre-trained relation prediction module outlined in Section 3.2. We sample 50 annotated documents for supervision along the pipeline. As expected, the supervised SJ model with 947 training examples gives the best scores. However, when the training size drops to 50, our pipeline exhibits better performance compared to SJ and AF in both link attachment (59.3% vs. 55.1%) and relation prediction (62.0% vs. 61.1%) tasks, bringing noteworthy improvement of resp. 5 and 14 points in full parsing, coupled with greater stability. As for GPT-3.5, both zero-shot and few-shot in-context learning perform abysmally, suggesting that ChatGPT still suffers from poor understanding of discourse structures and that we can not simply depend on powerful LLMs for this task (Chan et al., 2023a). Using predicted EDUs, our full parsing score drops nearly 6 points. A similar loss is also observed for end-to-end RST-style parsing in Nguyen et al. (2021).

Pipeline Error Analysis: We examine the relation composition in each task module: correct (orange) and wrong relation prediction (blue), and missing relations due to lack of link attachment (green) and false EDU segmentation (gray), as displayed in Figure 3. The results show that errors in link attachment account for 40.8%. Among the correctly attached pairs, 61% are assigned proper relations. Notably, relations such as *QA pair*, *Elaboration*, and *Acknowledgement* are accurately pre-

Train / Test	Train	STAC/STAC				STAC/Molweni-clean			STAC/Molweni		
	#Doc	EDU	Link	Rel	Full	Link	Rel	Full	Link	Rel	Full
SJ	947	-	$70.7_{0.5}$	$77.3_{1.2}$	$54.6_{0.7}$	$61.5_{3.4}$	$59.5_{4.3}$	$36.6_{3.8}$	$49.8_{3.6}$	$57.5_{2.9}$	$28.9_{2.8}$
SJ	50	-	$55.1_{3.5}$	$61.1_{2.1}$	$33.6_{2.2}$	$51.1_{6.4}$	$33.6_{9.5}$	$17.2_{5.3}$	$42.9_{5.6}$	$35.2_{10.1}$	$15.3_{5.3}$
AF	50	-	$42.7_{2.8}$	$56.4_{2.5}$	$24.0_{1.0}$	$53.7_{2.1}$	$38.8_{2.9}$	$20.9_{1.1}$	$45.9_{1.5}$	$41.4_{1.0}$	$19.0_{0.7}$
$GPT3.5_{few\ shot}$	3	-	20.7	24.1	7.3	-	-	-	-	-	-
$GPT3.5_{zero\ shot}$	-	-	20.0	22.8	4.4	-	-	-	-	-	-
Ours (gold EDU)	50	-	**$59.3_{0.7}$**	**$62.0_{1.1}$**	**$38.6_{0.7}$**	**$75.6_{0.7}$**	**$41.3_{3.8}$**	**$31.2_{2.9}$**	**$61.5_{0.7}$**	**$42.8_{2.9}$**	**$26.3_{1.7}$**
Ours (pred EDU)	50	94.8	$52.2_{0.4}$	$61.2_{1.6}$	$32.8_{0.9}$	~	~	~	~	~	~

Table 4: Left: in-domain parsing results (STAC/STAC) with supervised parsers Structured Joint (SJ) (2022) and Arc-Factored (AF) (2022), unsupervised model ChatGPT (GPT-3.5) with few-shot ($n = 3$) in-context learning and zero-shot (2023a), and our semi-supervised pipeline (with gold and predicted EDU). Right: cross-domain parsing results on Molweni-clean (STAC/Molweni-clean) and original Molweni (STAC/Molweni). Scores are average micro-F_1 over 10 runs. In 50 train setup, best scores are in bold. "-" not applicable. "~" same as previous row.

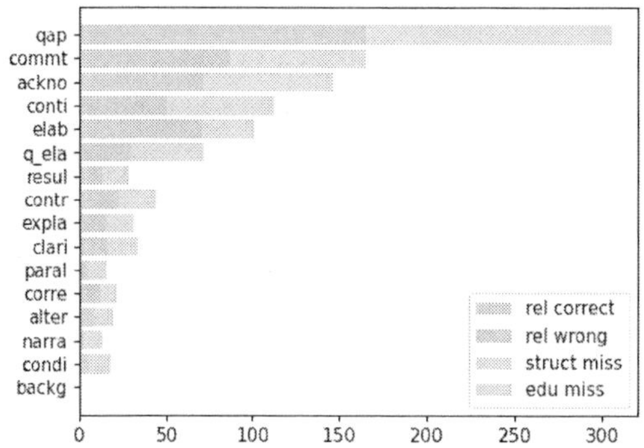

Figure 3: Full parsing result decomposition in relation prediction (orange and blue), link attachment (green), and EDU segmentation (grey). Numbers in Appendix E.

dicted, while less frequent relations such as *Result*, *Explanation*, and *Correction* require further improvements. We notice that the missing links often involve relation types that are accurately predicted (*QA pair* and *Acknowledgement*). This suggests that there is a high likelihood of accurately determining the discourse relations of connected pairs - a potential avenue for future improvement.

7.2 Cross-Domain Evaluation and Analysis

Cross-domain parsing is evaluated on the original Molweni test set and Molweni-clean, with SJ model and our pipeline trained on 50 STAC documents. Results are shown in Table 4 (right part).

Parsing Results: Our pipeline exhibits excellent performance on all tasks, outperforming the SJ model in terms of link (+24%), relation (+8%), and full parsing (+14%) on Molweni-clean dataset. Our pipeline for link attachment is particularly remarkable, surpassing even the fully trained SJ model (75.6 vs. 61.5). On relation prediction, SJ considers the tree structure and relation jointly, while our approach focuses on individual relation pairs. As texts across various genres demonstrate various structures, our approach, although more localized, is less influenced by the pre-existing structures, making it more suitable for general application. Furthermore, our model shows greater stability, whereas the SJ model is highly influenced by a particular domain. We notice similar behaviour on the original Molweni test set. Curiously, both SJ model and our pipeline exhibit improved performances on Molweni-clean, revealing the problem of inconsistencies in the initial annotation.

Molweni Cross-domain Annotation: We acknowledge that semi-supervised learning has an affinity for domain transfer. Taking one step further, we investigate automatic annotation on Molweni using STAC-trained model. The inconsistency of annotations in the original Molweni benefits this setup. We first de-duplicate repetitive documents in Molweni training and validation sets by taking one document per cluster (Sec. 4.1), which results in resp. 1865 and 107 documents. Trained on 50 STAC examples, our pipeline produces 1972 pseudo-labeled Molweni documents. These documents are used to train SJ in a supervised manner with the proposed hyper-parameters. In comparison, we also train the SJ model with Molweni's original annotation. Both models are evaluated on Molweni-clean, with results given in Table 6.

SJ model trained on pseudo-labeled Molweni gives better results on structure attachment (+9%) but under-performs its counterpart on relation pre-

Train / Test	Aug	STAC/STAC			STAC/Molweni-clean			STAC/Molweni		
	#Doc	Link	Rel	Full	Link	Rel	Full	Link	Rel	Full
SJ	-	$55.1_{3.5}$	$61.1_{2.1}$	$33.6_{2.2}$	$51.1_{6.4}$	$33.6_{9.5}$	$17.2_{5.3}$	$42.9_{5.6}$	$35.2_{10.1}$	$15.3_{5.3}$
SJ +self-train	50	$57.5_{2.2}$	$\mathbf{63.3_{1.4}}$	$36.4_{1.5}$	$51.6_{5.5}$	$34.3_{7.1}$	$17.6_{4.1}$	$42.9_{4.7}$	$34.5_{8.1}$	$14.8_{3.9}$
SJ +self-train	120	$57.2_{3.2}$	$62.7_{3.3}$	$35.9_{2.3}$	$54.3_{7.8}$	$40.3_{7.7}$	$21.9_{5.3}$	$45.7_{6.5}$	$39.2_{6.3}$	$18.0_{4.5}$
SJ +self-train	200	$57.4_{2.9}$	$63.1_{2.6}$	$36.2_{1.7}$	$56.4_{8.2}$	$38.4_{9.2}$	$21.8_{6.7}$	$46.6_{6.3}$	$38.7_{8.9}$	$18.1_{5.3}$
Ours	120	$\mathbf{59.3_{0.7}}$	$62.0_{1.1}$	$\mathbf{38.6_{0.7}}$	$\mathbf{75.6_{0.7}}$	$\mathbf{41.3_{3.8}}$	$\mathbf{31.2_{2.9}}$	$\mathbf{61.5_{0.7}}$	$\mathbf{42.8_{2.9}}$	$\mathbf{26.3_{1.7}}$

Table 5: Comparison between augmented SJ model (2022) (SJ +self-train) and ours in self-training setup across in-domain and cross-domain scenarios. SJ model is re-trained with the combination of 50 gold-standard data and {50, 120, 200} pseudo-labeled documents (Aug #doc). We show the best scores (average micro-F_1) in 3 loops.

Train on	#Doc	Link	Rel	Full
Molweni-pseudo	1865	$\mathbf{54.1_{0.6}}$	$56.3_{2.0}$	$30.6_{1.2}$
Molweni	1865	$45.7_{1.6}$	$\mathbf{82.7_{1.9}}$	$\mathbf{37.8_{1.1}}$

Table 6: SJ parsing results on Molweni-clean, trained on auto-annotated and original Molweni (resp. Molweni-pseudo, Molweni). Scores are average micro-F_1.

diction (-26%). Although the overall parsing score is inferior, the naked discourse structures in auto-annotated Molweni (Molweni-pseudo) are of better quality. This is encouraging, especially in the difficult cross-domain setup. As previous studies have shown, discourse structures alone are valuable features and can be employed in some downstream applications (Louis et al., 2010; Jia et al., 2020).

7.3 Self-Training the SJ Model

To understand the effectiveness of our relation prediction module, we conduct ablation studies by comparing our pipeline and SJ model with similar data volume, namely, we augment SJ model with self-training. Results are given in Table 5.

For the data augmentation, we select the pseudo-labeled documents with the highest average confidence scores, i.e., the average of predictive probabilities over all link and relation decisions in a document. Previous analysis (Sec. 6.2) shows that iterative training is beneficial, so we re-train SJ in a total of 3 loops. We test different sizes of augmentation data: {50, 120, 200} documents which correspond to resp. {800, 1800, 2800} relation pairs in our case. Over 3 loops, the largest augmentation attains 600 documents ($\approx$ 8000 relation pairs). It is important to note that although the SJ model jointly predicts structure and relation, our augmentation technique only focuses on relation prediction. Therefore, the augmentation would provide the SJ model with more structured supervision. Furthermore, our approach operates on a narrower scope, concentrating on relation pairs rather than entire conversations. In contrast, the SJ model's data augmentation is done at the document level. Hence, the comparison between our augmented model and the augmented SJ model would only be similar in terms of data volume, but not necessarily in terms of identical examples.

Given extra training data, SJ surpasses its base version in both in-domain (full +3%) and cross-domain (full +4%) contexts, with similar improvement in link attachment and relation prediction. This emphasizes the advantages of our self-training approach, apt for both basic and complex models. However, with the same augmented data size, the SJ model lags behind our pipeline, showcasing a 3 points difference in-domain and a sizable 10 points gap cross-domain, further attesting to the effectiveness of our simple approach.

8 Conclusion

In this study, we introduce a substantial extension to semi-supervised discourse parsing in dialogues by incorporating relation predictions into the established naked structures. We define simple yet effective sample selection strategies in self-training, achieving SOTA results with a minimal training set. Importantly, the efficacy of our discourse parsing pipeline is fully demonstrated across in-domain and cross-domain settings. We also contribute a small expert-annotated discourse dataset, along with semi-supervised benchmarks for subsequent comparisons. Future work should explore the use of more out-of-domain raw data and investigate bootstrapping methods for relation prediction, while also improving on structure prediction, possibly with the same strategies.

Limitations

Following DISRPT shared task, we focused on individual EDU pair relation prediction for general application. This setting captures local coherence in dialogues and has shown great generalizability in cross-domain experiments. We based our work on a semi-supervised link attachment module and predicted relations only for linked EDU pairs. Showing effective, there is potential for further improvement in attachment performance by considering (high confident) predicted relations for unattached EDU pairs. By extending the self-training strategy to include link attachment, we could enhance the overall parsing performance and achieve better results in full parsing.

Facing the data sparsity issue, we utilized all relation pairs in STAC for self-training. However, we only tested small sizes of k in the iterative training due to the limited size of STAC. With more data, we should explore the re-training outcomes with larger values of k. It is thus intriguing to expand the set of un-annotated relations by considering out-of-domain data, obtained for instance from weak supervision (Sileo et al., 2019), or from monologues such as PDTB (Prasad et al., 2008).

Ethics Statement

We carefully selected the corpora to work with to mitigate any potential hateful and biased language. Before the re-annotation process, we provided instructions to the annotators, emphasizing the importance of being vigilant for any biased or insulting language in the data. In the event of encountering such language, they were instructed to immediately cease annotation and report the issue. Throughout the re-annotation of all 77 dialogues, no instances of inappropriate language were found. We have confidence that these dialogues are free from harmful content that may insult the annotators.

All the annotators are PhD students. They did not receive any specific compensation for their work on annotation. We recorded the time taken for the re-annotation process, which consisted of an initial training period of 3 hours followed by an average of 1.5 hour for every 10 dialogues. All annotation work was conducted during regular working hours. The annotators are free to utilize the annotations and any discourse-related content in this project for their studies.

Acknowledgements

This work is supported by the AnDiaMO project (ANR-21-CE23-0020). Our work has benefited from the AI Interdisciplinary Institute ANITI. ANITI is funded by the French "Investing for the Future – PIA3" program under the Grant agreement n°ANR-19-PI3A-0004. Chloé Braud is part of the programme DesCartes and is also supported by the National Research Foundation, Prime Minister's Office, Singapore under its Campus for Research Excellence and Technological Enterprise (CREATE) programme. The work is also supported by the ANR grant SUMM-RE (ANR-20-CE23-0017).

References

Stergos Afantenos, Eric Kow, Nicholas Asher, and Jérémy Perret. 2015. Discourse parsing for multiparty chat dialogues. In *Proceedings of the 2015 Conference on Empirical Methods in Natural Language Processing*, pages 928–937, Lisbon, Portugal. Association for Computational Linguistics.

Yusuf Arslan, Kevin Allix, Lisa Veiber, Cedric Lothritz, Tegawendé F Bissyandé, Jacques Klein, and Anne Goujon. 2021. A comparison of pre-trained language models for multi-class text classification in the financial domain. In *Companion Proceedings of the Web Conference 2021*, pages 260–268.

Nicholas Asher, Nicholas Michael Asher, and Alex Lascarides. 2003. *Logics of conversation*. Cambridge University Press.

Nicholas Asher, Julie Hunter, Mathieu Morey, Benamara Farah, and Stergos Afantenos. 2016. Discourse structure and dialogue acts in multiparty dialogue: the STAC corpus. In *Proceedings of the Tenth International Conference on Language Resources and Evaluation (LREC'16)*, pages 2721–2727, Portorož, Slovenia. European Language Resources Association (ELRA).

Katherine Atwell, Junyi Jessy Li, and Malihe Alikhani. 2021. Where are we in discourse relation recognition? In *Proceedings of the 22nd Annual Meeting of the Special Interest Group on Discourse and Dialogue*, pages 314–325.

Sonia Badene, Kate Thompson, Jean-Pierre Lorré, and Nicholas Asher. 2019. Data programming for learning discourse structure. In *Proceedings of the 57th Annual Meeting of the Association for Computational Linguistics*, pages 640–645, Florence, Italy. Association for Computational Linguistics.

Parminder Bhatia, Yangfeng Ji, and Jacob Eisenstein. 2015. Better document-level sentiment analysis from RST discourse parsing. In *Proceedings of the 2015*

Conference on Empirical Methods in Natural Language Processing, pages 2212–2218, Lisbon, Portugal. Association for Computational Linguistics.

Glenn W Brier. 1950. Verification of forecasts expressed in terms of probability. *Monthly weather review*, 78(1):1–3.

Chunkit Chan, Jiayang Cheng, Weiqi Wang, Yuxin Jiang, Tianqing Fang, Xin Liu, and Yangqiu Song. 2023a. Chatgpt evaluation on sentence level relations: A focus on temporal, causal, and discourse relations. *arXiv preprint arXiv:2304.14827*.

Chunkit Chan, Xin Liu, Jiayang Cheng, Zihan Li, Yangqiu Song, Ginny Y Wong, and Simon See. 2023b. Discoprompt: Path prediction prompt tuning for implicit discourse relation recognition. *arXiv preprint arXiv:2305.03973*.

Jiaao Chen and Diyi Yang. 2021. Structure-aware abstractive conversation summarization via discourse and action graphs. In *Proceedings of the 2021 Conference of the North American Chapter of the Association for Computational Linguistics: Human Language Technologies*, pages 1380–1391, Online. Association for Computational Linguistics.

Junxuan Chen, Xiang Li, Jiarui Zhang, Chulun Zhou, Jianwei Cui, Bin Wang, and Jinsong Su. 2020. Modeling discourse structure for document-level neural machine translation. In *Proceedings of the First Workshop on Automatic Simultaneous Translation*, pages 30–36.

Mingda Chen, Zewei Chu, and Kevin Gimpel. 2019. Evaluation benchmarks and learning criteria for discourse-aware sentence representations. In *Proceedings of the 2019 Conference on Empirical Methods in Natural Language Processing and the 9th International Joint Conference on Natural Language Processing (EMNLP-IJCNLP)*, pages 649–662.

Ta-Chung Chi and Alexander Rudnicky. 2022. Structured dialogue discourse parsing. In *Proceedings of the 23rd Annual Meeting of the Special Interest Group on Discourse and Dialogue*, pages 325–335.

Jacob Devlin, Ming-Wei Chang, Kenton Lee, and Kristina Toutanova. 2019. BERT: Pre-training of deep bidirectional transformers for language understanding. In *Proceedings of the 2019 Conference of the North American Chapter of the Association for Computational Linguistics: Human Language Technologies, Volume 1 (Long and Short Papers)*, pages 4171–4186, Minneapolis, Minnesota. Association for Computational Linguistics.

Jingfei Du, Édouard Grave, Beliz Gunel, Vishrav Chaudhary, Onur Celebi, Michael Auli, Veselin Stoyanov, and Alexis Conneau. 2021. Self-training improves pre-training for natural language understanding. In *Proceedings of the 2021 Conference of the North American Chapter of the Association for Computational Linguistics: Human Language Technologies*, pages 5408–5418.

Jason Eisner. 1996. Three new probabilistic models for dependency parsing: An exploration. In *COLING 1996 Volume 1: The 16th International Conference on Computational Linguistics*.

Yaxin Fan and Feng Jiang. 2023. Uncovering the potential of chatgpt for discourse analysis in dialogue: An empirical study. *arXiv preprint arXiv:2305.08391*.

Yaxin Fan, Peifeng Li, Fang Kong, and Qiaoming Zhu. 2022. A distance-aware multi-task framework for conversational discourse parsing. In *Proceedings of the 29th International Conference on Computational Linguistics*, pages 912–921.

Luke Gessler, Shabnam Behzad, Yang Janet Liu, Siyao Peng, Yilun Zhu, and Amir Zeldes. 2021. Discodisco at the disrpt2021 shared task: A system for discourse segmentation, classification, and connective detection. In *Proceedings of the 2nd Shared Task on Discourse Relation Parsing and Treebanking (DISRPT 2021)*, pages 51–62.

Qi Jia, Yizhu Liu, Siyu Ren, Kenny Zhu, and Haifeng Tang. 2020. Multi-turn response selection using dialogue dependency relations. In *Proceedings of the 2020 Conference on Empirical Methods in Natural Language Processing (EMNLP)*, pages 1911–1920.

Zhengbao Jiang, Jun Araki, Haibo Ding, and Graham Neubig. 2021. How can we know when language models know? on the calibration of language models for question answering. *Transactions of the Association for Computational Linguistics*, 9:962–977.

Hamid Karimi and Jiliang Tang. 2019. Learning hierarchical discourse-level structure for fake news detection. In *Proceedings of the 2019 Conference of the North American Chapter of the Association for Computational Linguistics: Human Language Technologies, Volume 1 (Long and Short Papers)*, pages 3432–3442.

Mike Lewis, Yinhan Liu, Naman Goyal, Marjan Ghazvininejad, Abdelrahman Mohamed, Omer Levy, Veselin Stoyanov, and Luke Zettlemoyer. 2020. BART: Denoising sequence-to-sequence pre-training for natural language generation, translation, and comprehension. In *Proceedings of the 58th Annual Meeting of the Association for Computational Linguistics*, pages 7871–7880, Online. Association for Computational Linguistics.

Chuyuan Li. 2023. *Facing Data Scarcity in Dialogues for Discourse Structure Discovery and Prediction*. Ph.D. thesis, Université de Lorraine.

Chuyuan Li, Patrick Huber, Wen Xiao, Maxime Amblard, Chloé Braud, and Giuseppe Carenini. 2023. Discourse structure extraction from pre-trained and fine-tuned language models in dialogues. In *Findings of the Association for Computational Linguistics: EACL 2023*, pages 2517–2534.

Jiaqi Li, Ming Liu, Min-Yen Kan, Zihao Zheng, Zekun Wang, Wenqiang Lei, Ting Liu, and Bing Qin. 2020.

Molweni: A challenge multiparty dialogues-based machine reading comprehension dataset with discourse structure. In *Proceedings of the 28th International Conference on Computational Linguistics*, pages 2642–2652, Barcelona, Spain (Online). International Committee on Computational Linguistics.

Yinhan Liu, Myle Ott, Naman Goyal, Jingfei Du, Mandar Joshi, Danqi Chen, Omer Levy, Mike Lewis, Luke Zettlemoyer, and Veselin Stoyanov. 2019. Roberta: A robustly optimized bert pretraining approach. *arXiv preprint arXiv:1907.11692*.

Zhengyuan Liu and Nancy Chen. 2021. Improving multi-party dialogue discourse parsing via domain integration. In *Proceedings of the 2nd Workshop on Computational Approaches to Discourse*, pages 122–127, Punta Cana, Dominican Republic and Online. Association for Computational Linguistics.

Annie Louis, Aravind K Joshi, and Ani Nenkova. 2010. Discourse indicators for content selection in summaization.

Ryan Lowe, Nissan Pow, Iulian Serban, and Joelle Pineau. 2015. The Ubuntu dialogue corpus: A large dataset for research in unstructured multi-turn dialogue systems. In *Proceedings of the 16th Annual Meeting of the Special Interest Group on Discourse and Dialogue*, pages 285–294, Prague, Czech Republic. Association for Computational Linguistics.

Ryan McDonald, Fernando Pereira, Kiril Ribarov, and Jan Hajic. 2005. Non-projective dependency parsing using spanning tree algorithms. In *Proceedings of human language technology conference and conference on empirical methods in natural language processing*, pages 523–530.

Yu Meng, Yunyi Zhang, Jiaxin Huang, Chenyan Xiong, Heng Ji, Chao Zhang, and Jiawei Han. 2020. Text classification using label names only: A language model self-training approach. In *Proceedings of the 2020 Conference on Empirical Methods in Natural Language Processing (EMNLP)*, pages 9006–9017.

Thanh-Tung Nguyen, Xuan-Phi Nguyen, Shafiq Joty, and Xiaoli Li. 2021. Rst parsing from scratch. In *Proceedings of the 2021 Conference of the North American Chapter of the Association for Computational Linguistics: Human Language Technologies*, pages 1613–1625.

Noriki Nishida and Yuji Matsumoto. 2022. Out-of-domain discourse dependency parsing via bootstrapping: An empirical analysis on its effectiveness and limitation. *Transactions of the Association for Computational Linguistics*, 10:127–144.

Long Ouyang, Jeffrey Wu, Xu Jiang, Diogo Almeida, Carroll Wainwright, Pamela Mishkin, Chong Zhang, Sandhini Agarwal, Katarina Slama, Alex Ray, et al. 2022. Training language models to follow instructions with human feedback. *Advances in Neural Information Processing Systems*, 35:27730–27744.

Fabian Pedregosa, Gaël Varoquaux, Alexandre Gramfort, Vincent Michel, Bertrand Thirion, Olivier Grisel, Mathieu Blondel, Peter Prettenhofer, Ron Weiss, Vincent Dubourg, et al. 2011. Scikit-learn: Machine learning in python. *the Journal of machine Learning research*, 12:2825–2830.

Jérémy Perret, Stergos Afantenos, Nicholas Asher, and Mathieu Morey. 2016. Integer linear programming for discourse parsing. In *Proceedings of the 2016 Conference of the North American Chapter of the Association for Computational Linguistics: Human Language Technologies*, pages 99–109, San Diego, California. Association for Computational Linguistics.

Rashmi Prasad, Nikhil Dinesh, Alan Lee, Eleni Miltsakaki, Livio Robaldo, Aravind Joshi, and Bonnie Webber. 2008. The penn discourse treebank 2.0. In *Proceedings of the Sixth International Conference on Language Resources and Evaluation (LREC'08)*.

Chuck Rosenberg, Martial Hebert, and Henry Schneiderman. 2005. Semi-supervised self-training of object detection models.

Wei Shi and Vera Demberg. 2019. Next sentence prediction helps implicit discourse relation classification within and across domains. In *Proceedings of the 2019 conference on empirical methods in natural language processing and the 9th international joint conference on natural language processing (EMNLP-IJCNLP)*, pages 5790–5796.

Wei Shi, Frances Yung, and Vera Demberg. 2019. Acquiring annotated data with cross-lingual explicitation for implicit discourse relation classification. *NAACL HLT 2019*, page 12.

Zhouxing Shi and Minlie Huang. 2019. A deep sequential model for discourse parsing on multi-party dialogues. In *Proceedings of the AAAI Conference on Artificial Intelligence*, volume 33, pages 7007–7014.

Damien Sileo, Tim Van De Cruys, Camille Pradel, and Philippe Muller. 2019. Mining discourse markers for unsupervised sentence representation learning. In *Proceedings of NAACL-HLT*, pages 3477–3486.

Mark Steedman, Rebecca Hwa, Stephen Clark, Miles Osborne, Anoop Sarkar, Julia Hockenmaier, Paul Ruhlen, Steven Baker, and Jeremiah Crim. 2003. Example selection for bootstrapping statistical parsers. In *Proceedings of the 2003 Human Language Technology Conference of the North American Chapter of the Association for Computational Linguistics*, pages 236–243.

Hugo Touvron, Louis Martin, Kevin Stone, Peter Albert, Amjad Almahairi, Yasmine Babaei, Nikolay Bashlykov, Soumya Batra, Prajjwal Bhargava, Shruti Bhosale, et al. 2023. Llama 2: Open foundation and fine-tuned chat models. *arXiv preprint arXiv:2307.09288*.

Ante Wang, Linfeng Song, Hui Jiang, Shaopeng Lai, Junfeng Yao, Min Zhang, and Jinsong Su. 2021. A structure self-aware model for discourse parsing on multi-party dialogues. In *Proceedings of the Thirtieth International Conference on International Joint Conferences on Artificial Intelligence*.

Bonnie Webber, Rashmi Prasad, Alan Lee, and Aravind Joshi. 2019. The penn discourse treebank 3.0 annotation manual. *Philadelphia, University of Pennsylvania*, 35:108.

Thomas Wolf, Lysandre Debut, Victor Sanh, Julien Chaumond, Clement Delangue, Anthony Moi, Pierric Cistac, Tim Rault, Remi Louf, Morgan Funtowicz, Joe Davison, Sam Shleifer, Patrick von Platen, Clara Ma, Yacine Jernite, Julien Plu, Canwen Xu, Teven Le Scao, Sylvain Gugger, Mariama Drame, Quentin Lhoest, and Alexander Rush. 2020. Transformers: State-of-the-art natural language processing. In *Proceedings of the 2020 Conference on Empirical Methods in Natural Language Processing: System Demonstrations*, pages 38–45, Online. Association for Computational Linguistics.

Yang Xu, Yu Hong, Huibin Ruan, Jianmin Yao, Min Zhang, and Guodong Zhou. 2018. Using active learning to expand training data for implicit discourse relation recognition. In *Proceedings of the 2018 Conference on Empirical Methods in Natural Language Processing*, pages 725–731.

Jingxuan Yang, Kerui Xu, Jun Xu, Si Li, Sheng Gao, Jun Guo, Nianwen Xue, and Ji-Rong Wen. 2021. A joint model for dropped pronoun recovery and conversational discourse parsing in chinese conversational speech. In *Proceedings of the 59th Annual Meeting of the Association for Computational Linguistics and the 11th International Joint Conference on Natural Language Processing (Volume 1: Long Papers)*, pages 1752–1763.

David Yarowsky. 1995. Unsupervised word sense disambiguation rivaling supervised methods. In *33rd annual meeting of the association for computational linguistics*, pages 189–196.

Yue Yu, Simiao Zuo, Haoming Jiang, Wendi Ren, Tuo Zhao, and Chao Zhang. 2021. Fine-tuning pretrained language model with weak supervision: A contrastive-regularized self-training approach. In *Proceedings of the 2021 Conference of the North American Chapter of the Association for Computational Linguistics: Human Language Technologies*, pages 1063–1077.

Amir Zeldes, Yang Janet Liu, Mikel Iruskieta, Philippe Muller, Chloé Braud, and Sonia Badene. 2021. The disrpt 2021 shared task on elementary discourse unit segmentation, connective detection, and relation classification. In *Proceedings of the 2nd Shared Task on Discourse Relation Parsing and Treebanking (DISRPT 2021)*, pages 1–12.

A Class Distribution in STAC Corpus

See Table 7 for the relation distribution in train, development, and test sets in STAC.

	Labeled train		Validation		Test	
Relation	#	%	#	%	#	%
QA pair	175	25.0	152	22.89	305	27.04
Comment	108	15.43	110	16.57	165	14.63
Ack	86	12.29	87	13.1	148	13.12
Continuation	65	9.29	69	10.39	113	10.02
Elaboration	64	9.14	52	7.83	101	8.95
Q-elab	36	5.14	30	4.52	72	6.38
Result	26	3.71	29	4.37	29	2.57
Contrast	32	4.57	29	4.37	44	3.9
Explanation	34	4.86	31	4.67	31	2.75
Clarif-Q	23	3.29	20	3.01	33	2.93
Parallel	10	1.43	14	2.11	15	1.33
Correction	12	1.71	11	1.66	21	1.86
Alternation	5	0.71	8	1.2	19	1.68
Narration	8	1.14	7	1.05	13	1.15
Conditional	12	1.71	10	1.51	18	1.6
Background	4	0.57	5	0.75	1	0.09
Total	700	100.0	664	100.0	1,128	100.0

Table 7: Rhetorical relations and frequencies in train subset, validation subset, and test sets in STAC. QA pair: question answer pair; Ack: acknowledgement; Q-elab: question elaboration; clarif-Q: clarification question.

B Molweni-clean Case Study

B.1 Inter-Annotator Agreement Detail

We calculate inter-annotator agreement scores on the 10 common documents using Cohen's Kappa metric from Scikit-learn library (Pedregosa et al., 2011). The results are given in Table 8. Our final subset contains 50 documents. Annotator 1 and 3 (R1 and R3) have the highest agreement scores, so we include their individual annotations (a total of 39 documents). We also take the 8 training examples where all the annotators have aligned annotations and 3 documents from annotator 2.

	Link	Link&Rel
R1-R2	79.3	51.8
R1-R3	80.6	57.0
R2-R3	76.6	54.3

Table 8: Cohen's Kappa inter-annotator agreement scores. R1, R2, R3 represent resp. annotator 1, 2, and 3.

B.2 Relation Distribution Comparison

See Table 9 for relation distribution in original Molweni subset and Molweni-clean. We show the same 50 documents for a fair comparison. More precisely, we decompose each relation into intra- and inter- speaker categories to refer the relation within the same and different speakers, respectively. Note that the difference in the total number of relations (370 vs 373) is due to the incomplete annotation in the original annotation of documents 7048, 8018, and 9042 where one document contains multiple roots, i.e., some nodes miss an incoming edge.

	Molweni test			Molweni-clean		
Relation	#	%intra	%inter	#	% intra	%inter
Comment	99	2.0	98.0	104	2.9	97.1
Clarif-Q	89	0	100	84	2.4	97.6
QA pair	86	0	100	91	1.1	98.9
Continuation	28	17.9	82.1	27	92.6	7.4
Q-elab	11	9.1	90.9	18	22.2	77.8
Result	11	0	100	10	20.0	80.0
Explanation	9	11.1	88.9	5	40.0	60.0
Ack	7	0	100	6	0	100
Elaboration	7	42.9	57.1	14	85.7	14.3
Narration	7	0	100	1	100	0
Conditional	5	20.0	80.0	2	0	100
Contrast	3	0	100	2	50.0	50.0
Correction	3	0	100	6	16.7	83.3
Background	3	0	100	2	0	100
Parallel	2	50.0	50.0	0	0	0
Alternation	0	0	0	1	100	0
Total	370	3.8	96.2	373	14.7	85.3

Table 9: Relations distribution in original Molweni test subset and Molweni-clean.

B.3 Case Study

We present a comparison of the original annotation and our revised version for document #1035, as shown in Figure 4 and 5, respectively. This dialogue happens between two speakers: cr1mson (short in C) and APT-GET_INSTALL_ (short in A). C is asking A about the "apt" command. We show the number of speech turn after the speaker marker. Speech turns start from 0:

C0: *apt-get i doubt my apt thing is bad though , i just installed ubuntu today*

A1: *wait ! i found a much easier way*

A2: *well , i want you to read all of that*

A3: *before you start mucking around in system files*

C4: *there was only a couple lines in it*

C5: *most of it was rem 'd out*

A6: *you are going to learn what all of them all from the url i just pasted*

C7: *i can always use more than one terminal*

C8: *okay , so i have to add or change a 'repository'*

The main difference is in the annotation of *Complex Discourse Units* (CDUs) – several EDUs group together to form a common rhetorical function (Asher et al., 2016). In this example, the first CDU consists of three speech turns (A1, A2, A3) where A2 and A3 elaborate A1 by presenting a "much easier way". Between A2 and A3 it is a continuation. We can write as *Elaboration*(A1, *Continuation*(A2, A3)). This is a similar case with the example (58) in STAC annotation manual[6]. The original annotation, on the other hand, does not capture the accurate inner-CDU relations and roughly attaches every EDU inside the CDU with the first utterance C0.

Another CDU contains the speech turns C4 and C5. C5 continues C4 and together they provide a comment to A. Furthermore, we believe that CDU (C4, C5) should be linked to A2 instead of A3 since A2 and A3 are attached with a subordinating conjunction marker "before", which makes A3 *head* of this CDU. Semantically, "only a couple lines" also echos with "all of that". However, the original annotation does not capture the relationship between C4 and C5 and only link them individually to the previous utterance A3.

For each training document, annotators went through a similar discussion in order to reach consensus on difficult or ambiguous cases. We believe that this stage contributes to our improved understanding of dialogue content and the SDRT framework, and facilitate the production of more reliable annotations.

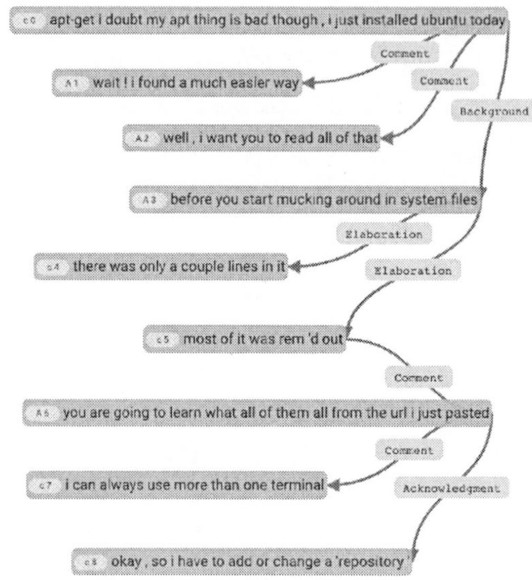

Figure 4: Original annotation of document 1035.

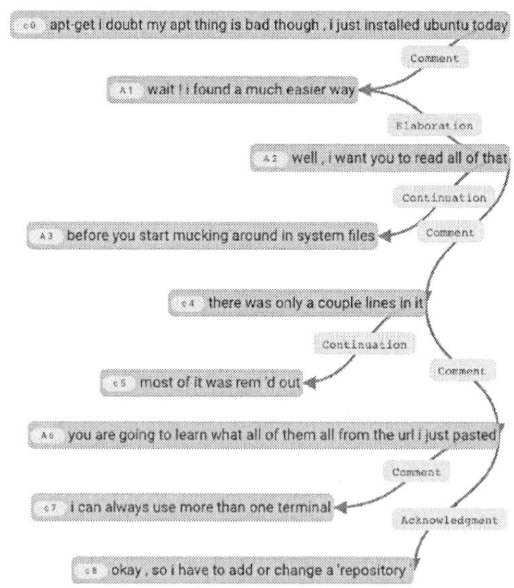

Figure 5: Re-annotated structure of document 1035.

C Class-wise Correlation Between Confidence and Accuracy

C.1 Correlation with Base Model

We investigate the correlation between class-wise confidence scores and prediction accuracy. For better readability, we divide 16 relations into 3 groups based on their frequency in the STAC corpus, as shown from top to bottom in the Figure 6. Recall

[6] https://www.irit.fr/STAC/stac-annotation-manual.pdf.

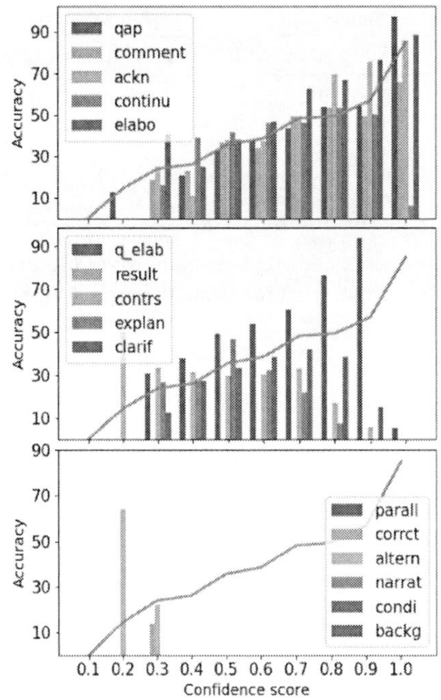

Figure 6: Relation class-wise accuracy and confidence score correlation in the base BERT-ft model. From top to bottom: the 5 most frequent, 5 medium-frequent, and 6 *infrequent* classes. The gray line is the aggregated score of all 16 relations.

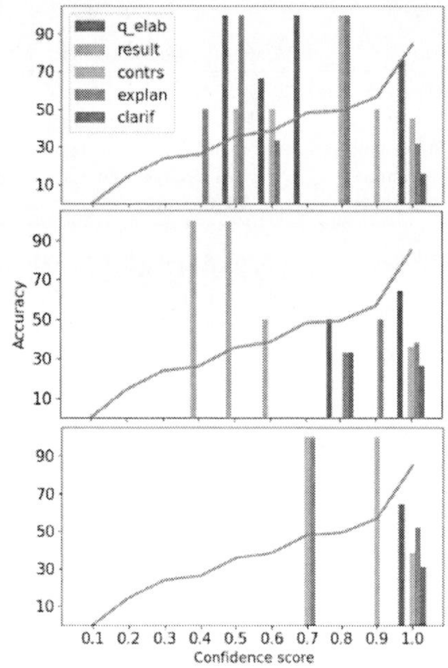

Figure 7: Accuracy and confidence score of the five medium-frequent relations in loop $\{1, 2, 3\}$.

that we translate confidence score with model's prediction probability.

The top plot in Figure 6 shows the first 5 relations: *QAP*, *Comment*, *Acknowledgement*, *Continuation*, and *Elaboration*. They are the most frequent relations. They show good positive correlation between the confidence and accuracy.

The middle plot in Figure 6 shows 5 medium-frequent relations: *Question elaboration*, *Result*, *Contrast*, *Explanation*, and *Clarification*. These relations have a frequency less than 10% and higher than 2% in STAC. The density of the bars moves towards the center compared to that with frequent relations, suggesting that the model is less *confident* to give predictions for these relations.

Finally, the last group contains six *infrequent* relations, as shown in bottom in Figure 6. They are the least present and the most difficult to predict. From this plot, we see that *Parallel*, *Narration*, *Conditional*, and *Background* are completely missing, while *Alternative* and *Correction* are correctly predicted with rather low confidence ($\in [0.2, 0.3]$).

C.2 Iterative Self-training Enhance Correlation for *Infrequent* Classes

Figure 7 and Figure 8 shows the changes of correlation during three loops. During iterative training, we observe that medium and the least frequent labels typically gain better correlation between accuracy and confidence scores, demonstrating that iterative training is good reinforcement for *infrequent* classes.

This observation is further proved in the confusion matrices, as displayed in Figure 9. A clear observation is that the *infrequent* classes has some recall improvement along self-training, typically for *Correction* and *Alternation*. For medium-frequent classes, *Result*, *Contrast*, and *Explanation* also obtain higher recall.

D SJ Model Reproduction Experiments

Table 10 shows the reproduction results on SJ model. Tellingly, removing the dummy roots leads to a noticeable drop, from around 59 to 54.6 in full parsing, which is even larger (-8 points) in cross-domain setting.

E Full Parsing Result Decomposition

Table 11 reports scores per class in each step of discourse parsing.

Train / Test		STAC/STAC			STAC/Molweni-clean			STAC/Molweni		
	#Train	Link	Rel	Link&Rel	Link	Rel	Link&Rel	Link	Rel	Link&Rel
(1) SJ reported scores	947	74.4	-	59.6	-	-	-	64.5	-	38.0
(2) SJ w dummy	947	$73.4_{0.4}$	$80.1_{1.1}$	$58.8_{0.7}$	$66.0_{3.0}$	$66.8_{3.5}$	$44.1_{3.3}$	$55.2_{3.1}$	$66.2_{2.7}$	$36.9_{2.4}$
(3) SJ w/o dummy	947	$70.7_{0.5}$	$77.3_{1.2}$	$54.6_{0.7}$	$61.5_{3.4}$	$59.5_{4.3}$	$36.6_{3.8}$	$49.8_{3.6}$	$57.5_{2.9}$	$28.9_{2.8}$
(4) SJ w dummy	50	$58.6_{2.7}$	$66.8_{1.8}$	$38.9_{1.9}$	$56.8_{5.6}$	$47.6_{7.5}$	$27.0_{4.7}$	$49.3_{5.0}$	$50.2_{7.1}$	$24.9_{4.7}$
(5) SJ w/o dummy	50	$55.1_{3.5}$	$61.1_{2.1}$	$33.6_{2.2}$	$51.1_{6.4}$	$33.6_{9.5}$	$17.2_{5.3}$	$42.9_{5.6}$	$35.2_{10.1}$	$15.3_{5.3}$

Table 10: SJ model reproduction (row 2-5) in different setups: in-domain and cross-domain, with different train sizes, and with or without dummy root. Scores are average F_1 over 10 runs. First row from the paper (2022).

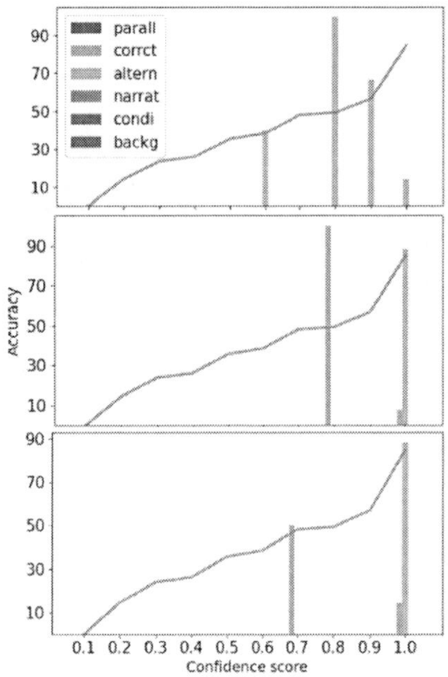

Figure 8: *Infrequent* relation accuracy and confidence scores, loop {1, 2, 3}.

Relation	#(%) correct	#(%) False relation	#(%) False link	#(%) False EDU
qap	143 (**46.9**)	22 (7.2)	127 (41.6)	13 (4.3)
commt	42 (25.5)	45 (27.3)	63 (38.2)	15 (9.1)
ackno	60 (40.5)	13 (8.8)	71 (48.0)	4 (2.7)
conti	20 (17.7)	30 (26.5)	55 (48.7)	8 (7.1)
elab	46 (**45.5**)	25 (24.8)	24 (23.8)	6 (5.9)
q_ela	20 (27.8)	9 (12.5)	41 (**57.0**)	2 (2.8)
resul	5 (17.2)	9 (**31.0**)	14 (48.3)	1 (3.5)
contr	10 (22.7)	12 (27.3)	17 (38.6)	5 (11.4)
expla	4 (12.9)	11 (**35.5**)	16 (51.6)	0 (0)
clari	6 (18.2)	10 (30.3)	13 (39.4)	4 (12.1)
paral	1 (6.7)	4 (26.7)	8 (**53.3**)	2 (**13.3**)
corre	2 (9.5)	10 (**47.6**)	7 (33.3)	2 (9.5)
alter	8 (**42.1**)	0 (0)	7 (36.8)	4 (**21.1**)
narra	0 (0)	3 (23.1)	10 (**76.9**)	0 (0)
condi	3 (16.7)	2 (11.1)	2 (11.1)	11 (**61.1**)
backg	0 (0)	0 (0)	1 (100)	0 (0)
Total	370 (32.8)	205 (18.2)	476 (42.2)	77 (6.8)

Table 11: Class-wise performance on relation prediction, link attachment, and EDU segmentation modules.

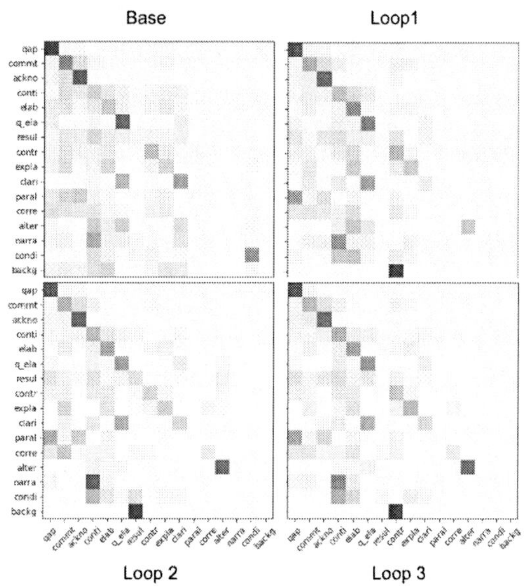

Figure 9: Confusion matrices in the base model and self-trained model with multiple loops. Relations (top to bottom, left to right): *QA pair, comment, acknowledgement, continuation, elaboration, question elaboration, result, contrast, explanation, clarification question, parallel, correction, alternation, narration, conditional, background.*

With a Little Help from my (Linguistic) Friends: Topic Segmentation of Multi-party Casual Conversations

Amandine Decker
Université de Lorraine, CNRS,
Inria, LORIA, F-54000 Nancy, France
University of Gothenburg, Sweden
amandine.decker@loria.fr

Maxime Amblard
Université de Lorraine, CNRS,
Inria, LORIA, F-54000 Nancy, France
maxime.amblard@univ-lorraine.fr

Abstract

Topics play an important role in the global organisation of a conversation as what is currently discussed constrains the possible contributions of the participant. Understanding the way topics are organised in interaction would provide insight on the structure of dialogue beyond the sequence of utterances. However, studying this high-level structure is a complex task that we try to approach by first segmenting dialogues into smaller topically coherent sets of utterances. Understanding the interactions between these segments would then enable us to propose a model of topic organisation at a dialogue level. In this paper we work with open-domain conversations and try to reach a comparable level of accuracy as recent machine learning based topic segmentation models but with a formal approach. The features we identify as meaningful for this task help us understand better the topical structure of a conversation.

1 Introduction

Topics play a crucial role in understanding and interpreting conversations. When participants have a wrong understanding of the current topic, their contributions can become irrelevant (Grice, 1975) or even incoherent, leading to confusion among the addressees. Similarly, misinterpreting the topic can hinder a participant's ability to understand others' interventions accurately. While topics are more constrained and easily identifiable in controlled settings, such as formal work meetings, open-domain casual conversations have a greater flexibility, allowing participants to switch topics with minimal indication and still be followed by others in the conversation. The larger the number of participants, the more challenging it becomes to maintain control, as everyone contributes to the context.

Understanding how topics interact in dialogue is thus essential when it comes to modelling dialogue structure beyond the sequence of utterances. However, analysing this structure requires insight on the topics themselves. Being able to segment a dialogue into topically coherent segments seems to be a first step towards modelling high level dialogue structure. The segments could later be linked inside a structure that describes the interactions between them. This task, called dialogue topic segmentation (DTS), finds utility in dialogue generation (Xu et al., 2021a) and summarising (Chen and Yang, 2020), among other applications.

DTS has received less attention compared to monologue or written text topic segmentation, primarily due to the scarcity of annotated data but some DTS approaches get good results on task-oriented dialogues (Takanobu et al., 2018) or conversations with a restricted set of possible topics such as meeting minutes (Hsueh et al., 2006; Georgescul et al., 2008). Xing and Carenini (2021) suggest another method to tackle more varied dialogues. They use the *TextTiling* algorithm (Hearst, 1997), that relies on a similarity metric between subsequent blocks of text to identify topic boundaries, and enhance it with a learned utterance-pair coherence scoring model based on BERT (Devlin et al., 2019) as similarity metric. They obtain good results in English and Chinese when evaluating their model on three datasets: DialSeg_711 (Xu et al., 2021b), Doc2Dial (Feng et al., 2020), and ZYS (Xu et al., 2021b). Even though these datasets cover different domains, they all contain task-oriented conversations. Evaluating this model on more open-domain dialogues would provide insight on the limits of its generalisation capability.

In this paper we present an improved version of the original TextTiling algorithm[1], where we use linguistics properties of dialogue to identify the topic shifts. Our aim is to reach a comparable level of accuracy as the model proposed by Xing and Carenini (2021) but with a formal approach. Since we are interested in the structure of topical

[1]Our code is available at https://gitlab.inria.fr/adecker/topicsegmentationtexttiling.git.

Proceedings of the 5th Workshop on Computational Approaches to Discourse (CODI 2024), pages 177–188
March 21, 2024 ©2024 Association for Computational Linguistics

interactions, an explainable model would help us better understand what features play a role in perceiving topic shifts. A rule-based approach also has the advantage of minimising the amount of computation required by our model, which is more sustainable. Following our goal to build a general model of interaction, we work with multi-party casual conversations, characterised by their more chaotic nature.

To summarise our contributions in this work: we (1) reproduced Xing and Carenini (2021)'s model; (2) trained a Bert-based model to improve the TextTiling algorithm; (3) improved the TextTiling algorithm based on linguistic properties; (4) evaluated topic segmentation in multiparty casual conversations using the *Friends* corpus.

2 Related work

2.1 Topic segmentation

As explained by Purver (2011), while defining a topic may seem straightforward in well-defined tasks such as news broadcasts (each news item), business meetings (agenda items), or court transcripts (arguments), trying to get a finer segmentation can make the task quite complex. Annotators often exhibit disagreement, and finer-grained segmentation leads to even poorer agreement.

DTS presents additional challenges compared to monologue topic segmentation. In dialogue settings, interactions create more complex exchanges where the points that are central to the topic under discussion are not necessarily explicit. As a result, producing topic segmentation annotations of great quality is even more complicated and applying technical approaches developed for monologue topic segmentation to DTS is not always successful, these methods are not yet able to tackle open domain conversations (Xing and Carenini, 2021).

Existing methods can be broadly categorised into unsupervised techniques (i.e. feature-based approaches) that rely on lexical co-occurrence (Hearst, 1997; Galley et al., 2003a; Eisenstein and Barzilay, 2008) or latent topical distribution (Eisenstein and Barzilay, 2008; Riedl and Biemann, 2012; Du et al., 2013) with the assumption that a significant change in vocabulary corresponds to a change in topic (Halliday and Hasan, 1976), and supervised methods(Arguello and Rosé, 2006; Takanobu et al., 2018). However, the lack of annotated dialogue data hinders the progress in neural-based approaches for DTS (Hearst, 1997).

One prominent technique used in dialogue topic segmentation is the *TextTiling* algorithm and its extensions. TextTiling was originally introduced by Hearst (1997) and relies on a similarity metric between subsequent blocks of text to identify the topic boundaries. It has been widely employed for topic segmentation in various domains as it is unsupervised. It relies on a similarity metric between subsequent blocks of text to identify the topic boundaries. This method, described in more details in Section 2.2, has been improved in different ways. Galley et al. (2003b) introduce lexical chains. Song et al. (2016) use word embeddings to measure the similarity of successive sentences, which is more adapted to dialogue than lexical similarity at a block level. Xu et al. (2021b); Xing and Carenini (2021) use BERT (Devlin et al., 2019) to capture deeper semantic relations at the utterance level.

However, these approaches may not be as reliable when applied to casual and open-domain conversations. Multi-party dialogues and long-term conversations add additional complexities to the topic segmentation task. Such conversations can involve multiple simultaneous discussions, references to past conversations that shape the current topic without clear indications, and a shared history among participants that influences the language and references used, potentially deviating from standard usage (Yule, 2013). Additionally, external interruptions by other characters can further disrupt the ongoing topic.

In summary, DTS presents a complex task, due to the inherent chaos introduced by interactions and the scarcity of annotated data. Technical approaches for DTS include feature-based approaches, and neural-based techniques. The adaptations of TextTiling to dialogue and the extensions proposed these past years have shown promising results in the field of dialogue topic segmentation.

However, further advancements are needed to address the unique challenges posed by open-domain casual conversations and achieve topically coherent segmentation.

2.2 TextTiling Approach

TextTiling (Hearst, 1997) is a topic segmentation algorithm that predicts topic boundaries for a given text. It relies on lexical distribution information and its execution follows three main steps: (1) tokenization, (2) lexical score determination, (3) boundary

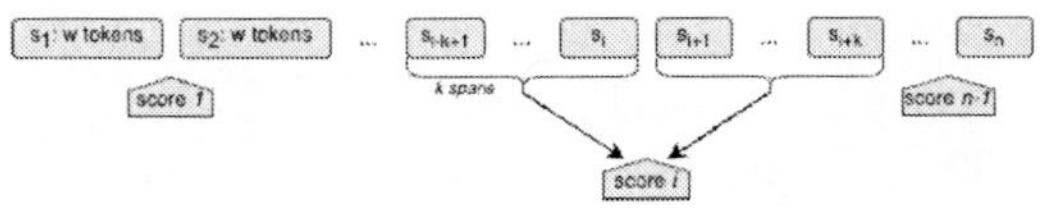

Figure 1: Segmentation in spans of w tokens and computation of the lexical scores in the TextTiling algorithm.

identification. The text is first split in spans of w tokens, then a lexical score is computed at the boundary between each span. For instance as represented on Figure 1, for a text of n spans $\{s_1, s_2, ..., s_n\}$, there are $n-1$ boundaries and thus $n-1$ lexical scores to compute.

Two approaches are suggested in the original paper to measure this score. One is based on the lexical similarity between the two blocks of k spans on each side of the boundary. As Figure 1 shows, the lexical score $score(i)$ (corresponding to the boundary i) would correspond to the portion of tokens present in both blocks, *i.e*, both in the set of spans $\{s_{i-k+1}, ..., s_{i-1}, s_i\}$ and in the set $\{s_{i+1}, s_{i+2}, ..., s_{i+k}\}$. The other approach focuses on new words in a segment of text. The lexical score $score(i)$ would be the ratio of never-yet-seen words in an interval of $2k$ spans centred around the boundary i divided by the total number of tokens in this interval. Stemming and Lemmatisation are suggested to improve the lexical similarity scores.

The maximal changes in the lexical scores are then computed thanks to "depth scores" by looking at the depth of the "valley" in which a given lexical score falls. A deeper valley means that the observed lexical score is more different from previous and later scores, which indicates a higher chance of topic shift. Formally, given a boundary i, we measure the depth of this valley by retrieving the first lexical score on the left that forms a pic, *i.e.* $hl(i)$ such that it is greater than the score directly on its left. We retrieve $hr(i)$ similarly on the right. The depth score of the boundary i is then computing by adding the depths on both sides: $dp(i) = \frac{(hl(i)-score(i))+(hr(i)+score(i))}{2}$. A smoothing of the lexical scores prevents small perturbations to impact the depth computation. Figure 2 shows two cases of depth score computation. The first one (i) is classical, where $hl(i)$ and $hr(i)$ are the first pics on the left and right of the considered score. The second case (j) illustrates the role of smoothing, as their is a very small pic between $score(j)$ and the $hr(j)$ we actually consider. Without smoothing, $score(j+1)$ would have been used

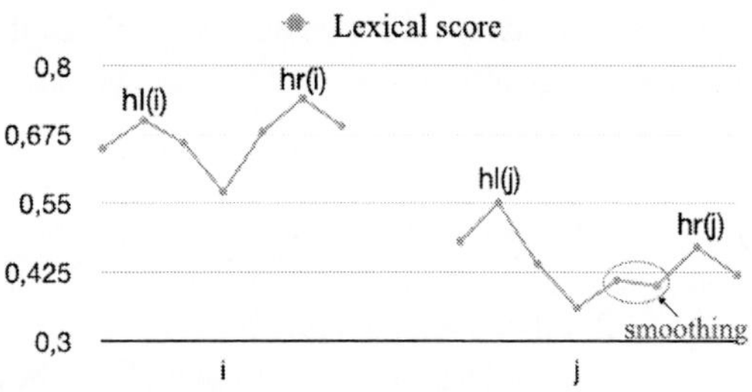

Figure 2: Examples of lexical scores used in the depth scores computation.

to compute the depth score while it would not be representative of the real lexical similarity at this point.

The local maxima of the depth scores are then chosen as topic boundaries. In practice these boundaries are shifted to the closest gap between two paragraphs because the first split into tokens of length w erases this structure.

3 Methodology

3.1 Models

We compare two enhancements of the original TextTiling algorithm, one developed by Xing and Carenini (2021) based on BERT and one based on linguistic properties. Our goal is to see if a feature-based approach can compete with one based on a language model on complex data such as our *Friends dataset*.

We use Xing and Carenini (2021)'s original dataset for training but also compare the results when adaptating their approach to our dataset. The adaptations and results are detailed in Section 4.

Our main contribution is the feature-based approach where we adapt the original TextTiling algorithm to dialogue and use more linguistic properties to identify the topic shifts.

3.2 Baselines

As baselines, we use the original TextTiling algorithm that exists in the Python library Nltk[2] as well as the *random* baseline used by Xing and Carenini (2021) which assigns boundaries with a probability $\frac{b}{k}$ where k is the number of utterances and $b \in [\![0, k-1]\!]$ is a randomly chosen number of segment boundaries. We ran ten iterations of this random baseline where only the F_{k1} and F_{k2} had significant differences from one iteration to the

[2]https://www.nltk.org/_modules/nltk/tokenize/texttiling.html

other. We thus chose the iteration with the best result on these scores for the final comparisons.

3.3 Evaluation Metrics

We use three evaluation metrics for each experiment: P_k error score (Beeferman et al., 1999), which is calculated by comparing the model's prediction within a certain sliding window to the ground-truth segments, the standard F_1 measure, and a relaxed version of it that we call F_k. This adapted F-measure considers that a boundary is correctly identified by the model if there is a ground-truth one at most k utterances before or after the predicted one, the corresponding ground-truth boundary cannot count a second time. In other words, we shift the predicted boundaries that are close to a ground-truth one so that they are considered accurate. We also give twice as much weight to precision compared to recall as we consider that finding right boundaries is more important than finding all of them, which decreases the performance of a model that would suggest boundaries between most utterances.

3.4 Dataset

For these experiments we use transcriptions in English of the episodes of the TV show *Friends*. Transcripts for all ten seasons (236 episodes), annotated in scenes and with additional notes, were used for the Character Mining project (Chen and Choi, 2016) and their dataset is available online[3] (Apache License, Version 2.0).

Casual conversations are central to human interactions but finding suitable data to analyse them, in particular at the topical level, remains complicated (Gilmartin and Campbell, 2016). For this reason, using transcriptions from a TV show seemed like a good idea for a first approach of our problem as it enabled us to have a sufficient amount of data to work with ML tools, while remaining close enough to real-life dialogues. Studies have indeed shown that spoken language in fiction is quite similar to spontaneous speech (Forchini, 2009).

The *Friends* dataset is not annotated in topics but we chose to rely on its segmentation in scenes to create the annotations. Additionally, we consider that the notes in the transcripts indicate an important enough change to create a topic shifts. As a result, our assumption is that the topic boundaries coincide with the notes and change in scene. This annotation method is far from perfect but it has the advantage of being objective.

The example below is an extract of our dataset. We can see that five different characters appear in this short extract, as well as what we consider as two different topics as there is a note between the second and third intervention of this extract. The note explains that a new character enters the room, which is a sufficient disruption to create a topic shift. However in practice, the first speech turn after the note remains on the previous topic and the shift happens right after. This is quite common in the dataset and not unexpected based on real life dialogues, especially when they involve many people. Moreover, the format of the transcriptions is such that concurrent events and/or speech turns are written down in a given order and overlapping are not represented. For this reason, evaluating a topic segmentation solely based on the exact place boundaries should have been placed does not necessarily reflect the quality of a model as we discussed earlier in Section 3.3.

> **Joey Tribbiani:** Strip joint! C'mon, you're single! Have some hormones!
>
> **Ross Geller:** I don't want to be single, okay? I just... I just- I just wanna be married again!
>
> *(Rachel enters in a wet wedding dress and starts to search the room.)*
>
> **Chandler Bing:** And I just want a million dollars!
>
> **Monica Geller:** Rachel?!
>
> **Rachel Green:** Oh God Monica hi! Thank God! I just went to your building and you weren't there and then this guy with a big hammer said you might be here and you are, you are!

4 Adapting Xing and Carenini (2021)'s BERT-based model to our Dataset

Xing and Carenini (2021) enhanced the original TextTiling algorithm by replacing the similarity metric by a trained utterance-pair coherence scoring model based on BERT. They use the *Next Sentence Prediction* BERT and fine-tune it with a pairwise ranking loss so that the model learns what pairs of sentences are more or less coherent. They use *DailyDialog* conversations[4] to train their model

[3] `https://github.com/emorynlp/character-mining`

[4] Xing and Carenini (2021) also trained a model for Chinese on *NaturalConv* but our own work being done with English dialogues we will not discuss this further.

by feeding it pairs of utterances that they indicate as relatively more or less coherent: Two adjacent utterances (based on Conversation Analysis, Schegloff and Sacks (1973)) are more coherent than two utterances randomly taken from a given conversation (and thus not necessarily adjacent or even subsequent), which in turn are more coherent than two utterances belonging to different conversations. Figure 3 in Appendix is a representation of these different levels of coherence.

This model replaces the original lexical similarity and thus outputs the lexical scores used to compute depth scores and then topic boundaries. It is important to note that the model itself is trained on a pairwise coherence ranking task, which means that it learns to judge how likely two utterances are to follow each other based on the coherence of the pair. The final goal is however to segment a dialogue into topics, the model is thus used with the TextTiling method and evaluated on its ability to produce the valid topic segmentation.

We applied these enhancements on our own dataset and ran different experiments to assess the performance of the model on multi-party casual conversation such as the ones in the *Friends* dataset.

We compare the results when Xing and Carenini (2021)'s and our data is used for training. We expect better results with our own training data as it would be more similar to the texts we try to segment.

For our first experiments, we used all seasons except for one as training data and evaluate on the remaining season. However, for a fairest comparison with the feature-based model, which can be evaluated on all seasons, we later worked with models trained on three seasons and evaluated on the seven remaining ones.

4.1 Learning Curve

Since we evaluate the model on a different task as the one it is trained on, *i.e.,* we evaluate it on the topic segmentation task while it was trained for utterance pair coherence scoring, we wanted to know how much training was needed for the model to show consistent results. We thus trained different models for 10 epochs to see how the results evolved with the training. Even though the loss decreases along training, the results on the actual topic segmentation task do not improve consistently. Table 1 shows the results for one model and we can see that the evolution in the scores is not consistent but also that the best epoch is not the same for all the measures. Moreover, while for model c-3 (Table 1) the best results can be found among the last epochs, other models found in Appendix give better results in their first epochs (Tables 5 and 6).

Experience	F1 ↑	F_{k1} ↑	F_{k2} ↑	P_k ↓
Epoch 1	19.25	44.05	51.36	50.26
Epoch 2	19.39	45.98	52.53	51.55
Epoch 3	19.53	46.14	53.49	50.44
Epoch 4	17.83	41.04	49.53	**48.97**
Epoch 5	20.18	46.10	53.58	51.47
Epoch 6	20.47	46.10	52.60	50.84
Epoch 7	19.66	43.91	51.64	51.94
Epoch 8	20.50	**46.76**	**54.09**	51.01
Epoch 9	20.53	45.34	51.87	51.51
Epoch 10	**20.73**	45.90	52.93	51.71

Table 1: Average results of 10 epochs for the model c-3.

4.2 Coherence Layers

Regarding the coherence layers, our dataset is not annotated in dialogue acts nor topics, which makes it impossible to use adjacency pairs or utterances from different topics as Xing and Carenini (2021) suggest. However, we believe that the annotation in scenes, episodes and seasons, as well as the additional notes in the transcripts, provide sufficient information to build utterance pairs of different coherence. As mentioned earlier, we consider that a note usually indicates an important enough change to create a topic shift, for this reason they are another type of boundary we consider when building our pairs and we subdivide each scene in smaller spans of utterances based on the note boundaries. As a consequence, we consider the following types of boundaries in decreasing order of coherence: note, scene, episode, season. In practice, it means that we have six levels of coherence ranked in decreasing order:

- a subsequent utterances within the same note span;
- n randomly picked utterances within the same note span;
- c randomly picked utterances within the same scene;
- e randomly picked utterances within the same episode;
- s randomly picked utterances within the same season;

d randomly picked utterances within different seasons.

As Xing and Carenini (2021) only had three levels of coherence, we try several settings with our own data. We include the subsequent utterances [a] and the randomly picked utterances within the same note span [n] in all our settings to reproduce the 'adjacent' and 'same dialogue' coherence levels from Xing and Carenini (2021). We try different layers for the third coherence level (within the same scene [c], within the same episode [e] and within different seasons [s]), and we also train one model with more layers: [c], [e], [s], and [d]. Table 2 shows the results of different models after one epoch of training. The models named X-1 were trained on a dataset containing utterances from all the seasons except the first one (and thus evaluated on season 1), while the models named X-3 were trained on all the seasons except the third one. We can see that in both cases, the model [d] shows the best results. However, if we have a look at the results for the second epoch, model [c]-1 gets better results.

We see again that the results are not consistent throughout the epochs and choosing the best setting in terms of layers of comparisons is complicated.

However, we can see that having more layers does not seem to provide better results so we decided to work with three layers like Xing and Carenini (2021). We worked with subsequent utterances within the same note span [a], randomly picked utterances within the same note span [n] and randomly picked utterances within the same episode [e]. [a] and [n] to reproduce the first two layers of Xing and Carenini (2021) as said before, and [e] because it is the middle coherence layer that we have.

Another problem of the models we have discussed so far was that they were trained on nine out of the ten seasons of the dataset, which leaves only one season for the evaluation while the feature-based model can be evaluated on all of them. We thus trained some models for two epochs on one, three and four seasons and saw that using only one season produced significantly worse results. We eventually decided to work with three seasons for our comparisons with the feature-based model.

4.3 Model Stability

To assess the stability of our model we trained different versions of it on different training subsets based on the same coherence layers. We built three subsets (based on seasons 2, 3 and 4, and with the coherence layers a, n and e as stated above) and trained three models per subset for two epochs. The results can be seen in Appendix in Table 7. When compared with a t-test, about half of the models gave significantly different results whether the comparison was done between epochs, between models trained on the same training subset or on different subsets. Some models performed well in terms of F-measure (the classical one as well as our adapted version) but worse than the others in terms of P_k.

To do the fairest comparison with our feature-based model, we chose to work with the best version of this model. Since none of the models was performing the best on all of the measures we considered, we chose the best one in terms of P_k among the ones with best F-measures (*d2 m2 e2* in Section 6.1). While the results seem lower than those of other models we presented in this section (see Table 2 for example), this model was trained on three seasons (instead of nine for the previous models) and can thus be evaluated on seven seasons (instead of one), which can explain the lower results.

Experience	F1 ↑	F_{k1} ↑	F_{k2} ↑	P_k ↓
ML [c]-1	25.96	57.49	62.74	51.97
ML [d]-1	**27.18**	**58.69**	**63.61**	**50.20**
ML [cd]-1	21.94	51.06	62.33	53.37
ML [cesd]-1	25.95	56.34	61.89	50.54
ML [c]-3	19.25	44.05	51.36	50.26
ML [d]-3	**20.42**	**48.22**	**54.15**	54.22
ML [cd]-3	20.37	45.06	53.03	**47.32**

Table 2: Average results for different models trained on *Friends* with different coherence layers (Epoch 1).

5 Improving the original TextTiling algorithm with Linguistic Features

In parallel to the experiments with the BERT-based model, we worked on enhancing the original TextTiling algorithm with more linguistic features. Such a model has the advantage of being explainable, as opposed the BERT-based one.

Two basic ideas are discussed in the literature when it comes to identifying changes in topics (Purver, 2011). The first one is that a change in topic implies an important change in terms of content. For example, it corresponds to the introduction of a new vocabulary (Youmans, 1991) which is more or less constant inside a topic (Morris and Hirst, 1991). Additionally in a dialogue, the most active participants can change based on the topic. The second insight is that there exist distinctive topic boundary features such as discourse markers or aspects of the prosody. Questions can also indicate a continuity of the current topic.

We decided to include both approaches in our version of TextTiling. Our idea was to complexify the similarity metric by taking more features of the text into account.

5.1 Adaptations of the Original TextTiling Algorithm

The original TextTiling algorithm proposes two approaches to segment a text. In the Block Comparison approach, the lexical scores represent the similarity between two blocks in terms of tokens. Two blocks with numerous tokens in common will have a higher score than a block that has unique tokens compared to the other block. The Vocabulary Introduction method focuses on the amount of new tokens in two consecutive blocks compared to the number of non stop-word tokens in the blocks. Instead of considering only never-yet-seen words we use a memory parameter m: a word is considered new if it did not appear in the m last sentences of the text. We set this parameter to 20. This adaptation accounts for the fact that in a long dialogue, a topic can be resumed after talking about something else.

Moreover, the original TextTiling algorithm splits the text in spans of w tokens which we supposed was not the most relevant for dialogue. For this reason, our adaptation splits the text in sequences of utterances such that the number of tokens is the closest possible to w (with $w = 12$ as it seems to be a reasonable length for an informative utterance). In practice, most of the spans contain only one utterance, they can contain more when the utterances are very short and are thus less likely to be informative.

5.2 New Feature-Based Additions

We also wanted to consider other features of dialogue when computing the similarity scores. We considered the changes in speakers throughout the conversation (Nguyen et al., 2012). We tried two different ways to modify the depth scores obtained after the block comparison or vocabulary introduction. In one case we increased the depth scores following each utterance that introduced a new speaker. The other modification we tried was inspired from the Block Comparison method. We computed a depth score for each speaker of the conversation based on their proportion of interventions in a block. It means that on top of considering great changes in the lexicon (original Block Comparison method), we also consider changes in terms of speaker distribution (speaker depth scores). The mean of all these scores was then averaged with the original depth scores, where the original scores weight twice as much as the speaker scores.

We took questions into considerations with the assumption that a topic shift would not directly follow a question. This hypothesis is rather naive but we decided to see what results a very basic implementation could produce.

And lastly we used the *coreferee* Python library to take coreference chains (Schnedecker, 1997) into account in the computation of our depth scores. Our assumption was that a topic shift is less likely to exist inside a coreference chain. For this reason, we smoothed the gap scores between the first and last mention of a given reference.

5.3 Comparison of the Features

We tried these features separately and combined them in different ways to see which combinations would give us the best results. The experiments are summarised in Table 3.

Experience	F1 $\uparrow$	F_{k1} $\uparrow$	F_{k2} $\uparrow$	P_k $\downarrow$
BC	10.78	30.57	45.60	49.58
VI	9.78	27.55	43.29	52.40
BC+VI	11.00	30.50	45.85	49.51
BC+SI	10.89	29.95	46.14	48.57
BC+SD	**14.94**	**39.55**	**52.38**	**46.70**
BC+SD+Q	**14.94**	**39.55**	**52.38**	**46.70**
BC+SD+S	**14.94**	**39.55**	**52.38**	**46.70**
BC+VI+Co+SD	**15.45**	**40.32**	**53.63**	**47.43**

Table 3: Results of different feature based models. *Block Comparison (BC), vocabulary introduction (VI), coreference chains (Co), speaker introduction (SI), speaker depth (SD), questions (Q), stemming (S)*

The best results are obtained with the Block Comparison method augmented by the Speaker Depth feature. The results are equivalent to the model that combined Block Comparison, Vocabulary Introduction, Coreference chains and Speaker Depth. However, coreference chains are computationally expensive to retrieve, which makes the model BC + SD more interesting.

We can also see that stemming the text does not improve the results. Lemmatisation gave the same result. This could be due to the data being artificial in the sense that scenarists may avoid repetitions when it is not for the sake of humour.

In the following, we will hence use BC + SD for comparisons with other models.

6 Final Comparisons and Conclusion

6.1 Comparison of All the Models

Table 4 summarises the results for the best feature-based model, the best ML-based model trained on *Friends* and the best ML-based model trained on the original data from Xing and Carenini (2021), as well as the two baseline models discussed above (random baseline and original TextTiling algorithm). These results are based on the evaluation on season one and five to ten only as the ML-based model was trained on the seasons two to four.

Experience	F1 ↑	Fk1 ↑	Fk2 ↑	P_k ↓
BC + SD	15.06	40.36	**52.94**	**46.44**
ML *Friends*	**18.98**	**42.71**	48.45	48.43
ML OG data	15.07	38.33	47.79	56.41
OG TextTiling	10.90	32.43	46.90	52.45
Random	13.95	37.74	42.28	55.74

Table 4: Comparison of the different models (Evaluation: Seasons 1, 5, 6, 7, 8, 9, 10 only).

As we expected, using the *Friends* dataset for training gives significantly better results than a less relevant dataset, as the one used originally by Xing and Carenini (2021). Nevertheless, we can note that in terms of F1-score, our feature-based model and the ML-based model trained on the original data are equivalent. As we have explained earlier, the F1-score is not the most meaningful measurement for the topic segmentation task but this result still shows a certain generalisation capacity from Xing and Carenini (2021)'s model.

We also see a clear improvement between the original TextTiling algorithm and our enhanced version, especially for the P_k, which shows that the linguistic properties we considered and described in Section 5.2 are relevant for our task.

The best model is the ML-based model trained on *Friends* when we look at the F1 and the F_{k1}. However, our feature-based model is better in terms of P_k and F_{k2}. This shows that for the Topic Segmentation task a feature-based model can compete with language models on certain types of dialogues. Moreover, the BERT-based model is not very stable on our dataset, which we believe is due to the complexity of multi-party casual conversations as opposed to the more controlled dialogues usually used in Topic Segmentation. Our approach based on linguistic features provides an explainable baseline.

6.2 Conclusion and Future Work

In this paper we investigated the task of linear topic segmentation on multi-party casual conversations. Since this kind of data is complicated to obtain, we chose to work on transcriptions of the TV-show *Friends* as this dataset is available online. The number of speakers and the context of the dialogues creates the possibility for various types of topic shifts which can be challenging for a model. We used the TextTiling approach which uses a similarity metric between subsequent parts of a text to identify the topic shifts. We enhanced it with more linguistic properties that could play a role in identifying topic shifts, and compared it to the same approach but enhanced with a trained utterance-pair coherence scoring model based on BERT.

As BERT has been trained on the next sentence prediction task, it seems like a relevant model for topic segmentation and in particular to improve the TextTiling approach. Other similar models such as BART (Lewis et al., 2020) or T5 (Raffel et al., 2020) did not seem as suitable for our work as they have not been explicitly trained for the next-sentence prediction task. The generalisation capabilities of T5 would probably make it able to produce similar results to BERT, or even better ones, but it would be more complicated to understand the dialogue features used to identify topic shifts. These reasons explain why we chose to use BERT, as Xing and Carenini (2021) had done.

While the BERT-based improved model showed good results, it did not significantly outperform the enhanced feature-based approach with all the measures we considered. It would be interesting in a future work to see if T5 or newer models produce better results. Our concern on explainability was however central in this first set of experiments. For this reason, working on improving even more our feature-based approach by investigating the different types of topic shifts and their linguistic specificities could be very insightful. It would provide us more clues on the structure of interaction and help us create a model of it at the topic level.

Limitations

In this study, we used the model BERT for one aspect of our experiments. We acknowledge that this model is not the most recent one but we considered it suitable for our task thanks to its specific training for next-sentence prediction. Working with more recent models would imply a higher energy cost while we believe these models would lack the explainability we are looking for in terms of structure.

We also chose to work on transcriptions from fictional dialogues, which creates two limitations. We discussed one of them in the paper when we explained that the fictional aspect of these conversations was likely not the source of huge differences with natural casual conversations. The second limitation however concerns the lack of multi-modality of our work. Transcriptions cannot contain all the information (visual, prosodic, etc.) required to capture fully a conversation. In particular, our dataset did not contain any prosodic information and lacked most of the visual context one may need to understand topic shifts that rely on a change in the context. While the notes could have brought some additional information, we chose to focus on linguistic information in this study. But future work on topic identification should include more modalities to be complete.

Ethical Statement

For this experiment, we did not employ any people and we used tools that were free to use.

We have taken care to ensure that the data used is representative of a certain diversity. For example, the corpus is the corpus is balanced in terms of gender. However, we acknowledge that working with the TV show *Friends* covers little cultural diversity.

References

Jaime Arguello and Carolyn Rosé. 2006. Topic-segmentation of dialogue. In *Proceedings of the Analyzing Conversations in Text and Speech*, pages 42–49, New York City, New York. Association for Computational Linguistics.

Doug Beeferman, Adam Berger, and John Lafferty. 1999. Statistical models for text segmentation. *Machine learning*, 34:177–210.

Jiaao Chen and Diyi Yang. 2020. Multi-view sequence-to-sequence models with conversational structure for abstractive dialogue summarization. In *Proceedings of the 2020 Conference on Empirical Methods in Natural Language Processing (EMNLP)*, pages 4106–4118, Online. Association for Computational Linguistics.

Yu-Hsin Chen and Jinho D. Choi. 2016. Character identification on multiparty conversation: Identifying mentions of characters in TV shows. In *Proceedings of the 17th Annual Meeting of the Special Interest Group on Discourse and Dialogue*, pages 90–100, Los Angeles. Association for Computational Linguistics.

Jacob Devlin, Ming-Wei Chang, Kenton Lee, and Kristina Toutanova. 2019. BERT: Pre-training of deep bidirectional transformers for language understanding. In *Proceedings of the 2019 Conference of the North American Chapter of the Association for Computational Linguistics: Human Language Technologies, Volume 1 (Long and Short Papers)*, pages 4171–4186, Minneapolis, Minnesota. Association for Computational Linguistics.

Lan Du, Wray Buntine, and Mark Johnson. 2013. Topic segmentation with a structured topic model. In *Proceedings of the 2013 Conference of the North American Chapter of the Association for Computational Linguistics: Human Language Technologies*, pages 190–200, Atlanta, Georgia. Association for Computational Linguistics.

Jacob Eisenstein and Regina Barzilay. 2008. Bayesian unsupervised topic segmentation. In *Proceedings of the 2008 Conference on Empirical Methods in Natural Language Processing*, pages 334–343, Honolulu, Hawaii. Association for Computational Linguistics.

Song Feng, Hui Wan, Chulaka Gunasekara, Siva Patel, Sachindra Joshi, and Luis Lastras. 2020. doc2dial: A goal-oriented document-grounded dialogue dataset. In *Proceedings of the 2020 Conference on Empirical Methods in Natural Language Processing (EMNLP)*, pages 8118–8128, Online. Association for Computational Linguistics.

Pierfranca Forchini. 2009. Spontaneity reloaded: American face-to-face and movie conversation compared. *Corpus linguistics 2009 proceedings*, pages 1–27.

Michel Galley, Kathleen McKeown, Eric Fosler-Lussier, and Hongyan Jing. 2003a. Discourse segmentation of multi-party conversation. In *Proceedings of the 41st Annual Meeting on Association for Computational Linguistics - Volume 1*, ACL '03, page 562–569, USA. Association for Computational Linguistics.

Michel Galley, Kathleen R. McKeown, Eric Fosler-Lussier, and Hongyan Jing. 2003b. Discourse segmentation of multi-party conversation. In *Proceedings of the 41st Annual Meeting of the Association for Computational Linguistics*, pages 562–569, Sapporo, Japan. Association for Computational Linguistics.

Maria Georgescul, Alexander Clark, and Susan Armstrong. 2008. A comparative study of mixture models for automatic topic segmentation of multiparty dialogues. In *Proceedings of the Third International Joint Conference on Natural Language Processing: Volume-II*.

Emer Gilmartin and Nick Campbell. 2016. Capturing chat: Annotation and tools for multiparty casual conversation. In *Proceedings of the Tenth International Conference on Language Resources and Evaluation (LREC'16)*, pages 4453–4457, Portorož, Slovenia. European Language Resources Association (ELRA).

Herbert Paul Grice. 1975. Logic and conversation. In *Syntax and Semantics*, volume 3, page 45–47. New York: Academic Press.

Michael Alexander Kirkwood Halliday and Ruqaiya Hasan. 1976. *Cohesion in english*. Longman: London.

Marti A. Hearst. 1997. Text tiling: Segmenting text into multi-paragraph subtopic passages. *Computational Linguistics*, 23(1):33–64.

Pei-Yun Hsueh, Johanna D. Moore, and Steve Renals. 2006. Automatic segmentation of multiparty dialogue. In *11th Conference of the European Chapter of the Association for Computational Linguistics*, pages 273–280, Trento, Italy. Association for Computational Linguistics.

Mike Lewis, Yinhan Liu, Naman Goyal, Marjan Ghazvininejad, Abdelrahman Mohamed, Omer Levy, Veselin Stoyanov, and Luke Zettlemoyer. 2020. BART: Denoising sequence-to-sequence pre-training for natural language generation, translation, and comprehension. In *Proceedings of the 58th Annual Meeting of the Association for Computational Linguistics*, pages 7871–7880, Online. Association for Computational Linguistics.

Jane Morris and Graeme Hirst. 1991. Lexical cohesion computed by thesaural relations as an indicator of the structure of text. *Computational Linguistics*, 17(1):21–48.

Viet-An Nguyen, Jordan Boyd-Graber, and Philip Resnik. 2012. SITS: A hierarchical nonparametric model using speaker identity for topic segmentation in multiparty conversations. In *Proceedings of the 50th Annual Meeting of the Association for Computational Linguistics (Volume 1: Long Papers)*, pages 78–87, Jeju Island, Korea. Association for Computational Linguistics.

Matthew Purver. 2011. *Topic Segmentation*, chapter 11. John Wiley & Sons, Ltd.

Colin Raffel, Noam Shazeer, Adam Roberts, Katherine Lee, Sharan Narang, Michael Matena, Yanqi Zhou, Wei Li, and Peter J. Liu. 2020. Exploring the limits of transfer learning with a unified text-to-text transformer. *J. Mach. Learn. Res.*, 21(1).

Martin Riedl and Chris Biemann. 2012. TopicTiling: A text segmentation algorithm based on LDA. In *Proceedings of ACL 2012 Student Research Workshop*, pages 37–42, Jeju Island, Korea. Association for Computational Linguistics.

Emanuel A. Schegloff and Harvey Sacks. 1973. Opening up closings. 8(4):289–327.

Catherine Schnedecker. 1997. *Nom propre et chaînes de référence*. Librairie Klincksieck.

Yiping Song, Lili Mou, Rui Yan, Li Yi, Zinan Zhu, Xiaohua Hu, and Ming Zhang. 2016. Dialogue session segmentation by embedding-enhanced texttiling. *CoRR*, abs/1610.03955.

Ryuichi Takanobu, Minlie Huang, Zhongzhou Zhao, Fenglin Li, Haiqing Chen, Xiaoyan Zhu, and Liqiang Nie. 2018. A weakly supervised method for topic segmentation and labeling in goal-oriented dialogues via reinforcement learning. In *Proceedings of the Twenty-Seventh International Joint Conference on Artificial Intelligence, IJCAI-18*, pages 4403–4410. International Joint Conferences on Artificial Intelligence Organization.

Linzi Xing and Giuseppe Carenini. 2021. Improving unsupervised dialogue topic segmentation with utterance-pair coherence scoring. In *Proceedings of the 22nd Annual Meeting of the Special Interest Group on Discourse and Dialogue*, pages 167–177, Singapore and Online. Association for Computational Linguistics.

Jun Xu, Zeyang Lei, Haifeng Wang, Zheng-Yu Niu, Hua Wu, and Wanxiang Che. 2021a. Discovering dialog structure graph for coherent dialog generation. In *Proceedings of the 59th Annual Meeting of the Association for Computational Linguistics and the 11th International Joint Conference on Natural Language Processing (Volume 1: Long Papers)*, pages 1726–1739, Online. Association for Computational Linguistics.

Yi Xu, Hai Zhao, and Zhuosheng Zhang. 2021b. Topic-aware multi-turn dialogue modeling. *Proceedings of the AAAI Conference on Artificial Intelligence*, 35(16):14176–14184.

Gilbert Youmans. 1991. A new tool for discourse analysis: The vocabulary-management profile. *Language*, 67(4):763–789.

George Yule. 2013. *Referential communication tasks*. Routledge.

A Appendix

A.1 Computational Resources Used

We tried to limit our use of heavy computational powers. Our feature-based model was run on a local machine and except for the experiments that involved co-reference chains identification, creating the topic segmentation of one episode of *Friends* takes less than a few seconds.

As for the experiments using Machine Learning, we did our best to optimise the batch sizes and the number of experiments we could run in parallel to reduce the training time as much as possible. We ran our experiments on the Lark servers from CLASP (Gothenburg University) where we used one Nvidia Titan RTX GPU. Our model is based on the *Next Sentence Prediction* BERT model (Devlin et al., 2019), each epoch took about one hour of training.

A.2 Different Coherence Levels Considered by Xing and Carenini (2021)

Figure 3 illustrates the three levels of coherence Xing and Carenini (2021) used in their experiment. As explained above, we had the possibility to use more different layers thanks to the segmentation in notes of our dataset.

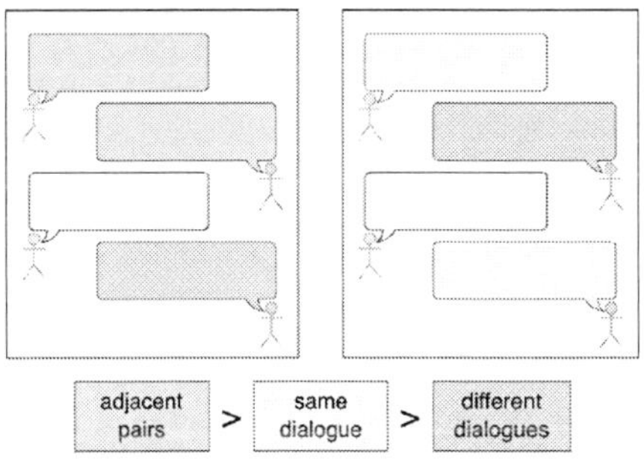

Figure 3: Levels of coherence considered by Xing and Carenini (2021)

A.3 Additional results of the Machine-learning-based Approach

Learning Curve Tables 5 and 6 show the results when training one model on nine out of the ten available seasons of *Friends* for ten epochs. We can see that the results do not consistently improve from one epoch to another and the differences between each epochs are not very big. A t-test indicates that the results are significantly different from one epoch to another, however the evaluation set is small due to the fact that these models were trained on nine seasons. Hence, we decided to stop training our models for such a long time and trained them for only two epochs in our later experiments.

Experience	F1 ↑	F_{k1} ↑	F_{k2} ↑	P_k ↓
Epoch 1	20.42	**48.22**	**54.16**	54.22
Epoch 2	19.92	44.50	51.38	53.09
Epoch 3	18.90	43.76	51.68	**51.40**
Epoch 4	19.91	46.13	52.11	52.54
Epoch 5	19.96	47.19	53.59	53.49
Epoch 6	19.81	46.08	51.69	52.67
Epoch 7	20.54	46.49	53.09	53.71
Epoch 8	**20.75**	47.23	52.47	53.39
Epoch 9	20.50	46.88	52.44	53.93
Epoch 10	20.14	47.00	52.44	54.18

Table 5: Resutls of 10 epochs for the model d-3.

Experience	F1 ↑	Fk1 ↑	Fk2 ↑	P_k ↓
Epoch 1	25.96	57.49	62.74	51.97
Epoch 2	**27.48**	**59.19**	**63.84**	50.71
Epoch 3	26.31	58.50	62.81	52.44
Epoch 4	27.18	58.03	63.03	51.90
Epoch 5	27.42	58.01	62.71	51.37
Epoch 6	27.09	58.50	**63.89**	51.12
Epoch 7	26.53	57.24	62.44	**50.56**
Epoch 8	26.51	57.72	62.50	52.04
Epoch 9	26.72	57.71	62.83	51.51
Epoch 10	26.81	57.54	62.96	51.61

Table 6: Results of 10 epochs for the model c-1.

Model Stability To assess the stability of our model we trained different versions of it on different training subsets based on the same coherence layers. We built three subsets (seasons 2, 3 and 4, coherence layers a, n and e) and trained three models per subset for two epochs. Table 7 shows that about half of the models gave significantly different results when compared with a t-test whether the comparison was done between epochs, between models trained on the same training subset or on different subsets. Some models performed well in terms of F-measure but worse than the others in terms of P_k.

Experience	F1 ↑	F_{k1} ↑	F_{k2} ↑	P_k ↓
d1 m1 e1	**17.66**	**44.82**	**48.66**	54.22
d1 m1 e2	**17.91**	**44.97**	**49.04**	54.00
d1 m2 e1	12.26	31.69	42.09	56.93
d1 m2 e2	12.76	33.48	43.20	56.95
d1 m3 e1	15.35	38.27	**47.30**	53.10
d1 m3 e2	14.78	38.16	**47.52**	53.35
d2 m1 e1	16.92	39.59	45.94	50.78
d2 m1 e2	16.20	35.42	42.78	50.21
d2 m2 e1	**18.94**	**42.93**	**48.57**	49.21
d2 m2 e2	**18.98**	**42.73**	**48.47**	48.43
d2 m3 e1	**18.36**	41.99	**47.58**	49.55
d2 m3 e2	**18.67**	41.37	**47.44**	48.54
d3 m1 e1	**17.43**	36.53	43.79	**46.88**
d3 m1 e2	**18.74**	38.15	44.52	**45.63**
d3 m2 e1	14.61	34.03	42.33	50.58
d3 m2 e2	10.70	28.29	42.97	54.82
d3 m3 e1	**17.94**	**43.75**	**48.87**	52.44
d3 m3 e2	**18.10**	**42.70**	**48.11**	51.23

Table 7: Results of different models trained on three training subsets (d1, d2, d3) for two epochs each.

Author Index

Amblard, Maxime, 161, 177

Barić, Ana, 64
Bourgonje, Peter, 39
Braud, Chloé, 91, 105, 161

Camilleri, Maris, 127
Carenini, Giuseppe, 161
Carretero Garcia, Paloma, 127
Chernyavskiy, Alexander, 149
Conrad, Stefan, 27
Costa, Nelson Filipe, 120

Decker, Amandine, 177
Dorgeloh, Heidrun, 27

Gao, Yingqiang, 12
Godunova, Mary, 78
Gu, Nianlong, 12

Hahnloser, Richard H.r., 12

Ilvovsky, Dmitry, 149

Jahangir, Khushnur, 105

Kawaletz, Lea, 27
Kiepura, Anna, 12
Kosseim, Leila, 120

Lam, Charles, 71
Lam, Jessica, 12
Li, Chuyuan, 161
Lin, Pin-Jie, 39

Metheniti, Eleni, 91
Muller, Philippe, 91, 105
Müller, Mark-Christoph, 127

Nnamoko, Nonso, 71

Oostdijk, Nelleke, 139
Ostyakova, Lidiia, 149

Padó, Sebastian, 64
Papay, Sean, 64
Pastor, Martial, 139
Poesio, Massimo, 127
Potter, Andrew, 1
Prévot, Laurent, 50

Stein, Simon, 27
Stodden, Regina, 27

Voloshina, Ekaterina, 78

Wang, Sheng-Fu, 50

Yu, Juntao, 127

Association for Computational Linguistics
209 N. Eighth Street
Stroudsburg, Pennsylvania 18360

ISBN 978-1-7138-9451-3

CURRAN ASSOCIATES INC.
proceedings.com